Photoshop® CS
Complete Course

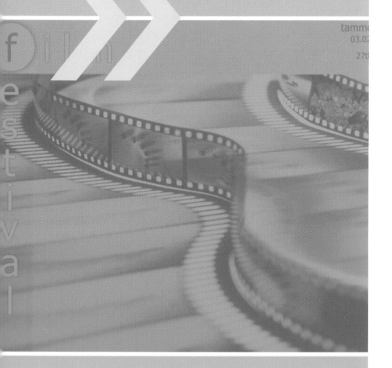

Jan Kabili

with Donna L. Baker

D1399061

WILEY

Wiley Publishing, Inc.

Photoshop® CS Complete Course

Published by:

Wiley Publishing, Inc.
111 River Street
Hoboken, NJ 07030
www.wiley.com/compbooks

Published simultaneously in Canada

For general information on our other products and services or to obtain technical support please contact our Customer Care Department within the U.S. at 800-762-2974, outside the U.S. at 317-572-3993 or fax 317-572-4002.

Library of Congress Control Number: 2004101452

ISBN: 0-7645-4175-7

Manufactured in the United States of America

10 9 8 7 6 5 4 3 2 1

» Credits

Publisher: Barry Pruett

Project Editor: Cricket Krengel

Acquisitions Editor: Michael Roney

Editorial Manager: Robyn Siesky

Technical Editor: Stephen M. Burns

Copy Editor: Elizabeth Kuball

Production Coordinator: Nancee Reeves

Proofreader: Vicki Broyles

Layout and Graphics: Beth Brooks
Lauren Goddard
Jennifer Heleine
Lynsey Osborn
Heather Pope

Cover Design: Anthony Bunyan

Quality Control: John Greenough
Susan Moritz
Angel Perez

Indexer: Anne Leach

» Dedication

To my beautiful, independent children, Ben, Coby, and Kate Kabili.

» Table of Contents

Introduction

Almost every Photoshop user I know is self-taught. Anyone who has tried to learn this program on his or her own eventually realizes that there's more to knowing Photoshop than understanding how to work some of its tools. The real trick is in knowing how to use the program in context to create a professional-looking product—be it a page layout, a typographic logo, a Web design, a color-corrected photograph, or an art collage.

That's where this book comes in. It uses a project-based approach to teach you Photoshop in a way that takes into account context as well as technique. Here you learn not only how to use the many exciting tools that Photoshop offers, but also how to use those tools together to construct a design project from beginning to end. Each lesson builds on those that came before, giving you a chance to practice what you've learned and reinforcing those skills that you use over and over.

In short, this is more than just a book. It really is a complete, structured course that leads you through the intricacies of Photoshop while keeping an eye on the bigger creative picture. If you put your nose to the grindstone and work your way through the lessons in this book, I can assure you that you'll come away with a deeper understanding of Photoshop than you already have, whether you're a Photoshop beginner or a user with some experience. In the process, I hope you enjoy yourself and give yourself a pat on the back each time that you complete a piece of the final project, which you work on throughout the book.

Is This Book for You?

The answer to this question is definitely yes if you're a serious student or teacher of Photoshop or if you're a designer, photographer, artist, architect, or other creative professional. The lessons offered in this course were designed with you in mind.

What's in This Book?

This course is divided into seven sections—the introductory Confidence Builder and six substantive parts. There are also two bonus sessions on the CD-ROM at the back of the book. Here's an overview of what's in each of these sections:

> » "Confidence Builder" introduces you to how Photoshop works, while leading you through the creation of a simple collage.

> » **Part I: Course Setup.** This is the only narrative section in the book. It contains introductory material about Photoshop and about this course.

> » "Photoshop Basics" includes an overview of what you can do with Photoshop and a summary of the features that are new in Photoshop CS.

> » "Project Overview" explains the project that you create as you work through this course and introduces the tutorial files that are provided for you on the CD-ROM at the back of the book.

> » **Part II: Getting to Know Photoshop.** This is where you find the first of the tutorials that make up the format of the rest of the book. There are three sessions (chapters) in this part.

> » Session 1, "Customizing Photoshop," uses tutorials to teach you how to access tools and commands, set preferences, assign keyboard shortcuts, and create custom-built workspaces and tool presets.

> » Session 2, "Managing Documents," shows you how to create and save files, how to use the File Browser to view and manage files, and various ways of fixing the mistakes that you're bound to make in Photoshop.

> » Session 3, "Viewing Documents," covers image magnification, navigation in the document window, multiple document windows image information, screen display modes, image size, canvas size, cropping, and video features.

» **Part III: Painting and Drawing.** This part covers how to paint and fill pixel-based images and how to draw vector-based objects.

> » Session 4, "Choosing and Using Color," introduces Photoshop's color-management system, foreground and background colors, the Color Picker, the Color palette, and the color Swatches palette.

> » Session 5, "Painting and Filling with Pixels," covers various methods of filling pixel-based artwork with color, patterns, and gradients. It introduces the Brushes palette and shows you how to define a custom brush. It also covers stroking and erasing.

> » Session 6, "Drawing with Vectors," addresses a side of Photoshop that's less well-known—its vector-drawing capabilities. You explore the Pen tools, paths, and the easy-to-use Shape tool.

» **Part IV: Image Editing.** This part addresses the image-editing capabilities that are at the heart of Photoshop.

> » Session 7, "Selecting," covers selection tools and commands, the Quick Mask mode, feathering and anti-aliasing, storing selections in Alpha channels, and the Extract feature.

> » Session 8, "Using Layers," explains everything you'll need to know about creating layers, layer visibility, layer locks, layer opacity, layer comps, linking layers, layer sets, adjustment layers, and fill layers.

> » Session 9, "Compositing Images," is all about making collages. You learn how to make images compatible and how to use layer masks, vector masks, blending sliders, rulers and guides, and blending modes.

> » Session 10, "Filters, Layer Styles, and Special Effects," shows you how to add decorative effects to your images using filters, the History Brush, the new Filter Gallery, the new Photo Filter adjustment, and customizable layer styles.

» **Part V: Text.** Here you learn all about using text in Photoshop.

> » Session 11, "Creating and Formatting Text," covers the Type tools, point type, paragraph type, type formatting features, the Check Spelling command, and the Find and Replace Text feature.

> » Session 12, "Special Text Effects," is the place to practice some typographic effects, including warping text, using curves to make text visible on a photograph, rasterizing type, and displaying an image in text.

» **Part VI: Working with Photographs in the Digital Darkroom.** This part covers how to retouch and correct photographs in Photoshop.

» Session 13, "Using Darkroom Tools," looks at retouching with the Clone Stamp tool, the Healing Brush tool, and the Patch tool. It also addresses adjusting exposure, saturation, and focus in photographs and the new Crop and Straighten command.

» Session 14, "Controlling Tone," is about correcting tonal imbalance in photographs using auto-correction commands, levels, and curves.

» Session 15, "Adjusting Color," covers color correction with color balance, hue/saturation, curves, and variation adjustments.

» Session 16, "Editing High-Bit Images," covers the new integrated Camera Raw interface and editing 16-bit images.

» **Part VII: CD-ROM Bonus Material: Preparing Art for Print and Web.** These sessions, located in PDF format on the CD-ROM, address output on the Web and in print.

» Bonus Session 1, "Using Photoshop and ImageReady for the Web," is a comprehensive look at the many Web-related tasks that you can accomplish with Photoshop and its sister program, ImageReady.

» Bonus Session 2, "Printing," offers pointers for preparing images for desktop and commercial printing as well as the Picture Package contact sheet, and PDF Presentation features.

Conventions Used in This Book

Each session in this book is made up of step-by-step tutorials. The bold type in a step indicates what you should do. Non-bold type following a step offers further explanation of that step.

A hot-pink step number indicates that a step is illustrated. Look for a matching hot-pink number on the nearby illustration. Steps with blue numbers are not illustrated.

Additional useful information is offered in hot-pink Notes, Cautions, and Tips and in larger blue boxes called Sidebars that are scattered through the text.

If you find any errors in this book, please let me (author Jan Kabili) know about them by e-mail addressed to kabili@saga2.com. Any errors we learn about will be posted at www.photoshopcourse.blogspot.com or by link to this book's site from www.complete-course.com.

Confidence Builder

Introduction

The Confidence Builder gives you a chance to try out some of Photoshop's basic tools and commands as you build a simple collage. You get a quick look at features that are addressed in more detail in later sessions, including layers, selections, brushes, type, filters, layer styles, vector shapes, image adjustments, and combining images from multiple files. This hands-on overview of Photoshop basics will build your confidence as a Photoshop user and whet your appetite for future sessions.

Tutorial
» Getting Started

This is the first of several progressive tutorials in which you create a collage from two images. Here you make sure the tutorial files are installed on your hard drive, launch Photoshop, and open your first file.

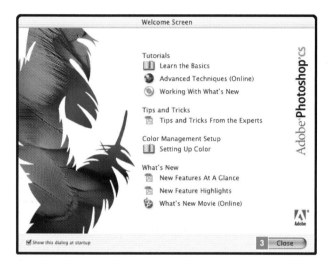

1. **Make sure that the Confidence Builder folder of tutorial files is on your hard drive.**
   The Confidence Builder files are included with the tutorial files on the CD-ROM at the back of the book. Before you get started, turn to Appendix A to find out how to put these files on your hard drive and how to prepare them for use with the tutorials.

   <CAUTION>
   Windows users may not be able make and save changes to the tutorial files copied to their hard drives from the CD-ROM. If you face that problem, follow the instructions in Appendix A for removing the read-only setting from the tutorial files on your hard drive.

2. **Launch Photoshop.**
   The Welcome Screen appears.

3. **Click the Close button at the bottom of the Welcome Screen.**
   The Welcome Screen offers links to information about Photoshop CS for new and experienced users. When you have a moment, reopen it by choosing Help→Welcome Screen and explore its links.

   <TIP>
   If you don't want the Welcome Screen to reappear every time you launch Photoshop, deselect the Show this Dialog at Startup check box before closing the Welcome Screen.

   <CAUTION>
   When the Welcome Screen is open, you cannot work in the program, so be sure to close the Welcome Screen instead of just sliding it out of the way.

4. **Choose Window→Workspace→Reset Palette Locations from the menu bar at the top of the screen.**
   This resets all the program's palettes to their default locations.

5. **Click the Tool icon on the far left of the Options bar at the top of the screen.**
   Your Tool icon may look different from the one in the illustration, depending on which tool you have selected in your toolbox. This opens the Tool Presets picker.

6. **Click the small arrow at the top right of the Tool Presets picker to open a side menu.**

7. **Choose Reset All Tools from the side menu and click OK at the prompt.**
   This resets all the program's tools to their default settings.

<TIP>
It's a good idea to reset palettes and tools to their default settings when you start each new session in this book and when you begin new projects of your own, particularly if you're not working on your own computer.

8. **Choose File→Open.**

9. **Navigate to** cb_filmslate.psd **in the Confidence Builder folder on your hard drive and click Open.**

<CAUTION>
If you're a Windows user, you may not see the .psd file extension in the tutorial files. See Appendix A for instructions on how to reveal the hidden file extensions in Windows.

10. **If you're confronted with an Embed Profile Mismatch warning, put a check mark in the box labeled Don't Show Again and click OK.**
    This tells the program to display tutorial files with the color settings profile that was attached when the files were created, rather than according to the color settings in your copy of Photoshop. The document window opens with a photograph of a film slate. Leave the file open for the next tutorial.

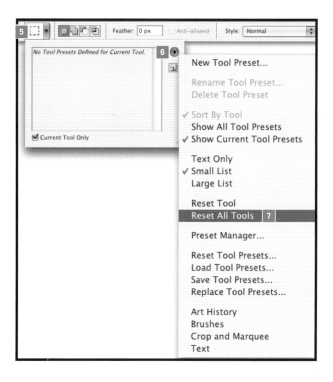

Tutorial
» Adding a Type Layer

In this tutorial you add, move, and format a layer of type.

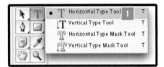

1. **With** cb_filmslate.psd **open from the last tutorial, click the Horizontal Type tool in the toolbox.**
   This selects the tool so it is ready to use. The Type tool has several variations. If a variation other than the Horizontal Type tool is showing in the toolbox, click and hold that Type tool and choose the Horizontal Type tool from the fly-out menu.

<TIP>
If you're not sure what a tool icon or any other icon means, move your cursor over the icon to reveal a ToolTip that identifies the icon and its keyboard shortcut.

2. **Click the Default Colors icon (the small black and white squares) in the toolbox.**
   This sets the Foreground Color box in the toolbox to black and the Background Color box to white.

3. **Click the Switch Colors icon (the double-pointed arrow) in the toolbox.**
   This switches the colors in the Foreground and Background color boxes so that white is now the Foreground color, which is the color the Horizontal Type tool applies by default.

4. **In the Options bar at the top of your screen, click the Font down arrow and choose Courier TT (Windows: Courier T1) from the drop-down list. Click the Font Size down arrow and choose 14 pt. Leave the other options at their defaults.**
   The Options bar is context sensitive, so it changes depending on the tool selected. It currently displays options for the Horizontal Type tool.

5. **Click on the black film slate in the document window and type** Jigsaw **as the production name. Press Return or Enter, and type** Chavez **as the director's name.**
   Two lines of type appear where you inserted your cursor in the document. When you use the Type tool, Photoshop automatically creates a separate type layer in the Layers palette and names that layer based on the words that you typed.

<CAUTION>
If you don't see your white text in the image, it's probably hidden against the background of the same color. In that case, select the Move tool in the toolbox and drag toward the black film slate where the text will show up.

6. **Click the Move tool in the toolbox.**

7. **Check that the Jigsaw Chavez type layer is highlighted in the Layers palette. In the document, click and drag to position the text near the lines in the film slate.**

   You can move the text separately from the rest of the image because the text is isolated on its own layer.

8. **Click the Type tool in the toolbox again. In the document, click and drag to highlight both lines of text.**

   You can select all or just some of the characters on a Type layer this way. Characters must be selected before they can be reformatted.

< T I P >

A shortcut for selecting all the characters on a Type layer is to double-click the T icon on the Type layer in the Layers palette.

9. **In the Options bar, click the Palettes icon to open the Character palette.**

   The Character palette offers options, in addition to those accessible from the Options bar, for formatting point type (independent lines of type, as distinguished from paragraph type, which is created inside a bounding box).

10. **In the Character palette, click the Leading down arrow and choose 18 pt from the drop-down list.**

    Increasing leading expands the amount of space between the two lines of type so that they more closely match the lines on the film slate.

11. **Click the Check Mark icon on the right of the Options bar.**

    Clicking the Check Mark icon commits the type edits that you just made and takes you out of type edit mode, enabling you to access the many menu commands that are unavailable when you're editing type.

12. **Choose File→Save As from the menu bar.**

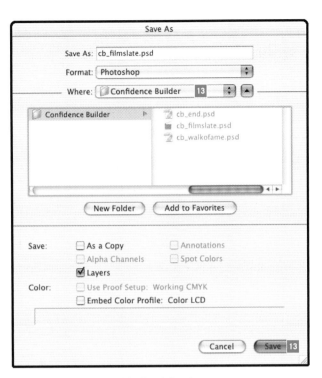

Macintosh Interface

13. **In the Save As dialog box, navigate to the Confidence Builder file on your hard drive and click Save. Click Replace (Windows: OK) in the warning box that appears. If you see a Maximize Compatibility prompt, remove the check mark next to Maximize compatibility and click OK. You learn how to disable this prompt later. Leave this file open for the next tutorial.**

The original of this file on your hard drive is replaced with this modified version. If you ever need the original again, you can reinstall it to your hard drive from the CD-ROM. Windows users: Your Save As dialog box looks different than the Save As dialog box on a Mac. You have the same settings, but in a slightly different configuration, as you can see in the illustration from Windows XP.

Windows Interface

Tutorial
» Painting

In this tutorial, you add some paint to your image with the Brush tool.

1. **With** cb_filmslate.psd **open from the last tutorial, check that the type layer, Jigsaw Chavez, is still selected in the Layers palette and click the New Layer icon at the bottom of the Layers palette. (If your Layers palette isn't open, first choose Window→Layers.)**

   This creates a new layer of transparent pixels above the layer that was selected in the Layers palette. Think of each layer as a piece of clear glass stacked one upon the other. You can add pixels of content to each layer, and wherever there is no content, you can see through to the layers below.

2. **In the Layers palette, double-click directly on the new layer's name, Layer 1. Rename the layer by typing** take **and press Return or Enter.**

   Be sure to double-click directly on the layer name, or you inadvertently cause the Layer Style palette to open.

3. **Click the Brush tool in the toolbox.**

4. **Click the Brush Sample in the Options bar to open the Brush pop-up palette.**

   You see a scrolling list of brush tips with previews of a stroke made with each brush.

5. **Click the arrow on the right of the Brush pop-up palette to display the palette menu and choose Large List from the menu.**

   This changes the view of the Brush pop-up palette to display each brush tip with its size and name.

6. **Scroll to the bottom of the Brush pop-up palette and choose the Rough Round Bristle brush.**

7. **Drag the Brush Size slider at the top of the Brush pop-up palette to 50 px (pixels).**

8. **Make sure the Foreground Color box in the toolbox is still set to white, and then click and drag a line of white paint under the word TAKE on the film slate.**

   Notice the painterly look this brush gives to your brushstroke. You can find many more natural media brushes like this in Photoshop.

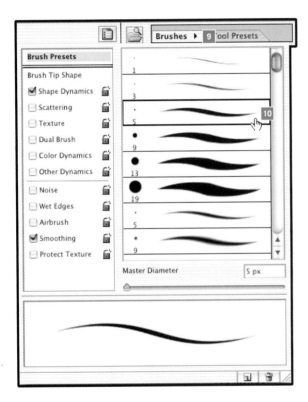

9. **Click the Brushes tab in the palette well on the right of the Options bar to open the Brushes palette.**

   This is another palette from which you can select a brush. It has more controls for configuring brush tips than the simpler Brush pop-up palette.

10. **Use the Scroll Bar to scroll up to the top of the Brushes palette, and choose the Hard Round 5 pixel brush from there.**

11. **Click the New Layer icon in the Layers palette. Double-click the name of the new layer and rename it** date scene**.**

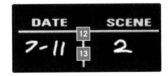

12. **Paint a date and scene number on the film slate in the document window.**

    You selected the Hard Round brush for this in Step 10.

13. **Select the Move tool in the toolbox, and click and drag to position the date and scene on top of the film slate.**

14. **Choose File→Save.**

    This saves over the last saved version of the file. The Save command is not available until you've used Save As at least once, as you did in the preceding tutorial.

Tutorial
» Selecting

Here you learn one of the many ways to select an area in Photoshop so that you can edit just that area. You also learn how to fill a selected area with color.

1. **Click the Magic Wand tool in the toolbox.**
   You have to select pixels in an image before you can affect them with many of Photoshop's tools and commands. The Magic Wand tool is one of several ways of selecting pixels.

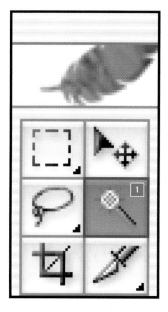

2. **Type** 18 **in the Tolerance box on the Options bar and make sure that there are check marks in the Anti-aliased and Contiguous fields.**
   Tolerance determines the color range of the pixels that the Magic Wand selects, based on color brightness. The lower the number, the narrower the range of colors that are selected. Anti-aliased softens the edges of the selection. Contiguous limits the selection to pixels that are adjacent to one another.

3. **Make sure that the Background layer is selected in the Layers palette and click inside one of the white polygons on the film slate arm to select that polygon.**
   The animated dashes that appear around the polygon are called marching ants. They identify the selected area of an image. If your selected area is bigger than the area shown here, decrease Tolerance in the Options bar. If your selected area is smaller than the white polygon, increase Tolerance. Then choose Select→Deselect and click again in the white polygon to reselect it with the new tolerance setting.

4. **Click the Foreground Color box in the toolbox to open the Color Picker.**
   The Color Picker is one of several tools that you can use to select colors in Photoshop.

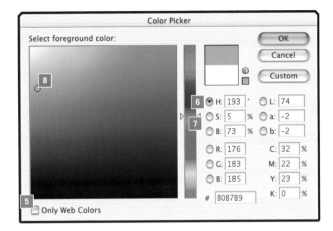

5. **Make sure that Only Web Colors is unchecked in the Color Picker.**

6. **Click the H radio button in the Color Picker.**
   This displays colors arranged by hue. S displays colors by saturation and B displays colors by their brightness.

7. **Move the Color slider in the Color Picker to the blue area of the hue bar.**

8. **Click a light gray-blue in the color field on the left side of the Color Picker and then click OK.**
   Alternatively, type the following values in the R, G, and B fields at the bottom of the Color Picker: R:**176**, G:**183**, B:**185**. These are the values of the red, green, and blue components of the color you are choosing.

9. **Check that the Background layer is still selected in the Layers palette. Press Option+Delete (Mac) or Alt+Backspace (Windows) to fill the selected area on that layer with the gray-blue color in the Foreground Color box.**

10. **Choose Select➜Deselect from the menu bar.**

11. **Repeat Steps 3 through 9 to color two more of the white polygons on the film slate arm. Try using khaki (R:213, G:148, B:96) and light olive (R:195, G:199, B:143) or colors of your choice.**
    You may have to tweak the Tolerance setting in the Options bar to get an accurate selection of each polygon.

12. **Choose File➜Save and leave the file open for the next tutorial.**

Tutorial
» Creating Shapes

This tutorial introduces you to the Shape tools, which are useful for drawing geometric shapes and graphics on special shape layers.

1. **Make sure the file** cb_filmslate.psd **that you saved at the end of the last tutorial is open. Click and hold the Shape tool in the toolbox and choose the Custom Shape tool from the fly-out menu of hidden tools.**

2. **Click the Shape sample in the Options bar.**

3. **Click the arrow on the top right of the Shape pop-up palette to open the palette menu and choose Objects from that menu. Click OK at the prompt.**
This replaces the default set of shapes with a different set of shapes.

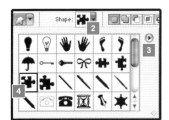

4. **Click one of the puzzle pieces in the Shape pop-up palette.**

5. **Click the Foreground Color box and choose a purple in the Color Picker (try R:124, G:90, B:123). Click OK.**

6. **Click and drag in the document to draw a puzzle shape, adjusting its size and shape as you drag.**
The Shape tool automatically creates a new shape layer in the Layers palette, labeled Shape 1. The shape layer has two thumbnails representing the two components of a shape—a pixel-based layer of color that fills the shape and a vector-based mask that outlines the shape. A shape has crisp edges and can be scaled and adjusted without losing those sharp edges.

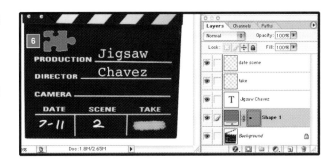

7. **Select the Path Selection tool (the black arrow) in the toolbox.**

8. **Click and drag in the document window to position the puzzle piece on the left side of the film slate.**

9. **Double-click the name of the shape layer—Shape 1—in the Layers palette. Type** puzzle shape **to rename the layer.**

< T I P >

I recommend that you always give each of your layers a meaningful name to make the layers easy to identify.

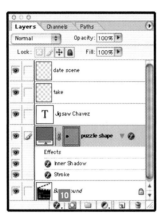

10. **With the puzzle shape layer still selected in the Layers palette, click the Layer Style icon at the bottom of the Layers palette and choose Stroke from the drop-down list.**
    This causes the Layer Style dialog box to open, displaying options for the Stroke layer style.

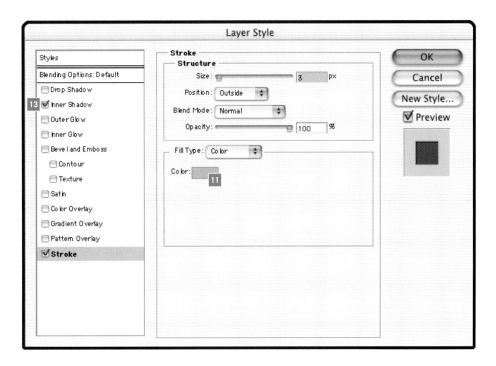

11. **With the Stroke effect highlighted on the left side of the Layer Style dialog box, click the Color option in the middle of the Layer Style dialog box.**
    This causes the Color Picker to open. Make sure the Stroke effect is highlighted, not just checked.

12. **Move your cursor out of the Color Picker, causing it to change to an eyedropper. Click in the document window on the polygon you filled with light olive to sample that color. Click OK in the Color Picker.**
    This fills the Stroke Color option with the color sampled from the image and creates a stroke of that color around the puzzle shape.

13. **Click the Inner Shadow check box on the left side of the Layer Style dialog box.**
    This adds an inner shadow to the layer style that you applied to the puzzle shape. In the Layers palette, the puzzle shape layer now displays sublayers of Stroke and Inner Shadow effects.

14. **Click OK to close the Layer Style dialog box and apply these styles to the puzzle shape.**

15. **Choose File→Save and leave the image open for the next tutorial.**

< T I P >
If you have trouble seeing the stroke that you applied to the image, click a different layer in the Layers palette. This hides the vector outline around the puzzle shape, making it easier to see the stroke that you just added.

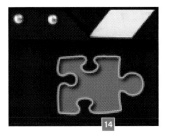

Tutorial
» Combining Images

In this tutorial you combine the filmslate image you've been working on with another image.

1. **With** cb_filmslate.psd **open from the last tutorial, click and hold the Eraser tool in the toolbox and choose the Magic Eraser tool from the fly-out menu.**

2. **Select the background layer in the Layers palette and click the white area of the image in the document window.**
   This causes the white pixels that were on the background layer to disappear, revealing a gray-and-white checkerboard pattern. The checkerboard is the symbol for transparent pixels.

3. **Double-click the layer named Layer 0 in the Layers palette and rename the layer by typing** slate.
   You may be wondering where Layer 0 came from. Making the bottom layer transparent automatically converted that layer from a special background layer (which cannot include transparency) to a regular layer named Layer 0.

<N O T E>
The Magic Eraser tool selects pixels within a range of color (just like the Magic Wand tool) and deletes those pixels—all in one step. It's great for knocking out solid color backgrounds like this one.

4. **With the slate layer still selected in the Layers palette, click inside the empty link field (the square just to the right of the eye icon) on each of the other layers.**
   This links the other layers to the slate layer so that you can move all the layers together into a second file.

5. **Choose File→Open and navigate to** cb_walkofame.psd **in the Confidence Builder folder on your hard drive. Click Open. If you see an Embedded Profile Mismatch, click OK.**

<N O T E>
Windows users, don't be surprised if you don't see the .psd extension on the end of the cb_walkofame file. Open it anyway.

6. **Select the Move tool in the toolbox.**

7. **Click inside the film slate document window and drag into the walkofame document window.**
   The film slate appears in the walkofame image, and all the layers from the film slate image appear in the Layers palette of the walkofame image.

8. **While the slate layer is still selected in the walkofame image, choose Edit→Transform→Rotate.**

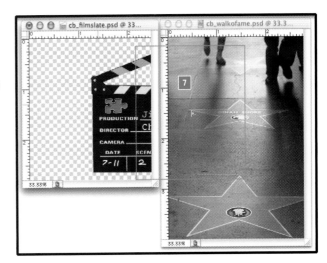

A bounding box appears around the film slate in the walkofame image.

9. **Move the cursor outside the bounding box so that it becomes a curved, double-pointed arrow. Click and drag to rotate the film slate and move it into a position like that shown in the figure. Press Return or Enter to commit this transformation.**
   If you want to cancel the transformation while it's in progress, press Esc on your keyboard.

10. **Click in the cb_filmslate.psd document window to make that image active. Choose File→Close.**
    The file cb_filmslate.psd closes; cb_walkofame.psd remains open.

11. **With cb_walkofame.psd active, choose File→Save to save over the original file of that name. Leave cb_walkofame.psd open for the next tutorial.**

Tutorial
» Applying Special Effects

Your collage is really taking shape now. Here you add some special effects to your collage, colorizing the background with a Hue/Saturation Adjustment layer, applying multiple filters from the new Filter Gallery.

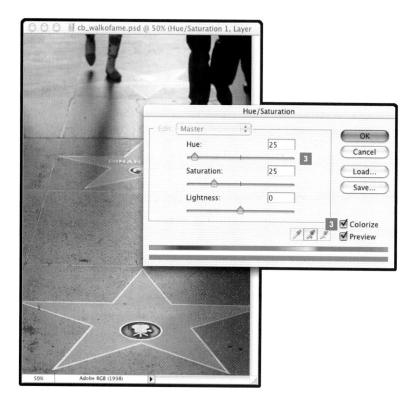

1. **With cb_walkofame.psd open from the last tutorial, select the Background layer in the Layers palette.**

2. **Choose Image→Adjustments→Hue/Saturation from the menu bar.**
   The Hue/Saturation dialog box opens.

3. **Click the Colorize check box in the Hue/Saturation dialog box. Move the Hue slider to 25 and the Saturation slider to 25. Click OK.**
   This changes the Background layer to sepia tones. Hue affects the color of the artwork and Saturation controls the intensity of the color.

4. **With the Background layer still selected in the Layers palette, choose Filter→Filter Gallery from the menu bar at the top of the screen.**
   The Filter Gallery dialog box opens. This is a new feature in Photoshop CS.

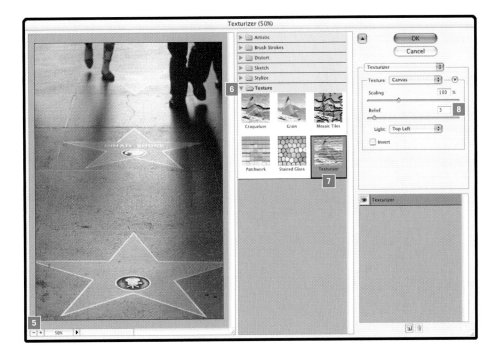

5. **Click the minus symbol at the bottom right of the preview pane in the Filter Gallery dialog box until you see most of the image in the preview window.**

   You see the Background layer of the image in the preview pane. The preview pane displays a preview of how your filtered image looks before you actually apply filters, giving you a chance to experiment with different filters.

<TIP>

You can reposition the image in the Filter Gallery preview pane by selecting the Hand tool in the toolbox and clicking and dragging in the preview pane.

6. **Click the arrow to the left of the Texture category in the middle of the Filter Gallery dialog box.**

   This displays thumbnails that represent each of the filters in the Texture category.

7. **Click on the Texturizer filter thumbnail.**

   The filter options on the right side of the dialog box change to settings for the Texturizer filter.

8. **Enter 3 in the Relief field. Leave the other filter settings at their defaults.**

   The Relief field controls the depth of the Texturizer filter effect.

9. **Click the New Effect Layer icon at the bottom of the Filter Gallery dialog box.**

   This adds another layer in the filter effects portion of the Filter Gallery dialog box.

10. **Click on the thumbnail of the Grain filter in the dialog box.**

11. **Click the Grain Type button in the options area on the right side of the dialog box and choose Soft.**

12. **Drag the Intensity slider to 30.**

13. **Click the Eye icons to the left of each filter effect layer off and on to see the effect of each filter in the preview pane of the Filter Gallery dialog box.**

    You can use the filter effect layers to make a filter effect invisible in the preview pane, rearrange the order in which filters are applied (which affects the appearance of the filtered image), and delete filter effects.

14. **Click OK to apply both the Texturizer and Grain filters to your image.**

< T I P >
Immediately after the Filter Gallery is applied, you have another chance to change the effect of the filters on the image by choosing Edit→Fade Filter Gallery and changing the opacity or blending mode in the Fade dialog box.

15. **Choose File→Save and leave** cb_walkofame.psd **open for the next tutorial.**

Tutorial
» Adding Text on a Path

This is the last tutorial in the Confidence Builder. Here you use another new feature, text on a path, to wrap a line of text around an elliptical path.

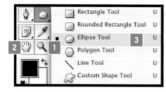

1. With cb_walkofame.psd open from the last tutorial, double-click the Zoom tool in the toolbox to magnify your view of the image to 100%.

2. Select the Hand tool in the toolbox, and then click and drag in the document window to position the image so that you have a good view of the movie projector symbol at the bottom of the image.

3. Select the Ellipse shape tool from the flyout menu of Shape tools in the toolbox.

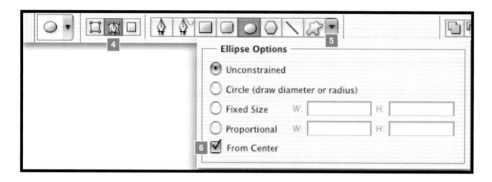

4. **In the Options bar, click the Paths icon.**
   This is an important step. If you don't do this, you end up drawing a shape filled with color rather than an empty path.

5. **Click the arrow to the right of the shape tool icons in the Options bar to open a palette of shape options.**

6. **In the shape options palette, add a check mark next to From Center. Click on a blank space in the Options bar to close the shape options palette.**
   This allows you to draw an ellipse shape from the center outwards, which is easier than the default behavior of starting from one edge of the ellipse.

7. **Click and drag an ellipse around the movie projector symbol in the image.**
   The ellipse should be slightly bigger than the symbol.

8. **If your ellipse isn't located exactly where you want it, select the Path Selection tool (the black arrow) from the flyout menu of selection tools in the toolbox and click and drag the path into place.**

9. **In the toolbox, click the Default Colors icon and then click the Switch Colors icon to set the Foreground color to white.**

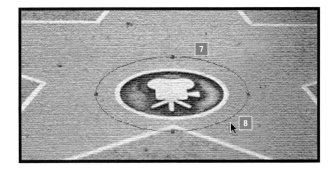

10. **Select the Horizontal Type tool in the toolbox. In the Options bar, set Font Family to Verdana, and Font Size to 8 pt. Click the Center Alignment button in the Options bar. Leave the other options at their defaults.**

11. **With the Background layer selected in the Layers palette, move your cursor over the elliptical path in the image until you see a wavy line in the middle of the I-beam cursor. Then click to set the starting point for your type.**

I-beam cursor

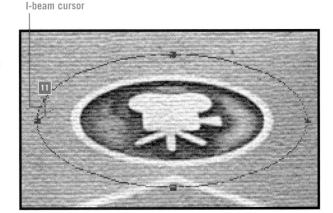

12. **Type the phrase** walk of fame**. Leave the cursor inside the flow of text so that the type remains uncommited.**
    The presence of a large check mark on the right side of the Options bar indicates that the type is not yet commited.

<TIP>
If text does not appear on the path, it's probably because the Right Alignment button was selected in the Options bar. Undo and try it again with the Center Alignment button selected.

13. **Select the Path Selection tool (the black arrow) in the toolbox and move your cursor over the type to display double-pointed arrows. Then click and drag the type around the circle to position it to match the illustration.**
    If you cannot drag the text, it's because you inadvertently committed the type before this step. You can fix this by clicking again in the text with the Type tool. Then select the Path Selection tool and drag the text into position.

<CAUTION>
When you drag the type around the ellipse, be careful not to drag across the path toward the center of the ellipse. This causes the type to flip to the inside of the ellipse, which is a nice effect but not the one you're after in this tutorial.

14. **Press the Return (Windows: Enter) key to make the path invisible.**

15. **Choose File→Save As to save your collage as** cb_end.psd **in the Confidence Builder folder on your hard drive. If a prompt appears, click Maximize Compatibility to remove the checkmark and click OK.**
    You completed your first Photoshop collage using many of the program's fundamental features. The figure shows what the final result should look like. In the sessions that follow, you find out more about the tools and commands that you tried out here.

Part I
Course Setup

Photoshop Basics

An Overview of Photoshop CS

Photoshop is, hands down, the most comprehensive image-editing program available. It offers tools to satisfy the graphic needs of a wide range of professionals and hobbyists—from photographers and artists to print designers and Web developers.

The breadth and depth of Photoshop's features are unmatched. You can use it for lots of different tasks. Here's a list of the kinds of things that you can do with Photoshop. You get a chance to try these as you work through this book, but don't stop with these ideas. Your imagination and creativity are the only real limits on how you use this expansive program.

- » Paint with pixel-based tools, including a variety of brushes, selections, fills, and layer masks.

- » Draw with vector-based tools, including shape tools, pen tools, and vector masks.

- » Retouch and manipulate photographs with toning, focus, and painting tools and with image adjustments.

- » Collage images using layers, masks, and blending modes.

- » Add special effects with filters and layer styles.

» Create editable, vector-based type, and arrange the text on a path.

» Use 16-bit images for high definition output.

» Work with an image's camera data using the Camera Raw feature.

» Create special types of output such as panoramic images, contact sheets, and slideshows.

» Make still, animated, and interactive graphics for the Web in Photoshop's companion program, ImageReady.

Photoshop CS for Macintosh OS X and Windows XP

One big change in this version of Photoshop is that it requires a minimum of Macintosh OS X 10.2.4 to install and operate.

On the Windows side, Photoshop CS is fully compatible with Windows XP operating system and also runs under Windows 2000 with Service Pack 3 installed. The program works the same way across platforms and operating systems. I let you know about any small cross-platform differences you may encounter as you work through the tutorials.

From a stylistic viewpoint, Photoshop CS is like a chameleon that wears different skins depending on the operating system in which it's running. In Mac OS X, Photoshop CS reflects that operating system's aqua interface, three dimensional buttons, and drop shadows. It's a bright, clean look that I think creates an optimal environment for graphics work. In OS X, you see a Photoshop menu at the top of the screen, to which the Preferences, Color Settings, and Quit commands have been moved. In Windows XP, the program takes on the crisp new look of that operating system, but the interface generally is the same as in other Windows environments.

New features in Photoshop CS

There's lots of anticipation among Photoshop users every time Adobe announces a new version of the program. Photoshop CS, like previous versions, didn't disappoint its fans. It has some major new features and lots of small changes that make it easier to use than ever. This section provides an overview of the most important new features in Photoshop CS.

» **Expanded File Browser features.** The File Browser was a major addition to Photoshop 7. It's an image viewer with extra features for managing and organizing files, and viewing thumbnails and detailed information about images. In Photoshop CS, the File Browser has more capability to search and edit metadata (information about the image files) and keywords, and also includes batch functions and other processes.

» **Draw text on a path.** Photoshop CS lets you apply text to a drawn path or shape. You can continue to edit and configure the text after it is applied to a path.

» **Create layer comps.** You can save combinations of layers in the same image file as Layer Comps to create design variations.

» **Create PDF presentations.** Combine several files into a single, multipage Adobe PDF document or create a PDF slideshow that has page transitions and security options.

» **Macromedia Flash file export.** Now you can export Macromedia Flash animations from images created in ImageReady CS. You can export each layer in an image to its own SWF file, which lets you open each layer as a separate symbol on its own layer in Flash.

» **Histogram palette.** Photoshop CS includes a new palette, the Histogram palette, that monitors changes as you make adjustments to your images.

» **Work with camera raw files.** Using the Camera Raw plug-in incorporated into Photoshop CS, you can work with pristine, raw image data from your camera's sensor, bypassing in-camera processing adjustments.

» **Use 16-bit images.** In Photoshop CS, you can work with 16-bit images for precise retouching or editing. Most functions in the program also apply to 16-bit images, such as layers and brushes.

» **Customizable keyboard shortcuts.** You can customize and save your own personalized set of keyboard shortcuts designed for how you like to work.

» **Easily access and use multiple filters.** The new Filter Gallery allows you to preview and apply multiple art filters from a single, easy-to-use dialog box.

Miscellaneous features

There are other changes in the existing tools and palettes. Some changes are of interest to those working with video, others for those working with Web pages or graphics design, and some are useful regardless of your area of interest.

» Track your editing history and save it in a file for future use and as a record of your activities.

» Use the Match Color command to match the color scheme of one image to that of another.

» Change the color of an area on an image without altering the original texture and shading using the new Color Replacement tool.

» Use the Shadow/Highlight correction command to modify over- or underexposed areas of an image without changing the rest of the image.

» Produce the effect of highlights taking on the shape of a camera lens aperture with the new Lens Blur filter.

» Simulate photographic lens filter effects using Photo Filter adjustment layers.

» Crop and straighten a group of scanned images automatically with the Crop and Straighten Photos command.

» Combine several images into a panorama.

» Customize a picture package using the Picture Package command.

» Work with huge images—up to 300,000 x 300,000 pixels, and up to 56 channels per file.

» Create non-square pixel documents for use on video monitors using document presets, and preview non-square documents without distortion.

» Export layers in an image to separate files for use in other editing and compositing programs.

» Work with new Web Photo Gallery templates, including templates that display file information and allow for viewer feedback.

» Use the new Web Content palette in ImageReady CS to create interactive elements.

» Fine-tune your control over remote rollover slices in ImageReady CS with the new point-and-shoot targeting system.

» Select, group, move, and manipulate objects on multiple layers in ImageReady CS using new object-oriented layout freatures.

You get a chance to work with these new features in the sessions that follow.

Project Overview

The Complete Course Project

This book is a tutorial-based course in Photoshop for students, educators, and design professionals. It will teach you not only how to use the features of Photoshop and ImageReady CS, but also how to apply those features in a practical context as you create a design project—a multipaged brochure for a film festival.

You'll create the collages for the brochure as you work through the tutorials in the book. Your reward for finishing all the tutorials will be completed collages for the pages of a brochure that you can print out on your inkjet or color laser printer or prepare for commercial printing. Use the printed product to remind yourself of the Photoshop techniques that you've learned, stimulate ideas for future projects, or show off your Photoshop skills to clients and friends.

Required Software

Adobe Photoshop CS. All the instructions and figures in this book are based on Adobe Photoshop CS. You may be able to download a try-out version of Photoshop CS from the Adobe web site (www.adobe.com/products/tryadobe).

What if you're stuck with using an older version of Photoshop? You can still work through this book, but you'll find that some features discussed here aren't available or are somewhat different in your version of the program. Photoshop 7 users will have an easier time with this book than users of even older releases because there aren't many drastic differences between Photoshop 7 and CS.

It's easy to install Photoshop CS on any supported Mac platform. Photoshop CS runs only on OS X 10.2.4 and later versions of the OS X operating system, including OS X 10.3. You cannot use Mac OS 9 or any earlier operating system. To install, start up your computer in OS X and follow the installation instructions.

Setting Photoshop's maximum memory allocation. Windows and Max OS X operating systems automatically distribute memory among open applications according to what each program needs at any given time. The only control that you have over the dynamic allocation of memory in Photoshop is to limit the maximum percentage of total memory that Photoshop is allowed to claim. You learn how to do that here.

1. Choose Photoshop→Preferences→Memory & Image Cache.

2. Click the arrow on the field labeled Maximum Used by Photoshop, which you'll find in the Memory Usage area of the Preferences dialog box. Move the slider to 90% or lower. Click OK.
   This sets a cap on the maximum percentage of available RAM that OS X allocates to Photoshop. This stops Photoshop from hogging all the available RAM, which could negatively affect the performance of other open programs and of the operating system itself.

< N O T E >

It's a good idea to set Photoshop's maximum memory usage to something less than 100%, even if there are no other programs running, to avoid Photoshop interfering with the memory requirements of the operating system. However, there is no method other than experience for determining the exact size at which to set this preference. Simply try decreasing this setting if you plan to run other programs that handle big files at the same time as Photoshop, and raising the setting if you work only in Photoshop. If the performance of the operating system or of other programs seems to degrade, go back into the Preferences dialog box and lower this number.

Adobe ImageReady CS

Adobe ImageReady is a companion program to Photoshop that's designed for making images for the World Wide Web. ImageReady CS ships free with Photoshop CS. This is a significant upgrade from the previous version of the program. Learn how to use ImageReady to create rollovers, animations, and other graphics for the Web in bonus session 1, on the CD-ROM.

Internet Explorer 5.2+

You want a Web browser installed on your computer for use with the tutorials on Web graphics. Internet Explorer 5.2+ (for Mac OS X) and Internet Explorer 6 (for Windows) can be downloaded from www.microsoft.com.

Required Hardware

Macintosh computer. Macintosh users need a PowerPC G3, G4, or G5 processor, a minimum of 192MB of RAM (256MB recommended), at least 320MB of free hard-drive space, and a color monitor that displays at least 1,024 x 768 resolution and is powered by a 16-bit or stronger color video card.

Windows computer. Windows users should have an Intel Pentium class III or 4 processor, a minimum of 192MB of RAM, at least 280MB of free hard-drive space, and a color monitor with at least 1,024 x 768 resolution and a 16-bit color video card. An Internet or phone connection is required for product activation.

CD-ROM drive. You need an internal or external CD-ROM drive to use the files and software on the CD-ROM that accompanies this book. The CD-ROM and its files can be read on both Macintosh and Windows platforms.

Optional digital still camera; optional scanner. Neither a digital camera nor a scanner is necessary to work through the tutorials in this book. However, if you have access to either, you can use it to bring images into Photoshop as resource material for supplemental projects.

Required Operating Systems

Macintosh OS. Mac OS X v.10.2.4 and above, including 10.3.

Windows OS. Windows 2000 with Service Pack 3, or Windows XP.

Using this book with different operating systems. The instructions and figures in this book illustrate Photoshop CS on both a Macintosh running OS X 10.2 and on a Windows XP computer. The instructions for performing different functions list the Mac OS X action first followed by the Windows command in brackets. If there are any relevant and noteworthy cross-platform or cross-operating system differences, I bring them to your attention as you work through the tutorials.

Required Files

The CD-ROM at the back of the book contains a folder called Tutorial Files. That folder holds the prebuilt files that you use as starting points for many of the tutorials in the book. Before you start work on any tutorial, open the Tutorial Files folder on the CD-ROM, find the folder for the current tutorial, and copy that folder to your computer, following the instructions in Appendix A. Use the files copied to your computer, rather than those on the CD-ROM, as you do the tutorial.

In each tutorial you work on a piece of the final project, a program guide for a film festival. In the course of working through the tutorials and sessions, you create collaged artwork for the pages of the brochure. The Tutorial Files subfolder for each session contains one file that contains the word _end in the filename. The _end file is an example of the collage that you work on in that session, showing the collage as it looks at the end of the session. (You may work on the same collage for more than one session.) Some of the Tutorial Files subfolders contain iteration files that give you an idea of how a collage should look at an intermediary point.

See Appendix A for more instructions on how to use the CD-ROM files.

As you work through the tutorials, you make changes to the prebuilt tutorial files you copied from the CD-ROM to your hard drive. When prompted to save a file, I suggest that you save right over the version you copied to your computer. That way, you always know where the latest version of the file is located. If you need to start over with a clean copy of a file, just go back to the CD-ROM and copy the file again.

Bonus Sessions

The CD-ROM at the back of the book contains two full bonus sessions in PDF format that I urge you to open and work through when you finish with Session 16. In Bonus Session 1, Using Photoshop and ImageReady for the Web, you learn how to lay out a Web page, slice images, create rollovers, make animations, create an entire Web site using Photoshop's Web Photo Gallery, and more. Bonus Session 2, Printing, covers how to print the cards you make throughout this book, and how to output Contact Sheets, Picture Packages, and PDF Presentations.

To read the bonus sessions, drag the files BS01.pdf and BS02.pdf from the CD-ROM onto your hard drive and open them in Adobe Reader. You can read these sessions on your screen or print them out on your desktop printer. Work through the tutorials in each bonus session using the BS01 and BS02 tutorial files that are included with the other tutorial files you install into your hard drive from the CD-ROM.

Stepping through the Project Stages

Photoshop CS Complete Course is divided into parts, sessions, and tutorials. The parts are general subject matter categories that contain chapters called sessions. The tutorials in each session are the heart of the book. Each tutorial focuses on a handful of related Photoshop features. It walks you through the steps of using those features to create part of the brochure project that you develop throughout the book.

Each tutorial builds on and assumes that you know the skills taught in the preceding tutorials. So if you're a beginning Photoshop user, I strongly suggest that you work through the tutorials in order. At the same time, each session can stand on its own. So if you already have Photoshop's basics under your belt, you may be comfortable approaching the sessions on a piecemeal basis (although you won't end up with all the printable pieces of the brochure project).

I've become a true believer in the tutorial method after teaching Photoshop to hundreds of students. I've found that most people learn better with their hands on a keyboard, trying out the features of the program, rather than just reading about them. To get the most out of this book, I recommend you do the same. I don't mind if you cozy up with the book in bed, but in the morning please take it with you to your computer and actually work through the tutorials.

I hope that you make this book yours by giving it a real workout. I like to picture your copy of *Photoshop CS Complete Course* fondly dog-eared and worn, a familiar companion on your way to learning Photoshop.

Part II

Getting to Know Photoshop

Customizing Photoshop

Session Introduction

Photoshop is a flexible program that you can customize to suit your own needs. In this session, you'll be introduced to Photoshop's work area, learning how to access the basic tools and commands, which are located in the toolbox, Options bar, menu bar, and palettes. Then you'll find out how to make the program your own by changing preferences, arranging palettes to your liking, saving reusable workspace configurations, and creating and saving tool presets.

TOOLS YOU'LL USE
Menu bar, toolbox, Options bar, palettes, Preferences, custom workspaces, and Tool Presets

CD-ROM FILES NEEDED
01_oldcamera.psd and 01_velvetrope.psd

TIME REQUIRED
90 minutes

Tutorial
» Accessing Tools and Commands

Take a tour of the Photoshop CS work area to see how to access the program's tools and commands, which are located in the menu bar, the toolbox, the Options bar, and the palettes. You'll be amazed at how easy it is to find what you need in this economical workspace.

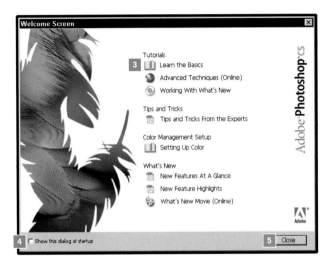

1. **Make sure that the Session 01 Tutorial Files folder from the CD-ROM that accompanies this book is on your hard drive.**
   See Appendix A for information about working with the CD-ROM files.

2. **Launch Photoshop CS from the OS X Dock (Windows: Start menu).**
   The Welcome Screen displays.

3. **Click Learn the Basics in the Welcome Screen.**
   The Photoshop CS Help files open, displaying a list of tutorial topics. Close the Help files to return to the Welcome Screen.

< N O T E >

Explore the other options available in the Welcome Screen. The icons indicate the type of file and where it is located. For example, you can view a movie online describing the new features or open an Acrobat PDF document describing tips and tricks.

4. **Click Show this dialog at startup to deselect the option.**
   The next time you open the program, the Welcome Screen is bypassed.

5. **Click Close to close the Welcome Screen.**
   You can't access Photoshop's commands when the Welcome Screen is open. To reopen the Welcome Screen choose Help→Welcome Screen.

6. **Choose File→Open from the menu bar at the top of your screen.**
   The menu bar contains a series of menus that have commands for executing tasks in Photoshop. You'll work with many of these commands in this book.

7. **Navigate to the Session 01 Tutorial Files folder on your hard drive. Choose** 01_oldcamera.psd **and click OK in the Open window.**
   Click Don't Show Again and OK if you get a warning about unreadable information when you open this or any file from the CD-ROM. You can safely ignore all such warnings.

Menu Differences for Macintosh and Windows Users

Macintosh OS X users have a menu labeled Photoshop on the left of the menu bar, next to the File menu. Click it, and you see that Photoshop Preferences, Color Settings, Quit Photoshop, About Photoshop, and About Plug-In are included in this menu. Windows users won't see a Photoshop menu in Photoshop CS. In Windows, Preferences and Color Settings are in the Edit menu, Quit is in the File menu, and About Photoshop and About Plug-In are in the Help menu.

8. **Move your cursor over the Eraser tool in the Photoshop toolbox to see that icon light up.**
   This tool rollover effect works with all the tools in the toolbox, and on all platforms.

9. **Leave your cursor hovering over the Eraser tool to reveal a Tool Tip that tells you the name of that tool.**
   Most of the Tool Tips also display a letter, which is a keyboard shortcut that you can click for quick access to a tool. If you're a beginning Photoshop user, I don't suggest that you bother learning lots of keyboard shortcuts, but they can be real time-savers for more advanced users. I point out the shortcuts that I think are most valuable throughout the book.

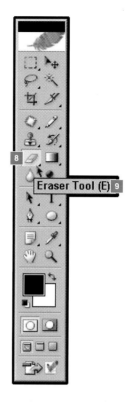

10. **Click once on the Eraser tool in the toolbox to make that tool active.**

11. **Click and drag on the white background of the image to erase some pixels.**
    After you make a tool active in the toolbox, you can use it to affect an open image, as you did here. By the way, the gray-and-white checkerboard pattern you now see in the image indicates that the erased area is transparent.

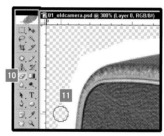

12. **Click the Eraser tool to reveal a menu of extra eraser tools.**

<NOTE>

Any tool that has an arrow in its bottom-right corner is hiding extra tools. Try clicking some other tools that display such an arrow to see for yourself.

13. **Click the Magic Eraser tool in the menu of extra tools.**
    The extra tool menu disappears, and the Magic Eraser icon appears in the toolbox.

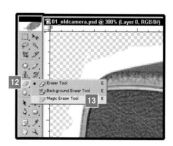

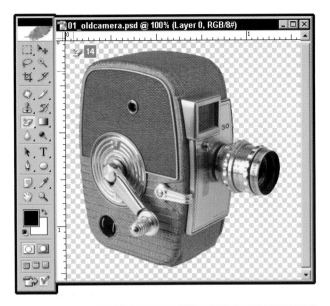

14. **Click anywhere on the white background of the image to apply the Magic Eraser tool.**

The Magic Eraser deletes all pixels that are similar in color to the pixel that you clicked. This is a great tool for eliminating solid color backgrounds, such as this one, with a single click. You'll work more with the Magic Eraser tool in future tutorials.

15. **Click the Dodge tool in the toolbox and keep your eye on the Options bar near the top of the screen.**

You can see that the content of the Options bar changes as you switch tools. Each tool has its own options, which determine how the tool behaves. You work with many tool options as you go through the tutorials in this book.

16. **Change the Dodge tool options so that they match those in the illustration.**

To make those changes, click the Brush sample in the Options bar to open the Brush Picker, and drag the Master Diameter slider in the Brush Picker to set the tip of the brush that you'll be using to 50 px. Click the Range option and choose Midtones from that menu. Click inside the Exposure option and type 80%.

<TIP>

You see some of the same options in the Options bar for more than one tool. For example, the Brush sample appears in the Option bar for the Clone Stamp, Pattern Stamp, Eraser, Magic Eraser, Background Eraser, Blur, Sharpen, Smudge, Brush, Pencil, History Brush, Art History Brush, Dodge, Burn, and Sponge tools.

17. **Click once in the image inside the camera viewfinder to lighten that area with the Dodge tool settings that you just chose.**

The Dodge tool in Photoshop acts just like an exposure dodging tool in a photographic darkroom; it lightens the dodged area.

18. **Locate the History palette among the palette groups on the right side of the screen. If you don't see it there, choose Window→ History from the menu bar.**

Contextual Menus

Hidden contextual menus are another place from which you can access certain Photoshop commands. To view a contextual menu, Ctrl+click (Windows: right-click) on an image. Depending on the tool you are working with, different options become available. For example, if you select the Pencil tool and then Ctrl+click (Windows: right-click) the image, you see the pencil options such as diameter and hardness display. You can also see some contextual menus in the palettes. For example, Ctrl+click (Windows: right-click) on any state in the History palette to see a contextual menu with some of the options related to that palette. The trick is knowing where and when to click to find a contextual menu. I'll let you know about the contextual menus I recommend as they come up in the course of tutorials.

19. **Click the arrow at the top right of the History palette to display a menu of palette options. Choose New Snapshot from the menu and click OK in the dialog box that appears.**

This creates a snapshot of the image as you edited it to this point. You can go back to this state at any point in the future by clicking this snapshot. Don't worry about understanding all the details of the History palette now. You learn more about it in the next session. The point of this step is to let you know about palette option menus.

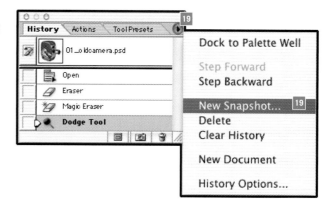

20. **Locate the Layers palette among the palette groups on the right side of the screen. If you don't see it there, choose Window→ Layers from the menu bar.**

The Layers for the image are listed in the palette.

<TIP>
All the palettes you can use in Photoshop CS are listed in the Window menu.

21. **Move the cursor over the Opacity label in the Layers palette.**

The cursor changes to a finger and a double-pointed arrow, indicating that the value in the Opacity field can be changed by scrubbing (clicking and dragging to the right or left) over the Opacity label.

22. **Click on the Opacity label and scrub to the left.**

This lowers the value in the Opacity field, making the image more transparent.

<NOTE>
Scrubby sliders are new to Photoshop CS. They are quicker to use than traditional pop-up sliders and are available wherever there is a labeled numerical field in a palette, in a dialog box, or in the Options bar. Holding the Shift key while you scrub over a label increases the value in the corresponding field by a larger increment. Holding the Option key (Windows: Alt key) while you scrub decreases the value by a larger increment.

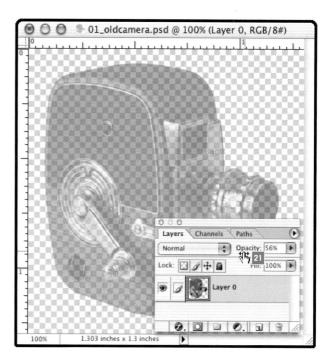

23. **Choose File→Close from the menu bar and click Don't Save at the prompt.**

Discussion
Extending the Help Menu

The Help menu in Photoshop CS and ImageReady CS is terrific. Even for those who don't ordinarily use Help much (and you know who you are!) there is a new feature that may change your thinking. You can access How To topics that explain how to accomplish common tasks. Suppose you want to learn to draw. Choose Help→How to Paint and Draw, and then choose an option from the list to learn how to draw shapes or work with tools.

You can create your own How To topics. How Tos are HTML files. Use any HTML editing program to modify the How To template file that comes with Photoshop or build an HTML file from scratch if you want. The new How Tos can be added to existing categories, or you can create your own new category.

Click the last option on the Help menu, How to Create How Tos, and then click How to Create Your Own How To tips. The command links you to a page of the main Help menu with a list of instructions. Here's an example:

1. **Open an HTML editing program. (You can use Word on Windows, Text Edit on a Mac, or any application that opens and edits HTML files on your platform.) Locate the template file** Add_001.html. **and open it in that program.**
   The file is in the hard drive folder: Photoshop CS\Help\Additional How To Content.

2. **Type the information for your tip, and then save the file.**
   The file must be saved in the Additional How To Content folder and given a name with an HTML extension. The example file is named when_to_use.html.

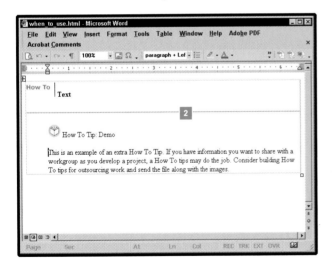

3. **Open the index file, Add_001.howto, also located in the Additional How To Content folder.**
   Type a category name, then a tip name, followed by the name of the HTML file. Make sure to enclose the names in quotation marks. Save the index file. Add _001.howto, into the Additional How To Content folder. The example uses a new category called "MY TIPS," and the tip is named "When to Use How Tos".

4. **Restart Photoshop.**
   You have to restart the program to attach your new file to the rest of the Help files.

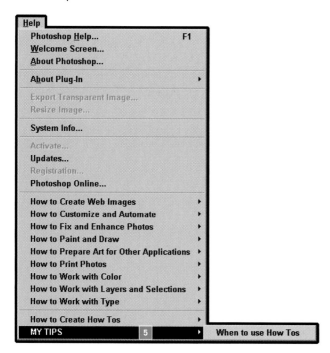

5. **Choose Help→MY TIPS.**
   The sample How To file is listed in its custom category. You can add as many files as you like to the custom category.

Tutorial
» Setting Preferences

Photoshop offers several Preference settings that you can use to customize the way your copy of the program runs, and you can easily change or reset the preference settings as necessary. This tutorial isn't intended to be an exhaustive look at all of the Photoshop Preferences. Instead, I show you those that deserve special attention when you do a print project, like the project in this book. The remaining tutorials assume that you made the changes suggested here, but whether you change these permanently in your copy of Photoshop is, of course, your preference.

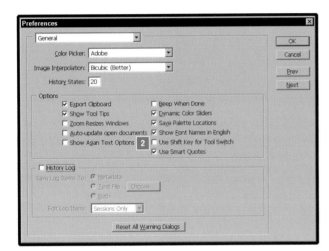

1. **Choose Photoshop→Preferences→General (Windows, Edit→ Preferences→General) from the menu bar.**
   This takes you to the General Preferences set, the first of nine sets.

2. **Click the Use Shift Key for Tool Switch check box to remove the check mark.**
   This Preferences change makes it easier to find a particular hidden tool in the toolbox. Now you can cycle through a group of hidden tools by repeatedly clicking the keyboard shortcut for that group (without having to hold the Shift key). Rather than setting a preference to use or not use system shortcut keys as in previous versions, Photoshop CS automatically uses the shortcuts, which you can customize. That's coming up in the next tutorial.

< N O T E >

The General Preferences include an option for choosing the way Photoshop CS interpolates, or mathematically adjusts the pixels in an image you resize or transform. There are five interpolation options. Nearest Neighbor is the fastest but least precise; it is useful for illustrations. Bilinear is a higher quality method, and Bicubic is the slowest but most precise for photographs and other images. Use Bicubic Smoother for enlarging images and Bicubic Sharper for reducing the size of an image.

3. **Click the Preferences Set button (currently labeled General) at the top of the Preferences dialog box and choose File Handling to reveal that set of preferences.**

4. **Click the drop-down list to open the Maximize PSD File Compatibility options and choose Never.**
   The reason to set this preference to Never is to keep the files you save in Photoshop's native PSD format as small as possible. Otherwise, when you save a layered file as a PSD, Photoshop creates and saves a flattened version of the file along with the layers—which increases file size.

<NOTE>

The File Handling preferences include an option for enabling the large document format, PSB. If this option is left unchecked, PSB does not appear in the list of file formats in the Save dialog box. If you are working with very large files (those over about 2 GB and 30,000 pixels in any dimension), select this option. Only Photoshop CS supports this file format.

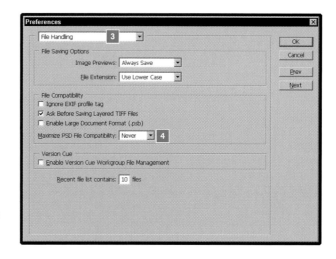

5. **Click the Preferences Set button and choose Displays & Cursors to reveal that set of preferences.**
   I suggest that you leave all the Displays & Cursors preferences at their defaults, as shown here. Leaving the Painting Cursors set to Brush Size displays the exact size of any brush tip that you use with the Brush tool, Eraser tools, and other painting tools. Leaving Other Cursors set to Standard displays an icon of the tool that you use. You can change any cursor temporarily to Precise (a cross-hair through which you can see the image) while you work by pressing the Caps Lock key.

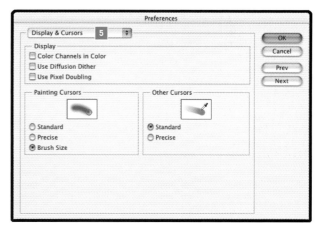

6. **Click the Preferences Set button and choose Transparency & Gamut.**
   This is another preference pane to leave at its defaults. The Transparency Settings are responsible for the way transparent pixels are displayed in an image—as a checkerboard of gray-and-white squares by default.

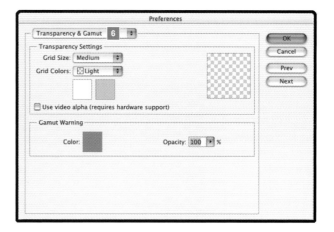

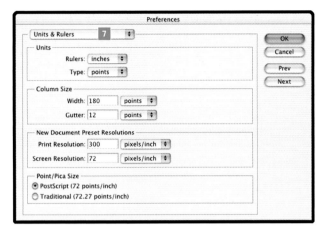

7. Click the Preferences Set button and choose Units & Rulers.

If you work on a print project, as you do for most of this book, leave these settings as they are so that the unit of measurement in the document window rulers and in dialog boxes is inches. However, if you create images for the Web or the screen, change the Rulers setting from inches to pixels. New Document Preset Resolutions determine the default resolutions of document presets in the New file dialog box. You learn about document presets in the next session.

\<TIP>

You can change rulers temporarily from inches to pixels when you're working on a document by choosing View→Rulers to display rulers. Then Ctrl+click (Windows: right-click) in a ruler and choose pixels from the contextual menu that appears.

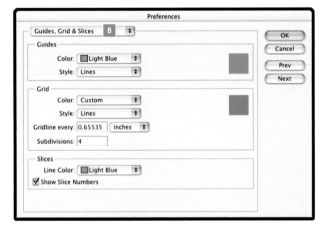

8. Click the Preferences Set button and choose Guides, Grid & Slices.

These are cosmetic preferences that you can leave at their defaults.

\<TIP>

If you ever want to revert to the default preferences, quit Photoshop, relaunch, and just after launching, press and hold Option+⌘+Shift (Windows: Alt+Ctrl+Shift). Click Yes when you're prompted to delete the Adobe Photoshop Settings file. This is something to try if Photoshop is behaving strangely, which sometimes is a result of damaged Preferences. In Mac OS, you can also remove the preferences file. Open the Preferences folder in the Library folder, and drag the Adobe Photoshop CS Settings folder to the Trash.

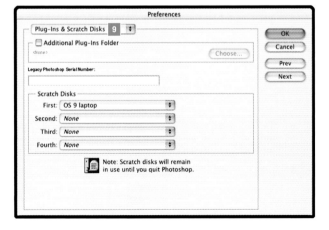

9. Click the Preferences Set button and choose Plug-Ins & Scratch Disks.

If you have an additional hard drive or a drive partition with lots of free space other than the one on which you're running Photoshop CS, click First and choose that drive or partition as your First scratch disk. If you have additional drives or partitions, you can set them as Second, Third, and Fourth scratch disks the same way.

\<NOTE>

A scratch disk is what Photoshop uses as virtual memory if it runs out of RAM when you're working on a big file. Instead of stopping the processing of the file, the program converts some of the unused memory on your computer's hard drive to a virtual memory or scratch disk, that simulates more processing power. By default, Photoshop uses the drive that contains the operating system as the first scratch disk.

<NOTE>

There is one more Preferences set—Memory & Image Cache. See
Part I, Project Overview to learn more about this preference.

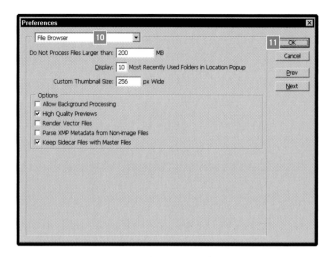

10. **Click the Preferences Set button and choose File Browser.**

    The File Browser feature is used to organize your images. It
    includes a set of palettes to use for sorting, selecting, and so
    on, as well as a toolbar. Leave the default settings as is.

11. **Click OK to close the Preferences dialog box.**

    A final word of advice on changing preferences: I suggest that
    you change only those preferences you understand and are
    sure that you want to change, so you don't cause any unex-
    pected modifications that may be hard to diagnose later.

Storing Image Information in the History Log

In some cases you need to keep a complete record of what operations have been performed on a file. Click History Log at the bottom
of the General Preferences dialog box to turn on the log function, as
shown in this figure. Choose from one of several options depending
on the extent and precision of information you need for your records.
For example, choose Sessions only to generate a log of when files
are opened and closed, or choose Detailed to create a history of
commands applied to the file. You can export the log file as a text
file. You can also store log data with other file information inside
the file, although the more data you save, the larger the file becomes
and the longer it takes to open and close the file. The History log is
not available for JPEG files.

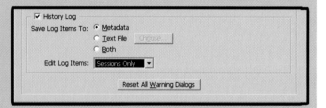

Tutorial
» Assigning Keyboard Shortcuts

Keyboard shortcuts can save a great deal of time. Rather than using the mouse to select a tool or a menu item and then using it on the image, you can quickly select a tool or command using keys. You can use the default keyboard shortcuts, or create custom shortcuts by modifying existing shortcuts or adding them to items that have none. In this tutorial, you learn how to create and remove custom keyboard shortcuts.

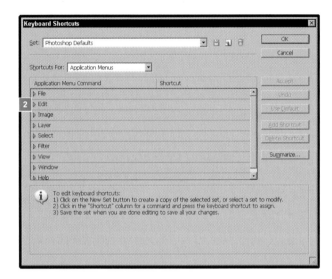

1. **Choose Edit → Keyboard Shortcuts.**
   The Keyboard Shortcuts dialog box opens. The Photoshop Defaults settings are shown.

<TIP>
If you import or create a new set of shortcuts, you can save them as a new collection of settings. To choose your collection, click the Set drop-down arrow and select your custom set.

2. **Click the arrow to the left of Edit in the Application Menu Command list to display the commands that appear in the program's Edit menu.**
   The Application Menu Command list is shown by default.

3. **Scroll down the list to display the Stroke command.**
   It currently has no assigned shortcut.

4. **Click the blank area to the right of the Stroke listing.**
   The Stroke command is selected and a field for adding the keystrokes is activated.

5. **Hold the ⌘ key (Windows: Ctrl Key) and type O (zero).**
   A notice displays saying that the shortcut key combination is already in use with another command (View→Fit to Screen) and that if you accept it here it will be removed from the other command.

6. **Click off the field anywhere on the dialog box or click Accept to accept the new shortcut key combination.**
   The key combination is removed from the View→Fit to Screen command and is attached to the Edit→Stroke command.

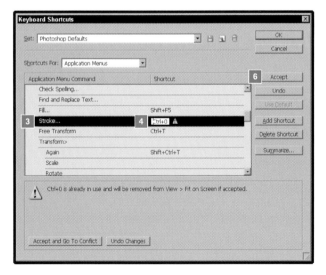

<TIP>
Alternatively, you can click Accept and Go to Conflict, which then opens the View menu highlighting the Fit to Screen option. This way you can set an alternate keystroke combination for that command if it is one you would commonly use.

<NOTE>

After you make any changes to the Photoshop Defaults settings,
the word "(modified)" appears in the Set title at the upper part of
the dialog box. You can save your modified shortcuts as a new set
that will appear in the Set menu at the top of the dialog box by
clicking the disk icon immediately to the right of the menu, giving
your new set a name, and clicking Save.

7. **Click the Shortcuts For menu and choose Tools.**
   The list of tools displays in the dialog box.

8. **Click the blank area to the right of the Single Row Marquee Tool
   listing.**
   The tool currently has no assigned shortcut while the previous
   two marquee tools in the list use the letter *M* as a shortcut key.

9. **Click off the field or click Accept to assign the key to the tool.**

<TIP>

Assign shortcut keystroke combinations to the Palette menus in the
same way; select the Palette Menus from the Shortcuts For menu,
choose the command, and type the keystrokes.

10. **Click Cancel to close the dialog box and return the settings to
    their original values.**
    You learned how to set custom keystroke commands for pro-
    gram functions. As your Photoshop skills and your own way
    of working develop, remember you can customize commands
    or change commands with assigned keystrokes that you use
    most often.

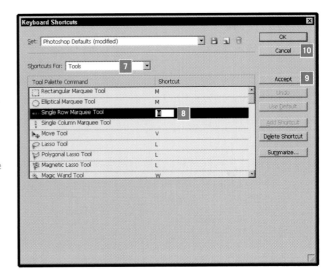

Tutorial

» Creating Custom Workspaces

Photoshop has several palettes, which you can arrange to meet your individual needs. In this tutorial, you'll learn how to close, collapse, move, and group palettes and how to store palettes in the Options bar. Then you'll practice using the Photoshop CS Workspace feature, with which you can save multiple arrangements of palettes as reusable, custom workspaces.

1. **Open** 01_velvetrope.psd **from the Session 01 Tutorial Files folder on your hard drive.**
   If you get a warning dialog box about this file, click OK to ignore it.

2. **Choose Window→Workspace→Reset Palette Locations from the menu bar.**
   This reopens any palette that you may have closed and resets all palettes to their default locations. You should do this at the beginning of each session in this book.

3. **Locate the palette group that contains the Navigator palette. Click the Info tab to bring the Info palette to the foreground in that palette group.**
   This is the fastest way to switch between palettes that are grouped together.

<NOTE>
You can display any palette at any time by choosing its name from the Window menu at the top of the screen. In Photoshop CS, palettes are listed alphabetically in the Window menu, and all currently open documents are listed at the bottom of the Window menu.

4. **Click the red button at the top left (Windows: the Close button at the top right) of the Info palette group to close that group of palettes.**

5. **Locate the History palette and click the green Zoom button at the top left of its palette group (Windows: the Minimize button at the top right of the palette group).**
   The palette group collapses so that only its title bar is showing. This is a good way to conserve screen real estate, while keeping all your palettes accessible. To re-expand the palette group, click the Zoom button (Windows: Minimize button) again.

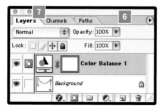

6. **Locate the Layers palette, click the title bar of its palette group, and drag the palette group away from the edge of your screen.**

7. **Click the green Zoom button at the top left of the Layers palette group (Windows: the Minimize button at the top right of the palette group).**
   The Layers palette resizes to fit its existing content. As you can see, the Zoom button (Windows: Minimize button) has slightly different effects on different palettes. To collapse the Layers palette to just its title bar, you'd have to Option+click (Windows: Alt+click) this button.

8. **Click and drag from the bottom-right corner (Windows: any corner) of the Layers palette to resize the palette by hand.**
   You can make it narrower, wider, longer, or shorter.

9. **Click and drag the Channels tab to separate the Channels palette from its palette group.**

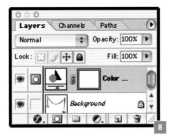

10. **Click and drag the Paths tab from its current palette group into the Channels palette group. Release the mouse button when you see a black box around the inside perimeter of the Channels palette.**
    This adds the Paths palette to the Channels palette group.

11. **Click and drag the Layers tab from its current palette group to the bottom of the Paths/Channels palette group. Release the mouse button when you see a thin black box at the bottom of the palette group.**
    This joins the Layers palette to the top of the Paths/Channels palette group. Now when you click and drag from the title bar of the joined palettes, all of them move together. I suggest that you join palettes you often use together so that you don't have to hunt for any of them.

<CAUTION>
Joining palettes can be tricky. You have to release the mouse button when you see the thin black box, rather than the black box around the inside perimeter of the palette.

12. **Shift+click the title bar of the Layers palette group to snap the joined palette groups to the nearest edge of your screen.**
    This is a quick way to tidy up your workspace. Palettes also snap to any edge of the screen if you drag them near the edge.

13. **Click the title bar of the toolbox and drag the toolbox to the right side of your screen.**
    You can also drag the Options bar anywhere on your screen.

14. **Click the Color tab and drag it into the gray Palette well on the right side of the Options bar (which contains the Brushes palette, Tool Presets palette, and Layer Comps palette by default).**
    The Palette well is a great place to store palettes that you use frequently. Another way to send a palette to the Palette well is to click the arrow at the top right of any palette and choose Dock to Palette Well from the palette options menu. Try this with the Swatches palette.

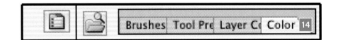

<NOTE>
The Palette well is not resizeable. As you add more tabs to it, the width of the tab decreases, but the Palette well doesn't increase in width. As you move your mouse over the tabs, the full name displays so you can easily find the tab you are looking for.

<CAUTION>
You won't be able to see the Palette well if your computer's resolution is set to less than 800 pixels wide, but it is difficult to design at resolutions less than 800 pixels in width, so you aren't likely to have a problem.

15. **Click the tab of the Color palette in the Palette well to open that palette. Click the tab again to close the palette.**

To remove a palette from the Palette well, click and drag the palette by its tab.

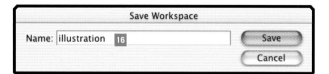

16. **Choose Window→Workspace→Save Workspace. Give this work-space a name in the Save Workspace window. (I chose the name** illustration **to represent the task for which I use this palette con-figuration.) Click Save.**

This saves a custom workspace with your palettes, Palette well, Options bar, and toolbox arranged as you set them.

<NOTE>

You can also save a custom File Browser workspace. Arrange the File Browser components as you like, and then save the workspace as described in Step 16.

17. **Rearrange and close some of the palettes on your screen. Then choose Window→Workspace→illustration to reuse your illustra-tion workspace.**

All your palettes snap back to the configuration that you saved as the illustration workspace.

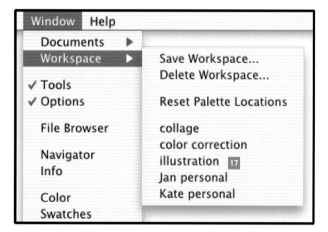

<NOTE>

You can create and save multiple workspaces. I suggest that you make separate workspaces for each task you perform, such as col-lage, color correction, illustration, and type.

18. **Click Window→Workspace→Reset Palette Locations to restore the default palette configuration before moving on to the next tutorial.**

19. **Close** 01_velvetrope.psd **without saving.**

You learned how to work with the palettes in the program, how to reset the default configuration, and how to save a custom workspace.

Using Two Monitors

If you are using a graphics card that supports it, you can run Photoshop CS on two monitors. The monitors are recognized and configured through the operating system. You can then split the content of your workspace over two monitors, such as having the image display on one monitor, and some of the palettes on the other (although on Windows you can't put the file browser on a separate monitor from the rest of the application). The mouse moves from monitor to monitor as if it were one unit. Both moni-tors do not have to be at the same resolution.

Tutorial
» Customizing Tools with Presets

The Tool Presets feature saves a copy of a tool with whatever tool options you choose, giving you the ability to create custom tools. In this tutorial, you'll create several Type tool presets, which you can use to quickly create headlines and text in a document.

1. **Click the Type tool in the toolbox.**
   The Options bar changes to display options for the Type tool.

2. **Click the Font option in the Options bar and choose Arial Black. Click the Size option in the Options bar and choose 36.**
   The fonts used in this tutorial are common ones, but if you don't have them in your computer, use fonts of your choice.

3. **Click the Type tool on the far left of the Options bar to open the Tool Preset picker.**

4. **Click the Create New Tool Preset icon on the Tool Preset picker.**

5. **Give your new tool preset a name and click OK in the New Tool Preset dialog box.**
   Photoshop suggests a name for the new tool preset that describes the tool options. You may prefer to give your tool preset a meaningful name that relates to the project in which you plan to use it (such as **Program Guide Headline 1**, which I suggest that you use here).

6. **Click the Size option in the Options bar and choose 18, leaving the Font option set to Arial Black.**

7. **Repeat steps 3 through 5 to create another tool preset. Name this one** Program Guide Subhead 2.

8. **Click the Font option in the Options bar and choose Arial. Click the Size option in the Options bar and choose 12.**

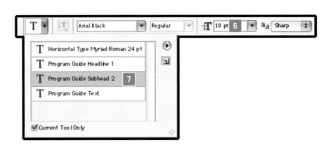

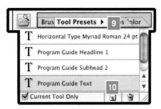

9. **Click the tab of the Tool Presets palette in the Palette well to open that palette.**

This is an alternative way to make a new tool preset. You can create and apply tool presets from either the Tool Presets palette or the Tool Presets Picker on the Options bar.

10. **Click the Create New Tool Preset icon at the bottom of the Tool Presets palette.**

11. **Name this tool preset Program Guide Text in the New Tool Preset dialog box and click OK.**

Another Type tool preset appears in both the Tool Presets palette and the Tool Presets Picker on the Options bar, along with all the other presets for the Type tool. If you ever want to delete a tool preset from this list, select it in either location, click the arrow on the top right of that palette or picker, and choose Delete Tool Preset.

12. **Make sure that the Type tool is still selected in the toolbox. Click the Type tool icon on the Options bar to reopen the Tool Presets Picker. Click the tool preset labeled Program Guide Headline 1 to select that tool preset for use.**

This is all that you have to do to use a tool preset. If you were to type inside an image now, the type would appear with the options that you built into this custom tool preset. You can select a tool preset from the Tool Presets palette the same way.

13. **Click the arrow on the top right of the Tool Presets Picker and choose Reset Tool from the menu.**

The Type tool is restored to its default settings—Helvetica, Medium, 12 pt—which display in the Options bar. You can also choose Reset All Tools from this menu to restore all tools to their default settings.

<N O T E>

I strongly suggest that at the beginning of each session in this book you Reset All Tools as explained here. This is also a good thing to do whenever you're working on a computer that has multiple users.

<N O T E>

The Tool Presets menu also offers options for saving and loading sets of tool presets. For example, you can click Save Tool Presets to save your Type tool presets as a .tpl format file and share that file with other users. Or you can use tool presets that another user created and saved as a .tpl file by downloading that .tpl file to your computer and clicking Load Tool Presets. By the time you're reading this book, there will probably be Internet sites offering Photoshop CS tool presets for free or for sale.

14. **Click the Current Tool Only check box in the Tool Presets Picker to remove the check mark.**

You see a list of the main set of tool presets that ship with Photoshop, as well as those you just created. Check some of these out when you have some free time.

15. **Click the arrow on the top right of the Tool Presets Picker, choose Text from the menu, and click OK at the prompt to replace the main set of tool presets with a set of Type tool presets that ships with Photoshop CS.**

Photoshop CS also ships with sets of Art History, Brushes, Cropping, and Marquee tools that you can load from this menu.

16. **Click the arrow on the top right of the Tool Presets Picker again; choose Reset Tool Presets from the menu to restore the main set of tool presets.**

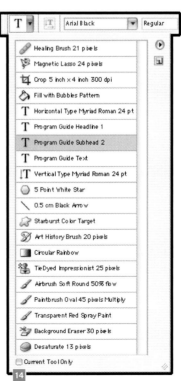

» Session Review

This session introduces Photoshop's work area and shows how to access tools and commands using the Menu bar, the toolbox, the Options bar, and palettes. The opening figure in this session shows you one of the images you are working with in this book. You also learned how to customize Photoshop CS to suit your personal work habits by setting preferences, rearranging palettes, and using the new custom workspace and tool preset features. The final figure in this session shows you the same image, but with some of Photoshop's tools and options active.

Use the following questions to review what you learned in this session. You can find the answer to each question in the tutorial noted.

1. What does an arrow on the bottom right of a tool icon in the toolbox signify? (See "Tutorial: Accessing Tools and Commands.")

2. How do you access the menu of palette-related options associated with each palette? (See "Tutorial: Accessing Tools and Commands.")

3. How do you display a contextual menu? (See "Tutorial: Accessing Tools and Commands.")

4. Where is the template file and the index file for new How To components stored? (See "Discussion: Expanding the Help Menu.")

5. Can you add additional sets of custom How To files to your program? (See "Discussion: Expanding the Help Menu.")

6. Why would you turn off Use Shift Key for Tool Switch in General Preferences? (See "Tutorial: Setting Preferences.")

7. Which drive should you choose as the first scratch disk in Plug-Ins & Scratch Disks Preferences? (See "Tutorial: Setting Preferences.")

8. What is the default collection of keyboard shortcuts named after you modify any of the command short-cut key combinations? (See "Tutorial: Assigning Keyboard Shortcuts.")

9. Can you remove a keyboard shortcut after you have added it? (See "Tutorial: Assigning Keyboard Shortcuts.")

10. How do you separate a palette from its palette group? (See "Tutorial: Creating Custom Workspaces.")

11. How do you add a palette to a palette group? (See "Tutorial: Creating Custom Workspaces.")

12. How do you snap a palette group to the edge of the screen? (See "Tutorial: Creating Custom Workspaces.")

13. How do you save a custom workspace? (See "Tutorial: Creating Custom Workspaces.")

14. Can you save multiple custom workspaces? (See "Tutorial: Creating Custom Workspaces.")

15. How do you reset all the palettes to their default locations? (See "Tutorial: Creating Custom Workspaces.")

16. How do you create a new tool preset? (See "Tutorial: Customizing Tools with Presets.")

17. How do you reset all tools? (See "Tutorial: Customizing Tools with Presets.")

Managing Documents

tammeron international experimental cinema

03.02.03 < 03.05.03
tammeron england
27th annual festival
2003

film schedule

fallen on wallstreet
03.02 5pm
finish line
03.02 7pm
territorial velvet
03.02 9pm
arising to the end
03.03 7pm
four large squares
03.04 7pm
frozen with steak
03.05 7pm
reason to cry
03.05 9pm

Session Introduction

This session teaches fundamental lessons about creating, managing, and saving files in Photoshop CS. You learn about bringing documents into Photoshop and saving them. You practice viewing, opening, rotating, ranking, sorting, organizing, and naming documents in one of Photoshop's more impressive features—the File Browser. Then you find out how to fix your Photoshop mistakes using the History palette and related features.

TOOLS YOU'LL USE
Open dialog box, Save dialog box, Save As dialog box, File Browser, Photomerge command, Search dialog box, Undo command, Revert command, Fade command, and History palette

CD-ROM FILES NEEDED
02_films.psd and the photos and Photomerge folder

TIME REQUIRED
90 minutes

Discussion
Resolution and Color Mode

Resolution Primer

Image resolution for print is one of the more difficult subjects you run into in this book. You don't have to know everything about resolution to work with Photoshop, but you'll feel more comfortable in the long run if you know the following terms and concepts.

A pixel, which stands for picture element, is a tiny rectangle of color information that is the basic building block of a bitmap digital image. Image resolution in Photoshop is the number of pixels that make up each printed inch of the image. The higher the resolution of an image, the more clear and detailed the image looks when it's printed, at least up to the limitations of the printer.

The downside of a high resolution is that it increases file size. An image with a large file size can be slow to edit in Photoshop and takes relatively longer to print and to transfer electronically. The larger the file size, the more storage space the file requires, but that's becoming less of an issue as storage becomes cheaper and easier.

Image resolution also affects the amount of space an image takes up on your computer screen. An image with a high resolution may take up more space than you can see all at once. For example, in the next tutorial you create an image that is 1440 pixels wide by 1080 pixels high (240 pixels per inch x 6 inches = 1440 pixels, and 240 pixels per inch x 4.5 inches = 1080 pixels). If your computer monitor can display only 1024 x 768 pixels, you won't see the whole image on your screen when you work on it in Photoshop. Although this may be uncomfortable, it isn't fatal because you can use the Hand tool to scroll around the image or you can set Photoshop's magnification to less than 100% (which you learn to do in the next session).

So how do you pick a resolution setting when you create a new document in Photoshop or scanning? Aim for the highest resolution that your printer can reproduce, as long as you have enough RAM, scratch disk space, and monitor resolution to work on the image efficiently in Photoshop. There's no reason to go to a higher image resolution because it won't improve the printed image and it inflates your file size and screen size. On the other hand, you don't want the resolution to be too low, or your printed image looks fuzzy, lacks detail, and may look pixelated.

The best resolution for a color image destined for a current inkjet printer is between 240 and 300 pixels per inch (ppi). Don't be confused by the advertised resolution of your inkjet printer. The printer uses several dots of ink to create the color of each pixel, so you only need about one-third as much image resolution as the printer's advertised dots per inch (dpi). For example, the tutorial files for this book were created at 240 ppi, which is an optimal image resolution for printing on my 720 dpi inkjet.

Resolution for images that are printed commercially is determined differently. Commercial printers usually use a halftone screen and measure screen frequency as lines per inch (lpi). Ask your print shop what lpi setting will be used to print your image and set a resolution in Photoshop that's no more than two times that lpi setting.

<NOTE>

If you were creating an image for the Web or other on-screen delivery, rather than for print, you'd set the unit of measurement to pixels and type in the desired number of pixels of width and height. Then just ignore the Resolution field. It doesn't matter what number appears there when you set the physical dimensions of the image in pixels. Honest!

RGB Color Mode

Color mode is the set of colors from which an image is built. RGB Color mode offers 16.7 million colors. Each pixel in RGB mode is described by a combination of red, green, and blue color values. RGB is the mode you'll use most often, whether you create an image in Photoshop's New dialog box or scan an image yourself for editing in Photoshop. RGB is the way to go if you prepare an image for output to an inkjet printer because most inkjet printers use RGB color drivers (even if they print with CMYK inks). Web graphics must be RGB because that's the only kind of image that can be seen on the Web. Images for other kinds of on-screen display should be RGB because color monitors always display all images in RGB. Most images you bring into Photoshop from digital cameras and scanners (other than high-end, professional CMYK scans) are already RGB because that's the mode those devices generate. Even if you're making a grayscale image, you often get the best results by starting with an RGB image and converting to grayscale later using one of several methods (Image→Adjustments→Desaturate; Image→Mode→Grayscale; the Channel Mixer; or one of the channels from the Channels palette).

RGB or CMYK Mode for Commercial Printing?

CMYK mode simulates the cyan, magenta, yellow, and black inks used in commercial printing. Some Photoshop users prefer to edit in CMYK mode when they prepare an image for a commercial printer. However, there are good arguments in favor of working in RGB rather than CMYK mode in that situation. Not all filters are available in CMYK mode. Other Photoshop features, such as layer blending, adjustments, and layer effects, often give better results when applied to an RGB image than a CMYK image. CMYK files are bigger than RGB files because they have four instead of three color channels. If you use CMYK mode, your monitor translates those colors to RGB for display anyway. And, as mentioned earlier, most digital photographs and nonprofessional scans are RGB in the first place. So it makes sense to edit in RGB mode, unless you are working with a high-end CMYK scan and can handle the larger file size.

If you do work in RGB, you can view an image to get an idea of how it looks in CMYK without permanently changing its colors. The process of looking at an image in another color space is called soft proofing. Choose View→Proof Setup and select Working CMYK to see how your image looks in the CMYK working space defined in Photoshop's Color Settings (which you learn about in Session 4). Or choose Custom to load a custom proof setup for another printer. Turn the soft proof display off and on by choosing View→Proof Color to display the color values of a soft proof in the Info palette. (Click the arrow on the top right of the Info palette, click one of the Readout Mode buttons, and choose Proof Color.)

You can convert an image to CMYK for printing after you finish editing it in RGB by choosing Image→Mode→CMYK Color. Remember to flatten the image first (Layer→Flatten Image), or layer blending may not work the way you intended. Be prepared to see a color change when you convert from RGB to CMYK.

Tutorial
» Creating Images

In this tutorial, you create a Photoshop file from scratch, learning important information about filenaming, image resolution, and color modes along the way. You are also introduced to other methods of getting images into Photoshop.

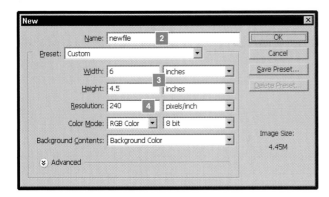

1. **Choose File→New.**

   This opens the New dialog box. The default settings that you see on your screen are likely different than those shown here. They come either from your virtual Clipboard, which remembers the settings of the last image you copied, or if there's nothing in the Clipboard, from the last image you created.

2. **Type a name for the new file in the Name field.**

   Don't bother adding a file extension (such as .psd or .tiff) to the name at this point. Photoshop does that for you automatically when you save the file.

3. **Click the button to the right of the Width field and choose inches as the unit of measurement. Type** 6 **in the Width field and** 4.5 **in the Height field.**

   This sets the physical dimensions of the image as it prints— 6-inches wide by 4.5-inches high. Document units change together unless you press Shift as you type the numbers. If you choose inches in one dimension, inches is automatically set in the other dimension as well.

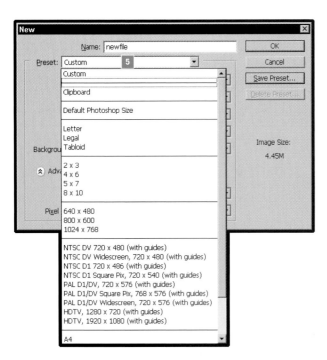

< T I P >

As soon as you type the first number for your settings, the Preset changes to Custom.

4. **Check that the button to the right of the Resolution field is set to pixels/inch and type** 240 **in the Resolution field.**

   This tells Photoshop to put 240 pixels of information in every inch of width and height in this image.

5. **Click the Preset button in the New dialog box and take a look at the list of preset document sizes. You can close this menu without making a choice for now.**

   The Preset list offers presets for the physical dimensions and resolution of a new document.

< N O T E >

You can create and save custom presets as well. When you create settings for a new file, the Save Presets button becomes active. Click the button to open a small dialog box. Name the preset, choose the settings you want to store, and click OK.

6. **Click the Color Mode button and choose RGB Color.**

   The mode is the set of colors from which your image is built. RGB Color mode offers 16.7 million colors. Each pixel in RGB mode is described by a combination of red, green, and blue color values.

7. **Click the Bit Depth option and choose 8-bit color.**

   The bit depth is the amount of color data contained in each channel of color (red, green, and blue). A higher bit depth means you can store more color information.

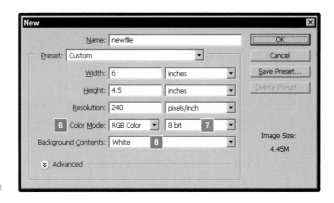

< N O T E >

Setting the bit depth of an RGB image to 8 bit creates an image with 24 bits of color information (8 bits x 3 channels), accommodating over 16 million possible colors. Photoshop CS provides significantly expanded support for editing high bit documents that have 16 bits of information in each channel, offering even more color data. See Session 16 for more information on high bit depth images.

< T I P >

When you create and save a new file, the color mode and bit depth are shown at the top of the document window along with the file's name.

8. **Click the Background Contents drop-down menu and choose White.**

   The background of your image becomes white. You can also choose the Background Color option, which creates a background for the image that's filled with whatever color is currently in the Background Color box in the toolbox. A background looks like a layer in the Layers palette, but it acts differently than a regular layer, as you find out in Session 8. The third option creates a transparent background.

9. **Click OK to close the dialog box.**

   A new document window opens containing an image with a plain background and the other settings that you chose.

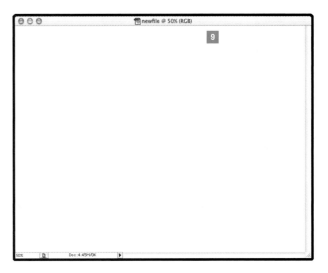

< T I P >

To create a new image with a regular layer instead of a special background, choose Transparent as the image content, rather than Background Color or White. You are able to save the image at that point only in a format that supports layers—PSD, TIFF, or PDF—unless you flatten the image first (Layer→Flatten Image).

10. **Leave the image open for the next exercise.**

    If you were to close the document at this point, you wouldn't find a trace of it on your hard drive. That's because a new document is not automatically saved at the time it's created. So it's smart to save each document soon after creating it and to resave often. You learn all about saving in the next tutorial.

Setting Pixel Aspect Ratio for Non-Square Documents

In Photoshop CS, you can work with files designed for video that don't use square pixels. When you create a file with any of the non-square presets in the Preset menu of the New dialog box, you can also specify a pixel aspect ratio appropriate to your video requirements. In the New dialog box, click the Advanced arrow to display an additional segment of the dialog box. Click the Pixel Aspect Ratio drop-down arrow and choose the required ratio.

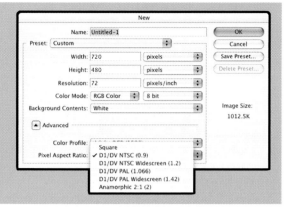

<NOTE>

Creating an image from scratch has taught you about resolution, color mode, and other basic concepts of digital imaging. Making a new image is a fundamental Photoshop skill, but it's not the only way to get an image into Photoshop for editing. Table 2-1 introduces other ways to bring images into Photoshop. You use some of these methods, such as opening an existing image in Photoshop, many times in this course and as you work on your own. Others are more esoteric. So rather than walk you through each method, I offer this summary as a reference list.

Table 2-1: Other Ways to Get Images into Photoshop

Method	Photoshop Command	Tips
Open an existing image in Photoshop	File→Open and navigate to the file in the Open window	Click Open or just double-click the filename in the Open window. To reopen a file you've opened recently, choose File→Open Recent. To locate and open files visually, use the File Browser, which you learn about in this session.
Scan an image into Photoshop	File→Import and choose Twain driver or File→Import→WIA Support (Windows XP only)	Alternatively, scan using your scanner's software and open the resulting image in Photoshop.
Bring photographs from a digital camera into Photoshop	File→Import→WIA Support (Windows XP only)	Alternatively, use your digital camera's software or iPhoto on a Mac to bring photographs into your computer and open the photographs in Photoshop.
Bring an EPS or Illustrator file into Photoshop	File→Open or File→Place	Both methods rasterize the file (convert it from a mathematically defined, vector format into pixels, so you can no longer scale and edit it as vector data). Use Open to open the file as a new image in Photoshop at the resolution you choose. Use Place to bring the file into an open image in Photoshop at the resolution of that image.
Copy an object from an Illustrator file into an image in Photoshop	Edit→Paste→Paste As Pixels, Paths, or Shape Layer	Pasting as paths or as a shape layer keeps the artwork in vector format, so you can scale and edit it in Photoshop without degrading its appearance.
Open images contained in a PDF (Adobe Acrobat format) file in Photoshop	Import→PDF Image or File→ Automate→ Multi-Page PDF to PSD	Use the Import method to bring a single image contained in a PDF into Photoshop. Use the Automate method to open multiple images from a PDF as new images in Photoshop.

Tutorial
» Saving Files

In this tutorial, you find out all about saving files, including how to save a new file for the first time, how to save a file as you work on it, how to save an open file in a new format, and how to save a file with layers. It's crucial to get in the habit of saving your work often. If your computer crashes or Photoshop freezes, you lose all the work you've done since the last save. So save frequently as you go through the tutorials in this book and as you work on your own projects.

1. **Check that your newfile image is still open from the previous tutorial. If it's not, create a new document following the steps in the preceding tutorial, "Creating Images."**

2. **Try to choose File→Save. You see that that command is grayed out, meaning that it's unavailable.**
   You can't use the Save command if you haven't made a change to the image since you created or last saved it.

3. **Choose Layer→New→Layer and click OK to add a layer to this image.**

<NOTE>
You add a layer to this image so that you can see how to save a file with layers. Don't bother trying to figure out other aspects of layers now. You find out more about them in Session 8.

4. **Click the Paintbrush tool in the toolbox and draw on the image in the document window.**
   You can leave the default settings for the brush and the color at this point. You are experimenting with the saving process.

5. **Choose File→Save.**
   Now that you've made some changes to the file, the Save command is available. This opens the Save As dialog box.

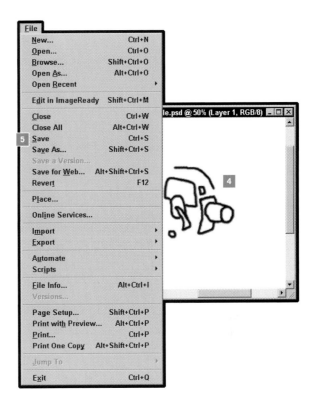

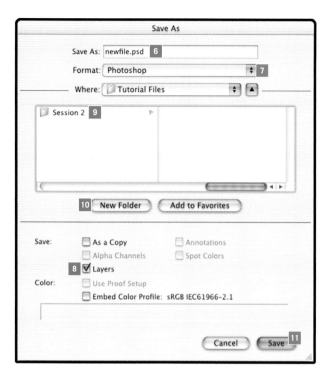

6. **Make sure that there's a filename in the Save As field (Windows: File Name field).**
   Photoshop uses the name that you gave the image when you created it. If you didn't name the image then, type **newfile** over the portion of the default filename before the dot.

<NOTE>
Photoshop automatically adds a three letter extension to the filename to match the format of the file. That's because you left Append File Extension set to its default—Always—in Preferences➜File Handling.

7. **Click the Format button to see the formats in which you can save a file in Photoshop. Leave this file set to the default Photoshop format.**
   The Photoshop format (PSD) is Photoshop's and ImageReady's native format. It retains all the Photoshop features that you may add to an image—layers, masks, styles, and so on. The TIFF format also saves the image's features such as layers.

8. **Make sure that there's a check mark in the Layers check box.**
   This ensures that layers are saved with the file.

9. **In the Save As dialog box navigate to the Session 2 Tutorial Files folder on your hard drive.**

10. **Click the New Folder button. Type** saving files **as the name for this folder and click Create in the New Folder window. (Windows: Click the yellow New Folder icon at the top right of the Save As dialog box, and type the new folder name**—saving files—**over the default folder name.)**
    You don't have to create a new folder when you save a file. It's simply a way of organizing files.

11. **Click Save in the Save As dialog box. Click OK if a warning appears about maximizing compatibility.**
    Your open file is now saved in PSD format. That's all there is to saving a new file for the first time.

<CAUTION>
In Session 1 you learned about the Maximize PSD File Compatibility settings in the File Handling Preferences. If you use the default setting, "Ask," you are warned about the compatibility issues that can arise in future versions of the program. If you're confused about the pros and cons of that choice, review the discussion of the Always Maximize Compatibility preference in Session 1. Unfortunately, the price of standing by that choice is having to see this warning every time you save a PSD file.

<TIP>
After you have saved the file, you cannot save it again unless some changes are made. If you save the file and then reopen the File menu, the Save option is grayed out. You can still choose the Save As command if you want to save the file with another name, in another format, or with the same format but in a different location.

12. Make another change to your image (such as drawing some more with the Paintbrush tool). Then choose File→Save.

Photoshop saves over the last-saved file, replacing it with the changed version. You use File→Save, or its shortcut ⌘+S (Windows: Ctrl+S), often as you work on an image.

< T I P >

Whenever you create a file in PSD fomat, save it as a PSD before flattening, converting to another file format, or saving for the Web. Store the full-featured PSD version in a safe place. That way you always have a source file with all its layers and other Photoshop features intact to modify or use as a template in the future.

< N O T E >

There are only four formats in which you can save layers—PSD, TIFF, PDF, and PSB. You work with PSD and TIFF in this tutorial. PDF is Adobe's Portable Document Format for sharing and editing digital files, which you probably use less often than PSD or TIFF. PSB is a new format for very large documents.

< T I P >

Don't panic if you save over a file by mistake. As long as you haven't closed the file, you can go back to the saved-over version by clicking ⌘+Z (Windows: Ctrl+Z). You find out more about fixing mistakes later in this session.

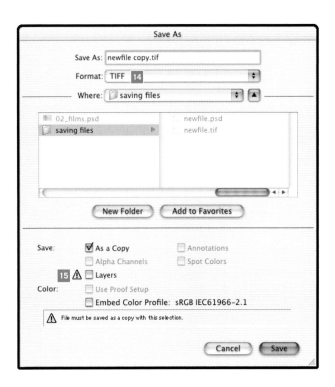

13. Choose File→Save As.

In the next steps, you learn how to use the Save As command to save an open file in a different file format.

14. Click the Format button in the Save As dialog box and choose TIFF.

This automatically changes the extension on the filename to .tif. TIFF preserves layers and can accommodate files up to 4 GB.

15. Uncheck Layers temporarily to see what happens.

Layers is checked by default when you save a TIFF in Photoshop CS. If you uncheck Layers, you see a warning that the file must be saved as a copy, and a check mark appears in the Save As a Copy check box. If you were to click Save (but don't do so now), Photoshop would save a flattened TIFF as a copy, and the original layered file would remain open. This is what Photoshop does whenever you try to save a file in a format that doesn't support all the file's features.

< N O T E >

If you are working with the Adobe Version Cue Workspace, available only as part of the Adobe Creative Suite, you can save separate versions of your image. If Version Cue is installed, your Save As dialog box displays an additional button that toggles between saving to the Version Cue workspace and saving to the local file structure on your hard drive.

< N O T E >

You can use numerous file formats to save a file. One fairly new format is the JPEG 2000 format, which adds more options and flexibility to the standard JPEG format, such as better compression and quality control. You must install the plug-in first before you can save images in this format. The plug-in is on the Photoshop CS installation CD in the Goodies/Optional Plug-Ins/Photoshop Only/File Formats folder. If you are working with very large files, you should activate the Large Document Format (PSB) option. As described in Session 1, you have to enable the option in the File Handling Preferences. The PSB format supports documents up to 300,000 pixels in any dimension and maintains all Photoshop features, such as layers and effects. However, a PSB document can only be opened in Photoshop CS.

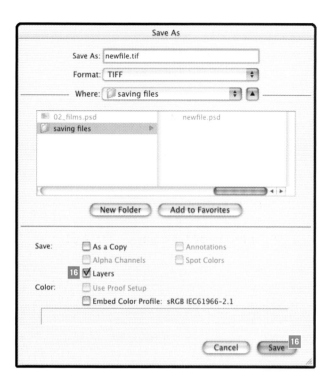

16. **Recheck the Layers box before continuing. Leave the other settings in the Save As dialog box as they are and click Save.**
A TIFF Options dialog box opens. Some, but not all, file formats display a dialog box like this with extra options.

17. **Leave the settings in the TIFF Options dialog box at their defaults for purposes of this tutorial and click OK.**
Photoshop CS defaults to saving a TIFF with layers and to offering relatively advanced options for compressing TIFFs. If you're preparing a TIFF for commercial printing and you're not sure whether to save with layers or how to set TIFF Options, be sure to consult your printer.

18. **Click OK again when you see a warning that including layers will increase the file size.**
The open file is now saved in the same location as the PSD file you originally saved, but with a different file format. Notice that the currently open file is a TIFF.

19. **Choose File→Close.**

< T I P >
Another potential use for Save As is to save a file with the same format as the original but in a different location.

Tutorial

» Viewing and Opening Images with the File Browser

The File Browser is one of the hottest features in Photoshop CS. It's an image viewer, a source of file information, and a file organizer. The File Browser is great for organizing photos from a digital camera, which often come into your computer without thumbnails, with meaningless names, and with vertical images rotated the wrong way. It's just as good for managing any folder full of image files for print or Web. This tutorial introduces you to the File Browser and teaches you how to use it to view and open documents. In the next tutorial, you delve into the file management features of the File Browser—rotating, organizing, ranking, sorting, and renaming files.

1. **Click the Toggle File Browser button on the Options bar.**
   You can also choose Window→File Browser, or File→Browse, and the File Browser opens as a standalone window. The File Browser comes complete with its own set of menus and tools across the top of its window.

2. **Navigate through the file tree in the Folders palette on the top left of the File Browser to the Session 2 Tutorial Files folder that you transferred to your hard drive.**
   The instructions for transferring Tutorial Files folders to your hard drive are located in Appendix A if you haven't already moved the files. You see thumbnails of the contents of the Session 2 folder on the right side of the File Browser. You can scroll down to see all the thumbnails or change the thumbnail view.

3. **In the File Browser menu bar, choose View→Medium Thumbnail.**
   You see thumbnails of all the image files and one folder contained in the Session 2 folder. If you don't see the photos folder, choose View→Show Folders in the File Browser menu bar.

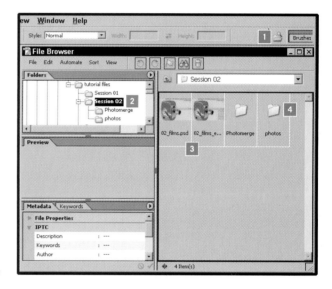

<TIP>
Depending on the numbers of files you're working with, and how clearly you have to see them, you can choose from a range of thumbnail sizes. If you set a custom thumbnail size in the File Browser preferences, you can display the custom size by selecting the Custom Thumbnail Size option in the File Browser's View menu.

<NOTE>
Another way to quickly navigate to a folder on your hard drive so that you can see thumbnails of its contents is to drag and drop the folder from the hard drive onto the navigation button above the thumbnails area in the File Browser.

4. **Double-click the thumbnail of the photos folder on the right side of the File Browser.**
   The File Browser displays thumbnails of all the images in the photos folder.

<TIP>
Choose View→Refresh in the File Browser menu bar to reorganize and update the contents of a folder display in the File Browser. The view is also refreshed if you close and reopen the File Browser.

<NOTE>
You can see the entire contents of a folder, even files that Photoshop can't open like spreadsheets. Choose View → Unreadable Files in the File Browser menu bar. If you work with large numbers of files and folders, deselect this option to save the screen space for the thumbnails you actually want to work with. If you also check Render Vector Files in the File Browser Preferences, you can view thumbnail previews of Illustrator files and PDF files.

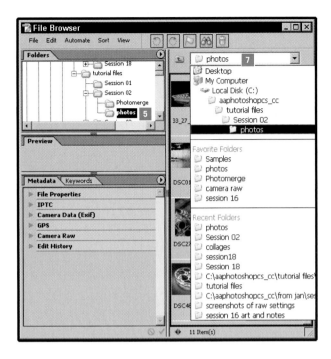

5. **Make sure the photos folder name is selected in the File Browser Folders palette.**

   You add this folder to your favorites.

6. **Choose File→Add Folder to Favorites in the File Browser menu bar to add the selected photo folder to your Favorites list.**

   You can also Ctrl+click (Windows: right-click) the folder name and choose the Add Folder to Favorites command from the contextual menu.

7. **Click the Navigation button above the thumbnail area of the File browser to display your Favorite Folder list.**

   The photos folder is added to the Favorite Folders listing. The next time you want to reopen the folder, instead of using the File Browser Folders palette, you can just select it from the list. The list also includes the last folders you have accessed in the File Browser.

   <NOTE>

   You can easily move or copy files between folders on your hard drive using the File Browser. Select a file in your Finder (Windows: Explorer), and drag and drop the file into the thumbnail area of the File Browser window. The file is moved to the open folder. If you hold the Option (Windows: Alt) key, the file is copied, rather than moved to the new folder.

8. **Click the thumbnail of the landscape photo on the right side of the File Browser.**

   A larger preview of that image appears on the left side of the File Browser in the Preview palette. Information about the image is shown in the Metadata palette.

9. **Click the diagonal lines at the bottom-right corner of the File Browser and drag down. Click and drag up on the borders above and below the larger preview to reveal more of the metadata on the bottom left of the File Browser.**

   The File Browser displays a great deal of information, including EXIF information from a digital camera. EXIF information can include anything from image resolution to whether the camera's flash fired when the picture was taken. If you want to see only the EXIF information, drag the scrollbar at the right of the Metadata area until you see the EXIF heading.

<NOTE>

The File Browser can be configured just the way you like it in Photoshop CS. You can resize the individual palettes (the Folders, Preview, Metadata, and Keywords palettes) by clicking and dragging their borders. You can change palette groupings by clicking and dragging palettes by their tabs. You can collapse a palette to make more room for others by double-clicking the palette's tab. You can combine these techniques to display very large previews of thumbnails in the Preview palette, feeling confident that those large previews will look good, because File Browser previews are full resolution in the Photoshop CS. Or if you want to see thumbnails only, you can click the double-pointed arrow at the bottom of the File Browser to toggle to expanded view. When you've configured your File Browser just the way you like it, save it as a workspace for quick reuse, as you learned to do in Session 1.

10. **Double-click the landscape thumbnail in the File Browser to open the full image in a document window.**

    This is a feature that I use often to open images. It's the quickest way of identifying which image I want to open.

< T I P >

If you want to hide the File Browser when you open an image, Option+double-click (Windows: Alt+double-click) the image thumbnail. If you open an image when the File Browser is maximized, the opened image is maximized as well.

11. **Leave the File Browser open and move on to the next tutorial.**

Tutorial
» Managing Files with the File Browser

Now that you're familiar with the File Browser and know how to use it to view and open images, you find out how to use its file management features—rotating, organizing, ranking, sorting, and renaming images—all from one convenient window and with visual feedback.

1. **Click the File Browser button on the Options bar to open it if you closed it at the end of the previous tutorial.**

2. **Increase the size of the File Browser by clicking the Maximize button at the top left (Windows: top right) of the File Browser.**
   Alternatively, you can resize the File Browser horizontally, vertically, and diagonally by clicking and dragging the diagonal lines on the bottom-right corner.

<TIP>
To see the File Browser without any other program palettes or toolbars, press the Tab key. Repeat to return to normal view.

3. **Choose View→Large Thumbnails.**
   You want to see the images more clearly to sort them.

4. **⌘+click (Windows: Ctrl+click) each of the image thumbnails that is rotated the wrong way to select them all.**
   Vertical photographs usually are rotated horizontally when they come into your computer from a digital camera. The File Browser's rotate feature saves you all the time that you used to spend opening, rotating, and resaving photos one at a time.

<NOTE>
⌘+click (Windows: Ctrl+click) selects noncontiguous thumbnails. Shift+click selects thumbnails that are next to one another. Ctrl+click (Windows: right-click) any thumbnail and choose Select All to select all thumbnails in the File Browser.

5. **Click the Rotate Clock Wise icon in the File Browser toolbar.**
   This rotates the images clockwise. You can also choose Edit→Rotate 90°CW.

6. **A message displays explaining that the rotation is shown only in the File Browser until you open the images or choose the Apply Rotation Command. Click OK to close the message, and rotate the images.**

   When you have seen the message a few times and are aware of how rotation functions, click Don't Show Again at the bottom-left of the message dialog box.

7. **Each rotated thumbnail displays an icon at the bottom right. Right-click one of the selected thumbnails and choose Apply Rotation from the contextual menu, or choose Edit→Apply Rotation.**

   A message dialog box explains that the files are being resaved. Click OK; you can also click Don't Show Again at the bottom-left of the message dialog box. The group of selected thumbnails are rotated 90 degrees.

<N O T E>

Rotating an image that is in JPEG format may cause some loss of image quality, even if rotation is done in the File Browser. That's because JPEG is a lossy format that throws away some image information every time a file is acted upon and recompressed. However, unless you're preparing a file for high end commercial or fine art output, you can usually get away with some rotation without a noticeable loss of quality.

8. **Choose View→Show Rank.**
   A rank label is displayed below each image's name.

9. **⌘+click (Windows: Ctrl+click) the thumbnails of your four favorite images to select them. Then Ctrl+click (Windows: right-click) one of the selected files and choose Rank. In the small dialog box that opens, type A, and click OK.**
   All the selected thumbnails display the label Rank A. This is a quick way to give multiple thumbnails the same rank for sorting.

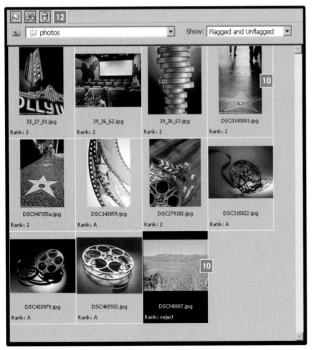

10. **Ctrl+click (Windows: right-click) the landscape image. Choose Rank, rank and type reject in the Rank field. Select the remaining thumbnails and assign the Rank label 2.**
    You can give individual thumbnails any name or number up to 15 digits as a custom rank. This enables you to sort images by any category that you find relevant.

11. **Choose Sort→Rank to sort the thumbnails numerically and then alphabetically by rank.**

<NOTE>
Rank enables you to sort by your own criteria. Alternatively, you can sort by any of the categories in the Sort By menu—File Size, File Type, Date Created, and so on.

12. **Click and drag the landscape image to the File Browser's Trash icon. Click Yes at the prompt.**
    This deletes the corresponding file from your hard drive. Be sure before you invoke this command!

<NOTE>
Another way to reorder thumbnails is to click and drag them around in the thumbnail area of the File Browser. This allows you to use the File Browser like a lightbox—reorganizing image previews without having to rank them first. This is new to Photoshop CS.

Using Flags for a Simple Image Sort

Another way you can easily sort the images in a folder is by flagging them. Select the images you want to flag and then click the Flag icon in the File Browser toolbar. A flag is displayed at the bottom-right of the thumbnail as you can see in the image.

Click the Show menu and choose Flagged, Unflagged, or both to display subsets of the image thumbnails. If you want to remove a flag from an image, select its thumbnail, and then click the Flag icon on the toolbar.

Flagging is useful as a way to sort through a roll of photographs to narrow down those you want to use. It allows you to isolate and preview selected images without having to move them into individual folders.

13. **In the Folders palette of the File Browser, click the photos folder to select it.**

    You create a new folder inside this folder.

14. **Choose File→New Folder to add a new folder within the photos folder. The folder is named Untitled by default. Click the default name to activate the field and type** best photos.

    This names the new folder on your hard drive. You can rename the folder in the Folders area or the thumbnails area of the File Browser.

15. **Shift+click all the thumbnails labeled Rank A and drag them onto the thumbnail of the best photos folder.**

    This moves the actual files into the best photos folder on your hard drive.

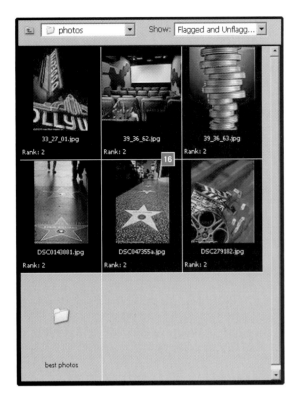

16. **Shift+click all the thumbnails labeled 2. Choose Automate→Batch Rename to open the Batch Rename dialog box.**

<CAUTION>
If you are viewing thumbnails in the File Browser of files that are located on a digital camera, on a memory card, or on a CD, you can't rename them, because you can't write to those media.

<NOTE>
You can rename individual files using the File Browser by clicking on a file name in the thumbnail area of the File Browser and typing a new prefix. However, you can't change the file extension suffix (such as .jpg or .tiff) when you rename individual files this way.

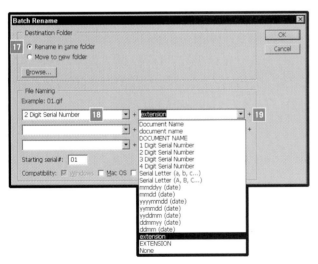

17. **Click Rename in same folder in the Batch Rename dialog box.**
Once the files are renamed, they remain in the same location. You can also run a batch that renames the files and puts them in a different folder.

18. **Click the first button in the File Naming area of the dialog box and choose 2 Digit Serial Number.**
This adds a different two digit serial number as part of the new name of each selected thumbnail and corresponding file.

19. **Click the next button in the File Naming area and choose extension. Click OK.**
This renames each of the selected thumbnails and corresponding files with the two variables that you chose. You could have added more information to each filename by clicking the other buttons in the File Naming area and choosing from the same menu of variables. You could even type a word or phrase into one of the fields that will appear in each of the file names. If you've ever slogged through a folder of files from a digital camera, manually changing meaningless filenames one by one, you'll love what the File Browser's Batch Rename feature can do for you.

20. **Open the photos folder on your hard drive to see that your files have been moved, sorted, and renamed to reflect all the changes that you made to the thumbnails in the File Browser.**

A quick way to open the photos folder on your hard drive is to select one of the thumbnails in that folder in the File Browser and choose View→Reveal Location in Finder (Windows: Reveal Location in Explorer). Close the photos folder.

21. **Choose File→Export Cache.**

If you move or rename the photos folder before you export the cache, all the rotating and ranking instructions that you applied in the File Browser are lost. Exporting the cache copies that information into the photos folder, so it stays with the affected files. After the cache is exported, you can move the photos folder or even burn it onto a CD-ROM to give to a coworker or client without losing the work that you did to the files in the File Browser.

22. **Choose File→Purge Cache.**

The File Browser created a cache in your system files, so thumbnails load faster the next time you access the photos folder. Purging the cache frees up space on your hard drive.

<CAUTION>

Purging the cache eliminates all the rotating and ranking data in the original cache. So don't purge the cache until you've clicked Export Cache.

23. **Close the File Browser window to return to Photoshop if you have the File Browser maximized, or click the Toggle File Browser icon on the Options bar to close the window.**

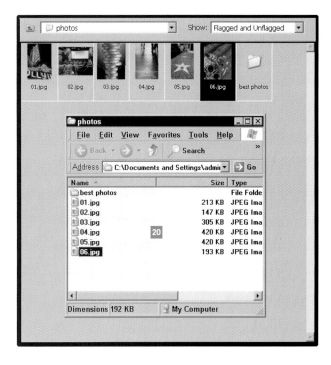

Tutorial

» Automating Tasks in the File Browser

You have learned a lot about working with the File Browser so far, including how to view and manage your images and files. You can also automate a number of tasks directly from the File Browser using selected thumbnails. In this tutorial, you learn how to use an automatic function, and you also learn how to use a new Photoshop CS feature, Photomerge, to stitch together multiple images into a wide, panoramic image.

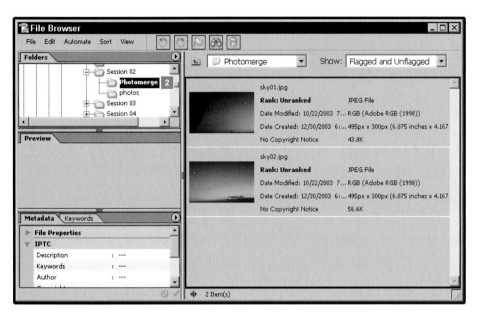

1. Click the Toggle File Browser button on the Options bar or choose File→Browse to open the File Browser.

2. In the Folders palette, click the Photomerge folder, which is located inside the Session 2 Tutorial Files folder on your hard drive. The contents of the folder display in the Details area. The images in the folder are selected automatically for the Photomerge process.

3. Choose Automate→Photomerge from the File Browser menu bar. Photoshop starts processing the images, and then displays the Photomerge dialog box displaying a preview of a panoramic combination of these images.

<NOTE>
The Automate options include Batch processing as well as specialty items like Photomerge and PDF Presentations.

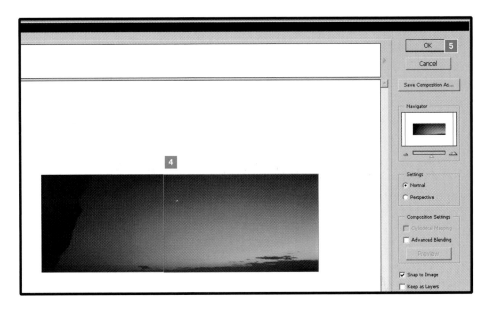

4. **Click the image segments in the work area of the Photomerge dialog box.**

   The active image displays a red bounding box; you can see how the two image segments overlay each other.

   <NOTE>

   You can save the components in their Photomerge arrangement so that you can open the composition again in Photomerge. Click Save Composition As, name the file, and save it. Photomerge files are saved with a .pmg extension.

5. **Click OK to close the Photomerge window.**

   The stitched image displays in the regular Photoshop window.

6. **Choose File→Save and close the file.**

   You can view a finished version of this panorama by opening bigsky.psd from the Session 2 folder in your Tutorial Files folder.

7. **Leave the File Browser open for the next tutorial.**

Using Photomerge Tools and Settings

Photomerge isn't always successful at combining source images. If it can't do the job for you automatically, it gives you a chance to combine your source images manually by dragging them from the lightbox area to the work area of the Photomerge dialog box. Tweak position and alignment of the source images using the Direct Select Image tool and the Rotate tool from the Photomerge toolbox. If you have trouble repositioning images, make sure the Snap to Image option is deselected. When this option is selected, Photomerge automatically tries to snap one image to another where they overlap.

Panoramic compositions sometimes appear flat and lacking in perspective. Counteract that tendency by modifying the vanishing point (which defaults to the centermost image in a composition).

Activate the Perspective setting in the lower-right corner of the dialog box, select the Vanishing Point tool (the star icon) from the Photomerge toolbox, and click on the location of the new vanishing point in the composition. If this causes distortion, try activating the Cylindrical Mapping option and clicking Preview. If you work with source images that differ in exposure, you may find that they don't blend together smoothly where they overlap. You can try to correct that problem by activating the Advanced Blending option. If that doesn't work, select the Keep as Layers option so that you can continue to blend the layered images in Photoshop's document window after exiting the Photomerge dialog box. And if you're just plain stuck, try reshooting the scene following the suggestions in the sidebar on Shooting Source Images for Photomerge.

Shooting Source Images for Photomerge

Photomerge works best with images that are similar in exposure and angle of view. Here are some tips to keep in mind when you shoot source images for use in a Photomerge panorama:

1. Use a tripod so that your images are level with one another. A tripod with a smoothly rotating head works best. If you're without a tripod, rest your camera on a steady, flat surface, like the top of a wall.

2. Overlap your images by 20% to 30%. You can use the tick marks on your tripod head or make a rough estimate by keeping track of the location of a landmark in your viewfinder. Pick a spot on the right side of the first image. When you rotate your camera to take the second image, place that spot in the leftmost 30 percent of the second image. Continue in this manner.

3. Try to shoot source images that are similar in brightness and contrast. The best way to ensure consistent exposures is to use a camera that has an auto-exposure (AE) lock feature. Set your exposure as you normally would for the first frame; engage the AE lock to take subsequent frames with the same exposure. If your camera does not have this feature, set the aperture and shutter speed of each frame manually to match the exposure of the others. Shoot in even light and avoid changing lighting conditions (for example, don't turn into and then away from the sun as you shoot). If your finished panorama displays diagonal banding where the source images overlap, the problem is most likely inconsistent exposures, and the solution is to shoot some more.

Tutorial
» Working with Metadata and Keywords

Before you leave the File Browser, there is one last area to look at metadata. In the first tutorial on the File Browser, you saw that selecting an image thumbnail displays information about the image in the Metadata area of the window. In this tutorial you take a closer look at the information stored in an image file as you learn how to customize an image file's metadata. You also learn how to work with keywords. You may be familiar with keywords used in searching documents or Web pages; the same concept applies to images. You add keywords and then use them as a way to search for images.

1. **In the File Browser, click the navigation button in the toolbar and choose photos from the list of Favorite Folders.**

   The content of the photos folder displays in the thumbnails area.

   <NOTE>
   You added the photos folder to your favorites list in an earlier tutorial. If you didn't do the tutorial, locate the Session 2 Tutorial Files on your hard drive and select the photos folder inside the Session 2 folder.

2. **Rearrange the margins of the display areas on the File Browser so you can see the contents of the Metadata tab.**

3. **Click one of the thumbnails to select it. Choose View→Details to view selected image information in the thumbnail area.**

4. **Click the spin-down arrows to open the File Properties and IPTC listing.**

   There are several categories of metadata, which is a fancy name for file information. Refer to Table 2-2 for a description of the categories. The File Properties category includes basic information about an image, such as name, date created, and size. The IPTC category, named after the standard-setting International Press Telecommunications Council, is the only category of metadata that you can edit and add to in the File Browser. The pencil icons next to the Description, Author, and Copyright fields indicate that those fields are editable.

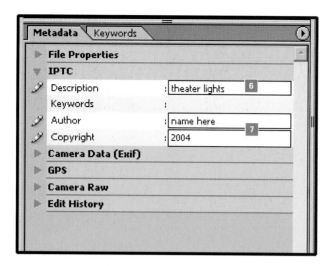

5. **Close the File Properties listing.**
   You have seen the information for the selected image.

6. **Click the Description field in the IPTC list.**
   You see all fields in the IPTC list are active except for the keyframes. Type a description for the image in the Description field. You work with the keyframes a bit later in the tutorial.

7. **Add an author name and copyright year in their respective fields.**

8. **Click anywhere off the field. When a confirmation dialog box opens, click Apply to close the dialog box and make the changes.**

Table 2-2: Types of Metadata

Category	Information about...
File Properties	Characteristics of the file such as size and creation date
IPTC	Custom captions for files and copyright information (the only editable data)
Camera Data (EXIF)	Images shot by a digital camera generate EXIF information such as camera settings
GPS	Navigational information from a Global Positioning System (GPS), added only by cameras using GPS technology
Camera Raw	Metadata for files in the Camera Raw format
Edit History	Changes made to the image stored in a log file

9. **Check the thumbnail information for the selected file.**
   You see the copyright date is added to the basic information for the image. If you don't see the date, choose View→Refresh to refresh the thumbnail information.

10. **Click the Keywords palette.**
    Keywords are useful tools for organizing lots of images. The key is to develop a set of custom keywords that works for you. Tag your images with subject matter keywords so you can search for and view files by subject matter regardless of where the files are on your computer.

11. **Collapse the default keyword categories.**
    You see there are categories for events, people, and places.

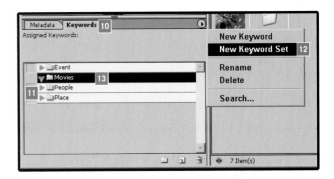

< T I P >

If you are planning a lot of work with keywords, you should delete the default categories to save space.

12. **Click the Keyword palette menu and choose New Keyword Set.**
    A field is added to the Keyword listing.

13. **Type Movies in the field and click off the field to add the keyword category.**
    Leave the word selected to add keywords to the category.

14. **Click the Keyword palette menu and choose New Keyword.**
    A blank field displays below the Movies category.

15. **Type film.**
    Click off the field to apply the keyword.

16. **Repeat Step 14 two more times, adding two more keywords. Type sidewalk and theater.**

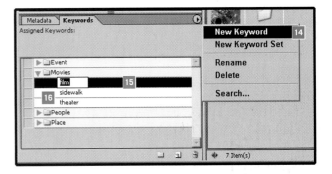

Creating and Applying a Metadata Template

You can quickly attach sets of metadata to multiple files by saving and applying a metadata template. This is useful for adding metadata other than the limited metadata fields you can edit from the File Browser's Metadata palette. For example, you can use a metadata template to add visible copyright symbols to the title bars of documents, rather than just embed copyright information in files as you can do from the Metadata palette.

Open an image in Photoshop and choose File→File Info. Enter some information about the image into the fields in the File Info palette. Choose Copyrighted from the Copyright Status menu, and add the year and artist in the Copyright Notice field. If you know the URL of a Web site that offers more copyright information about the piece, you can type that into the Copyright Info URL field. Click the arrow at the top right of the File Info dialog box and choose Save Metadata Template. Give the template a name and click OK. Close the image.

Now it's easy to append that set of information to a portfolio of images. ⌘+click (Windows: Ctrl+click) in the thumbnail area of the File Browser to select multiple thumbnails. Click the arrow on the top right of the Metadata palette, choose Append [template name] or Replace [template name], and click Yes at the prompt. All of the information in the metadata template you created is now attached to all of the selected images. Double-click one of those images to open it and notice that the title bar of its document window now displays a copyright symbol.

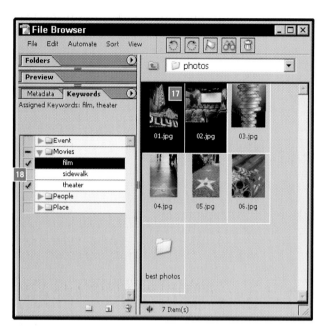

17. **Select View→Large Thumbnail from the File Browser menu bar. In the Thumbnail area, shift+click on the first two images to select them.**
    You apply the same keywords to the two images.

18. **In the Keyword palette, click film and theater.**
    Click OK to accept the message saying you are applying keywords to more than one image. Check marks are added to the selected keywords in the Keyword list, and a dash displays in the Movies keyword category.

19. **In the Thumbnail area, select the two sidewalk images.**
    You apply the same keywords to the two images.

20. **In the Keyword palette, click sidewalk and theater.**
    Click OK to accept the message saying you are applying keywords to more than one image. Check marks are added to the selected keywords in the Keyword list.

21. **Click the first thumbnail, 01.jpg, the theater lights at night.**

22. **Click the Metadata palette and open the IPTC list.**
    You see the keywords are now added to the metadata.

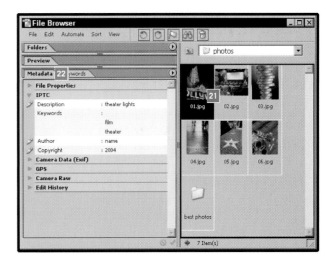

23. **Choose File→Search from the File Browser menu, or click the Search icon on the File Browser menu (the binoculars).**
    The Search dialog box opens. The current folder, photos, is listed in the Source field.

    < T I P >
    If you want to search elsewhere in your system, click Browse.

24. **In the Criteria area, click the first drop-down arrow and choose Keywords.**
    You can search using a range of options; nearly all the items listed in the details view for the thumbnail can be used as search criteria.

25. **In the third field, type theater.**
    You want to search the folder for files containing the keyword theater.

26. **Click Search to close the Search dialog box.**
    In the thumbnails area of the File Browser, you see all four files that have the keyword theater attached.

27. **Choose File→Search from the File Browser menu to open the Search dialog box again.**
    The settings you used are still displayed.

28. **Click the (+) at the end of the first row of criteria to add an additional line.**
    The new line is added, and the (-) and (+) icons move to the end of the second line.

29. **In the new line, click the first dropdown arrow and choose Keywords again. Type** sidewalk **in the third field.**

30. **Click Search to close the Search dialog box.**
    In the File Browser, only the two images showing the sidewalk display, as they are the only two that contain both keywords.

31. **Close the File Browser.**

Customizing Your Metadata View

You have worked with the default metadata arrangement in the tutorials. You can customize the metadata that is displayed depending on your project and its requirements. Choose Edit→Metadata Display Options or click the Metadata palette menu and choose Metadata Display Options. The dialog box shown here opens.

Select and deselect the items listed according to your requirements. To save screen space, leave the Hide Empty Fields option selected. Click OK when you are finished; the information is reset in the Metadata palette.

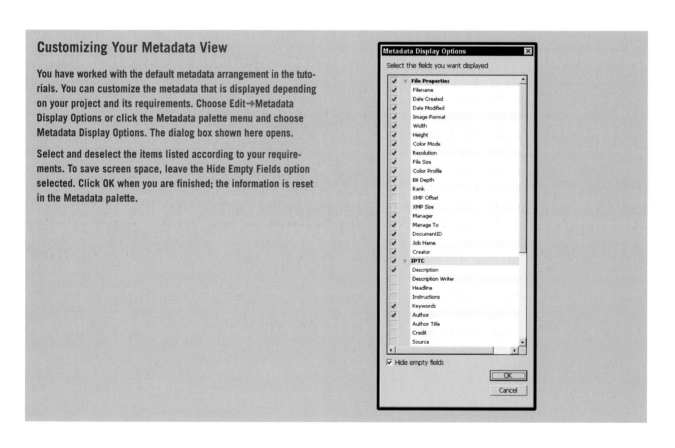

Tutorial
» Fixing Mistakes

This is one tutorial that you won't want to skip. You learn several different ways to go back in time to change what you've done to an image in Photoshop, using the Undo, Revert, and Fade commands and the History palette.

1. **Choose File→Open and navigate to** 02_films.psd **in the Session 2 Tutorial Files folder on your hard drive. Click Open.**

2. **Make sure that the Layers palette is showing. If it's not, choose Window→Layers.**

3. **Click in the empty box in the column of eye icons to the left of the film schedule layer.**
   This adds an eye icon to that box and makes the artwork on the film schedule layer visible in the image.

4. **Choose File→Save and click OK at the prompt.**
   Note the way the image looks at this point. You revert to this point later in this tutorial.

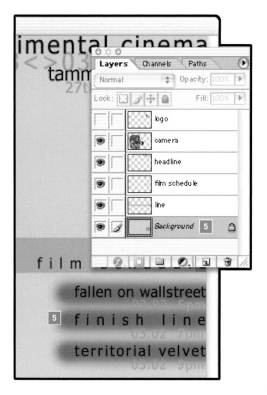

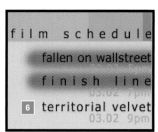

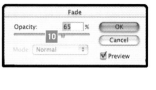

5. **Make sure that the Background layer is selected in the Layers palette. Select the Paintbrush tool in the toolbox and draw three lines anywhere in the image.**
Say that you change your mind and want to eliminate these brush strokes. The simple solution is to use multiple undo's, as you do in the next few steps.

6. **Press ⌘+Z (Windows: Ctrl+Z).**
This takes you back one step to the condition of the image as it was before your last action. This is commonly known as an *undo*. You use this shortcut so often that I used it as the instruction in this step, rather than the longhand command, which is Edit→Undo Brush Tool.

<N O T E>
⌘+Z (Windows: Ctrl+Z) undoes your last action even after you save or print a document, as long as you don't close and reopen the document.

7. **Choose Edit→Step Backward twice.**
All three of your brush strokes are now gone from the image. Thank goodness Photoshop offers multiple undo's. The shortcut for each undo after the first one is ⌘+Option+Z (Windows: Ctrl+Alt+Z).

<N O T E>
If you change your mind again, choose Edit→Step Forward to reapply your last action.

8. **Draw some more on your image, using lots of individual brush strokes.**
Don't spend too much time on this drawing because you're going to eliminate the result shortly.

9. **Select the Eraser tool and try to erase what you just drew.**
Notice that the Eraser tool erases back to the color that's currently in the Background Color box in the toolbox. The Eraser is not always the best choice for fixing mistakes because it doesn't really move your image back in time. The History palette, which you practice using shortly, does a better job. It's the most precise and flexible method of correcting mistakes in Photoshop.

10. **Choose Edit→Fade Eraser. In the Fade dialog box, move the Opacity slider to the left and notice that the erasure diminishes in your image.**
If you moved the slider all the way to 0%, all trace of the erasure would be gone from your image. This is another way of correcting mistakes in Photoshop.

11. **Make sure that the History palette is showing. If it's not, choose Window→History.**
Notice that each action you've taken since your multiple undo's is recorded as a state in this palette.

12. Click one of the Brush Tool states in the History palette.

Notice that your image changes to the condition it was in at the time you made that brush stroke. Alternatively, move the slider on the left side of the palette up to this state.

< N O T E >

The History palette records 20 states by default. To increase that amount, go to Preferences→General and type a different number in the History States field. Theoretically, you can have up to 1,000 history states in an image in Photoshop CS, but use some restraint here because each additional history state in an image increases file size.

13. Click the state at the very top of the History palette, labeled 02_films.psd.

This returns your image to the condition that it was in when you first opened it, as it appeared back in step 1.

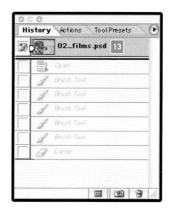

14. Choose File→Revert.

This takes you all the way back to the condition of the image as it was the last time it was saved, back in step 4. This is the most heavy-handed way to fix mistakes. Sometimes it takes you back in time farther than you'd like to go, so use it judiciously.

15. Choose File→Save As. Rename the file 02_films_end.psd. **Make sure that the format is set to Photoshop and Layers is checked. Navigate to the Session 2 Tutorial Files folder on your hard drive and click Save.**

This saves over the version of 02_films_end.psd that I provided for you. If you ever find that you want my version of 02_films_end.psd, you can always get a new copy of it from the CD-ROM.

Take a Snapshot for Later

Sometimes, as you work on an image, you get to a point to which you may want to return later. You can take a snapshot of the condition of the image at that point by clicking the arrow at the top right of the History palette and choosing New Snapshot, and then clicking OK. The snapshot appears near the top of the History palette. You can click it any time to return your image to that condition. A snapshot is active only for the session you are working in; you cannot return to the snapshot after closing and reopening the file.

» Session Review

This session covers getting images into Photoshop, saving images out of Photoshop, using the File Browser, and fixing mistakes using the History palette and the undo, revert, and fade commands. Use the following questions to help you review the materials in this session. You'll find the answer to each question in the tutorial noted in parentheses.

1. What is the rule of thumb when choosing a resolution for a new image? (See "Discussion: Resolution and Color Mode.")

2. What resolution should you use for images that are printed to an inkjet printer? (See "Discussion: Resolution and Color Mode.")

3. What does the number that you put in the Resolution field in the New dialog box mean? (See "Tutorial: Creating Images.")

4. Why don't you want to set image resolution higher than the resolution your printer can reproduce? (See "Tutorial: Creating Images.")

5. Which color mode do you use most often when you create a new image? (See "Tutorial: Creating Images.")

6. Name the three file formats in which you can save a file with layers. (See "Tutorial: Saving Files.")

7. How do you select and rotate multiple image thumbnails in the File Browser? (See "Tutorial: Managing Files with the File Browser.")

8. How do you rename multiple files at once in the File Browser? (See "Tutorial: Managing Files with the File Browser.")

9. Which variable from the File Browser's Batch Rename dialog box should you include to make sure that multiple files are given different names? (See "Tutorial: Managing Files with the File Browser.")

10. What is the function of the Export Cache feature in the File Browser? (See "Tutorial: Managing Files with the File Browser.")

11. What kinds of tasks can be automated in the File Browser? (See "Tutorial: Automating Tasks in the File Browser.")

12. What is the advantage of assembling segments of an image in the Photomerge window instead of the regular Photoshop window? (See "Tutorial: Automating Tasks in the File Browser.")

13. What kinds of metadata can be edited? (See "Tutorial: Working with Metadata and Keywords.")

14. What criteria can you use for searching images? (See "Tutorial: Working with Metadata and Keywords.")

15. What is the shortcut for undo in Photoshop? (See "Tutorial: Fixing Mistakes.")

16. What happens to an image when you click a state in the History palette? (See "Tutorial: Fixing Mistakes.")

tammeron international experimental cinema

03.02.03<>03.05.03

tammeron england

27th annual festival

2003

film schedule

fallen on wallstreet
03.02 5pm

finish line
03.02 7pm

territorial velvet
03.02 9pm

arising to the end
03.03 7pm

four large squares
03.04 7pm

frozen with steak
03.05 7pm

reason to cry
03.05 9pm

Session 3

Viewing Documents

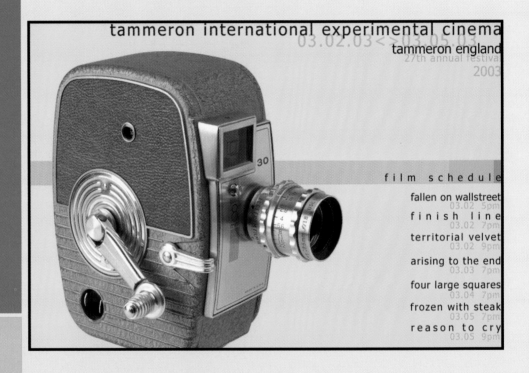

tammeron international experimental cinema
03.02.03 < > 03.05.03
tammeron england
27th annual festival
2003

film schedule

fallen on wallstreet
03.02 5pm
finish line
03.02 7pm
territorial velvet
03.02 9pm
arising to the end
03.03 7pm
four large squares
03.04 7pm
frozen with steak
03.05 7pm
reason to cry
03.05 9pm

Session Introduction

The Photoshop document window is the heart of the Photoshop interface. This session covers many aspects of viewing and handling an image that's open in the document window. You learn how to change your view of an image, move around in an image, access document information, display a document in different screen modes, change the size of an image and its canvas, and crop an image. You also learn how to create a new file designed for video use. Knowing how to use these features will make you a more adept and efficient Photoshop user.

TOOLS YOU'LL USE
Zoom tool, Hand tool, Navigator palette, New Window command, Patch tool, title bar, file information menu, Info palette, Eyedropper tool, Move tool, Measure tool, Notes tool, Screen Mode buttons, Canvas Size dialog box, Crop tool, and Image Size dialog box

CD-ROM FILES NEEDED
03_films.psd, 03_films_end.psd, sunflower.psd, and flower.psd

TIME REQUIRED
90 minutes

Tutorial
» Controlling Image Magnification

There will be times when you want to change the magnification at which you view an image you're working on in Photoshop. You can zoom in, increasing magnification, to get a close-up of part of an image for detail work. You can zoom out, decreasing magnification, to see the big picture. In this tutorial, you find out how to control image magnification using the Zoom tool, zoom settings on the Options bar, and some keyboard shortcuts.

1. **Choose File→Open and navigate to** `03_films.psd` **in the Session 3 Tutorial Files folder on your hard drive. Click Open.**
   `03_films.psd` is a replica of the finished file `02_films_end.psd` that you saved into your Session 2 Tutorial Files folder at the end of Session 2.

2. **Look at the title bar at the top of the document window or the zoom field at the bottom left of the document window to see the magnification at which the image is displayed.**
   Photoshop has some preset magnifications (such as 25%, 33.3%, 50%, 66.7%, and 100%). An image opens at the largest of the preset magnifications that fits on your screen between any open palettes, the toolbox, and the menu bar. On my screen, the image opened at 33.3%, although yours may be different. 33.3% magnification means that you're viewing the image at one-third of its actual size in pixels.

<CAUTION>
Do not confuse image magnification with image size. Magnification changes only the way you view the image; it has no effect on the actual size of the image. You learn how to change image size later in this session.

<TIP>
If you look closely at the figure, you see that the text in the image appears degraded. That's because it's being viewed at a magnification other than one of Photoshop's round-numbered presets. If you ever have an image that looks degraded on-screen, try changing the magnification to one of those round presets—such as 25%, 50%, or 100%. Chances are that it will look a lot better. The magnification you use on-screen is only that—on screen; it has no effect on the resolution used for printing an image.

3. **Double-click the Zoom tool in the toolbox to view the image at 100% magnification.**

   This changes the image magnification to 100%. Notice that there's no image distortion at this magnification. You won't be able to see this whole image at 100% without moving it around in the document window, which you learn to do in the next tutorial.

4. **Make sure that the Zoom tool is selected in the toolbox.**
   This causes the Options bar to display Zoom tool options.

<TIP>
Clicking the Actual Pixels button in the Options bar is another way to zoom to 100% magnification. I suggest that you ignore the other large buttons on the Options bar (Fit On Screen and Print Size) in favor of the control offered by the Zoom In and Zoom Out buttons and their shortcuts, which you try out in the next steps.

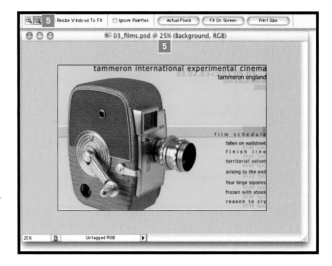

5. **Select the Zoom Out button (the one with the minus symbol) on the Options bar. Then click several times in the document window until you see in the title bar that the image magnification is 25%.**
   The Zoom Out button tells Photoshop to reduce the size at which the image is displayed. There's empty space around the image because the document window doesn't resize to match the image by default. You change this behavior in the next step.

<TIP>
A quick way to switch between zooming in and zooming out is to press the Option (Windows: Alt) key with the Zoom tool selected. If the Zoom In button is selected in the Options bar, you see the icon on the cursor change from + to –, and vice versa.

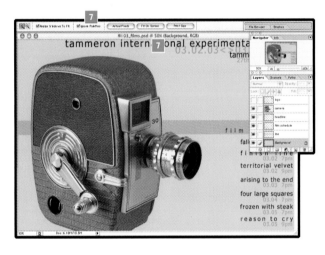

6. **Click in the Resize Windows To Fit box on the Options bar to add a check mark. Select the Zoom In button (the one with the plus symbol) on the Options bar. Click in the document window to increase magnification to 33.3%.**

   With the Resize Windows To Fit option checked, the document window grows or shrinks as necessary to fit the magnified image.

7. **Click in the Ignore Palettes box on the Options bar to add a check mark. Then click once more in the document window to increase magnification to 50%.**

   The Ignore Palettes option allows the enlarged document window to slip under any open palettes. Otherwise the document window would expand no farther than the left edge of the palettes.

< N O T E >

This setup (50% magnification, with the document window resized and palettes ignored) is the way I suggest that you view the tutorial files as you work through this book. You are able to see the entire contents of each file on most screens, and the images won't look degraded. If open palettes get in your way at any time, you can close them temporarily.

< T I P >

You often need to zoom in or out when you use another tool. The quickest way to do that is to hold the ⌘ (Windows: Ctrl) key and press the plus (+) key to zoom in or the minus (−) key to zoom out. In Windows, the document window doesn't resize itself with these shortcuts.

8. **Click and drag a selection around the number 30 on the camera in the image. Release the mouse button, and the selected portion of the image increases to the highest magnification that fits on your screen.**

   This technique is useful for doing detail work, such as painting in a mask.

<NOTE>

An image can be magnified to as high as 1600% and reduced as low as .05%, although I can't imagine why you'd go to those extremes.

9. **Leave this image open for the next tutorial.**

Tutorial
» Navigating the Document Window

Sometimes you can't see an entire image in your document window, as you just learned. Knowing how to move an image around in the document window is crucial in that situation. Here you practice using the Hand tool, its keyboard shortcuts, and the Navigator palette to navigate inside the document window.

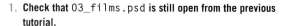

1. **Check that** 03_films.psd **is still open from the previous tutorial.**
   If it isn't, open 03_films.psd from the Session 3 Tutorial Files folder on your hard drive.

2. **Select the Hand tool in the toolbox.**
   This changes the Options bar to options for the Hand tool.

3. **Click the Actual Pixels button to return the image to 100% magnification.**

4. **Move the cursor over the image and notice that the cursor changes to a hand.**
   Click and drag the image around in the document window.

<NOTE>

You can access the Hand tool temporarily when you have another tool selected by holding down the spacebar and dragging in the image. This comes in handy when you paint, draw, or select inside a large image and need to move beyond the area that you can see in the document window.

5. **Choose Window→Navigator if you can't see your Navigator palette.**
   The Navigator palette acts like a combination Hand tool and Zoom tool to help you zero in on a specific part of an image. Notice there's a red box in the Navigator palette that defines the visible area of the image in the document window.

6. **Click inside the Navigator palette and drag the red box so that it's centered around the camera lens.**
   Notice that the image in the document window moves in sync with the red box in the Navigator palette, so the camera lens is now centered in the document window, too.

7. **Click the larger of the two mountain icons on the Navigator palette.**
   This magnifies to 200% the part of the image in the document window that corresponds to the area inside the red box on the Navigator palette. Clicking the smaller mountain icon reduces the corresponding area in the document window. You can accomplish the same thing by moving the slider on the Navigator palette.

8. **Close the Navigator palette and leave this image open for the next tutorial.**

Tutorial
» Displaying an Image in Multiple Windows

You can display an open image in more than one document window. This is useful when you've zoomed in to work on an area and want to see the results from a larger perspective as well. Any editing you do in one window appears in the other window too. You can also position multiple document windows in tiled or cascading arrangements and automatically scroll and zoom multiple windows simultaneously. In this tutorial you work with multiple windows.

1. **Make sure that** 03_films.psd **is still open from the previous tutorial. If it's not, open** 03_films.psd **from the Session 3 Tutorial Files folder on your hard drive and zoom in to 200%.**

2. **Choose Window→Arrange→New Window for** 03_films.psd**.**
   A second window opens displaying the same image.

< N O T E >

All open files are listed at the bottom of the Window menu. The active file, the one you are presently working with, is indicated by a check mark.

3. **Select the Zoom tool in the toolbox and the Zoom Out button in the Options bar.**
   Click several times in the new window to zoom it out to 25%.

4. **Select the Hand tool, click inside the larger window, and move the image until you see the words MADE IN U.S.A. on the camera.**
   Making the larger window active caused it to obscure the smaller window. You fix that in the next step.

5. **Choose Window→Arrange→Tile.**
   Use the tile view to see multiple windows regardless of their size. If you ever want to go back to your original multiple window arrangement, choose Window→Arrange→Cascade.

6. Click the Healing Brush tool (the one with the bandage icon) in the toolbox and select the Patch tool from the hidden menu that appears. Select the camera layer in the Layers palette. In the larger of the two image views, click and drag a selection around the words MADE IN U.S.A.

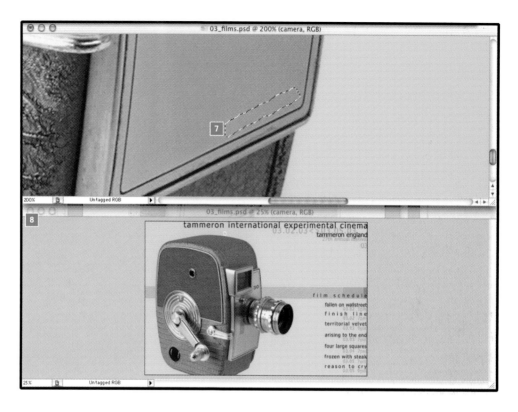

7. **Click inside the selection that you just made, drag it just above the words MADE IN U.S.A., and release the mouse button.**
   Wow! The words MADE IN U.S.A. have disappeared in both document windows. After you get over your amazement at how well the Patch tool works, focus on the fact that the change you made in the larger view also appears in the smaller view.

8. **Choose Select→Deselect to eliminate the Patch tool selection.**

<TIP>
Another good use for multiple document windows is to display the image in more than one color mode. For example, if you're preparing an image for commercial printing, you can work on it in RGB mode in one window and soft proof it in CMYK in another window at the same time. (If you don't remember how to soft proof, turn to the Discussion "Resolution and Color Mode" in Session 2.)

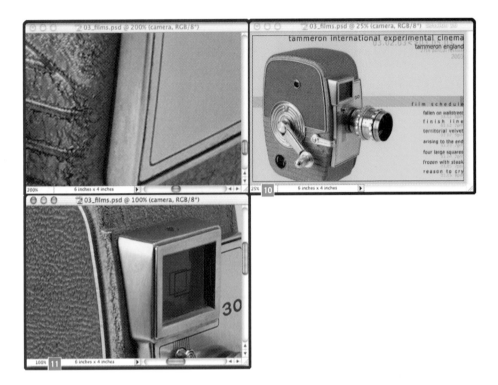

9. **Choose Window→Arrange→New Window for** 03_films.psd.
   You now have a third copy of the image open. Set the magnification of the third window to 100% by double-clicking the
   Zoom tool with that window active. The two copies you already
   have open are set at 25% and 200% magnification.

10. **Choose Window→Arrange→Tile to file all three images so that
    you can see them all on your screen.**

11. **Click the copy using 100% magnification to make it active.**
    You reset the zoom using the selected copy.

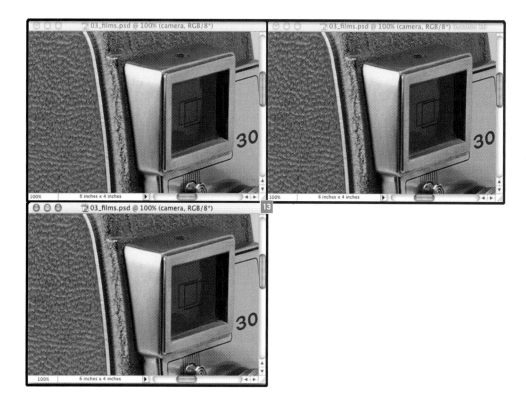

12. **Choose Window→Arrange→Match Zoom.**

    The copies using 25% and 200% magnification reset themselves to match the selected copy at 100% magnification.

13. **With any one of the three windows active, choose Window→ Arrange→Match Location.**

    The image in the other two windows automatically moves to the same location as the image in the selected window. This feature is handy if, for example, you use the three windows to view different channels in the same image and want to see the same area in all of the channels.

<TIP>

You can set multiple document windows to the same magnification and the same location all at once by choosing Window→Arrange→Match Zoom and Location.

<TIP>

To zoom multiple windows together in the same increments, select the Zoom tool in the Toolbox, activate the Zoom All Windows option in the Options bar, and click on any open window. To move an image around in multiple windows at the same time, select the Hand tool in the Toolbox, activate the Scroll All Windows option in the Options bar, and click and drag in any open window.

14. **Close all but one copy of the** 03_films.psd **image.**

15. **Use the Zoom tool and the Zoom Out option to reduce the magnification of the open document window back to 50% and leave that window open for the next tutorial.**

Tutorial
» Viewing Image Information

You can get all kinds of information about an image from Photoshop. Session 2 covers the image information available in the File Browser. After an image is opened, use the title bar, the file information menu at the bottom of the document window, and the Info palette to find out more about an image. Add your own information to the image with the Notes tool. You'll use all of these features in this tutorial.

1. **Check that** 03_films.psd **is still open from the previous tutorial. If it's not, open** 03_films.psd **from the Session 3 Tutorial Files folder on your hard drive and zoom out to 50%.**

2. **Take a look at the title bar at the top of the document window to get some basic information about the open document.**
   The title bar reveals the name of the file, the image magnification (50%), the layer that's selected in the Layers palette (the camera layer), the color mode of the image (RGB), and the bit depth of the image (8 bit).

3. **Click the arrow in the bottom border of the document window (Windows: the application window) to reveal the file information menu. Choose Document Sizes if it isn't already selected.**
   Document Sizes reveals two pieces of information in the information field to the left of the menu. The number on the left tells you that this file would contain 13.3 megabytes of information if you were to flatten its layers and save it. The number on the right tells you the true file size of this image—23.9 megabytes—which takes into account all the layers and channels in this image.

<NOTE>
The number of layers that you add to a file has a big impact on file size. The artwork, as well as the transparent pixels on each layer, affects file size.

4. **Click the arrow again and choose Document Dimensions.**
   You'll see that this image is 6 inches by 4 inches. This is the actual physical size of the document and has nothing to do with image magnification.

5. Click the arrow again and choose Current Tool.

This tells you which tool is currently selected in the toolbox. It's useful if you've closed your toolbox to gain more screen real estate or if you've moved your toolbox to a second monitor.

<TIP>

Option+click (Windows: Alt+click) the information field at the bottom of the document window, and a pop-up menu tells you fundamental information about the image—its width and height, the number of channels it has, and the image resolution in pixels per inch. Although you can get this information from the file information menu, this is a handy shortcut.

<TIP>

Click the information field, and you'll see a diagram of the position and orientation of the image as it will print. You can change these settings in the Print dialog box, which you access by choosing File➜Print with Preview.

6. Choose Window➜Info to display the Info palette.

7. Click the Eyedropper tool in the toolbox and move your cursor anywhere in the open image, keeping an eye on the Info palette.

The Info palette displays different information depending on which tool you work with. With the Eyedropper tool selected, the Info palette tells you the RGB and CMYK values of the color directly under the cursor.

8. Choose Window➜Layers if your Layers palette is not displayed on your screen. Click in the empty Visibility box to the left of the logo layer in the Layers palette to make the artwork on that layer visible. Click the logo layer to select it.

An eye icon appears in the Visibility box on the logo layer, indicating that that layer is now visible. You see a camera logo in the image.

9. Select the Move tool in the toolbox. Click and drag in the image to move the artwork on the selected layer so that it's in line with the left edge of the list of films. Keep your eye on the Info palette as you do so.

At the top right of the Info palette, you can see how far you moved the artwork from its original location and the angle of movement. At the bottom left of the Info palette, you can see the location of your cursor, measured from the top-left corner of the image.

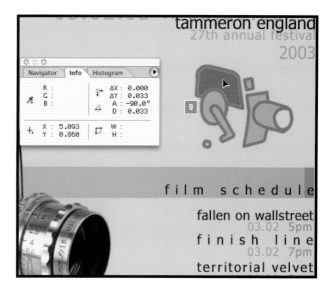

<NOTE>

You can change the color mode for either of the two mode readouts in the Info palette by clicking the arrow at the top right of the Info palette and choosing Palette Options. Click either of the Mode buttons, choose a color mode, and click OK. For example, you can choose Web Color if you're creating a Web graphic and want to know the hexadecimal code for a color in your image. Or you may choose Proof Color if you're soft proofing an image and have chosen a proofing mode under View➜Proof Setup. The proof color values are displayed in the Info palette in italics to distinguish them from the actual color values.

<TIP>

You run into lots of reasons to create individual pieces of artwork on separate layers as you work through this book. You just experienced one of those reasons. It's easiest to move pieces of artwork around if you have the foresight to create them on separate layers.

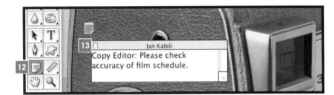

10. **Click the Eyedropper tool in the toolbox and select the Measure tool from the hidden menu that appears. Click and drag from one side of the camera to the other, while observing the Info palette.**

    The Info palette displays the distance that you just measured—3.7 inches. If you ever want to replace the camera with another image, you know exactly how big to size that image.

11. **Click any other tool in the toolbox to hide the measured line in the image.**

12. **Select the Notes tool in the toolbox. Click and drag in the image to create an annotation.**

    With the Notes tool, you can add your own information to an image—to remind yourself of something or share information with someone else.

13. **Type a message inside the annotation box. Then click the close box at the top-left corner of the annotation.**

    This leaves a note icon in the document. To read the annotation, double-click that icon.

    < N O T E >
    To hide all the note icons in a document, choose View➜Show➜ Annotations to remove the default check mark. To delete an annotation, Ctrl+click (Windows: right-click) its note icon, choose Delete Note, and click OK at the prompt.

14. **Choose File➜Save As. In the Save As window, make sure that the format is set to Photoshop and Save Annotations is checked. Click Save. (You can save over the** 03_films.psd **that you copied to your hard drive.)**

    You have to save the file as a Photoshop or Portable Document Format (PDF) file to retain the annotation. A person who receives your file can read the annotation if he or she opens the file in either Photoshop or Adobe Acrobat.

15. **Leave this image open and continue to the next short tutorial.**

Tutorial
» Changing Screen Display Modes

In this tutorial, you learn how to display an image in Photoshop without any distracting interface elements. Try this when you want to impress a client. Photoshop has three screen display modes—the regular one you work with all the time, one that places a solid background behind the image, and one that shows the image on a black background without menus and toolbars. You can access the options from the toolbar or by using shortcut keys, as you learn in this tutorial. You can also find the same options in the View→Screen Mode menu.

1. **Make sure that** 03_films.psd **is open from the previous tutorial.**

2. **Choose View→Show→Annotations to hide the note icon.**
   You used the Annotations in an earlier tutorial.

3. **Press F on your keyboard to display your image with a plain gray background.**
   Alternatively, click the middle of the three screen mode buttons near the bottom of the toolbox, or choose View→Screen Mode→Full Screen Mode with Menu Bar.

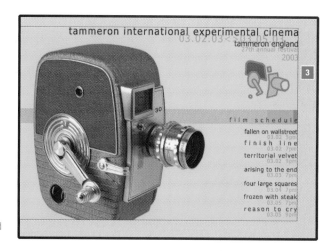

<NOTE>
You can move your image around the screen in Full Screen mode. Use this new feature to make room for palettes and tools so that you can work on an image even in Full Screen mode. Press F twice to enter Full Screen mode, hold the spacebar to switch to the Hand tool, and click and drag to move the image. If you zoom in and out after you do this, the image recenters itself on your screen.

4. **Press F a second time to display the image with a black background.**
   You can also click the rightmost screen mode button in the toolbox, or choose View→Screen Mode→Full Screen.

<TIP>
If you use the menu commands to change the screen mode, you see a message box that explains you have to use the shortcut key F to return to a regular menu-based view.

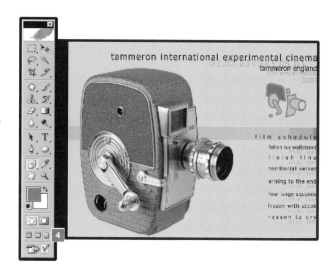

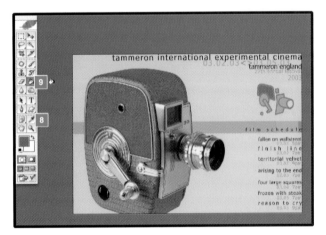

5. **Press the Tab key to hide the toolbox and menu bar.**

   This is an elegant way to display an image without distractions. However, at this point, the only way you could work on the image would be with keyboard shortcuts. So unless you're a Photoshop power user, click the Tab key again to bring back the toolbox and menu bar.

6. **Press F again to return to the gray background mode.**

7. **Select the Zoom tool, deactivate Resize Windows to Fit in the Options bar, and zoom out until you can see the gray area of the document window that surrounds the image.**

8. **Select the Eyedropper tool and click on the brown part of the camera in the image.**

   This sets the Foreground Color box in the toolbox to brown.

9. **Click the Gradient tool in the toolbox and Select the Paint Bucket tool from the hidden menu that appears. Hold the Shift key and click in the gray area that surrounds the image.**

   This fills the gray area with whatever color is in the Foreground Color box. It's another nice effect for displaying an image. Keep in mind that the brown border you see is not part of the image. It's the empty area of the document window.

10. **Click the leftmost screen mode button to return to regular screen mode.**

11. **Leave the image open for the next tutorial.**

Tutorial
» Changing Canvas Size

The canvas is an important part of a Photoshop image. Increasing canvas size adds to the image area without stretching the image itself. Decreasing canvas size can cut off part of the image without shrinking the whole image. You modify the canvas size relative to the existing canvas. Work through this tutorial to see what I mean.

1. **Make sure that** `03_films.psd` **is open from the previous tutorial.**

2. **Select the Eyedropper tool in the toolbox. Hold the Option key (Windows: Alt key) and click in the yellow area of the image.**
   This sets the Background Color box in the toolbox to yellow.

3. **Choose Image→Canvas Size.**

4. **Type** .5 **into both the Width and Height fields and leave the Relative box checked.**
   This tells Photoshop to add .5 inches to both the width and height of the canvas. This increases the canvas from its current 6 inches by 4 inches to 6.5 inches by 4.5 inches. If you were to uncheck the Relative box, you would type 6.5 into the Width box and 4.5 into the Height box to get the same result.

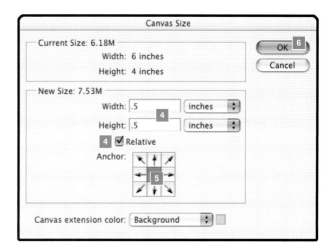

< T I P >
To decrease canvas size with the Relative box checked, type negative numbers into the Width and Height fields.

5. **Click the center anchor tile in the diagram in the Canvas Size dialog box.**
   This tells Photoshop where to position the image when it increases the canvas—in the center of this canvas. This causes .25 inches to be added to each side of the canvas.

6. **Click OK.**
   This increases the canvas and fills it with the yellow in the Background Color box in the toolbox.

< N O T E >
You can choose a color for an expanded canvas right in the Canvas Size dialog box. This avoids having to close the Canvas Size dialog box to return to the Background Color box if you forgot to set a color there first. In the Canvas Size dialog box, click the small color square to the right of the Canvas extension color field to open the Color Picker. Choose a color in the Color Picker, or move your cursor over the document window and click to sample a color from the image. This is another welcome new feature in Photoshop CS.

7. **Save the image. Leave it open for the next tutorial.**

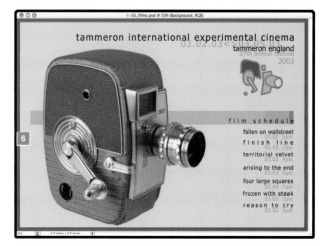

< N O T E >
The units of measurement for height and width both default to inches. Changing the unit of measurement for one dimension automatically changes it for the other unless you hold the Shift key. You find this new behavior in many locations in Photoshop CS, including the New dialog box and the Image Size dialog box.

Tutorial
» Cropping an Image

Cropping is similar to changing canvas size. In this tutorial, you'll practice using the Crop tool.

1. **Make sure that** 03_films.psd **is open from the previous tutorial.**

2. **Select the Crop tool in the toolbox. In the Options bar, type** 6 in **in the Width field and** 4.5 in **in the Height field. Photoshop adds in for inches by default. Type** 300 **in the resolution field, which is set to pixels/inch by default.**
   This causes Photoshop to resize whatever area remains after the crop to 6 inches by 4.5 inches at 300 dpi resolution. Leave the other options at their defaults for now.

<TIP>
If you don't know the size to which you want to crop an image, you can just drag out a bounding box to define the cropping area.

<NOTE>
The Width and Height fields in the options bar can be reversed by clicking the arrows in between those fields.

3. **Click in the image and drag out the bounding box that defines the area to be cropped.**

   The dark areas outside of the bounding box are the areas that will be cropped off. The Shield option in the Options bar causes them to look screened back so that you can evaluate how the rest of the image will look after cropping.

< N O T E >

The Hide option in the Crop tool Options bar gives you the chance to hide, but not completely eliminate, the cropped areas. Hide is the option to choose if you think you may change your mind about the crop.

4. **Adjust the bounding box that defines the area to be cropped so that its position matches that shown here.**

   To move the bounding box, click inside it and drag. You can also change the shape of the bounding box by clicking an anchor point and dragging. To rotate the bounding box, move the cursor outside of the box until it changes to a double-pointed area and drag.

< T I P >

You can use the Crop tool to extend the canvas, which is similar to increasing canvas size as you did in the previous tutorial. Draw a bounding box inside the image, click its anchor points, and drag the box out into the empty area of the document window (the brown area in this case).

5. **Click the big check mark icon at the right of the Options bar to commit the crop.**

   This crops away the area outside the bounding box and resizes the remaining area to a 6.5-inch by 4-inch 300 dpi image.

< N O T E >

You can also double-click the cropped area or choose Image➜Crop to commit the crop.

6. **Resize the document window to fit the image. Save and leave the image open for the next tutorial in this session.**

Tutorial
» Changing Image Size

There are two ways to change the actual size of an image. You can change the number of pixels in the image, which is called resampling. It's okay to resample down, but resampling up (increasing the amount of information in an image) is usually a bad idea. The other way to change the size of an image is to leave the total amount of information the same and just trade off a change in physical dimensions for a change in resolution. You learn how to do both in this tutorial.

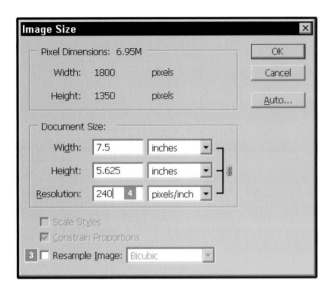

1. **Check that** 03_films.psd **is open from the previous tutorial.**

2. **Choose Image→Image Size.**

3. **Click the Resample Image check box to remove the check mark.**
   The Scale Styles and Constrain Proportions options are deselected and grayed out.

4. **Type** 240 **in the Resolution field.**
   This resolution field is just like the one in the New file dialog box that you used in Session 2. It tells Photoshop to include 240 pixels per inch in the printed image.

<NOTE>
Notice that when you decrease the Resolution field in the Image Size dialog box from 300 to 240, the physical dimensions of the image in the Width and Height fields increase (from 6 x 4.5 inches to 7.5 x 5.625 inches). However, the file size reported at the top of the dialog box remains the same (6.95M). All this is because you unchecked Resample Image, which told Photoshop not to change the total number of pixels in the image. That number is a function of physical dimensions and resolution, so changing one of those factors (changing resolution from 300 to 240) necessitated an automatic change in physical dimensions. However, in this case, you want the width and height to stay at 6.5 x 4 inches, and you want to reduce the resolution to 240, based on the assumption that that's the best resolution for your printer. (Turn back to the Discussion "Resolution and Color Mode" in Session 2 if you need a refresher on choosing print resolution.)

5. **Click the Resample Image check box to add a check mark.**

   The Scale Styles and Constrain Proportions options are active again.

< T I P >

Layer styles applied to layers in your image can be scaled with the rest of the image. Make sure the Scale Styles option is selected in the Image Size dialog box. You can also manage the layer scaling independently of the image scaling using layer effects.

6. **Type** 6 **in the Width field and** 4.5 **in the Height field. Leave the Resolution field at 240.**

   Notice that the total file size has changed. The dialog box tells you that it's now 4.45 megabytes, but it was 6.95 megabytes.

7. **Click OK.**

< C A U T I O N >

When the Resample Image box is checked, avoid increasing width, height, or resolution. If you add pixels, Photoshop has to make up image information for those pixels, and the result is almost always a degraded image. The rule is that it's okay to resample down, but not up.

< C A U T I O N >

Don't uncheck Constrain Proportions in the Image Size dialog box, unless you deliberately want to distort the shape of your image.

8. **Choose File→Save As, rename the file** 03_films_end.psd, **navigate to the Session 3 Tutorial Files folder on your hard drive, and click Save.**

   This saves over the version of 03_films_end.psd that I provided for you. If you ever find that you want my version of 03_films_end.psd, you can always get a new copy of it from the CD-ROM.

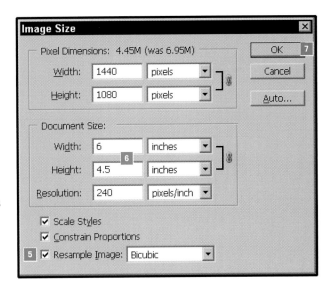

Interpolation Methods

Photoshop CS provides five different interpolation methods. Each is different, but they are all used to assign color values to new pixels based on the exisiting pixel colors when you resample the image. Choose a default interpolation method in the General Preferences. When you resize an image, you can choose an optional method from the Image Size dialog box. The five methods are:

» **Nearest Neighbor**—This is the fastest but least precise option. Use for illustration without anti-aliasing. This method can produce jagged effects.

» **Bilinear**—A generic option, medium quality, medium file size.

» **Bicubic**—Processes files slowly but precisely; a good option for photographs.

» **Bicubic Smoother**—Slow processing, but good for enlarging images. This new method was designed to facilitate upsizing and to replace stepped sizing that some use to try to avoid image degradation when upsizing.

» **Bicubic Sharper**—Slow processing, but good for reducing image size when you need to retain detail. Try this new method when you're drastically reducing image size, as you might do if you repurpose print images for the Web.

Tutorial

» Changing Pixel Aspect Ratio for Video Images

Most images you work with on a regular basis, and in this book, use square pixels. Each pixel has the same width and height, which makes scaling and other types of manipulation predictable. If you work with video editing software such as Adobe's Premiere Pro or Apple's Final Cut or iMovie, you often work with still images. Using a still image in digital video projects that use rectangular pixels distorts your image. Another common feature used in video editing is safe margins that define areas of the screen that can become distorted depending on the display monitor. In Photoshop CS, you can work with both pixel aspect and safe margins. In this tutorial you learn how to create a file with non-square pixels, bring a regular square-pixel file into a non-square image, and preview non-square files without distortion.

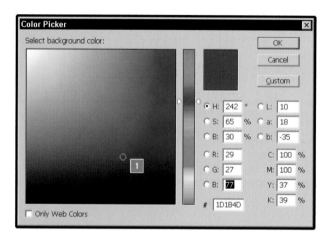

1. **Click the background color swatch in the toolbox to open the Color Picker. Choose a dark blue and click OK.**

   The Color Picker closes and the dark blue is used as the background for the new image.

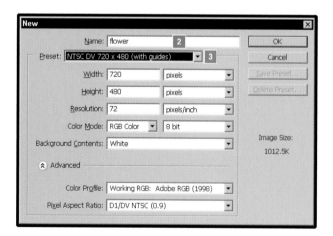

2. **Choose File→New to open the New File dialog box. Name the file flower.**

3. **Click the Preset menu and choose NTSC DV 720 x 480 (with guides).**

   This is a common digital video file format. The guides are used to help position content. When you choose the preset, the width and height of the image are automatically entered, and the color space and Pixel Aspect Ratio are listed in the Advanced section of the dialog box.

<NOTE>

The DV preset used in this tutorial has a 0.9 pixel aspect ratio; another common format is D1/DV NTSC Widescreen, which uses a 1.2 pixel aspect ratio.

4. Click the Background Contents menu and choose Background Color.

You use the dark blue color you set in step 1. Notice when you choose a custom color, the Preset at the top of the dialog box changes to Custom.

<TIP>

If you are creating a number of new files to use in a video and are planning to use a custom setting such as a background color, save the options as a custom preset. That way you can choose your custom options quickly from the preset list.

5. Click OK to close the dialog box.

6. Click OK to dismiss the message about image quality; to prevent seeing the message again, click Don't show again.

You are working with non-square pixels on a monitor displaying square pixels, so what you see is a preview. The message box closes and the new image opens.

<TIP>

Look at the top of the image window, you see the filename, as well as its color space and bit depth, and [scaled]. This means the image uses a non-square pixel aspect ratio.

7. Choose File→Open. Browse to your tutorial files and select sunflower.psd.

You add a copy of the file to your new DV-compliant image file.

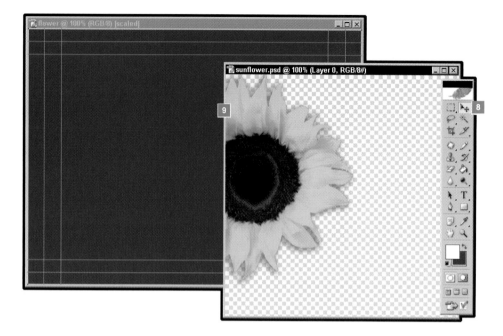

8. **Click the Move tool on the toolbar to select it.**

   You use the tool to drag a copy of the sunflower to your new file.

9. **Drag the picture of the sunflower over the border of its window and drop it on the new file window.**

   The sunflower image, which was originally created with square pixels, is automatically converted and scaled to the non-square pixel aspect.

10. **Close the** sunflower.psd **image**.

    If you are prompted to save changes, click No.

11. **Position the sunflower in the center of the new image file.**
    You see the petals of the flower extend to the safe-border guidelines. The outer guidelines define the Action-safe area; the inner guidelines define the Title-safe area.

<NOTE>
The Title-safe and Action-safe areas refer to areas of distortion that occur when the image is seen on a television screen, which has a convex surface. In order to show the image clearly, the center of the image is slightly magnified, and the outer edges are cut off as a result. *Action-safe* refers to the maximum space on the screen in which you can see activity occur; *Title-safe* refers to the maximum size of titles and images that display clearly. Unless you are intending to use your video project for television display, the safe margins aren't necessary.

12. **Choose File→Save. Save the file as** flower.psd.

Action-safe margin

Title-safe margin

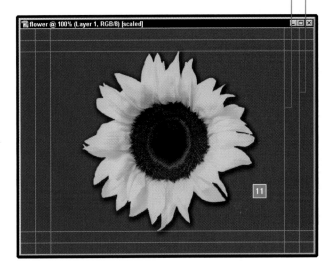

13. **Select View→Pixel Aspect Ratio Correction to remove the default check mark.**
    Your sunflower looks distorted because you are now viewing its non-square pixels in the square pixel environment of your computer monitor, without the benefit of Photoshop's Pixel Aspect Ratio Correction preview. When that preview is activated, non-square images look undistorted on your computer monitor.

<NOTE>
View→Pixel Aspect Ratio is a preview feature only. It just scales non-square pixels temporarily to make them look okay in a square pixel environment. To actually assign a different pixel aspect ratio to an existing image use the Image→Pixel Aspect Ratio command.

14. **Select View→Pixel Aspect Ration Correction again to activate the corrected preview.**
    Your sunflower no longer looks distorted.

15. **Close the file** flower.psd.

» Session Review

This session covers the many aspects of viewing documents in Photoshop. It includes lessons on zooming in and out to adjust image views, moving around an image with the Hand tool and the Navigator palette, displaying an image in multiple windows at once, viewing information about the image in the image information field and the Info palette, changing the screen display mode, adjusting canvas size, cropping, and changing image size. Here are some questions to help you review the information in this session. You'll find the answer to each question in the tutorial noted in parentheses.

1. Does image magnification affect actual image size? (See "Tutorial: Controlling Image Magnification.")

2. At what magnifications is your image least likely to appear degraded? (See "Tutorial: Controlling Image Magnification.")

3. What does double-clicking the Zoom tool do? (See "Tutorial: Controlling Image Magnification.")

4. What does the Actual Pixels button do? (See "Tutorial: Controlling Image Magnification.")

5. What tool would you use to navigate around an image in the document window? (See "Tutorial: Navigating the Document Window.")

6. What does the red box in the Navigator palette do? (See "Tutorial: Navigating the Document Window.")

7. What does the slider in the Navigator palette do? (See "Tutorial: Navigating the Document Window.")

8. When viewing an image in multiple windows, do changes you make to the image in one window appear in the other window? (See "Tutorial: Displaying an Image in Multiple Windows.")

9. What does the Notes tool do? (See "Tutorial: Viewing Image Information.")

10. What two formats can you save an image in if you want to preserve an annotation that you made with the Notes tool? (See "Tutorial: Viewing Image Information.")

11. How do you display an image in Photoshop without any menu bars, toolbox, or other distracting elements? (See "Tutorial: Changing Screen Display Modes.")

12. When you change canvas size, what is the function of the anchor tile in the Canvas Size dialog box? (See "Tutorial: Changing Canvas Size.")

13. When you change image size, what is the effect of unchecking the Resample Image check box in the Image Size dialog box? (See "Tutorial: Changing Image Size.")

14. When you change image size, is it best to resample an image up or down, and why? (See "Tutorial: Changing Image Size.")

15. Why is it important to match the pixel aspect ratio of your images to that of a video project? (See "Tutorial: Changing Pixel Aspect Ratio for Video Images.")

16. What are Action-safe and Title-safe margins? Do you always need to use them? (See "Tutorial: Changing Pixel Aspect Ratio for Video Images.")

tammeron international experimental cinem
03.02.03 <> 03.05.03
tammeron englan
27th annual festiv
200

A B C D
am be
is
are

Part III
Painting and Drawing

Session 4

Choosing and Using Color

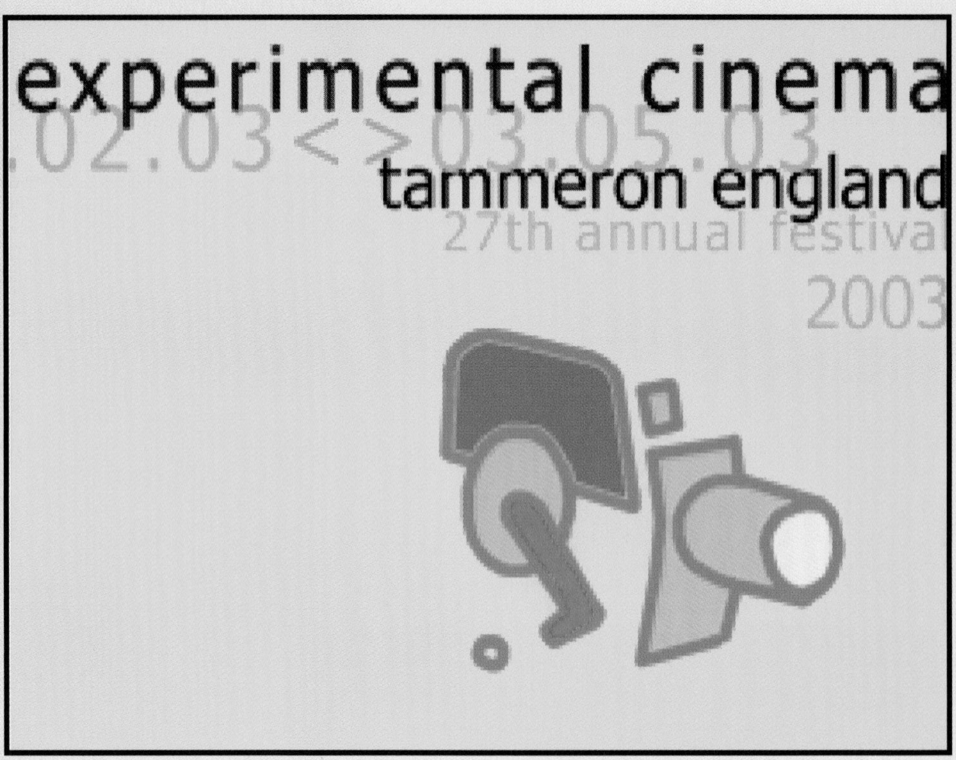

experimental cinema
.02.03<>03.05.03
tammeron england
27th annual festival
2003

Session Introduction

This session is all about color. You are introduced to Photoshop's color management system and learn how to set it up to keep the color of an image as consistent as possible as it moves from your screen to your printer. Then you practice using Photoshop's features for choosing colors—the Foreground and Background Color boxes, the Eyedropper tool for sampling colors, the Color Picker, the Color palette, and the Swatches palette.

TOOLS YOU'LL USE
Color Settings dialog box, Eyedropper tool, Foreground and Background Color boxes, Color Picker, Color palette, and Swatches palette

CD-ROM FILES NEEDED
04_films.psd and 04_films_end.psd

TIME REQUIRED
40 minutes

Discussion
Color Management Simplified

The goal of Photoshop's color-management system is to keep the colors in your images as consistent as possible from screen to print. This is no easy task because each piece of hardware takes the raw values that describe color and interprets them differently. You can do several things to help the process.

First, characterize your monitor, creating a monitor profile that describes to Photoshop how your monitor reproduces color. In Windows, you can use the Adobe Gamma utility that is installed with Photoshop for Windows. Go to the Program Files→Common Files→Adobe→Calibration folder on your hard drive, double-click on the Adobe Gamma Control Panel, and choose the Step by Step Wizard that will take you through the process. On a Mac, you can use the Apple Display Calibration utility, which has an assistant that walks you through the process. To access it in Macintosh OS X, go to System Preferences→Displays, select the Color tab, and click the Calibrate button. These utilities create a custom monitor profile for you. If you save the profile where the utility suggests, Photoshop can access it automatically.

Second, choose the color-management settings that your copy of Photoshop CS will use when you create or open a file in Photoshop. Access these settings by choosing Photoshop→Color Settings (Windows: Edit→Color Settings). You can choose a preset bundle of settings, such as North America General Purpose Defaults, which is the default bundle in Photoshop CS, or U.S. Prepress Defaults, which is generally useful for print work. Or you can set the fields individually. The Working Spaces fields are particularly important. They define how Photoshop interprets and displays color data during editing of an image that has no alternative embedded profile. In Photoshop CS you can override application of the default Working Space to a new document by choosing a different profile in the Advanced section of the New dialog box. Adobe RGB is a good all-around working space choice for print work, as you see in the upcoming tutorial. The Color Management Policies fields dictate how Photoshop handles images that have been tagged with color-management settings that don't match yours. In the tutorial, these are set automatically to warn you when there's a mismatch. If you find this bothersome, you can uncheck the Ask When Opening and Ask When Pasting check boxes.

Third, when you save a document in Photoshop, embed the color profile of its working space by checking the Embed Color Profile check box in the Save As dialog box. Profiles are the heart of Photoshop's color-management scheme. They tag an image with information about the working space in which the image was created. Printers that read color profiles can use that information to try to match the print output to the colors you see on-screen. If the image is opened on another computer in Photoshop or in some other program that reads color profiles, that program can use the profile to display the image as it looked when you created it. You can convert an open image to a different color profile at any time by choosing Image→Mode→Convert Profile.

Fourth, when you're ready to print your image, go to File→Print with Preview, click the Output button, and choose Color Management. Make sure that Document is selected as the source. Under Print Space, click the Profile down arrow and choose your printer's profile from the menu. This converts the colors in the image temporarily to the device-specific color space that your printer uses. There is a caveat: Keep in mind that the color-management setup recommended in the tutorial is not the only way to go. It assumes that you're preparing images in RGB for an inkjet printer. If you're working on files for commercial CMYK printing, consult your printer about choosing color-management settings and embedding profiles. If you want to know more about color management, read the Photoshop CS Help files, which have a pretty good explanation. You can quickly access the color topics using the Welcome Screen. Choose Help→Welcome Screen and click the book icon to the left of Setting Up Color.

Tutorial
» Managing Color for Print

Color management is a subject that makes many Photoshop users cringe. It's a complex, technical area that can be difficult to understand, so I've tried to make it as simple as possible for you. In this tutorial, I show you one way to approach color management when you work in RGB color mode preparing an image for print on an inkjet printer. In the process, you get a handle on what color management is and the steps to take to use Photoshop's color management system.

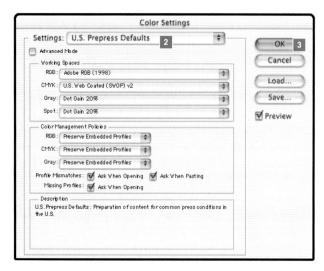

1. **Choose Photoshop→Color Settings (Windows: Edit→Color Settings). In the Color Settings dialog box, the Settings field defaults to North America Graphics Defaults.**
   In the next step, you use this field to choose a package of presets that are more appropriate for print work.

2. **Click the Settings button and choose U.S. Prepress Defaults.**
   This changes all the settings in the Color Settings dialog box. U.S Prepress Defaults is the best choice if most of your work is preparing images for print output according to U.S. printing standards. Table 4-1 briefly explains these settings.

3. **When you're done choosing color settings, click OK.**

4. **Open** 04_films.psd **from the Session 4 Tutorial Files folder on your hard drive.**
   04_films.psd is a replica of the finished file 03_films_end.psd that I asked you to save into the Session 3 Tutorial Files folder on your hard drive at the end of Session 3. You can use your file, 03_films_end.psd, in this session instead of 04_films.psd if you completed all the preceding tutorials.

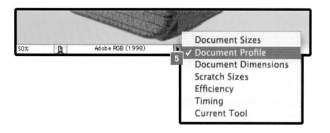

5. **Click the arrow at the bottom of the open document window (Windows: the application window) and choose Document Profile. Notice that the information field reads Adobe RGB (1998).**
   This tells you that this file has been tagged with the Adobe RGB (1998) color profile. There were no Profile Mismatch warnings when you opened this image because its color profile matches the Adobe RGB (1998) color environment that you chose as your working space in step 2.

6. **Leave this file open for the next tutorial.**

Table 4-1: Color Management Settings

Field	U.S. Prepress Default Setting	Explanation
RGB (in the Working Spaces area)	Adobe RGB (1998)	A working space is a color environment that determines how Photoshop interprets the raw color values in an image when it displays them on your screen. The most important working space setting for your purposes here is the RGB working space because the files that you use in these tutorials are RGB files. Adobe RGB (1998) is generally the best RGB working space setting for images destined for print because it contains a wide range of colors. Therefore, it matches the gamut (which means the range of reproducible colors) of most RGB printers, and it converts well to CMYK color mode if necessary. If you're interested in a description of the other RGB color spaces, select each color space from the Working Spaces RGB menu in the Color Settings dialog box and read the description that appears at the bottom of the dialog box.
Profile Mismatches	Ask When Opening	This instructs Photoshop to warn you when an image you open contains an embedded profile that's different than your working space. The best choice usually is the default—use the embedded profile instead of the working space—which maintains the color integrity of the image as it was created. You can choose to convert the colors to your working space, which changes the colors but may be useful if you plan to collage the image with other images created in your working space. Or you can discard the embedded profile entirely. Doing so creates an untagged image that doesn't carry a profile to tell other devices how you intended the colors to look. I don't recommend this option unless you're creating images for the Web. (Web browsers can't read color profiles anyway.)
Profile Mismatches	Ask When Pasting	This tells Photoshop to warn you when you paste a selection from one image into another image that has a different embedded profile. You are offered options for how to deal with that selection.
Missing Profiles	Ask When Opening	This instructs Photoshop to warn you when an image you open contains no embedded profile. The default choice is to leave the document as is (don't color manage). In that case, the image is left untagged, but is interpreted according to your working space while it's open. Alternatively, you can choose to assign the profile of your working space or to assign another profile.

Tutorial
» Setting Foreground and Background Colors

The Foreground and Background Color boxes in the toolbox are like paint wells that hold the colors that you use as you work on an image. You can select the colors that appear in these boxes several different ways. This short tutorial teaches you how to set Foreground and Background colors by sampling colors from an open image, and how to return the Foreground and Background Color boxes to their black and white defaults. In the tutorials that follow, you learn other ways to choose color: with the Color Picker, the Color palette, and the Swatches palette.

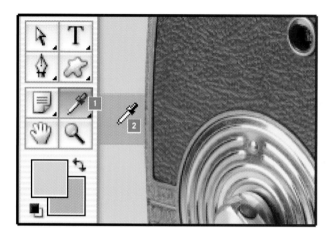

1. **Select the Eyedropper tool in the toolbox and click a color in the image.**

   This fills the Foreground Color box in the toolbox with the sampled color from the open image. The color in the Foreground Color box is used whenever you apply the painting tools, the Type tool, one of the Shape tools, or the Edit→Stroke command. You work with all these features in upcoming sessions.

   < T I P >

   Photoshop's Eyedropper tool can sample colors from any place on your screen. This means that you can sample a color from a document that's open in another program, from a Web page that's open in a Web browser, or even from image thumbnails in Photoshop's File Browser. To try this, click inside the Photoshop document window, keep the mouse button held down, and move the Eyedropper outside the Photoshop document window. Notice the Foreground Color box change as you move over colors anywhere on your screen. Release the mouse button to sample whatever color is under the cursor.

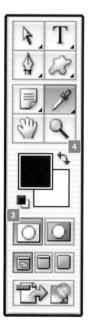

2. **Option+click (Windows: Alt+click) inside the image to sample another color.**

   This fills the Background Color box in the toolbox with this sampled color. The Background color appears when you erase a bottom layer with the Eraser tool, and it fills the blank area of the canvas when you increase the canvas size.

3. **Click the Default Colors icon (the small black and white squares) in the toolbox.**

   This changes the Foreground color to black and the Background color to white. The keyboard shortcut for this operation is the D key. This is a shortcut that you'll use often.

4. **Click the double-pointed arrows in the toolbox.**

   This switches the two color boxes, so that the Foreground color is now white and the Background color is black. The keyboard shortcut for this operation is the X key. This is another shortcut worth memorizing.

5. **Leave this image open for the next tutorial.**

Tutorial
» Choosing Colors with the Color Picker

The Color Picker is one of several features you can use to select colors in Photoshop. It's my favorite because it offers lots of different ways to view color. You learn how to use the Color Picker in this tutorial.

1. **Make sure that** 04_films.psd **is open from the previous tutorial.**

2. **Click the Foreground Color box to open the Color Picker.**

3. **Uncheck Only Web Colors if that box has a check mark in it.**
   This box limits the display of colors in the Color Picker to 216 Web-safe colors. There's no reason to limit your color choices this way when you design for print.

4. **Click the H radio button to display colors by hue.**
   The slider in the middle of the Color Picker now shows a rainbow of hues. The color area on the left of the Color Picker shows the hue that's selected in the slider at different combinations of brightness (from top to bottom) and saturation (from right to left).

5. **Move the slider to the blue-green area of the spectrum. Then click inside the color area to select a blue-green that you like.**
   The new color and the previous selected color appear in the square at the top of the Color Picker. If you like the new color, you could click OK at this point, but hold off for now so that I can show you some more features of the Color Picker.

6. **Click again in the color area, until you see a triangular alert icon to the right of the new color square.**
   This is an out-of-gamut warning, indicating that the color you chose is beyond the range of printable colors on a CMYK printer. The small square under the alert icon contains the closest color that's printable with CMYK inks.

7. **Click the triangular alert icon to change your selection to the nearest printable color.**

<N O T E>
You may be wondering about the cube icon just below the out-of-gamut warning. That indicates that you chose a non-Web-safe color and isn't relevant when you create an image for print. Another Web-only feature is the # field at the bottom of the Color Picker, where you can enter the hexadecimal code for a color if you want to match a color in a Web graphic to a color identified in the hexadecimal numbering system in a Web page's HTML code.

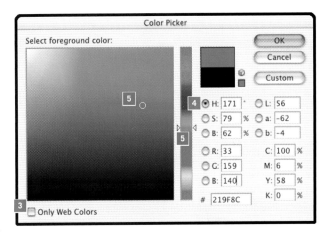

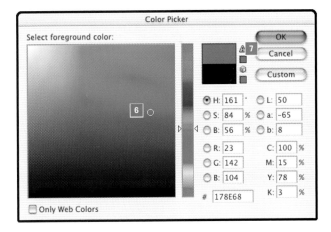

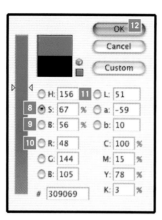

8. **Click the S radio button to display colors by saturation.**

9. **Click the first B radio button to display colors by brightness.**
   All these different displays show the same colors, but they're just arranged in different ways to help you select colors that go well together.

10. **Click the R, G, or B radio button to display colors by amount of red, green, and blue.**

<TIP>

If you know the exact RGB color value that you're after, you can type it into the R, G, and B boxes. For example, 0, 0, 0 are the RGB values for black, and 255, 255, 255 are the RGB values for white.

11. **Click the L, a, or b radio button to display colors by luminosity.**
    These displays suggest some nice color combinations that you may use when you try to come up with a palette for an image.

<NOTE>

If you ever try to select a Pantone or other custom color, click the Custom button and explore the options there. The Custom colors dialog box lists over 20 different custom color systems, or books. Choose a book and then select the color by number and swatch from the lists.

12. **When you finish exploring the Color Picker, click the OK button.**
    You see the color that you selected in the Foreground Color box in the toolbox.

13. **Select the Brush tool in the toolbox, choose a brush from the Brush Preset Picker on the left side of the Options bar, and select the Logo layer in the Layers palette.**
    Then have some fun coloring in the handle of the camera logo in the image.

<TIP>

You may want to zoom in, as you learned how to do in Session 3, to make it easier to see where you paint.

14. **Choose File→Save As. Navigate to the Session 04 Tutorial Files folder, and click Save, writing over the document of the same name that's already there. Leave the image open for the next tutorial.**

<NOTE>

Notice the Embed Color Profile command at the bottom of the Save As window. It's set to Adobe RGB (1998), which is the RGB working space you chose in your color management settings at the beginning of this session. It's checked by default, which causes Photoshop to embed this profile in the document when you click Save.

Tutorial
» Choosing Colors with the Color Palette

The Color palette is an alternative way of choosing colors. It offers the same colors as the Color Picker, arranged in a different interface. You may prefer the Color palette if you like to mix colors visually or if you don't have room on your screen for the bulky Color Picker. Try out the Color palette in this tutorial.

1. **Make sure that** `04_films.psd` **is open from the previous tutorial.**

2. **Choose Window→Color if the Color palette is not already displayed on your screen.**

3. **Click the arrow at the top right of the Color palette to reveal a menu of options.**

4. **Choose RGB Spectrum.**
   This sets the color bar at the bottom of the Color palette to RGB colors. You can set the color bar and the color sliders at the top of the palette to separate color modes.

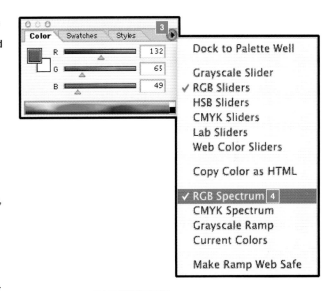

5. **Click in the Background Color box on the Color palette.**
   The Color palette has a Foreground and Background Color box, just like the toolbox.

6. **Move your cursor over the color bar.**
   Notice that the cursor changes to an eyedropper.

7. **Click to sample a color from the yellow area of the color bar.**
   Use the color bar as a starting point to get to the general color area that you want.

8. **Move the R, G, and B sliders to fine-tune your color selection to a light yellow.**
   Notice in the figure that the Color palette has a triangular alert icon for out-of-gamut colors, just like the Color Picker. It also has a non-Web-safe color alert and small black-and-white default icons, like the Color Picker.

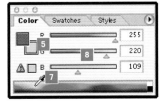

9. **Select the Eraser tool in the toolbox, select the Background layer in the Layers palette, and erase inside the lens of the camera logo.**
   The Eraser tool erases to the background color when you have the bottom-most layer selected in the Layers palette. You learn more about layers in Session 8.

10. **Make a new folder on your hard drive and name it collages.**
    This is where you store each final collage as you finish working on it in the tutorials. Keep this folder safe so that you can print its contents as the final project at the end of the book. Keep your collages folder on your desktop or anywhere else in your file system that's easy for you to find.

11. **Choose File→Save As and save the file as** `04_films_end.psd` **in the collages folder.**

12. **Close the image.**
    You don't need an open image for the next tutorial.

<NOTE>
Whatever color you choose as the Background color in the Color palette also will appear in the Background Color box in the toolbox.

Tutorial
» Choosing Colors with the Swatches Palette

The Swatches palette is yet another source of colors in Photoshop. Using the Swatches palette is similar to working with a painter's palette. You can limit your colors by loading preset swatches or swatches that you create yourself and see those colors in front of you as you work. Small custom palettes are handy for creating a series of images with the same colors. In this tutorial, you learn how to load a preset swatch and create and load your own color swatch.

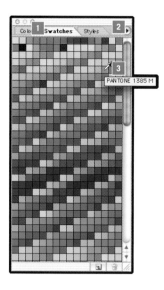

1. **Click the Swatches tab next to the Color palette or choose Window→ Swatches to bring the Swatches palette to the foreground.**

2. **Click the arrow on the top right of the Swatches palette and choose PANTONE Solid Matte from the menu of preset Swatches. Click OK at the prompt.**
   This replaces the default swatch with a swatch made up entirely of Pantone solid matte colors. If none of the preset swatches suit you, you can make your own.

3. **Move the cursor over any color in the Swatches palette to view the name of that color.**

4. **Click any color in the Swatches palette to set the Foreground Color box to that color.**

5. **Click the arrow on the top right of the Swatches palette and choose any of the smaller palettes, such as HKS E. Click OK at the prompt.**
   You use this preset palette as a starting point for creating your own custom palette.

6. **Option+click (Windows: Alt+click) any color in the Swatches palette to change the cursor to scissors and eliminate that color from the palette. Repeat this until you delete all the colors that you don't want to include in your custom swatch.**
   Alternatively, click any color and drag it to the Trash icon at the bottom of the Swatches palette to delete it from the palette.

7. **Use any of Photoshop's color selection methods (such as choosing a color from the Color Picker or Color palette) to select another color that you want to include in your custom swatch.**
   This places the selected color in the Foreground Color box in the toolbox.

8. **Move your cursor over the blank area of the Swatches palette until it changes to a Paint Bucket icon and click.**

9. **Type a name for your new swatch color in the Color Swatch Name dialog box and click OK.**

    This adds the Foreground color to your custom swatches. Alternatively, click the New Color icon at the bottom of the Swatches palette and name your new color.

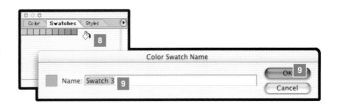

10. **Repeat Steps 7 through 9 until the Swatches palette contains all the colors that you want to include in your custom swatch.**

11. **Click the arrow at the top right of the Swatches palette and choose Save Swatches.**

12. **In the Save dialog box, name your new swatches file `filmfest.aco`, making sure to keep the `.aco` extension, and save it to the default location (the Color Swatches folder in the Presets folder inside the Photoshop Application folder on your hard drive).**

13. **Click the arrow at the top right of the Swatches palette and choose Reset Swatches.**

    This loads the default swatch into the Swatches palette. In the next steps, you find out how to replace this swatch with your custom swatch so that it's ready to use on any image.

14. **Click the arrow at the top right of the Swatches palette again and choose Replace Swatches.**

    This opens the Load window (Windows: Replace window), displaying all the swatches in the Color Swatches folder, including your custom swatch, `filmfest.aco`.

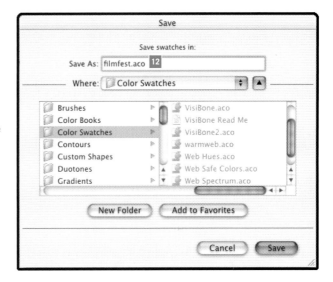

15. **Choose `filmfest.aco` in the Load window (Windows: Replace window) and click Load.**

    This replaces the default swatches in the Swatches palette with your custom-built swatches. Your custom swatches are now displayed in the Swatches palette, ready to use on any open image.

» Session Review

This session covers how to choose and use color in Photoshop. You were introduced to Photoshop's color management system and practiced selecting colors for image editing using a variety of methods—the Eyedropper tool, the Color Picker, the Color palette, and the Swatches palette. Work through these questions to review what you learned in this session.

1. What is the purpose of Photoshop's color management system? (See "Discussion: Color Management Simplified.")

2. Does Photoshop for Macintosh include the Adobe Gamma utility? (See "Discussion: Color Management Simplified.")

3. What does the RGB Working Space color management setting do? (See "Tutorial: Managing Color for Print.")

4. Where can you find information on the color used in an open image? (See "Tutorial: Managing Color for Print.")

5. How do you embed a color profile into a document? (See "Tutorial: Managing Color for Print.")

6. What does a color profile do? (See "Tutorial: Managing Color for Print.")

7. How do you convert the colors in an image to the color space that your printer uses? (See "Tutorial: Managing Color for Print.")

8. What does checking the Profile Mismatches Ask When Opening check box in the Color Settings dialog box instruct Photoshop to do? (See "Tutorial: Managing Color for Print.")

9. What tool do you use to sample a color from an image to fill the Foreground Color box? (See "Tutorial: Setting Foreground and Background Colors.")

10. How do you set the Background Color box in the toolbox to a sampled color? (See "Tutorial: Setting Foreground and Background Colors.")

11. What does clicking the Default Colors icon in the toolbox do? (See "Tutorial: Setting Foreground and Background Colors.")

12. Name four alternative tools/features that you can use to choose a color in Photoshop. (See all tutorials except "Managing Color for Print.")

13. What does the triangular alert in the Color Picker tell you about a selected color? (See "Tutorial: Choosing Colors with the Color Picker.")

14. What is the purpose of the color bar in the Color palette? (See "Tutorial: Choosing Colors with the Color Palette.")

15. How do you select a color to apply to an image from the Swatches palette? (See "Tutorial: Choosing Colors with the Swatches Palette.")

16. Are preset swatches the only kind of swatch that you can load into the Swatches palette? (See "Tutorial: Choosing Colors with the Swatches Palette.")

tammeron international experimental cinema

03.02.03<>03.05.03

tammeron england

27th annual festival

2003

film schedule

fallen on wallstreet
03.02 5pm

finish line
03.02 7pm

territorial velvet
03.02 9pm

arising to the end
03.03 7pm

four large squares
03.04 7pm

frozen with steak
03.05 7pm

reason to cry
03.05 9pm

Session 5

Painting and Filling with Pixels

03.02.03 < > 03.05.03
27th annual festival< > tammeron england

tammeron affliates and sponsors

SPIKE FILMS   CINEARTS   THE STUDIO

Session Introduction

You get your creative juices flowing in this session as you learn about Photoshop's pixel-based filling and painting features. You find out how to fill with color, pattern, and gradient. You try out Photoshop's Brushes palette, learn how to use preset brushes, edit preset buttons using Photoshop's many brush options, and define a new brush of your own. You paint away color with the Eraser, Magic Eraser, and Background Eraser, and you accent your collage by stroking with pixels.

TOOLS YOU'LL USE
Fill command, Lock Transparency button, Rectangular Marquee tool, Paint Bucket tool, Pattern Stamp tool, Define Pattern command, Pattern Maker, Gradient tool, Gradient Editor, Brush tool, Brushes palette, Brush pop-up palette, Define Brush command, Options bar, Stroke command, Eraser tool, Magic Eraser tool, and Background Eraser tool

CD-ROM FILES NEEDED
05_sponsors.psd, 05_sponsors_patt.psd, 05_sponsors_grad.psd, 05_sponsors_brush.psd, 05_camera.psd, 05_brush.psd, and 05_brush_end.psd

TIME REQUIRED
120 minutes

Tutorial

» Filling a Layer

This session begins on a simple note with this tutorial which teaches how to use Photoshop's Fill command to fill a whole layer with a solid color.

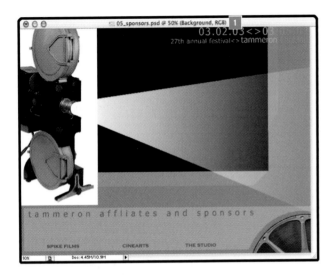

1. **Open** 05_sponsors.psd **from the Session 5 Tutorial Files folder on your hard drive.**

   05_sponsors.psd is a barebones image that you will develop into a page for your film festival program guide over the course of this and the following session. If you see a prompt about updating text layers, here or anywhere in this session, click Update.

2. **Choose Window→Layers to open the Layers palette if it isn't already visible on your desktop.**

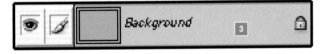

3. **Click the Background layer in the Layers palette to select that layer.**

An Introduction to Layers

The files that you use in this session have several layers, each of which contains separate pieces of artwork. Structuring an image this way makes it easy to fill and paint individual items. Don't worry that you haven't yet studied the subject of layers in detail. For now, it's sufficient to know that each layer in a PSD file can contain pixels of artwork, as well as transparent pixels. When you look at a layered image on your screen, it's as if you are looking down through the stack of layers from top to bottom. So you can see through transparent areas on a layer to the layers below. In addition, each layer and its artwork can be made temporarily visible and invisible, can be edited separately, and can be moved up or down in the stack of layers. You experiment with these and other qualities of layers when you get to Session 8.

4. **Click the Foreground Color box in the toolbox to open the Color Picker, and then select a yellow-green color in the Color Picker and click OK.**

   If you want to use the exact same color that I did, type its RGB values in the RGB fields in the Color Picker. Those values are R: 199, G: 181, B: 20.

5. **Go to the menu bar at the top of the screen and choose Edit→Fill.**

   This opens the Fill dialog box.

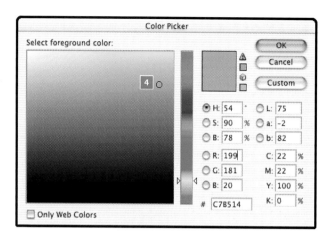

<NOTE>

In Photoshop CS you can select a fill color directly from the Fill dialog box. Click the Use menu inside the dialog box and choose Color to open the Color Picker. Choose a color from the Color Picker using any of the methods you learned in Session 4. This saves you from having to exit the Fill dialog box if you forget to set the Foreground Color in Photoshop's toolbox first.

6. **Check that the Use setting in the Fill dialog box is set to Foreground Color.**

   This instructs Photoshop to use the contents of the Foreground Color box in the toolbox as the fill color. Leave the other fields at their default settings for now.

7. **Click OK to fill the Background layer with yellow-green.**

<NOTE>

Another way to fill an image with a solid color is by applying a Fill layer (choose Layer→New Fill Layer→Solid Color and select a color from the Color Picker that opens). The advantage of using a Fill layer is that it can be easily modified without disturbing the original artwork, and its content can be quickly changed from a solid color to a pattern or gradient. Otherwise, using the Fill tool, your image's layer is changed. Fill layers are addressed in Session 8.

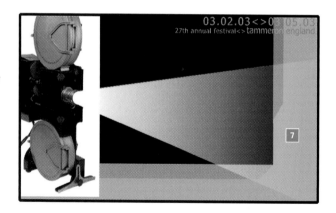

8. **Option+click (Windows: Alt+click) the eye icon in the Visibility box to the left of the Background layer in the Layers palette.**

   This hides the eye icons on all the layers except the Background layer, leaving only the contents of the Background layer showing in the document window. Now you can see that you've filled the entire Background layer with yellow-green. In the next tutorial, you'll learn how to restrict a fill to the artwork on a layer, leaving transparent pixels on that layer unfilled.

9. **Option+click (Windows: Alt+click) the eye icon on the Background layer again.**

   This makes all layers that were originally visible, visible again.

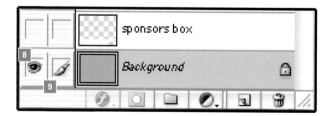

10. **Choose File→Save and leave this document open for the next tutorial.**

Discussion
Working with Pixels and Bitmapped Images

When you fill an area with color, as you did in this tutorial, you are modifying pixels in a bitmapped image. The same is true when you use Photoshop's painting tools and many of its other features and commands. This session focuses on filling and painting with pixels, so it's useful to have a basic understanding of what the terms pixel and bitmapped image mean.

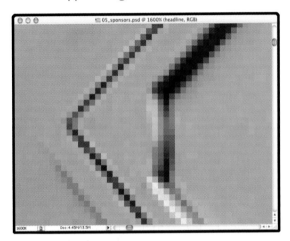

A pixel is a tiny rectangle that contains information about the color at a particular location in an image. A bitmapped image (sometimes called a rasterized image) is made up of pixels arranged on a grid. You can actually see image pixels and their grid-like arrangement if you zoom in on an image that's open in Photoshop, such as the one shown here.

A bitmapped image can display gradual changes between colors and subtle blends between foreground and background elements. This makes bitmapped images ideal for photographs, soft-edged graphics, and continuous tone artwork. On the downside, a bitmapped image contains a finite number of pixels. Therefore, the image won't look very good if you try to make it bigger. Scaling up a bitmapped image in a page layout program such as QuarkXPress or a drawing program such as Illustrator just stretches the existing pixels, creating a pixelated image. You learned in Session 3 that in Photoshop you can increase the number of pixels in an image by checking Resample Image and increasing the resolution or dimensions in the Image Size dialog box. However, that requires Photoshop to generate image information to fill in the gaps, which usually causes the printed image to look blurry.

<TIP>
If you must resample up, apply Photoshop's Unsharp Mask filter afterwards to increase contrast, which can make the image look more focused. If you use the Unsharp Mask, experiment with the settings to get the best focus appearance.

Photoshop is best known for its prowess at creating and editing bitmapped images. In addition, Photoshop CS has some useful vector-based features, which you learn about in Session 6.

Tutorial
» Filling the Artwork on a Layer

In this tutorial, you learn how to confine a color fill to the artwork on a layer, leaving transparent pixels on the layer unfilled. This is a useful technique for changing the color of all the artwork on a layer at once, without having to do any selecting.

1. **Make sure that** 05_sponsors.psd **is open from the preceding tutorial.**

2. **Click the main box layer in the Layers palette to select that layer.**
   Don't confuse selecting a layer so that you can edit its contents with making the layer visible or invisible by clicking its eye icon.

3. **Click the Lock Transparency button at the top left of the Layers palette.**
   The Lock Transparency button darkens, and a hollow lock icon appears on the main box layer, indicating that you can't paint, fill, or otherwise edit any transparent pixels on that layer.

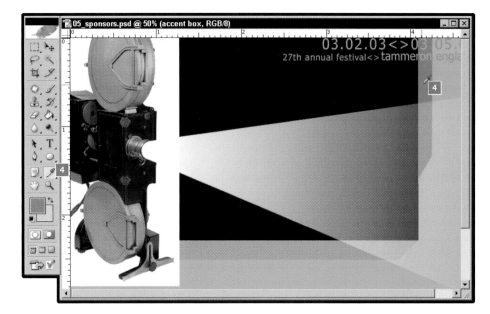

4. **Select the Eyedropper tool in the toolbox. Click the thin green polygon on the right side of the image.**
   This sets the Foreground Color box in the toolbox to green. You already practiced this technique in Session 4.

5. **Choose Edit→Fill, leave the Use field in the Fill dialog box set to Foreground Color, and click OK.**
   This fills the black rectangle on the main box layer with green.

<NOTE>
There are three other lock buttons in the Layers palette. The Lock Image button (with the paintbrush icon) prevents you from filling, painting, or otherwise changing existing artwork on a layer. The Lock Position button (with the arrows icon) prevents you from moving the artwork on a layer. The Lock All button (with the lock icon) freezes all these layer properties.

<NOTE>
Protecting transparent pixels while filling changes the color of all the artwork on a layer. To color just part of the artwork on a layer, you have to isolate that area before filling.

6. **Option+click (Windows: Alt+click) the eye icon on the main box layer in the Layers palette.**
   This makes all layers except the main box layer invisible. Notice that you filled the artwork, rather than the entire layer, with green. The transparent pixels on the main box layer (represented by the gray checkerboard pattern) were protected from the fill by the transparency lock feature. In the next steps, you try this again on another layer, using an efficient shortcut for the Fill command.

7. **Option+click (Windows: Alt+click) the eye icon on the main box layer again.**
   This makes all layers visible again.

8. **Select the accent box layer in the Layers palette.**

9. **Click the Lock Transparency button to protect the transparent pixels on the accent box layer.**

10. **Click the Foreground Color box in the toolbox to open the Color Picker, choose yellow (R:** 255, **G:** 204, **B:** 0), **and click OK.**

<CAUTION>
If you filled the entire layer with yellow by mistake, it's because you forgot to click the Lock Transparency button, which is a common oversight. Fix it by clicking ⌘+Z (Windows: Ctrl+Z) to undo, and try the last few steps again.

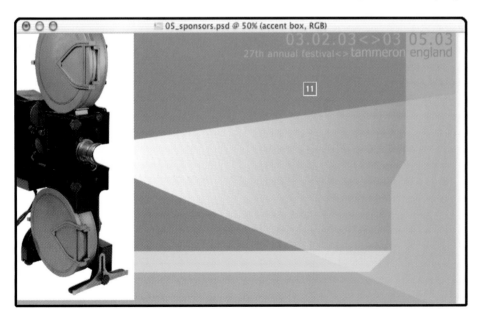

11. **Click Option+Delete (Windows: Alt+Delete).**
    This is a useful shortcut for filling with the foreground color. The artwork on the accent box layer is now filled with yellow.

12. **Choose File→Save and leave this image open for the next tutorial.**

Tutorial
» Filling Selected Artwork

In the preceding tutorial, you learned how to fill all the artwork on a layer. There will be times when you want to limit the extent of a fill even further so that only part of the artwork on a layer is affected by the fill. You do that in this tutorial.

1. **Check that** 05_sponsors.psd **is still open from the previous tutorial.**

2. **Click the Foreground Color box in the toolbox to open the Color Picker. Choose a bright blue-green (R: 153, G: 204, B: 153) and click OK.**

3. **Select the headline layer in the Layers palette.**

4. **Click the Lock Transparency icon.**
This prevents the transparent pixels on the headline layer (all the pixels except the text) from being filled.

5. **Click the Rectangular Marquee tool in the toolbox. If it's not visible, click whichever marquee tool is showing in the toolbox and choose Rectangular Marquee Tool from the hidden menu.**
The Rectangular Marquee is one of Photoshop's selection tools. You learn all about selection tools in Session 7.

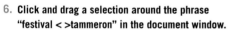

6. **Click and drag a selection around the phrase "festival < >tammeron" in the document window.**
This limits the area that you're about to fill to just the selected phrase on the headline layer. The animated broken lines around the selection are called *marching ants*.

<NOTE>
The headline layer isn't a type layer. If it were, you couldn't isolate and change the color of words on the layer the same way. This is just a regular layer that contains artwork in the shape of text. The technique that you learned here would work the same way if this layer contained images rather than words.

7. **Click Option+delete (Windows: Alt+backspace) to fill the selected phrase "festival < > tammeron" with blue-green.**

8. **Click anywhere outside the selection to deselect.**
This causes the marching ants to disappear.

9. **Choose File→Save. Leave the image open.**

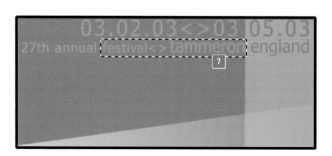

Tutorial
» Filling with the Paint Bucket Tool

The Paint Bucket tool offers another method of filling that's different than the Fill command or fill shortcut. Those methods are useful for filling an area of solid color or an area that you've defined. The Paint Bucket tool comes in handy when you want to fill pixels of a related color. Try it in this tutorial.

1. **Make sure that** 05_sponsors.psd **is open from the previous tutorial.**

2. **Click the reel layer in the Layers palette.**

3. **Click the Lock Transparency button in the Layers palette.**

4. **Click the Eyedropper tool in the toolbox and click in the purple box at the bottom of the image to set the Foreground Color to purple.**

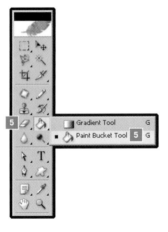

5. **Click the Paint Bucket tool in the toolbox. If you don't see it, click the Gradient tool to reveal a hidden tool menu and choose Paint Bucket Tool from that menu.**
   The Options bar changes to display options for the Paint Bucket tool.

6. **Click in the Tolerance field in the Options bar and type** 40.
   The Paint Bucket fills all pixels that have color values sufficiently similar to the pixel on which you click with that tool.
   Increase tolerance if you want to expand that range to fill a
   larger area; decrease tolerance if you want to fill a smaller
   area. This is one of those settings that demands experimentation. I found that 40 worked fine here.

7. **Click in the Mode field in the Options bar and choose Overlay.**
   The mode determines how the Paint Bucket's fill blends with
   the underlying image. I found that Normal produced a fill that
   was too solid for my taste. Overlay allows the tones in the
   underlying image to show through. Many tools have blending
   mode options, and they usually require lots of experimentation.

8. **Make sure that Contiguous and Anti-aliased are checked in the
   Options bar.**
   The Contiguous option tells the Paint Bucket to fill only pixels
   that are touching. The Anti-aliased option gives your fill a
   graduated edge that blends nicely into surrounding pixels. You
   see these options on the Options bar for other tools too.

9. **Click in the metal part of the film reel in the document window to
   fill that area.**
   You may have to try several times, clicking in different spots,
   to get the look you want.

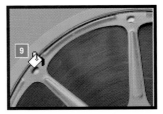

10. **Choose File→Save and leave** 05_sponsors.psd **open if you
    want to use it in the next exercise.**
    You have the option of starting the next exercise with a fresh
    prebuilt file.

Tutorial
» Filling with a Pattern

You can fill a layer, artwork, or a selection with a pattern, instead of a solid color. Both the Fill command and the Paint Bucket give you the option of filling with a pattern. In this tutorial, you use the Fill command to fill the artwork on a layer with a pattern. Another way to fill an image with a pattern is to use a Fill layer. Patterns are potential attention-grabbers that can overpower an otherwise balanced design. To protect against this, consider using subtle patterns and keeping patterned areas small, as in this tutorial.

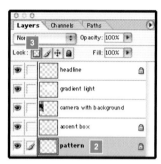

1. **Check that** 05_sponsors.psd **is still open from the previous tutorial. Alternatively, you can open** 05_sponsors_patt.psd **from the Session 5 Tutorials folder on your hard drive.**
   05_sponsors_patt.psd is a replica of how 05_sponsors.psd should look if you completed all the preceding tutorials in this session. If you skipped any of the tutorials in this session or if you messed up your file along the way, feel free to start with this fresh file.

2. **Select the pattern layer in the Layers palette.**

3. **Click the Lock Transparency button in the Layers palette.**
   This protects the transparent pixels on the pattern layer from filling with a pattern.

4. **Choose Edit→Fill. In the Fill dialog box, choose Pattern from the Use menu.**

5. **Click in the Custom Pattern sample in the Fill dialog box to open the Pattern Picker.**
   The pattern picker displays a default set of patterns that ship with Photoshop.

6. **Click the arrow on the top right of the Pattern Picker and choose Patterns 2.**

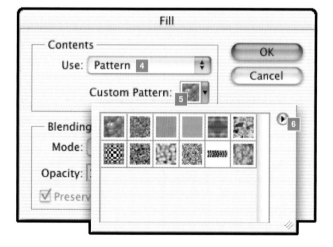

7. **At the prompt, click OK.**
   This replaces the default set of patterns with another set of patterns.

8. **Select the Stone pattern in the Pattern Picker and click anywhere inside the Fill dialog box to close the Pattern Picker.**

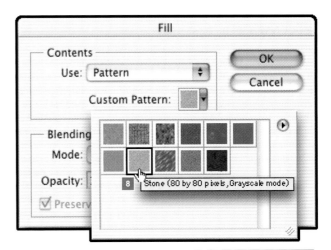

9. **Click in the Mode field under Blending in the Fill dialog box and choose Soft Light from the menu.**

   The blending mode determines how the pattern fill blends with pixels on other layers. The Soft Light blending mode creates a combination of the gray stone pattern and the colors on other layers, darkening some pixels and lightening others. The result is a textured green-gray appearance. It's difficult to predict the outcome of different blending modes on different artwork. The best method for choosing a blending mode is trial and error.

10. **Click OK in the Fill dialog box to apply the pattern fill to the pattern layer.**

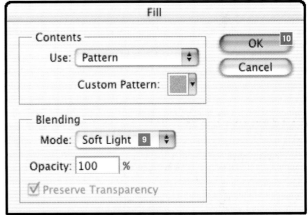

11. **Click the eye icon on the gradient light layer to get a better view of your pattern fill. Leave the gradient light layer hidden.**

12. **Choose File→Save As. Save the file as** 05_sponsors_patt.psd **(whether you used your own file or the fresh file provided for you for this tutorial). Leave the file open for the next exercise.**

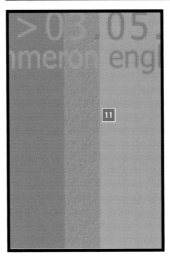

Tutorial
» Defining and Applying a Custom Pattern

If you have a creative spirit, you likely prefer your own custom-made pattern over the canned patterns that come with Photoshop. The traditional way of creating a pattern in Photoshop is with the simple Define Pattern command, which you use in this tutorial. You can fill an area with a custom-made pattern using the Fill command or the Paint Bucket tool. Another option, which you try here, is to paint with your pattern, using the Pattern Stamp tool.

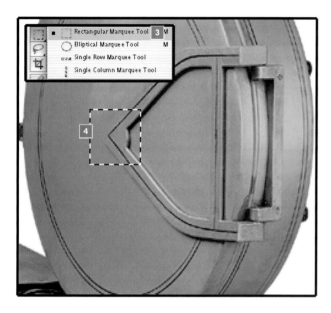

1. **Make sure that** `05_sponsors_patt.psd` **is open from the previous tutorial. Hold the spacebar to switch to the Hand tool, and click and drag to bring the top reel on the movie projector into view.**

2. **Double-click the Zoom tool in the toolbox to magnify the image to the 100% view.**

3. **Select the Rectangular Marquee tool in the toolbox.**

4. **Click and drag a small selection around the design on the movie projector in the image.**
   Be sure not to feather, expand, or otherwise modify your selection.

5. **Choose Edit→Define Pattern.**

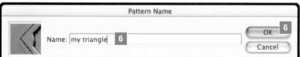

6. **Give your pattern a name (such as** my triangle**) and click OK.**

7. **Click anywhere in the image to deselect.**
   That's all there is to defining a custom pattern. The pattern now appears in the Pattern Picker, which is accessible from the Fill command and from the Paint Bucket tool Options bar. You could use either of those methods to fill an area with your pattern. The pattern repeats itself in a grid pattern. In the following steps, you learn another, more controlled way to apply your pattern—painting it into your image with the Pattern Stamp tool.

8. **Click the Clone tool in the toolbox to display a hidden tool menu. Select the Pattern Stamp tool from that menu.**

9. **Click the camera with background layer and click the New Layer button at the bottom of the Layers palette. Click the layer name and type** pattern stamp **as the name of the layer.**
   This creates a new layer on which to draw with the Pattern Stamp tool. Drawing on a separate layer protects the existing artwork and makes it easy to delete your drawing if you don't like it.

10. **Click the Brush sample in the Options bar to open the Brush pop-up palette.**

    The Brush pop-up palette is one place to select a brush style and size for any of Photoshop's brush tools (which include the Paint Brush tool, the Pencil tool, the Healing Brush tool, the Clone tool, the Stamp tool, the Eraser tools, the History brushes, and the Darkroom tools). It's sufficient when you want quick access to one of the preset brush tools that come with Photoshop. But if you want to vary brush options to create a custom brush, use the Brushes palette, which you learn about later in this session.

11. **Select a hard-edged brush from the Brush pop-up palette. Then move the Master Diameter slider until your brush tip is around 30 px.**

12. **Click anywhere in the Options bar to close the Brush pop-up palette.**

13. **Click the Pattern field in the Options bar to open the Pattern Picker. Click on the custom pattern you defined earlier in this tutorial, which appears in the last slot in Pattern Picker.**

14. **Click and drag in the image to paint the camera reel with your custom pattern.**

    You can change the size of the brush as you paint. Click the left bracket key on your keyboard to reduce brush size or the right bracket key to increase brush size.

15. **Click your pattern stamp layer in the Layers palette and drag it to the Trash icon.**

    This is one reason that it makes sense to create different pieces of artwork on different layers. It makes it so easy to change your mind!

16. **Choose File→Save and leave the image open for the next tutorial.**

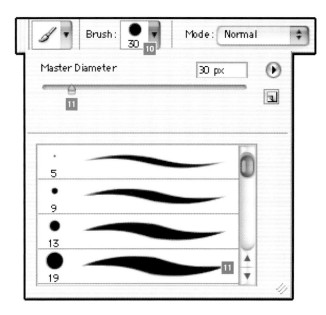

Tutorial
» Using the Pattern Maker

The Pattern Maker has its own interface (like the Extract tool or the Liquify feature), but it's not as complicated as it may look at first. What the Pattern Maker does is create pattern tiles from rectangular selections of artwork and arrange those tiles in repeating patterns. It attempts to make those patterns look seamless, with more or less success depending on the source material. In this tutorial, you use the Pattern Maker to create a pattern and automatically apply it to your collage.

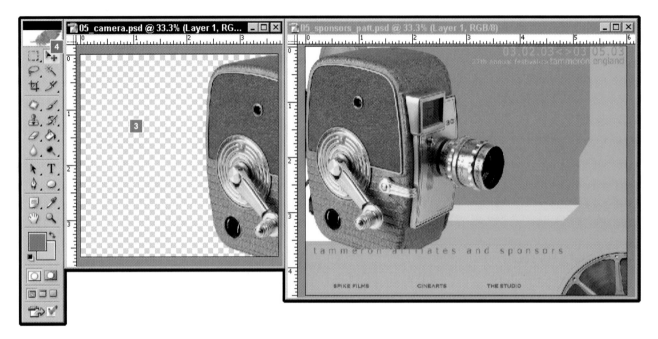

1. **Make sure that** 05_sponsors_patt.psd **is still open from the previous tutorial. Zoom out until you can see the whole image in your document window.**

2. **Click the top layer of the image in the Layers palette.**

3. **Open a second image,** 05_camera.psd, **from the Session 5 Tutorial Files folder on your hard drive.**

4. **Select the Move tool from the toolbox and click and drag the single layer of artwork from** 05_camera.psd **into** 05_sponsors_patt.psd.
   The camera image appears in your collage, on a new layer called Layer 1. It doesn't matter where the camera lands in the collage or whether it is centered.

5. **Click on** 05_camera.psd **and choose File→Close.**
   You won't need this file any longer.

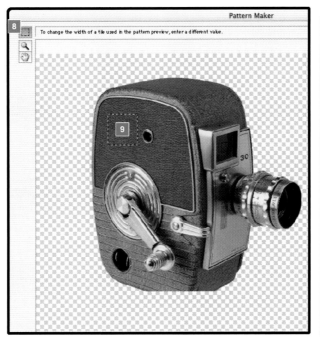

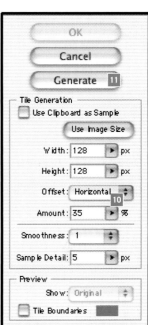

6. **Click the Layer 1 layer in the Layers palette and drag it down to just above the Background layer. Release the mouse button when a black line appears between the Background layer and the sponsors box layer just above it.**
Layer 1 is now located just above the Background layer in the Layers palette.

<TIP>
If you create a pattern from a layer you want to keep, make a copy of that source layer before you open the Pattern Maker (by dragging the layer onto the New Layer icon at the bottom of the Layers palette). The Pattern Maker completely fills the source layer with a pattern, obliterating any artwork on that layer. In this case, it isn't necessary to make a copy of the source layer because you won't be using it in this collage.

7. **With Layer 1 selected, choose Pattern Maker from the Filter menu at the top of your screen.**
This opens the Pattern Maker dialog box.

8. **Select the Rectangular Marquee tool at the top left of the Pattern Maker dialog box.**

9. **Click and drag a small rectangle around part of the brown leather on the camera in the preview area of the Pattern Maker.**
This defines the tile from which your pattern is built. Choose a relatively uniform part of the leather so that you don't get repeating lines in the pattern.

10. **Click the Offset button in the Pattern Maker and choose Horizontal. Type any number except for 50 into the Amount field.**
This offsets the tiles from one another in the pattern. You see this for yourself when you turn on Tile Boundaries after generating a pattern shortly.

11. **Leave the other settings as they are for now and click Generate.**
Photoshop generates a large preview of a pattern on the left side of the Pattern Maker.

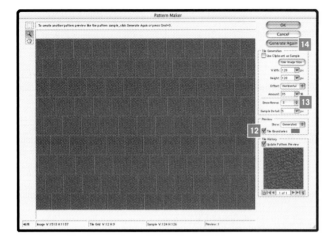

12. **Click the Tile Boundaries check box to see an overlay of the grid of tiles in the pattern.**

The tile boundaries preview where the edges of each tile are in the pattern. Although you can see some irregularities in the pattern, offsetting helps avoid symmetrical patterns.

13. **Click the Smoothness button and increase that field to 3.**

In some cases, this makes the transition between tiles less obvious.

14. **Click Generate Again.**

Photoshop makes a second pattern preview.

15. **Click the Tile Boundaries check box to remove the check mark.**

Now you can evaluate patterns without the boundaries obscuring your view.

16. **Click the arrows at the bottom of the Tile History preview on the right of the Pattern Maker to scroll through the previews that you just made.**

The pattern previews on the left change as you scroll if Update Pattern Preview is selected. If you come across a tile that you're sure you don't want, you can delete it by dragging it to the Trash icon at the bottom of the Tile History Preview area.

17. **Stop scrolling when you get to the tile that you want to use and click OK.**

Photoshop fills Layer 1 in your image with a pattern made from this tile. The Pattern Maker closes automatically.

< N O T E >

You can treat Layer 1 like any other layer. Try changing its opacity and blending mode from the controls at the top of the Layers palette. Or click the Move tool to reposition the layer in the image. I tried all of that and was still not satisfied with the look of this pattern layer. So I deleted it, as I recommend you do.

Creating Pattern Tiles with the Pattern Maker

In this tutorial, you learned how to use the Pattern Maker to create a pattern and apply it, all in the same image. You can also use the Pattern Maker to create and save a small tile to be made into a pattern elsewhere. After you generate several tiles as you did in this tutorial, choose one to save and click the Save button at the bottom left of the Tile History preview in the Pattern Maker. That tile automatically appears in the Pattern Picker that's accessible from the Fill command, the Paint Bucket tool, and the Pattern

Stamp. You can apply it from any of those features, just like the prebuilt patterns that you used in the preceding tutorials. You may wonder why you need the Pattern Maker, when you already know how to make a pattern tile using the Define Pattern command. The main advantage of the Pattern Maker is that it attempts to blend the edges of the tiles it makes so that the resulting pattern appears relatively seamless.

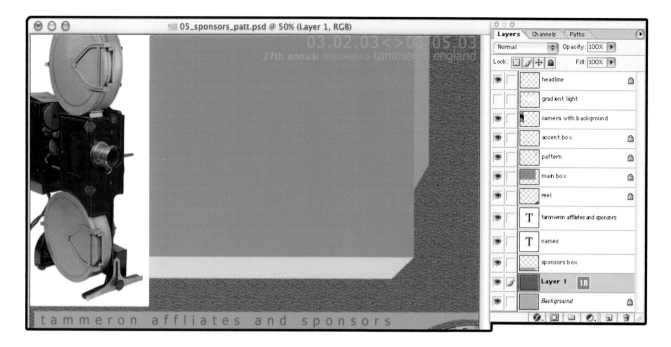

18. **Click Layer 1 in the Layers palette and drag it to the Trash icon at the bottom of the Layers palette.**

<NOTE>
Some settings in the Pattern Maker dialog box are probably new to you. Table 5-1 contains a summary of what each does.

19. **Leave** 05_sponsors_patt.psd **open for the next tutorial if you want to use it (instead of a fresh prebuilt file) in the next exercise.**

Table 5-1: Pattern Maker Settings

Setting	Function
Generate or Generate Again	Creates a pattern preview based on your settings.
OK	Fills the selected layer with a pattern made from the selected tile and closes the Pattern Maker.
Cancel	Closes the Pattern Maker without making a pattern.
Use Clipboard as Sample	Used when you've copied a selection from another image to use as a pattern tile.
Use Image Size	Makes a single pattern tile as big as the entire source image.
Width and Height	Determine the size of the pattern tile.
Offset	Offsets tiles from one another in the pattern.
Smoothness	Increasing this sometimes makes the edges between tiles in a pattern less obvious.
Sample Detail	Increasing this sometimes helps unify graphic details broken up by a pattern.
Show	Displays the original image or a pattern preview in the preview area.
Tile Boundaries	Indicates the location of tile edges in a pattern preview.

Tutorial
» Using the Gradient Tool

A gradient is a special kind of fill that is a gradual blend of colors and opacities. Photoshop offers several features that you can use to create gradients—the Gradient tool, the Gradient Fill layer, and the Gradient Overlay layer style. Fill layers and layer styles are special features that are addressed later in this book. In this tutorial, you get to know the basic Gradient tool, and use it to replace a selected area of solid color with one of the many preset gradients that ship with Photoshop CS.

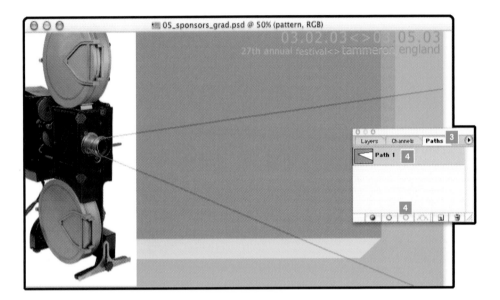

1. **Check that** 05_sponsors_patt.psd **is still open. Alternatively, you can open** 05_sponsors_grad.psd **from the Session 5 Tutorials folder on your hard drive.**
   05_sponsors_grad.psd is a replica of how 05_sponsors_patt.psd looks if you completed all the preceding tutorials in this session. If you haven't done that, start with this fresh file.

2. **In the Layers palette, select the gradient light layer. Choose Select→All from the menu at the top of the screen. Then choose Edit→Clear.**
   You replace this gradient with one of your own in this tutorial.

3. **Click the Paths tab to display the Paths palette.**
   The Paths tab is in the same palette group as the Layers tab. Alternatively, you can access the Paths palette by choosing Window→Paths.

4. **Select Path 1 in the Paths palette. Then click the Load Path as Selection icon at the bottom of the Paths palette.**
   You learn more about paths in the next session. So don't worry about understanding how they work now. This step is necessary because you can't recolor the transparent pixels in this semitransparent gradient using the lock transparency approach that you learned earlier. Instead, you need a selection to shape the area that you fill with a new gradient. Photoshop just made that selection for you from the vector outlines with which the projector light was originally drawn.

5. **Click Foreground Color box in the toolbox to open the Color Picker. Choose a yellow (such as R: 255, G: 204, B: 0) in the Color Picker and click OK.**
   This sets the foreground color to yellow.

6. **Click the Paint Bucket tool in the toolbox to display another hidden tool menu. Select the Gradient tool.**

7. **Click the drop-down arrow to the right of the gradient sample in the Options bar.**
   This opens the Gradient Picker, which displays some of the preset gradients that ship with Photoshop.

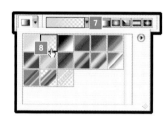

<TIP>
Photoshop ships with more preset gradients than you see here. To replace this default set of gradients, click the small arrow at the top right of the Gradient Picker and choose any of the eight sets of gradient presets listed at the bottom of the drop-down menu (Color Harmonies, Metals, Noise Samples, and so on). Click OK at the prompt to replace the current group of preset gradients, or Append to add more presets to this group.

8. **Select the Foreground to Transparent thumbnail in the Gradient Picker.**
   This thumbnail is yellow to transparent, because you set the Foreground Color to yellow in step 5.

9. **Click anywhere in the Options bar to close the Gradient Picker.**
   Your selected gradient appears in the gradient sample field of the Options bar.

10. **Type** 75% **in the Opacity field in the Options bar. Leave the other options at their defaults.**
    This lowers the opacity of the whole gradient. Try out the other Gradient tool settings on the Options bar when you get a chance. Table 5-2 is a rundown of what each does.

<NOTE>
Don't confuse lowering the opacity of a gradient in the Options bar with using opacity stops in the Gradient Editor to make some parts of a gradient more transparent than others (as you learn to do in the next tutorial). In fact, you can apply both features to the same gradient.

Table 5-2: Gradient Tool Options

Option	Function
Style buttons	The buttons on the left of the Options bar determine the style of shading in a gradient (linear, radial, angular, reflected, or diamond). Linear is the default. It lays down bands of color starting with the first color you specify and ending with the last.
Mode	This determines how the gradient blends with other colors in the image, just like the Mode setting for the Fill command and other painting tools.
Reverse	This switches the starting and ending colors of a gradient. It is off by default.
Dither	This mixes adjacent pixels in a gradient in an attempt to reduce the appearance of separate bands of color. Banding is a common problem in gradients. Bands often appear when a gradient is printed, even if they're not terribly obvious on the computer monitor. Dithering can help.
Transparency	This must be checked to allow different levels of opacity at different points in a gradient. In this example, if you unchecked Transparency, you would lose the realistic effect of light falling off as it moves away from the projector.

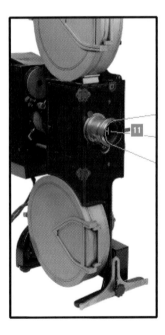

11. **Click inside the lens of the projector in the image and drag to the right edge of the document window.**

    As you drag, you see a blue line tracing your progress. The beginning point of that line represents the first color in this gradient (yellow) and the ending point of the line the last color in this gradient (transparency). The length and direction of the gradient depends on where you are in the image when you release the mouse button.

12. **Release the mouse button to fill the selected area with a yellow to transparent gradient.**

    If you didn't have an area selected, the gradient would have filled the entire layer. That's all there is to applying a preset gradient. In the next tutorial, you practice creating a custom gradient starting from one of the presets.

13. **Choose Select→Deselect from the menu bar at the top of the screen to turn off the marching ants.**

14. **Choose File→Save As. Save the file as** 05_sponsors_grad.psd **(whether you used your own file or the fresh file provided for you for this tutorial). Leave the file open for the next tutorial.**

Tutorial
» Creating a Custom Gradient

Photoshop's preset gradients are only a starting point for an infinite variety of custom gradients that you can create. In this tutorial, you learn how to custom build a gradient in the Gradient Editor.

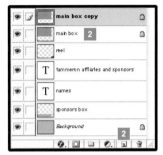

1. **Make sure that** 05_sponsors_grad.psd **is open from the previous tutorial.**

2. **Click the main box layer and drag it to the New Layer icon at the bottom of the Layers palette.**
   This creates a duplicate of the main box layer, called main box copy. You work on this duplicate layer so that you don't harm the underlying artwork. I'm a big fan of nondestructive editing like this because it keeps more options open.

   <NOTE>
   The fact that the Gradient tool is destructive of original artwork is one reason to consider using one of the alternative methods when you want to apply a gradient. A Gradient Fill layer places a gradient on a Fill layer that is separate from the original artwork layer and is easily editable or removable. A Gradient layer style adds a gradient in the form of a layer style that can be easily removed from a layer of artwork. Or you can use the Gradient tool on a duplicate layer, as you did here, in order to preserve the original art.

3. **Click inside the gradient sample on the Options bar to open the Gradient Editor.**
   Don't click the down arrow to the right of the gradient sample. That opens the Gradient Picker, not the Gradient Editor. You have to click right inside the gradient sample to open the Gradient Editor.

4. **Select one of the gradient thumbnails in the Gradient Editor as a starting point.**
   I chose the black to white gradient, which has only two defined colors, because I want to show you how to add color points to a gradient.

5. **Make sure that Gradient Type is set to Solid.**
   This is the setting for making a smooth gradient, as opposed to the choppy gradient that you get if you choose Noise from this menu.

6. **Select the color stop located underneath and to the far left side of the gradient preview bar in the Gradient Editor. Then click in the Color field at the bottom of the Gradient Editor to open the Color Picker.**

   A color stop is a device for setting a color at a designated point in a gradient. When a stop is selected, its triangular top turns black.

7. **Choose purple (R:** 109, **G:** 79, **B:** 158**) in the Color Picker and click OK.**

   This fills the selected color stop with purple and colors the nearby pixels in the gradient purple.

8. **Repeat the preceding two steps for the color stop on the right, choosing light yellow (R:** 243, **G:** 235, **B:** 171**) as its color.**

9. **Click the bottom edge of the gradient preview bar to add a third color stop to your gradient.**

   Adding color stops to a gradient enables you to define and control more colors.

10. **Move your cursor out of the Gradient Editor and over the purple box at the bottom of the open image. The cursor turns to an eye-dropper. Click to fill your new color stop with that purple.**

    Pulling colors from the image in which you plan to use a gradient is a good design strategy.

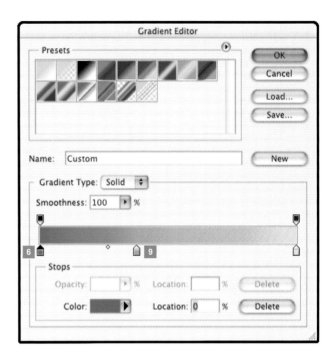

11. **Select the opacity stop that is located above and on the far right side of the gradient preview bar.**

    An opacity stop is used to vary the opacity of the colors in a gradient. It enables you to increase or decrease the opacity of the colors that are near that stop.

12. **Click the Opacity field at the bottom of the Gradient Editor and move its slider to 90%.**

    This reduces the opacity of the light yellow colors in this gradient. You can partially see through those colors on the right side of the gradient preview bar, down to the gray-and-white checkerboard pattern that indicates transparency.

13. **Click any of the color or opacity stops and drag them to the right or left on the gradient preview bar to adjust the arrangement of colors in the gradient.**

    You can also move the small diamonds on the gradient preview bar. They represent midpoints between colors and opacities.

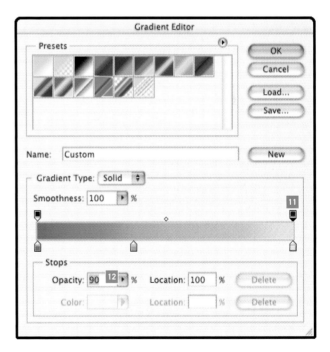

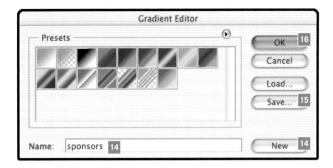

14. **Type a name** (sponsors) **for your custom gradient in the Name field and click the New button.**

    This adds a thumbnail of your sponsors gradient to the Gradient Editor. However, that thumbnail isn't fixed there permanently. It disappears if you replace this gradient set with another.

15. **Click Save in the Gradient Editor and save into Photoshop's Gradients folder on your hard drive a new gradient preset that includes the custom gradient you just made.**

    This safeguards your new custom gradient. You can now access it at any time by clicking the arrow at the top of the Gradient Editor, choosing Replace Gradients, and selecting this custom gradient set. You can customize this gradient set, eliminating those gradients you don't like and keeping those you do, by opening and editing the set in the Preset Manager.

16. **Click OK to close the Gradient Editor.**

17. **Make sure that the main box copy layer is selected in the Layers palette and that the Lock Transparency button is activated at the top of the palette.**

18. **Click near the top and drag toward the bottom of the image to apply your custom gradient to the box in the middle of the image.**

    I dragged from the top of the box to the bottom to create the gradient on the box, behind the projector light.

19. **After you admire your overlapping gradients, delete the gradient you just made by clicking on the main box copy layer in the Layers palette and dragging that layer to the trash.**

    This gradient isn't part of the final design of this collage.

20. **Choose File→Save and leave** 05_sponsors_grad.psd **open if you want to use it in the next exercise. (You have the option of starting with a fresh prebuilt file.)**

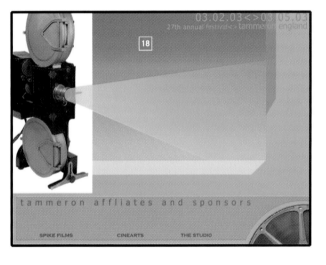

Tutorial

» Exploring the Brushes Palette

Photoshop has a number of painting features that put it in the big leagues as a professional painting program, including an extensive Brushes palette that you explore in this tutorial. You learn how to view and select brushes in the Brushes palette. You use the Master Diameter slider to resize brushes, and you have a chance to try out some of the many preset brushes that ship with Photoshop CS. The Brushes palette was introduced in Photoshop 7, and expanded in Photoshop CS.

1. **Use** 05_sponsors_grad.psd **from the previous tutorial or open the fresh file** 05_sponsors_brush.psd.
   The fresh file mimics 05_sponsors_grad.psd as it should look at this point if you did all the tutorials.

2. **Select the main box layer in the Layers palette and choose Layer→New→Layer to create Layer 1. Double-click Layer 1 and rename it** painting.
   You use this new layer to practice using some brush tools without destroying any existing artwork. This is another example of using layers for nondestructive editing.

3. **Select the Brush tool in the toolbox.**
   If you open the Brushes palette before you select one of the painting tools in the toolbox, the contents of the Brushes palette is grayed out and unavailable.

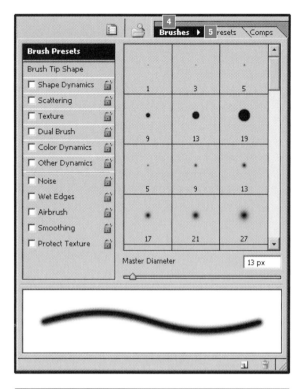

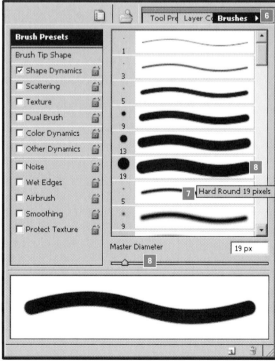

4. **Click the Brushes tab, which is docked in the Palette well at the right side of the Options bar.**

   This opens the Brushes palette, but leaves it docked in the Palette well.

5. **Make sure that your Brushes palette matches the figure. If your palette is displaying only brush tips, click the arrow on the right side of the Brushes tab and choose Expanded View.**

   Expanded View displays the currently loaded preset brushes on the right, a preview of the stroke that a selected brush draws on the bottom, and a list of brush options on the left. The brush preset options can be locked after you make adjustments.

6. **Click the arrow on the Brushes tab and choose Stroke Thumbnail from the Brushes palette menu.**

   This changes the view of currently loaded preset brushes on the right side of the palette, showing a stroke sample for each brush in addition to the brush tip. There are basically three ways to view brushes in the Brushes palette—by stroke sample, by thumbnail, and by list. All are accessible from the Brushes palette menu.

7. **Move your cursor over any stroke sample on the right side of the palette and wait a moment.**

   A larger preview of that stroke appears in the bottom pane of the Brushes palette, as well as a ToolTip with the name of the brush.

8. **Click any stroke sample on the right side of the palette to select a brush. Click and drag the Master Diameter slider to change the size of the brush.**

   You can change the diameter of any brush in Photoshop, including specialty brushes and custom brushes that you create yourself (which you learn to do shortly).

9. **Make sure that the painting layer is still selected in the Layers palette. Click and drag in the document window to try out your selected brush.**

   Don't worry about making a mess. You throw out this painting layer shortly anyway. It's just a place to practice.

10. **Click the arrow on the right side of the Brushes tab and choose any of the other sets of preset brushes at the bottom of the Brushes palette menu. Click OK at the prompt to replace the current set of brushes with the new set that you chose.**

    This is how you load sets of brushes.

11. **Try some of these other preset brushes by selecting them and drawing in the image. When you're done, click the eye icon to the left of the painting layer to hide what you've drawn for now.**

< N O T E >

Many of the new preset brushes are designed to help you paint with the look and feel of natural media. There are wet and dry brushes and natural brushes with which you can digitally simulate traditional art techniques. Give them a try.

12. **Choose File→Save As. Save the file as** 05_sponsors_brush.psd **(whether you used your own file or the fresh file provided for you for this tutorial). Leave the file open for the next tutorial.**

< T I P >

If all you need to do with a brush at any time is what you learned here—select, resize, and perhaps load a preset brush—you're just as well off using the simple Brush pop-up palette as the more elaborate Brushes palette. You learned how to use the Brush pop-up palette with the Pattern Stamp tool earlier in this session. It works just the same way with any of the painting tools. You can access the Brush pop-up palette by selecting one of the painting tools and clicking the Brush sample on the left side of the Options bar.

Tutorial
» Using Brush Options

The Brushes palette offers several options that you can use to modify and customize a preset brush. In this tutorial, you use some of those options to create new brushes, which you can save for reuse as tool presets. You also use brush options from the Options bar.

1. **Make sure that** 05_sponsors_brush.psd **is open from the previous tutorial.**

2. **Choose Layer→New→Layer. Double-click the Layer 1 title in the Layers palette and rename it** roses. **Click and drag the roses layer to just below the gradient light layer in the Layers palette.**

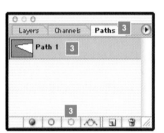

3. **Click the Paths tab and select Path 1 in the Paths palette. Click the Load Path as Selection icon at the bottom of the Paths palette.** You created a selection in the shape of the projector light in your image, just as you did in a previous tutorial in this session. Your roses layer should still be selected.

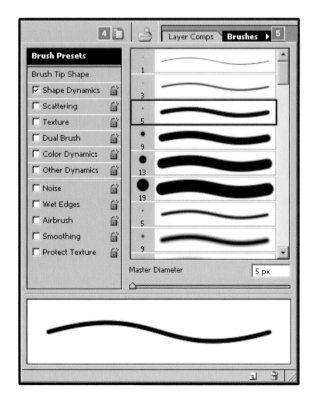

4. **Select the Brush tool in the toolbox. Click the Palette button on the far right side of the Options bar to open the Brushes palette.** This is an alternative to clicking the Brushes tab to open the Brushes palette. The Palette button appears on the Options bar for all the painting tools.

5. **Click the arrow on the right of the Brushes tab and choose Special Effect Brushes. Make sure Brush Presets is selected on the left side of the Brushes palette.** Click OK at the prompt to replace the current brush set with the Special Effects preset brushes.

6. **Select the Scattered Roses brush from the Brushes palette.**
   Notice that there is a check mark next to the Scattering option on the left side of the Brushes palette. This indicates that the Scattering option is active for this brush, but you can't see the settings for the Scattering option until you select that option.

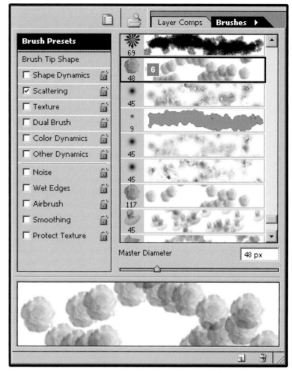

7. **Click the Scattering option on the left side of the Brushes palette.**
   The Scattering option is highlighted, and the Scattering option settings appear on the right side of the Brushes palette. When Scattering is activated, a brush makes more than one mark with each brush stroke. You control the number and placement of those marks with the Scattering settings.

<TIP>

Make sure to click on the word Scattering, rather than the checkbox to the left of the word to open the panel of Scattering settings. The checkbox just controls whether these settings are applied to a particular brush.

8. **Click the Scatter slider on the right side of the Brushes palette and move it up to around 685%. Leave Count at 1 and jitter at 0% to match this figure.**
   This increases the scattered placement of marks and instructs Photoshop to put one mark at each spacing interval. Jitter is a word that you see in many of the Brush options. Whenever you increase the jitter of a setting, you increase the random variation in the setting. Notice that the preview at the bottom of the settings area shows you what a stroke will look like with these settings.

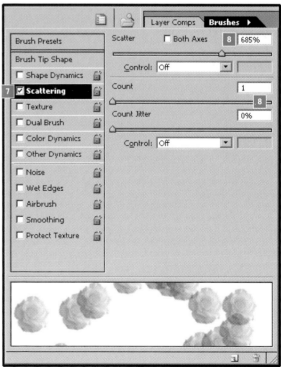

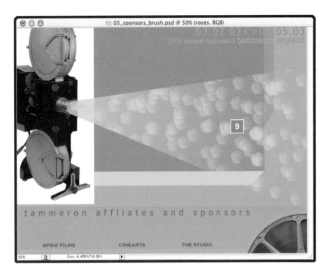

9. **Paint a few brush strokes in your image.**
   Notice how the roses are applied in a scattered pattern when you paint. If you're wondering why your strokes are confined to the shape of the projector light, remember that you selected this area back in step 3.

10. **Choose Select→Deselect.**

11. **Select the sponsors box layer in the Layers palette. Choose Layer→New→Layer to make another new layer. Double-click the new layer and name it** logos**.**

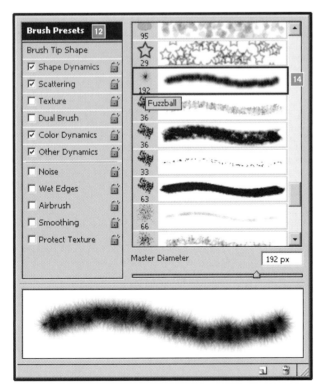

12. **Click Brush Presets at the top of the Brushes palette.**
    This returns the right side of the palette to a view of brush presets.

13. **Click the arrow on the Brushes tab and choose Reset Brushes. Click OK at the prompt.**
    This replaces the current set of brushes with the default preset brushes.

14. **Select the Fuzzball brush from the brush presets.**
    This brush comes with lots of options activated. Shape Dynamics control the size and shape of brush marks. Scattering controls the placement and number of brush marks. Color Dynamics allow variation in color in a brush stroke. Other Dynamics control opacity and flow in brush strokes. There is so much jitter in many of the option settings that each brush stroke you make in an image produces different combinations of color, size, opacity, and other attributes. So it's unlikely that copying the settings used in this example will give you the same result that you see here. It's up to you to experiment! I suggest that you leave all the options at their defaults and concentrate on the Color Dynamics setting, as covered in an upcoming step.

15. **Click in the Foreground Color box in the toolbox and set the foreground color to aqua. Click in the Background Color box and set the background color to purple.**
    Don't worry about matching my colors in this case.

16. **Click the Color Dynamics option.**

    Try increasing the amount of Foreground/Background Jitter
    and set Control for that option to Fade. This varies the color in
    a brush stroke between the foreground and background colors.
    Leave the level of Hue Jitter low to avoid lots of random colors
    in your brush strokes. Increase Saturation and Brightness
    Jitter to get some variation in saturation and brightness within
    a brush stroke. Leave Purity at 0% so that the colors you use
    keep their normal saturation.

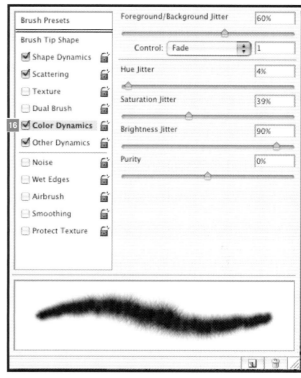

17. **Click in your image and draw a small logo. If you don't like the
    results, choose Edit→Step Backward and try again.**

18. **Click Brush Presets in the Brushes palette. Select the Dune Grass
    brush in the Brushes palette. Experiment with drawing a logo with
    that brush, varying some of the brush options.**

19. **Click Brush Presets again and select a hard round brush.**

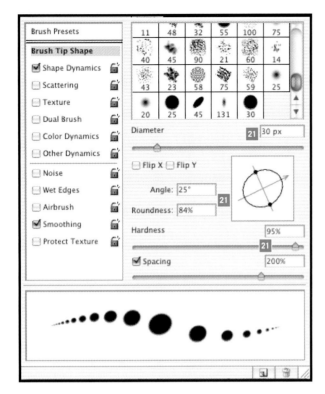

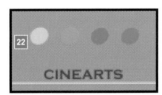

20. **Click the Brush Tip Shape option on the left side of the Brushes palette.**

    This opens a set of options for modifying the shape of any brush tip.

21. **Increase the Diameter of the brush to 30 px and increase the Spacing to 200%. Set Brush Roundness to 84%, Angle to 25°, and Hardness to 95%.**

    Spacing is a very useful setting. Use it to increase the amount of space between brush strokes to simulate a dotted line with a round brush.

22. **Set the foreground color in the toolbox to yellow and the background color to aqua. Click the Color Dynamics brush option in the Brushes palette. Increase Foreground/Background Jitter and set Control to Fade. Click and drag to draw a third logo in your image.**

    < N O T E >

    You can save any brush you create with brush options as a reusable tool preset. Take a look back at Session 1 to remind yourself how to make a new tool preset.

    < N O T E >

    A new feature in Photoshop CS allows you to lock brush attributes so that they don't change as you switch from one preset brush to another. For example, if you use a pressure sensitive Wacom tablet, you can make the size of all the preset brushes change with the amount of pressure you apply to the pen. With one brush selected, click on the word Shape Dynamics on the left side of the Brushes palette to display the Shape Dynamics settings. In the Shape Dynamics panel that appears on the right side of the Brushes palette, choose Pen Pressure from the menu of Controls under Size Jitter. Then click the lock icon next to the word Shape Dynamics. The new settings in the Shape Dynamics panel now apply to all brushes, regardless of any preset attributes a particular brush may have had. Each lock toggles on and off, and you can reset all locked panels from the palette options menu accessible from the arrow at the top right of the Brushes palette.

23. **Choose File→Save and leave** 05_sponsors_brush.psd **open for the next tutorial.**

Tutorial
» Defining a Brush

You aren't limited to using the preset brushes that ship with Photoshop or even brushes you make yourself by modifying those presets. You can create your own brush from scratch from a drawing or other image, as you do in this tutorial.

1. **Open** 05_brush.psd **from the Session 5 Tutorial Files folder on your hard drive.**

   Use this image as the source of your brush or draw your own image of the same size (50 x 50 pixels) with black paint on a white background. In most cases, you want to define a brush from a black-and-white line drawing. This results in a solid, opaque brush. You could use a color or grayscale image as the basis for a brush, but that brush would paint with semitransparency rather than solid outlines.

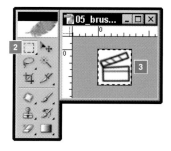

2. **Select the Rectangular Marquee tool in the toolbox. If it's not showing, click on the marquee that is displayed and select the Rectangular Marquee tool from the hidden menu that pops out.**

3. **Draw a selection around your image.**

   Draw your selection tight to the image. Don't leave extra white space surrounding your selection or that too becomes part of the brush.

4. **Choose Edit→Define Brush Preset from the menu bar at the top of the screen.**

5. **Type** 50 cut **in the Brush Name dialog box that appears and click OK.**

6. **Click the Brush tool in the toolbox.**

7. **Click the Brushes tab to open the Brushes palette. Click Brush Presets. Scroll to the bottom of the brush preview.**

   Your new brush should be there, ready to use!

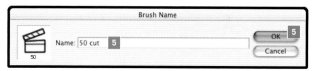

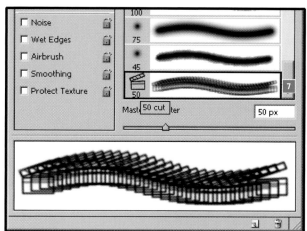

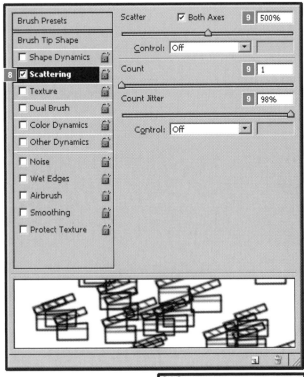

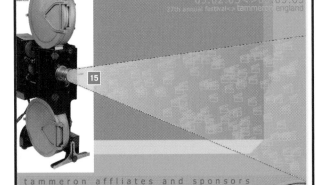

8. Click the Scattering option on the left side of the Brushes palette to display the Scattering settings.

9. Click the Scatter slider at the top of the right side of the Brushes palette and increase it to around 500%. Decrease the Count slider to 1. Increase the Count Jitter slider to around 98%.

10. Click the Foreground Color box in the toolbox and choose a light yellow color.

11. Click the Paths tab to display the Paths palette. Click Path 1 and then click the Load Path as Selection button at the bottom of the Paths palette.
This selection limits the area in which you paint to the shape of the projector light.

12. Click the roses layer in the Layers palette and drag it to the Trash icon at the bottom of the palette.

13. Choose Layer→New→Layer in the Layers palette. Double-click the new layer and name it cuts. Drag it to just below the gradient light layer.

14. Type 50% in the Opacity field.

15. Click and drag in the image 05_sponsors_brush.psd to paint with your new brush in the area of the projector light.

16. Choose Select→Deselect to eliminate the marching ants. If you still see blue path lines, click the Paths tab and click off Path 1 in the Paths palette.

17. Choose File→Save and keep 05_sponsors_brush.psd open for the next tutorial. Close the small image 05_brush.psd without saving.

Tutorial
» Using Brush Settings on the Options Bar

Given the variety of brush options available in the Brushes palette, it's hard to believe that there are more brush settings to consider. However, the Options bar has some important brush settings that you can use alone or in combination with options from the Brushes palette. You use some of them in this short tutorial.

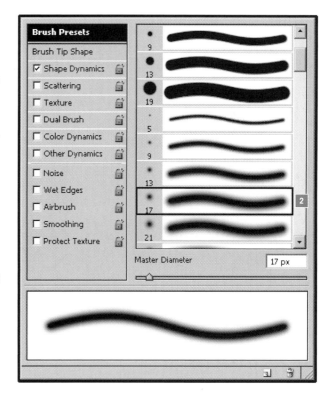

1. **Use** 05_sponsors_brush.psd **from the previous tutorial.**

2. **Select the Paint Brush tool in the toolbox and select a 17 px soft-edged brush in the Brushes palette.**

3. **Click the Mode button on the Options bar and choose Behind from the list of brush blending modes.**
   You've run into blending modes several times already in the context of other tools and fill features. You can also find blending modes in the Layers palette. The blending modes for the Paint Brush tool determine how the color applied by that tool interacts with the artwork on other layers. The Behind blending mode causes a brush to apply color only where there are transparent pixels on a layer. That creates a nice contour when you paint along the semitransparent pixels of the gradient light layer.

4. **Click the arrow on the Opacity field on the Options bar and drag the slider to the left to decrease Opacity to around 40%.**
   Opacity is the density with which a brush adds color. Lowering opacity this much gives a very transparent look to the painted area.

5. **Click the arrow on the Flow field on the Options bar and drag this slider to around 40%, too.**
   Flow is the speed with which paint is delivered by a brush. Reducing this parameter softens the stroke.

<NOTE>
The last icon on the Options bar is the Airbrush. The Airbrush offers a softening effect, but it also makes paint pool if you hold your cursor in one place, just like a real airbrush. That's an effect you don't want here, so don't click on the Airbrush option.

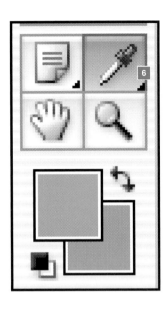

6. **Select the Eyedropper tool from the toolbox and click on a semi-transparent yellow area of the projector light in the image.**
   This sets the foreground color to a mustard yellow.

7. **Hold the Shift key down. Then click on the beginning of the top edge of the projector light in the image. (The edge of the shape should intersect your brush.) Click on the end of that edge (again with the edge intersecting the brush).**
   This draws a straight line down the top edge of the projector light, adding a subtle contour to that edge. Knowing how to draw a straight line in any direction comes in handy. You must hold the Shift key down before the first click and keep it held down through the second click, as you just did.

8. **Choose File→Save and leave** 05_sponsors_brush.psd **open for the next tutorial.**

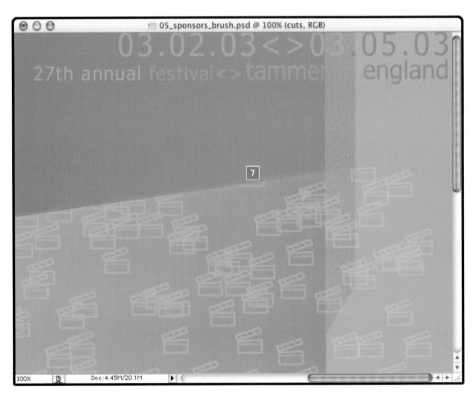

Tutorial
» Stroking

Stroking places a border around isolated artwork. It qualifies as a painting technique because it deposits color by way of pixels. In this short tutorial, you use the Stroke command along with the transparency lock to put a stroke around the artwork on a layer. You can also use this command to stroke a selection.

1. **Use** `05_sponsors_brush.psd` **from the preceding tutorial.**

2. **Select the accent box layer in the Layers palette.**

3. **Click the Lock Transparency button at the top left of the Layers palette if there isn't already a lock symbol in the accent box layer.**

4. **Choose Edit→Stroke from the menu bar at the top of the screen.**

5. **In the Stroke dialog box, type** 4 px **in the Width field.**

6. **Click the Color field in the Stroke dialog box to open the Color Picker. Move your cursor over the image; it becomes an eyedropper. Click in the green-blue text at the top of the page. Click OK in the Color Picker to set the Color field in the Stroke dialog box.**

7. **Choose Center as the location of the stroke.**
   This centers the stroke over the edge of the selected area.

8. **Click OK to create a green-blue stroke around the yellow accent box.**

9. **Choose File→Save and keep this image open for the next tutorial.**

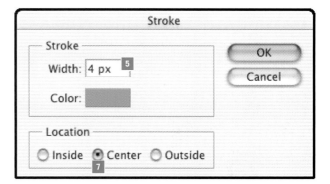

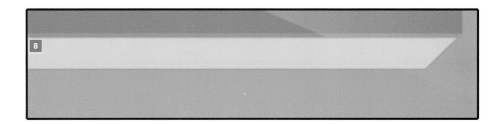

Tutorial
» Erasing

There are tools other than the Paint Brush tool that are technically brush tools, in that they paint with pixels and use brushes accessed from the Brush palette. The Eraser tools are a hybrid. The main Eraser tool acts like a brush. It paints with pixels and uses brushes just like the Paint Brush and other painting tools. The Magic Eraser is like a selection tool. It selects pixels and deletes them in one fell swoop. The Background Eraser distinguishes foreground elements from their surroundings and erases only the surroundings. You use all three Eraser tools in this tutorial.

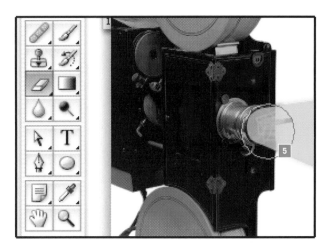

1. **Make sure that** 05_sponsors_brush.psd **is open from the previous tutorial.**

2. **Select the Eraser tool from the toolbox.**
   It's the one with the plain eraser icon. If it's not showing, click whichever Eraser tool is showing and select the Eraser tool from the hidden tool menu.

3. **Select the cuts layer in the Layers palette.**

4. **Choose a medium-sized brush (such as a 19-pixel hard round one) from the Brush pop-up palette.**

5. **Click and drag over any of the cut designs that you want to eliminate from your image.**
   The Eraser tool paints out pixels on a layer so that you can see what's on the underlying layers. If you erase on a Background layer, the Eraser erases to the background color identified in the toolbox.

6. **Select the camera with background layer in the Layers palette.**

7. **Click the Eraser tool in the toolbox and select the Background Eraser tool (the one with the Scissors icon).**

8. **Make sure that the settings in the Options bar match those shown in the figure.**

   There are quite a few settings in the Background Eraser's Options bar. Choosing Contiguous in the Limits field instructs the Background Eraser to only erase colors that touch the color that's at the center of the Background Eraser. Adjust Tolerance up to erase more pixels and down to erase fewer pixels. If there's a color you do not want erased, choose it as the foreground color in the toolbox and check Protect Foreground Color in the Options bar. Setting Sampling to Once tells the Background Eraser that it only has to decide what the background color is one time, which works here because the background is all one color.

9. **Zoom in to 200% with the Zoom tool.**

10. **Position the cursor so that the cross at its center is very near, but not touching, the camera. Move the cursor around the outside edge of the camera, being careful not to let the cross touch the camera.**

    The Background Eraser is smart enough to erase the white background, but not the camera, letting you see through to green pixels on the layer below!

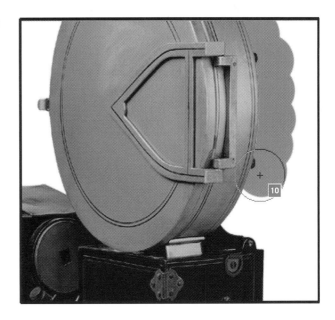

11. **Click the Background Eraser tool in the toolbox and select the Magic Eraser (the one with the asterisk) from the hidden menu.**

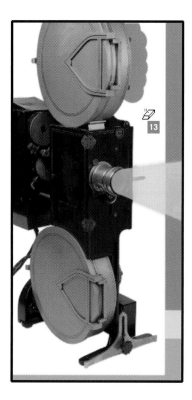

12. **Make sure that the settings in the Options bar are the same as the ones shown in the figure.**

13. **Click anywhere in the white area that surrounds the camera, and the entire white background will disappear at once!**

14. **Choose File→Save As. In the Save As dialog box, name this image** `05_sponsors_end.psd`. **Make sure that Layers and Embed Profile are checked. Save it in a safe place. You'll be working on this collage further in the next session.**

» Session Review

This session covers how to fill and paint with pixels. You learned to fill with the Fill command, the Paint Bucket tool, and the Pattern Stamp. You defined your own pattern using the Define Pattern command, and you learned how to use the new Pattern Maker to create a fill from artwork tiles. You filled an area with a prebuilt gradient, and you learned how to make a custom gradient in the Gradient Editor. Then you were introduced to Photoshop CS's Brushes palette, which has lots of preset natural media brushes and many options from which you can create custom brushes. You learned how to stroke artwork, and you were introduced to the three Eraser tools—the Eraser, the Background Eraser, and the Magic Eraser. There's a lot to remember from this session. Use these questions to jog your memory about what you learned here.

1. Why doesn't a bitmapped image look good if you try to make it bigger by resampling in Photoshop? (See "Tutorial: Filling a Layer.")

2. What is a pixel? (See "Discussion: Working with Pixels and Bitmapped Images.")

3. How can you confine a fill to the artwork on a layer and leave the transparent pixels on the layer unfilled? (See "Tutorial: Filling the Artwork on a Layer.")

4. If you want to fill only part of the artwork on a layer, what do you have to do? (See "Tutorial: Filling Selected Artwork.")

5. What command would you use if you wanted to fill an entire layer with color? (See "Tutorial: Filling the Artwork on a Layer.")

6. What is the shortcut for the command that you would use if you wanted to fill an entire layer with color? (See "Tutorial: Filling the Artwork on a Layer.")

7. Name two features that you could use to fill an entire layer with a pattern. (See "Tutorial: Filling with a Pattern.")

8. Name two features that you could use to create a pattern. (See "Tutorial: Defining and Applying a Custom Pattern" and "Tutorial: Using the Pattern Maker.")

9. What is a gradient? (See "Tutorial: Using the Gradient Tool.")

10. What feature do you use to create a custom gradient? (See "Tutorial: Creating a Custom Gradient.")

11. Name three ways that you can view brush presets in the Brushes palette. (See "Tutorial: Exploring the Brushes Palette.")

12. Other than the Brushes palette, what feature can you use to select preset brushes? (See "Tutorial: Exploring the Brushes Palette.")

13. In what two places are brush options located? (See "Tutorial: Using Brush Options" and "Tutorial: Using Brush Settings on the Options Bar.")

14. What command do you use to define a brush from another image? (See "Tutorial: Defining a Brush.")

15. What does the Magic Eraser do? (See "Tutorial: Erasing.")

16. What does the Background Eraser do? (See "Tutorial: Erasing.")

17. What feature do you use to put a border around artwork? (See "Tutorial: Stroking.")

Session 6

Drawing with Vectors

Session Introduction

Photoshop isn't just a bitmapped image editing program. It also includes vector-based drawing tools—the Pen tools and Shape tools—which you try out in this session. You are introduced to drawing and editing vector paths with the Pen tools. You see how easy it is to create a vector logo, resize it for use in another document, and color it by filling and stroking its path. You also practice converting a path to a selection so that you can further embellish it with bitmap editing features. Then you learn all about the Shape tools, which you can use to create geometric shapes or variations on the many prebuilt graphic shapes that ship with Photoshop 7.

TOOLS YOU'LL USE
Pen tools, Paths palette, Path Selection tool, Direct Selection tool, Shape tools, shape layers, Style Picker, and Custom Shape tool

CD-ROM FILES NEEDED
06_camera_paths.psd, 06_camera_edit.psd,
06_camera_magnet.psd, 06_camera_fill.psd,
06_camera_move.psd, 06_sponsors_move.psd,
06_sponsors_select.psd, 06_sponsors_shape.psd, and
06_sponsors_end.psd

TIME REQUIRED
90 minutes

Discussion
An Introduction to Vector Graphics

You learned about bitmapped images, which are composed entirely of pixels, in the previous session. Bitmapped images are resolution dependent and are best-suited for continuous tone images, such as photographs and soft-edged graphics.

Vector graphics, which are the subject of this session, are very different than bitmapped images. Vector graphics consist of mathematical instructions rather than pixels. They can be resized and reshaped without damaging image quality because they are resolution independent. Vector objects are easy to select and recolor even if they aren't located on separate layers. And vector objects have crisp edges if they are printed on a PostScript printer, saved as a PDF file, or exported to another vector program, such as Adobe Illustrator. All of this means that vector objects are useful for commercial graphics, and particularly for items such as logos that you may want to reuse at different sizes.

There are a couple ways to work with vector graphics in Photoshop—as paths created with Pen tools and managed in the Paths palette or as shapes created with Shape tools and located on shape layers—both of which are covered in this session. (You can also find paths or shapes located in vector masks, which are used to reveal or hide portions of an image. Vector masks are covered in Session 9.)

The outline of a vector graphic is called a path. A path consists of straight and curved line segments connected with points. You can leave a path open-ended to form a straight or curved line, or you can close a path to form a shape.

Paths are independent of any particular layer. So you can use a path to define shapes on more than one layer in a document, or you can copy and use a path in other documents, as you do in this session. Paths are created and edited with Photoshop's Pen tools and are managed from the Paths palette. In the Paths palette, you can convert a temporary work path into a saved path that stays with the image. You can activate a path so that it can be stroked with color or filled with color, a pattern, or a history state. You can convert a path to a selection. Or you can convert a selection to a path so that you can resize it or distort its shape. You learn how to do all of this as you work through the tutorials.

Tutorial
» Drawing with the Pen Tool

Paths are lines and curves that make up the outlines of vector graphics. The Pen tool is the most precise method of creating paths in Photoshop. In this tutorial, you learn the basics of using the Pen tool to draw and edit paths. If you're an illustrator, you'll love the flexibility and precision this tool offers. But if you're handier with a camera than with a sketch pad, you may not take to the Pen tool right away. You can look forward to the tutorials at the end of this session, where you learn an easier way to make vector graphics using the Shape tools.

1. **Open** 06_camera_paths.psd **from the Session 6 Tutorial Files folder on your hard drive.**
   This isn't one of the collages for your final film festival guide project. It's merely a source document in which you practice drawing and editing paths and from which you trace and copy a path for use in a final collage that you complete later in this session.

2. **Select the Pen tool in the toolbox. Click the Paths icon in the Options bar.**
   If one of the Pen tool variations is showing in the toolbox, click the tool that is displayed and choose the Pen tool from the hidden menu.

3. **Click once in the image to create a point. Release the mouse button and click again in another place to draw a path in the shape of a straight line. ⌘+click (Windows: Ctrl+click) anywhere else in the image to end the path that you just created.**

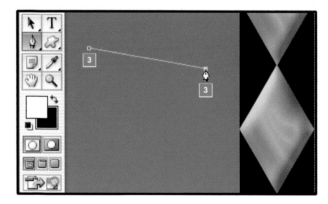

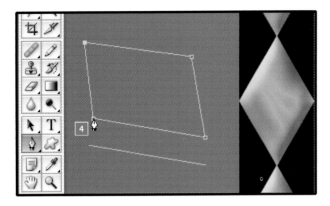

4. **Repeat the preceding step to draw another line, but this time don't end the path. Instead, click several more times to draw four connected straight lines that form a polygon. To close the polygon, move your cursor over the first point that you drew and click when you see a tiny circle that indicates you're back where you started.**
The lines that you've drawn so far look jaggedy. That's because they aren't drawn at 45° angles to conform to the invisible grid of pixels on your screen. (Even vector lines can look jaggedy on a computer screen because the screen has to use pixels to represent them.) If you hold the Shift key while you click, your lines are constrained to 45° angles and look straight and clean on-screen.

5. **Choose Window→Paths to open the Paths palette. Notice that it contains a path labeled Work Path. Double-click Work Path in the Paths palette to open the Save Path dialog box. Type the name** shapes **and click OK.**
You've converted a temporary work path, containing the objects you just drew, to a permanent saved path that will remain with the image unless the path is deliberately deleted. The work path was created automatically when you began drawing with the Pen tool. If you click off a work path in the Paths palette and then draw even one more point, the current work path is replaced, and you lose all the objects you've drawn to that point. So it's wise to convert a work path to a saved path as soon as you've drawn a path that you want to keep.

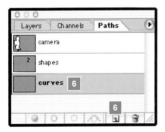

6. **Click the Create New Path button at the bottom right of the Paths palette to create a new path called Path 1. Double-click Path 1 and rename it** curves. **Make sure that the curves path is selected.**
Creating and selecting a permanent path before you start drawing is the way to avoid drawing on an automatically created work path, which is temporary and can be inadvertently replaced.

7. **Choose View→Show→Grid.**
Turning on the grid eases the job of drawing curves with the Pen tool because the points that you draw snap to the intersections of the grid and the grid lines help you judge the length and angle of your direction lines, as you see in the next steps.

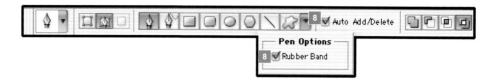

8. **With the Pen tool still selected, click the Options arrow in the Options bar and put a check mark next to Rubber Band in the Options menu.**
   The Rubber Band option previews each path segment for you as you draw.

9. **Click an intersection of the grid to begin drawing a curve. Drag in the direction that you want the curve to bow (to the left in this case).**
   As you drag, a direction line appears. Follow the horizontal line of the grid as you drag if you want to keep your curves uniform.

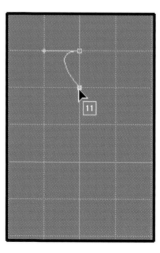

<NOTE>
I've changed the color of the grid lines in Photoshop's Grids, Guides & Slices Preferences to make the grid more noticeable for you.

10. **Release the mouse button when you reach the intersection one square to the left of the beginning point.**

11. **Click an intersection of the grid where you want your curve to end (try one square down from the beginning point).**

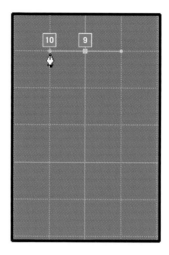

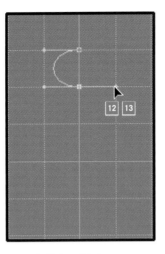

12. **Drag a direction line to the right, away from the bow of the curve.**

13. **Release the mouse button when you reach the intersection one square to the right of your ending point.**
    You could close the path at this point by ⌘+clicking (Windows: Ctrl+clicking) off the path. Instead, in the next steps you draw some more curves that are connected to this path.

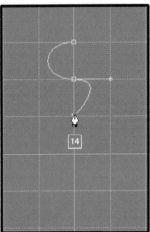

14. **Click the intersection one square below the ending point of the first curve.**

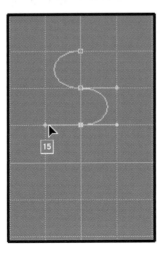

15. **Drag to the left. Release the mouse button at the intersection one square to the left.**

16. **Click the intersection one square below the beginning point of the curve that you're currently drawing. Drag to the right. Release the mouse button at the intersection one square to the right.**

<TIP>

When drawing a single curve with the Pen tool, place your first point where you want the curve to start. Also, drag from the start point toward the direction that you want the curve to bow. Place your second point where you want the curve to end, rather than in the middle of the curve. And finally, drag from the end point away from the bow of the curve.

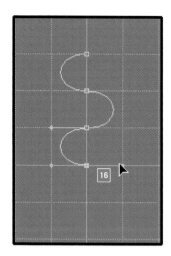

17. **Option+click (Windows: Alt+click) the end point of the preceding direction line you drew.**

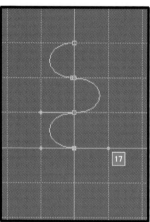

18. **Drag the direction line down and around to the left.**
This changes the direction so that the next curve you draw bows out to the left (the way the direction line is now pointing).

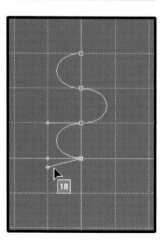

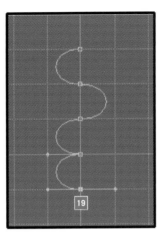

19. Click the intersection one square below the beginning point of this curve. Drag to the right. Release the mouse button at the intersection one square to the right. ⌘+click (Windows: Ctrl+click) anywhere in the image to close the path.

20. Choose File→Save and leave 06_camera_paths.psd **open if you want to use it for the next tutorial.**
    You have the option of starting the next tutorial with a fresh prebuilt file.

Tutorial
» Editing Paths

In the preceding tutorial, you learned the basics of drawing paths with the Pen tool. In this tutorial, you learn how to move and adjust paths.

1. **Check that** 06_camera_paths.psd **is open from the previous tutorial or open the fresh file** 06_camera_edit.psd **from the Session 6 Tutorial Files folder on your hard drive.**
   06_camera_edit.psd is a replica of how 06_camera_paths.psd should look at the end of the previous tutorial.

2. **Select the shapes path in the Paths palette.**

3. **Select the White Arrow tool from the toolbox. If you don't see it, click the Black Arrow tool to reveal a hidden menu and choose the White Arrow tool from that menu.**
   The official name of the White Arrow tool is the Direct Selection tool, and the official name of the Black Arrow tool is the Path Selection tool. To make things easier, I call them by their generic names.

4. **Click one of the corner points in the polygon-shaped path in the image and drag to reshape the attached line so that it's straight up and down. Repeat this on the other corner points to try to straighten all the lines so that the polygon becomes a rectangle.**

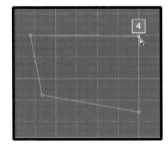

5. **Click any of the line segments in the shape and drag to reposition that line. Try to change the shape into a square.**
   Don't worry if you don't succeed in creating a perfect square. The point is for you to see that the White Arrow tool is used to select, reshape, and move individual line segments.

6. **Click the White Arrow tool in the toolbox and select the Black Arrow tool from the hidden menu.**

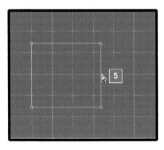

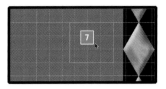

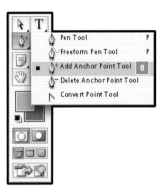

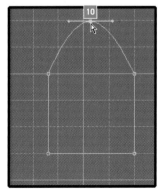

7. **Click anywhere inside the square and drag to move the whole shape to another location on the screen.**
The Black Arrow tool is used for selecting and moving whole objects, rather than line segments like the White Arrow tool.

8. **Click the Pen tool and select the Add Anchor Point tool from the hidden menu.**

9. **Click the top line of the square to add a point to that line segment.**

<TIP>
More than one object can exist in the same path, such as the square and the line you drew in this path. To select multiple objects in a path, hold the Shift key while you click those objects.

10. **Click the point that you added and drag to change the shape of the line segment on which the point is located.**
The Add Anchor Point tool acts like the White Arrow tool when you click a point (enabling you to reshape a line segment just as you can with the White Arrow tool).

11. **Click each end of the direction lines on the point you added and drag to further change the shape of the line segment.**

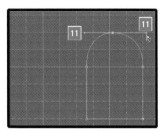

12. **Click the Add Anchor Point tool in the toolbox and choose the Convert Point tool from the hidden menu. Click the point that you added.**

    The Convert Point tool changes a curve from smooth to sharp.

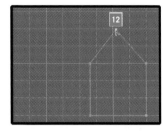

13. **Click the Convert Point tool in the toolbox and choose the Delete Point tool from the hidden menu.**

    Click the point you added to eliminate that point. The line segment returns to its original shape.

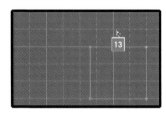

14. **Select the Black Arrow tool from the toolbox. Draw a marquee around all the shapes on the path and press the Delete key.**

15. **Choose File➜Save As. Save the file as** 06_camera_edit.psd **(whether you used your own file or the fresh file provided for you for this tutorial). Leave the file open for the next tutorial.**

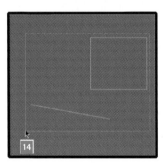

Tutorial

» Tracing a Path with the Freeform Pen Tool

You can use the path drawing and editing skills you learned in the preceding tutorials to create a vector graphic from scratch, or you can cut a few corners by tracing a path around an existing image. In this tutorial, you use the Freeform Pen tool, with its magnetic option activated, to trace around a photograph. A few tweaks with the path editing tools, and you have a crisp-edged vector shape that looks like it took you hours to draw.

1. **Make sure that** 06_camera_edit.psd **is open from the previous tutorial or open the fresh file** 06_camera_magnet.psd **from the Session 6 Tutorial Files folder on your hard drive.**
   06_camera_magnet.psd is a copy of 06_camera_edit.psd as it should look after the previous tutorial. You can use either file.

2. **Choose View→Show→Grid to turn off the grid if it's still showing.**

3. **Click the camera path in the Paths palette to see a prebuilt version of the path that you draw in the image. Click in the blank area of the Paths palette when you're done looking at this path.**
   Notice that this path hugs the contours of the image. You could draw this path by hand, using all the methods that you learned in the preceding tutorials. But a faster way to trace a path like this is to use the Freeform Pen tool with its magnetic option turned on, as you do in the next steps.

4. **Select the Zoom tool from the toolbox and click in the document window to zoom in to 200%.**

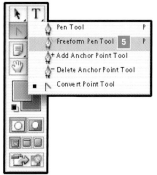

5. **Click whichever pen tool is showing in the toolbox and choose the Freeform Pen tool from the hidden menu.**
   Another way to access the Freeform Pen tool, if the Pen tool is active, is from the Freeform Pen tool icon on the Options bar.

6. **Make sure that the Path button is selected in the Options bar.**
   This ensures that you are drawing a path, as opposed to a shape or a bitmapped graphic, which are the other two choices in this area of the Options bar.

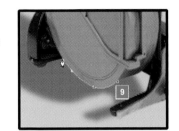

7. **Put a check mark next to Magnetic in the Options bar.**
   This changes the Freeform Pen tool into a Pen tool with magnetic properties, so it creates a path that automatically finds and snaps to the edge of any image. You see how this works in the next steps.

8. **Click the arrow to the right of the Shape tool icons on the Options bar to display the Freeform Pen options. Leave these options at their defaults for now.**

9. **Click anywhere on the edge of the camera to begin the path. Move, but don't drag, your cursor around the edge of the camera.**
   As you move, you see a path form, snapping to the edge of the camera. Points automatically appear on the path. If you don't like where Photoshop adds a point, follow the instructions in the next step.

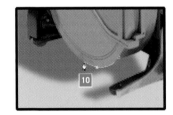

10. **Press the Delete or Backspace key on your keyboard and notice that the last point on the path disappears. You can delete more points if necessary, and then back up and continue forward again to redraw the path.**

11. **Click to add a point manually, if the Magnetic Pen doesn't add a point where you want it to.**
    If the path jumps away from the edge, press the left bracket key on your keyboard to decrease the width of the area the Magnetic Pen uses to locate an edge, as described in the sidebar "Freeform Pen Options."

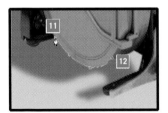

12. **Click the beginning point of the path, after you've gone all the way around the image, to close the path.**

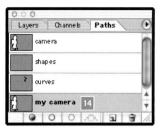

13. **Clean up the path, using the techniques that you learned in the preceding tutorial.**

    Use the White Arrow tool to select points that are too far afield and tuck them into the edge. Use the Add Anchor Point tool to add and drag a point when necessary and the Delete Anchor Point tool to delete a point that's distorting part of the path.

14. **Double-click Work Path in the Paths palette to save your work path as a permanent path. Name the path** my camera **and click OK.**

15. **Choose File➔Save As. Save the file as** 06_camera_magnet.psd **(whether you used your own file or the fresh file provided for you for this tutorial).**

    Leave the file open for the next tutorial.

Freeform Pen Options

If the Magnetic Pen doesn't work the way you'd like it to on a particular image, reopen the Freeform Pen Options menu and experiment with these options:

» Curve Fit. This controls how closely the path fits the image you trace, within a range of 0.5 to 10 pixels. If you like a closer fit than you get, decrease this value. The result is more points and a less smooth path. If you like a smoother path than you get, increase this value. The result is less points and a less exact fit.

» Width. This determines how many pixels the Magnetic Pen takes into account when it looks for the edge of an image, within a range of 1 to 256 pixels. Press the Caps Lock key on your keyboard to see a visual representation of this parameter. If you work on an edge that has lots of turns and crevices, decrease this number. If you want more latitude to trace farther away from the edge when you work on an larger, uncluttered edge, increase this number. You can change this parameter on-the-fly while you draw by clicking the left bracket key on your keyboard to decrease the width and the right bracket key to increase the width. If you draw with a stylus tablet, your pen pressure affects Width if there's a check mark in the Pen Pressure box on this Options menu.

» Contrast. Contrast is what the Magnetic Pen uses to find the edge of an image. If you work on a low contrast image, increase this value, which ranges between 1 and 100 percent.

» Frequency. This value, which ranges between 5 and 40, determines how often the Magnetic Pen sets a point as you move around the image. The lower the value, the more frequently the tool lays down points. The more points in the path, the rougher the path looks.

Tutorial
» Stroking and Filling a Path

You may have wondered what you can do with a path after you've created it. You can turn that path into a logo or other graphic by stroking its outline with color or filling it with color, a pattern, or an image from a previous history state. In this tutorial, you'll learn to stroke and fill a path.

1. **Use** 06_camera_magnet.psd, **which you saved from the previous tutorial, or open the fresh file** 06_camera_fill.psd **from the Session 6 Tutorial Files folder on your hard drive.**
   06_camera_fill.psd is a replica of
   06_camera_magnet.psd as it should look at the end of the previous tutorial. You can use either file.

2. **Click the Create New Layer button at the bottom of the Layers palette, double-click Layer 1, and rename that layer camera logo.**
   This is where the fill and stroke that you create with the path outline will be located. The path itself remains independent of any particular layer. If you try to fill a path without first selecting a layer, you find the Fill command unavailable.

3. **Select a Brush tool and a small brush (try 3 pixels) from the Brush pop-up palette on the Options bar.**

4. **Click the Foreground Color box in the toolbox and choose a dark gold color from the Color Picker. (I chose R:** 207, **G:** 143, **B:** 3.**)**

5. **Make sure that the my camera path is selected in the Paths palette.**

6. **Click the arrow at the top right of the Paths palette and choose Fill Path.**
   This opens the Fill Path dialog box.

7. **Make sure that the Use field is set to Foreground Color, Blending Mode is set to Normal, Opacity is set to 100%, and Rendering is set to Anti-aliased. Click OK.**
   This fills the selected path with the foreground color.

<NOTE>

The Fill Path dialog box has several options, most of which are probably familiar to you from other contexts, like options for brushes and layers. Blending Mode determines how the fill pixels blend with colors on other layers. Opacity controls the density of the fill. You usually want to leave Anti-aliased checked to ensure that your fill has gradual rather than jaggedy edges. Increasing the Feather Radius blurs the fill on both sides of the path, creating a soft watercolor effect. (See the discussion of anti-aliasing and feathering in Session 7.) There's no need to check Preserve Transparency because there are no transparent areas in the camera image encompassed by the path. If there were, checking Preserve Transparency would keep those transparent areas from being filled. The Use field gives you the option to fill with various colors, a pattern, or imagery from a prior history state. Experiment with these fill options on your own.

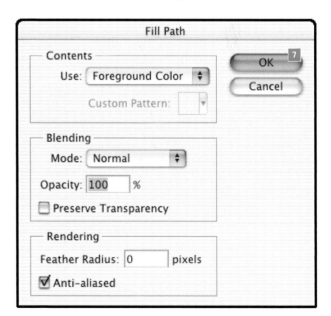

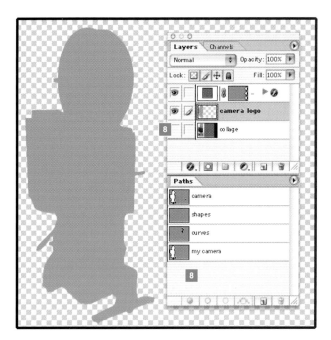

8. **Click off the my camera path in the Paths palette and turn the collage layer's eye icon off in the Layers palette so that you can get a better view of your filled path.**

<TIP>
You may want to separate and dock together your Layers and Paths palettes, as shown here, so that you can see them both. You learned how to do that in Session 2.

9. **Select the Brush tool in the toolbox. Select a brush in the Brushes palette.**
   I loaded the Natural Brushes brush set into the Brushes palette and selected a brush called Stipple 12 pixels. See Session 5 if you need to review how to use the Brushes palette.

10. **Click the Default Foreground and Background Color icons in the toolbox to set the foreground color to black.**

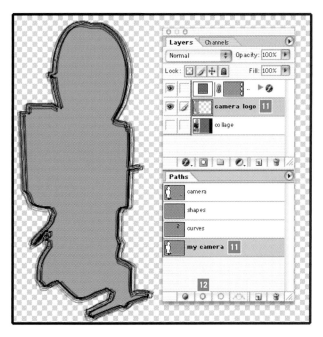

11. **Select the my camera path in the Paths palette and the camera logo layer in the Layers palette again.**

12. **Click the Stroke Path button at the bottom of the Paths palette.**

<NOTE>
Try stroking a path with a tool other than the Brush tool. Click the arrow on the top right of the Paths palette and choose Stroke Path from the menu. In the Stroke Path dialog box, choose Tools and try some of the options there. Try Dodge or Burn for some interesting effects.

13. **Choose Edit→Fade Stroke Path, lower the Opacity in the Fade dialog box, and click OK to decrease the intensity of the stroke effect. Lower the Opacity all the way to 0 to eliminate the stroke.**

14. **Choose File→Save As. Save the file as** 06_camera_fill.psd **(whether you used your own file or the fresh file provided for you for this tutorial). Leave the file open for the next tutorial.**

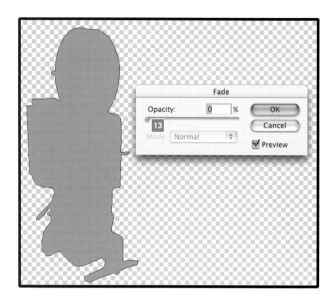

Tutorial
» Copying a Path between Documents

Now that you created a vector graphic by tracing it from a source document, how do you get it into one of the collages that you're making for the final project? In this tutorial, you learn how simple it is to copy a path from one document to another.

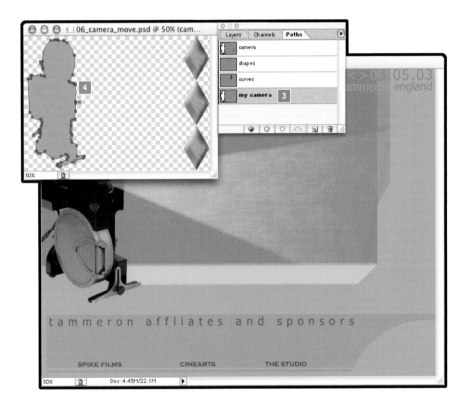

1. **Make sure that** `06_camera_fill.psd` **is open from the previous tutorial or open the fresh file** `06_camera_move.psd` **from the Session 6 Tutorial Files folder on your hard drive.**
   `06_camera_move.psd` is a copy of `06_camera_fill.psd` as it should look if you completed the preceding tutorial. This is the source document for the path that you're about to copy.

2. **Open** `06_sponsors_move.psd` **from the Session 6 Tutorial Files on your hard drive and click Update at the prompt.**
   Alternatively, if you prefer to use your own file, open `05_sponsors_end.psd` that you saved from the previous session and click the eye icons on the gradient light, reelblue, and logos layers to hide those layers. This is the target document.

3. **Select the my camera path in the Paths palette in the source document.**

<NOTE>
The source and target documents are set to 50% in this figure so that you can see both.

4. **Select the Black Arrow tool in the toolbox and click the path around the camera in the source document.**

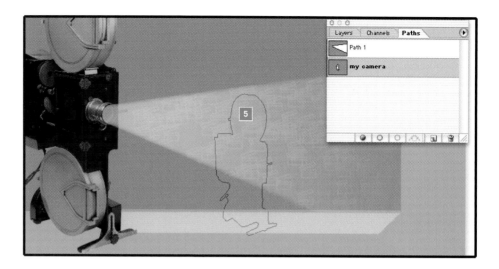

5. **Drag the path into the target document and release the mouse button.**
This pastes the my camera path into the Paths palette of the
target document and drops the path outline in the middle of
the target document. Notice that only the path, not its fill,
was copied.

6. **Close the source document without saving.**

7. **Select the path in the target document with the Black Arrow tool
and drag the path to the lower-right corner.**

8. **Put a check mark next to Show Bounding Box in the Options bar.**

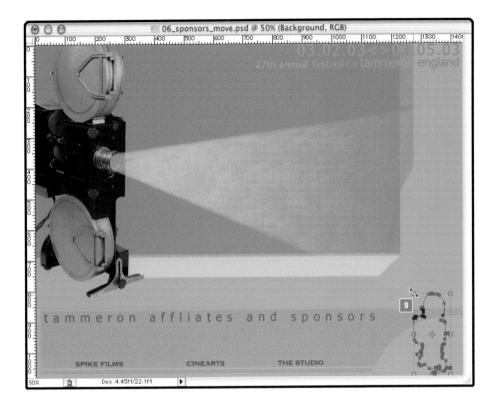

9. **Hold the Shift key to constrain the proportions of the path, click one of the corners of the bounding box, and drag to resize the path to match the figure. Click Return (Windows: Enter) to accept the transformation.**
Resizing a path doesn't degrade the path.

<TIP>
You can also use the Free Transform tool to resize the path. Choose Edit→Free Transform to display the bounding box, or resize using the Edit→Transform→Scale command.

10. **Select the accent box layer in the Layers palette. Click the Create New Layer button at the bottom of the palette. Double-click the new Layer 1, rename it camera graphic, and leave that layer selected.**

11. **Double-click the Foreground Color box and choose a dark olive-green color (try R:128, G:119, B:5) from the Color Picker. Click OK.**

12. **Make sure that the my camera path is selected in the Paths palette of the target document and click the Fill Path button at the bottom of the Paths palette.**

13. **Click off the my camera layer in the Paths palette to see the results—a detailed, smooth-edged logo!**

14. **Choose File→Save As. Save the target document as** 06_sponsors_move.psd **(whether you used your own file or opened a fresh file in step 2). Leave the file open for the next tutorial.**

Tutorial

» Converting a Path to a Selection

In this tutorial, you draw a simple triangular path for a projector light. In order to fill this area with a gradient, you must convert the path to a selection, as you do in this tutorial.

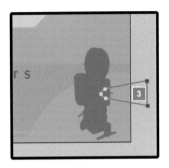

1. **Use** 06_sponsors_move.psd **from the previous tutorial or open the fresh file** 06_sponsors_select.psd **from the Session 6 Tutorial Files folder on your hard drive and click Update at the prompt.**
   06_sponsors_select.psd is a replica of 06_sponsors_move.psd as it should look after the previous tutorial.

2. **Select the Pen tool in the toolbox and click the Path icon on the left of the Options bar.**

3. **Draw a small triangular shape with a small curve on one end, in the shape of a projector light, as illustrated. Close the shape.**
   This is easiest if you expand the canvas by clicking and dragging its bottom-right corner. You can draw into the canvas, as shown in the figure.

4. **Double-click Work Path in the Paths palette to save the path and name the path** light.

5. **Click the Load Path as Selection button on the bottom of the Paths palette.**
   You have to convert this path to a selection in order to fill it with a gradient because there is no direct way to fill a path with a gradient.

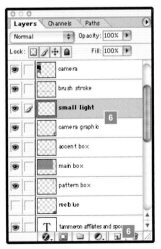

6. **Make sure that the camera graphic layer is selected in the Layers palette and click the Create New Layer button at the bottom of the palette. Name the new layer** small light**.**

7. **Select the Gradient tool in the toolbox. Create a lavender to light yellow gradient in the Gradient Editor.**
   If you need to review how to create a gradient, see Session 5.

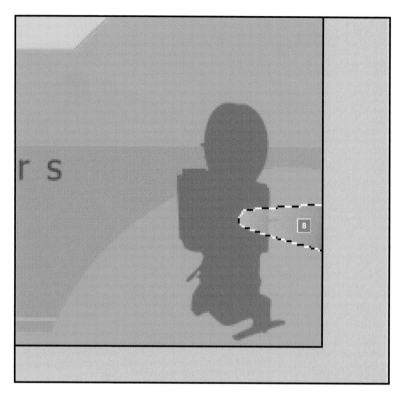

8. **Click and drag to fill the selection with the gradient.**

<NOTE>
You can go the other way and convert a selection to a path by clicking the Make Work Path from Selection button on the bottom of the Paths palette.

9. **Choose Select→Deselect from the menu bar at the top of the screen to deselect the filled area.**

10. **Choose File→Save As. Save the file as** 06_sponsors_select.psd **(whether you used your own file or opened the fresh file provided for you).**
Leave the file open for the next tutorial.

The Anatomy of a Shape Layer

Take a look at the new layer, labeled Shape 1, that was created in the Layers palette when you drew with the Shape tool. It has two thumbnails, representing the two components of a shape layer. The thumbnail on the left is a fill layer, which contains pixels of color. The thumbnail on the right is a vector mask, which contains a vector-based circle shape. That shape acts as a mask, hiding all the fill layer pixels outside of the white area of the mask. The link in between the thumbnails ties the fill layer to the vector mask layer. Clicking that line icon would unlink the two components of the shape layer.

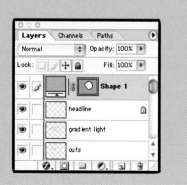

Tutorial
» Drawing a Geometric Shape with a Shape Tool

The Shape tools, introduced in Photoshop 6, are a godsend for Photoshop users who prefer not to draw graphics from scratch. In this tutorial, you practice using one of the geometric Shape tools (which come in five flavors—Rectangle, Rounded Rectangle, Ellipse, Polygon, and Line). You also learn how to apply a style to the shape.

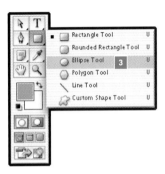

1. **Open the fresh file** 06_sponsors_shape.psd **from the Session 6 Tutorial Files folder on your hard drive and click Update at the prompt, or you can use** 06_sponsors_select.psd **that you saved from the previous tutorial.**
   06_sponsors_shape.psd is a replica of 06_sponsors_select.psd as it should look at the end of the previous tutorial.

2. **Double-click the Foreground Color box to open the Color Picker and choose a light purple.**
   Don't worry too much about the color. You change it in a minute.

3. **Click the Shape tool that is showing in your toolbox and choose the Ellipse tool from the hidden menu.**

4. **Click the Shape Layer icon on the left side of the Options bar.**
   If you leave this control the way it was set in preceding tutorials, you end up drawing a work path rather than a shape on a shape layer.

5. **Click the down arrow to the right of the shape icons on the Options bar. Enter the diameter of the circle that you want to draw (585 px) in both the Width and Height fields.**

<TIP>
If you're drawing a circle from scratch, click Circle to constrain the ellipse to a circle. It's also helpful to click From Center in order to draw the circle from the center, rather than from one side.

6. **Select the topmost layer in the Layers palette.**
   This causes the shape layer that you're creating to be located just above the selected layer, so you can see it clearly for the purposes of this tutorial.

7. Click in the document to create a circle shape.
If you hadn't chosen a fixed size, you would click and drag to create the circle shape.

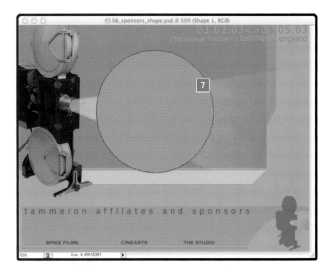

8. Select the White Arrow tool in the toolbox and click the thin vector outline around the circle. When you click that outline with the White Arrow tool, you'll see points. Click any of those points and drag to reshape the circle. When you're done, choose Edit→Step Backwards until your circle is restored. To hide the vector outline, click the vector mask thumbnail in the Layers palette. Are you noticing similarities between the vector mask on a shape layer and paths? They are edited the same way because they are both vector shapes. The difference is that the vector shape on a shape layer is located on a mask.

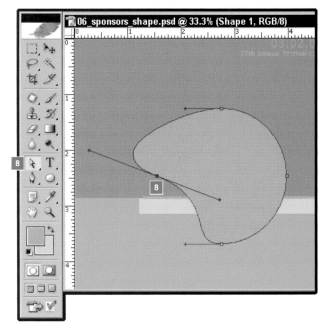

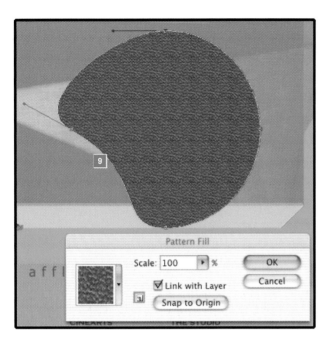

9. Choose Layer→Change Layer Content→Pattern or Layer→Change Layer Content→Gradient to change the fill side of the shape layer from a solid color to a pattern or gradient.
   When you're done, choose Edit→Step Backwards until your circle is a solid color again.

10. **Click the Style drop-down arrow on the Options bar to open the Styles palette. Click a style to see it applied to the circle.**
    Check the Layers palette after you apply the style; you see the effects that make up the style are listed below the shape's layer. When you're done, choose Edit→Step Backwards until your circle is a solid color again.

< N O T E >

Notice that the icon in the Style field contains a red slash, meaning that no layer styles are applied to the shape you're drawing; when you choose a style, it displays in the icon. You learn more about layer styles in Session 10. For now, know that you can choose a layer style from the Options bar to draw a shape with a special effect. The gold diamonds on the right side of the source file that you used earlier in this session are shapes created with a satin layer style.

11. **Select the Ellipse shape tool in the toolbox. Click the Color field on the right of the Options bar to open the Color Picker. Choose bright gold (try R: 255, G: 204, B: 0).**

    This is how you change the color of a shape.

12. **Select the Move tool or the Black Arrow tool. (Either works to move a shape on a shape layer.) Drag the now gold circle to the lower-right side of the document window, aligning it with the edge of the curve on the purple bar. Position it so that only part of it is inside the image boundaries, as shown.**

13. **Double-click the Shape 1 layer and name it** circle shape**.**

14. **Drag the circle shape layer to just above the sponsors box layer in the Layers palette so that the circle isn't obscuring other items in the image.**

15. **Choose File→Save As. Save the file as** 06_sponsors_shape.psd **(whether you used your own file or opened the fresh file provided for you).**

    Leave the file open for the next tutorial.

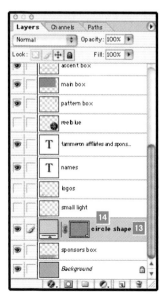

Tutorial
» Using Custom Shapes

Photoshop CS ships with a whole slew of custom shapes. These are exactly like the geometric Shape tools that you just mastered, except they are in the shape of icons, frames, and borders. They can be resized and modified as much as you like because they are vector-based.

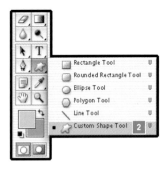

1. Use 06_sponsors_shape.psd, which you saved from the previous tutorial.

2. Select the Custom Shape tool from the hidden menu of Shape tools in the toolbox or from the Options bar.

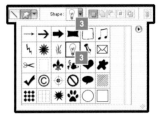

3. Click the arrow to the right of the Shape sample on the Options bar to open the Custom Shape Picker. Click the light bulb icon to select it.

4. Click in the image and drag to draw this shape to approximately the size shown.

   You can make a custom shape as big or small as you like without harming it.

5. Open the Custom Shape Picker again and click the arrow on its upper right. Choose All from the dropdown list and click OK at the prompt.

   This replaces the small default set of custom shape icons with all the custom shapes that come with Photoshop.

6. Click the bottom-right corner of the Custom Shape Picker and drag to see all the Custom Shapes. Select single pedestrian.

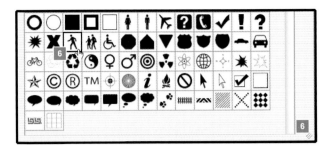

7. Click and drag in the image to the size shown in the figure.

8. Click the Add to Shape Area button in the Options bar.
   If these shape combination buttons are grayed out, make sure that the proper shape layer is selected in the Layers palette.

9. Open the Custom Shape Picker again and select the two pedestrians. Click and drag in the image.
   All three pedestrians are now located on the same shape layer. So if you were to change the nature or color of the fill, all would be affected.

10. Click the Ellipse Shape tool on the Options bar. Click the arrow to the right of the Shape icons in the Options bar and change the Options so that there is no fixed size and Circle is checked. Click and drag a small circle in the image.

11. Select the Custom Shape tool in the Options bar. Choose the dog print shape from the Custom Shape Picker. Click the Subtract from Shape Area button.

12. Click and drag on top of the small yellow circle to create a negative shape in that circle.

13. Choose File→Save As, name the image 06_sponsors_end.psd, and save this image in your collages folder.
    This is one of the final collages that you include in the film program guide you create in this course. There is a copy of 06_sponsors_end.psd in your Session 6 Tutorial Files folder.

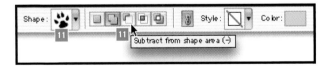

» Session Review

This session covers how to work with vector-based objects in Photoshop. You learned to create and edit paths with the Pen tools, how to fill and stroke paths, and how to copy a path between documents. Then you learned all about Shape tools and shape layers, including the geometric Shape tools and the Custom Shape tool. These questions will help you review this session.

1. What is the difference between vector graphics and bitmapped images? (See "Discussion: An Introduction to Vector Graphics.")

2. What is a path? (See "Tutorial: Drawing with the Pen Tool.")

3. What are vector graphics made up of? (See "Tutorial: Drawing with the Pen Tool.")

4. Can you resize a vector graphic without damaging its image quality? (See "Tutorial: Drawing with the Pen Tool.")

5. Name three things that you can use as a fill for a path. (See "Tutorial: Drawing with the Pen Tool.")

6. How do you end a straight path? (See "Tutorial: Drawing with the Pen Tool.")

7. How do you end a closed path? (See "Tutorial: Drawing with the Pen Tool.")

8. Why is it important to convert a work path to a saved path? (See "Tutorial: Drawing with the Pen Tool.")

9. What does the Pen tool's Rubber Band option do? (See "Tutorial: Drawing with the Pen Tool.")

10. What are the functions of the White Arrow tool (officially the Direct Selection tool)? (See "Tutorial: Editing Paths.")

11. What are the functions of the Black Arrow tool (officially the Path Selection tool)? (See "Tutorial: Editing Paths.")

12. What does the Convert Point tool do? (See "Tutorial: Editing Paths.")

13. How do you make the Freeform Pen tool act like a magnetic tool? (See "Tutorial: Tracing a Path with the Freeform Pen Tool.")

14. When you're using the Freeform Pen tool with its magnetic options, do you click and drag to move around the image? If not, what do you do? (See "Tutorial: Tracing a Path with the Freeform Pen Tool.")

15. How do you convert a path to a selection? (See "Tutorial: Converting a Path to a Selection.")

16. Describe what the two thumbnails on a shape layer represent. (See "Tutorial: Drawing a Geometric Shape with a Shape Tool.")

17. Can you resize custom shapes? (See "Tutorial: Using Custom Shapes.")

Part IV
Image Editing

Session 7

Selecting

Session Introduction

Selecting is a prerequisite for almost all bitmapped editing tasks in Photoshop. You have to select pixels in an image in order to fill, move, copy, cut, transform, adjust, or otherwise edit those pixels. There are many different tools for selecting in Photoshop, including Marquee selection tools for making geometric selections, Lasso tools for drawing selections, the Magic Wand tool and the Color Range command for selecting by color, the Extract feature for selecting complex images such as hair or foliage, and the Quick Mask feature for cleaning up selections. This session teaches how to use these tools and offers ideas about which selection tool to use when. You also learn how to save and reuse a selection, how to make aliased, anti-aliased, and feathered selections, and how to move, copy, hide, invert, modify, and transform selections. There's a lot to learn, but it's all pretty straightforward.

TOOLS YOU'LL USE
Marquee tools, Lasso tools, Quick Mask feature, Magic Wand tool,
Color Range command, Extract feature, Replace Color command,
Select menu, anti-aliasing, feathering, and Transform commands

CD-ROM FILES NEEDED
07_tix.psd, 07_fox.psd, 07_tix_copy.psd,
07_tix_wand.psd, 07_tickets.psd, and 07_tix_end.psd

TIME REQUIRED
90 minutes

Tutorial
» Selecting Geometric Forms with the Marquee Tools

It's relatively simple to recolor, transform, adjust, style, or filter artwork that is isolated on its own layer, as you learned elsewhere in this course. However, you are frequently confronted with an image in which pieces of artwork that you want to treat separately are located on the same layer. That's when you have to use one or more of Photoshop's selection techniques to isolate the areas you want to affect. When the areas to select are geometric forms, Photoshop's Marquee selection tools are the tools to reach for first. In this tutorial, you learn how to use the Rectangular and Elliptical Marquee tools.

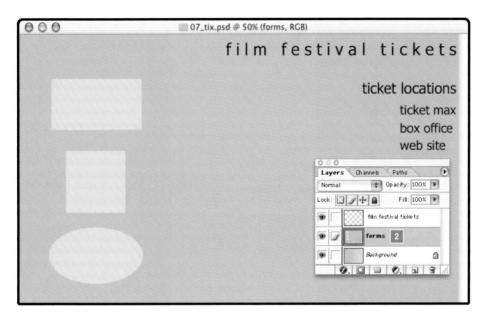

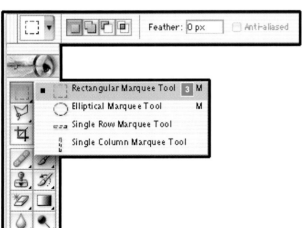

1. **Choose File→Open, navigate to** 07_tix.psd **in the Session 7 Tutorial Files folder on your hard drive, and click Open.**
   Notice that this image contains geometric forms merged with a color fill on the forms layer. In the next steps, you learn how to select each of these forms with a Marquee selection tool.

2. **Make sure that the forms layer is selected in the Layers palette.**

3. **Select the Rectangular Marquee tool from the toolbox. If it's not showing, click whichever Marquee tool is displayed there and choose the Rectangular Marquee tool from the hidden menu.**
   Leave the settings in the Options bar at their defaults for now.

4. **Click the top-left corner of the yellow rectangular shape and drag a rectangular selection around that shape.**
   Your selection is defined by an animated boundary of marching ants.

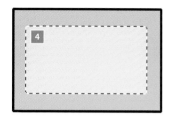

5. **Fill the selected rectangle with a color of your choosing, using any of the fill methods that you learned back in Session 5.**
   Don't worry about how the fill looks because this rectangle won't be part of your final collage. Now that the rectangle is selected, you can do any number of things to it without affecting the rest of the Background layer. You can fill the shape, as you did here, or copy it, cut it out, move it, transform it, add a layer style to it, filter it, and more.

6. **Choose Select→Deselect from the menu bar at the top of the screen to eliminate your selection.**
   Remember to deselect whenever you finish an operation on a selected area. If you don't, your next operation is limited to that area, or, in some cases, Photoshop refuses to perform the next operation.

7. **Hold the Shift key, click a corner of the yellow square, and drag with the Rectangular Marquee tool.**
   This constrains your selection to a square. Holding the Shift key doesn't constrain a selection to a square if there is another selection in the image. In that case, holding the Shift key has another function. It adds the second selection to the first, just like the Add Selection combination button, which you learn about later in this session.

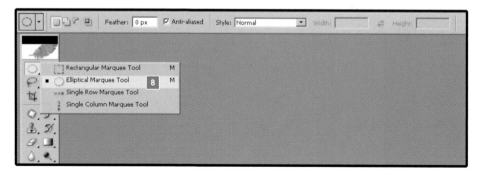

8. **Click the Rectangular Marquee tool and select the Elliptical Marquee tool from the hidden menu.**
   Leave the Options bar set to its defaults, as in this figure.

<NOTE>
Deselecting is something that you'll do frequently. So it's worth remembering two shortcuts for Deselect: The keyboard shortcut for deselecting is ⌘+D (Windows: Ctrl+D), and the physical shortcut for deselecting is to click anywhere else in the document (as long as none of the combined selection buttons are activated in the Options bar). If you change your mind after deselecting and want your last selection back, you can choose Select→Reselect. This restores the last selection that you made, even if you made other kinds of edits to your image in the meantime.

9. **Click any edge of the ellipse and drag. Part way through your drag, press the spacebar and reposition the selection to match the artwork. Release the spacebar and continue to drag. Repeat this several times to fit the selection to the form.**
   This creates an elliptical selection, beginning with one edge of the ellipse. This method can require quite a bit of fine-tuning with the spacebar to match the selection to the artwork.

10. **Click outside of the selection to deselect.**
    In the next step, you try a method that's similar, except that it draws from the center of the ellipse out, which you may find easier.

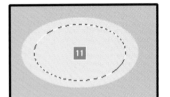

11. **Hold the Option (Windows: Alt) key, click in the center of the ellipse, and drag to create an elliptical selection from the center out. Part way through the drag, with the Option (Alt) key still held down, press the spacebar and reposition the selection to match the artwork.**
    This method usually requires less fine-tuning than the last method.

12. **Click outside of the selection to deselect.**
    In the next step, you draw a circular selection. You won't always be selecting an existing object when you draw a selection. Sometimes you draw a selection from scratch, as you practice doing in the next step.

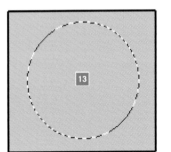

13. **Hold the Option (Windows: Alt) key to draw from the center out and at the same time hold the Shift key to constrain your selection to a circle. Click and drag in the green area toward the right side of the document window to draw a small circular selection.**
    Release the mouse button before you release the Option (Alt) and Shift keys.

14. **Press Option+Delete (Windows: Alt+Backspace) to fill the circular selection with a foreground color of your choice.**

15. **Choose File→Save and leave** 07_tix.psd **open for the next tutorial.**

Hints for Working with the Marquee Tools

The only way to learn to use the Marquee tools, like all other tools in Photoshop, is by experimenting. Here are some tips for mastering these tools:

» Use the Marquee tools when the selection you're making is a square, rectangle, ellipse, or circle—for example, when you're creating buttons for a Web page layout or making frames to set off photos. The Marquee tools also come in handy when the color-based selection tools, such as the Magic Wand or Color Range command, won't work due to lack of contrast between colors. You can start with a Marquee tool selection and then expand it to other parts of the image with the Grow command, which is covered later in this session.

» If you find that drawing a circular selection with the aid of the modifier keys, as you did in the tutorial, seems to require an extra pair of hands, you may prefer setting the Style button in the Options bar to Fixed Aspect Ratio and entering the same number in both the Width and Height fields (try 1). This constrains the Elliptical Marquee to a circle, freeing you from holding the Shift key. You can still use the Option (Alt) key and the spacebar with this feature. This trick also works to constrain a rectangular marquee to a square.

» There are two more marquee tools: the Single Row and Single Column Marquee tools. These draw horizontal or vertical lines one pixel wide, respectively. They are useful for drawing or cutting out thin rules for design interest. Try selecting the Single Column Marquee tool and clicking in the document window to the right of the shapes. Press Option+Delete (Alt+Backspace) to fill the thin line with color. Press ⌘+D (Windows: Ctrl+D) to deselect.

» If you find that you often switch between the Rectangular and Elliptical Marquee tools as you work, you'll like this shortcut. With either of the two tools selected in the toolbox, press Shift+M to toggle to the other tool.

Tutorial
» Moving and Copying Selections

In the previous tutorial, you learned how to move a selection as you drew it. It's more common that you want to move a selection after you draw it, which is what you learn to do in this tutorial. You also learn the important difference between moving a selection outline and moving the contents of a selection.

1. Use `07_tix.psd`, which should still be open from the previous tutorial.

2. Make sure that the forms layer is still selected in the Layers palette.

3. Select the Elliptical Marquee tool from the toolbox. If one of the other Marquee tools is showing, select it and click Shift+M to cycle through the Marquee tools to the Elliptical Marquee.

4. Use any of the techniques that you learned in the last tutorial to drag a selection around the circle in the document. Don't bother pressing the spacebar to move the selection into place as you draw.
   The trick to moving a selection outline, rather than the contents of the selection, is to have one of the selection tools selected in the toolbox. Resist the temptation to use the Move tool for this purpose because it moves the contents of the selection, as you see in step 7.

5. Leave the Elliptical Marquee tool selected, click inside the selection, and drag to move the selection into position over the circle graphic.

6. Press the arrow keys on your keyboard, with the Marquee tool still selected, to finish the job by nudging the selection into position one pixel at a time.
   Hold the Shift key while pressing an arrow key to move the selection ten pixels at a time, when a selection tool is active.

7. Select the Move tool in the toolbox. Click inside the selection and drag.
   This causes the contents of the selection, the colored circle, to move with the selection outline, leaving a hole in the fabric of the forms layer. (Your hole may not look as pronounced as the one shown here because you have a green layer underneath the forms layer.)

<TIP>
You can select the Move tool temporarily while another tool is active by clicking and holding the ⌘ key (Windows: Ctrl key).

8. Choose Edit→Undo and deselect.

<TIP>

If you want to move the circle graphic without cutting a hole in the forms layer, you have to make a copy of the selected graphic. There are two ways to do this, and the first is only temporary:

- Hold the Option (Windows: Alt) key while dragging the selected graphic with the Move tool. This creates a temporary "floating" copy of the graphic that you can move without consequence until you deselect it. Then it becomes part of the forms layer, and selecting and moving it again causes a hole in the layer. If you're a Photoshop old-timer, you may remember floating selections like this from back in Photoshop 4.

- Choose Layer➜New➜Layer Via Copy, with the circle graphic selected. This creates a new layer above the forms layer that contains a copy of the selected graphic, which you can move as much as you want without damaging other layers.

<NOTE>

You can copy the content of a selection between images, as well as within an image. This is a skill that you use often as you build collages in Photoshop. You learn how to do this in the following steps.

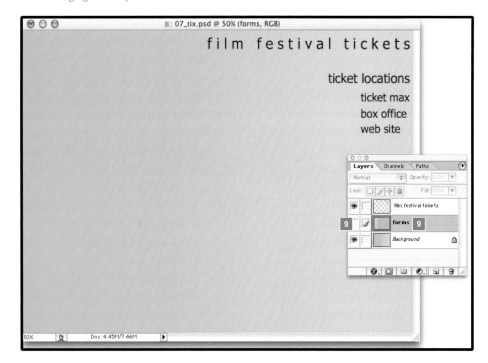

9. **Click the eye icon on the forms layer to hide that layer for now, and select the forms layer.**
   You can see the gradient background of the collage you're building in this session.

10. **Open a second image,** `07_fox.psd`, **from the Session 7 Tutorial Files folder on your hard drive.**

11. **Make sure that** `07_fox.psd` **is the active image and choose Select→All from the menu bar at the top of the screen, or use the shortcut ⌘+A (Windows: Ctrl+A).**
    A marching ants selection border surrounds the entire image.

12. **Choose Edit→Copy from the menu bar at the top of the screen.**

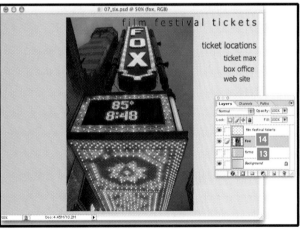

13. **Click in** `07_tix.psd` **to make that the active image, make sure that the forms layer is selected, and choose Edit→Paste.**
    This pastes the selection from `07_fox.psd` into `07_tix.psd` and creates a new layer for the pasted content above the selected layer. This technique would have worked the same way if the selection that you copied and pasted had been a portion of an image, rather than the entire image.

    <NOTE>
    Another way to copy a selection from one image to another is to click and drag the selection with the Move tool.

14. **Double-click the new layer in** `07_tix.psd` **and name it** fox.

15. **Select the Move tool in the toolbar and click and drag the pasted content to the bottom-left corner of the document.**

    By default, a selection is pasted into the center of the destination document, but you can move it wherever you like because it is automatically isolated on its own layer.

< T I P >

If you want a selected image to land somewhere other than the center of the destination document, make a selection elsewhere in the destination document and then choose Edit→Paste. The image centers on that selection, even if the selection is smaller than the image. Note that this is a different technique than the Paste Into technique discussed in the sidebar.

16. **Click in** 07_fox.psd **and choose File→Close.**

17. **Choose File→Save and leave** 07_tix.psd **open if you want to use it in the next exercise.**

    You have the option of starting the next tutorial with a fresh prebuilt file.

Pasting into a Selection

When you paste a copied selection into a document, you can paste into a space that's limited by another selection. This is a technique that's useful for creating vignetted images in a document.

To try it, select all or a portion of 07_fox.psd. Select the Rectangular Marquee tool and drag out a rectangular selection in your destination document 07_tix.psd. Choose Select→ Feather and add about 20 pixels to blur the edges of the selection. Choose Edit→Paste Into. The image is pasted into a layer with a layer mask in the shape of your selection. Select the Move tool and move the image around in the selected area until you're satisfied with the part that's showing.

You can use a prebuilt shape instead of a feathered selection for another look. Select the Custom Shape tool in the toolbox. Click the Paths button on the left of the Options bar. Choose a custom shape from the Custom Shape Picker on the menu bar and click and drag in the image. Click the Load Path as Selection button at the bottom of the Paths palette. Choose Edit→Paste Into and position the image in the shape with the Move tool. When you're done, choose Edit→Step Backwards to delete these experiments from your collage.

Tutorial
» Using the Lasso Selection Tools

In this tutorial, you learn how to use the Lasso selection tools, including the freeform Lasso, the Polygonal Lasso, and the Magnetic Lasso. The Lasso tool isn't a great tool for making precise selections. It is most useful for defining a rough area to limit the reach of other selection tools, such as the Magic Wand, that you can use in combination with the Lasso tool.

1. **Make sure that** `07_tix.psd` **is open from the previous tutorial or open the fresh file** `07_tix_copy.psd` **from your Session 7 Tutorial Files folder.**
   `07_tix_copy.psd` is a replica of the way `07_tix.psd` should look at the end of the previuos tutorial. You can use either file.

2. **Select the Lasso tool in the toolbox. If it isn't showing, click whichever Lasso tool is displayed and choose Lasso Tool from the hidden menu.**

3. **Click and drag a selection around the Fox sign in the image. Release the mouse button when you near the beginning of the selection.**
   Notice how difficult it is to draw a precise selection with the Lasso tool in its default mode, in which it acts like a freeform drawing tool. Notice also that as soon as you release your mouse button, the selection closes, which means that you can't release the mouse button until you complete the selection. In step 5, you learn how to use the Lasso tool with the Option (Windows: Alt) key to address both of these problems.

4. **Press ⌘+D (Windows: Ctrl+D) to deselect.**

5. **Press and hold the Option (Windows: Alt) key. Click and drag with the Lasso tool around the top of the Fox sign in the image. When you get to a straight section of the sign, release the mouse button. Click again at the bottom of the straight section of the sign to create a straight segment of the selection. Then click and drag again. Repeat this until you get near the beginning of the selection. Release the mouse button and the Option (Alt) key to close the selection.**
   Holding the Option key as you used the Lasso tool enabled you to add straight lines to your selection and to release the mouse button during the selection without closing the selection. This works better than using the freeform Lasso tool, but an even easier way to do the same thing is to select with the Polygonal Lasso tool, as you do in the next steps.

6. **Press ⌘+D (Windows: Ctrl+D) to deselect.**

7. **Select the Polygonal Lasso tool from the toolbox. If it isn't showing, click whichever Lasso tool is displayed and choose Polygonal Lasso Tool from the hidden menu.**
   This tool works just the opposite way from the Lasso tool. It defaults to drawing straight lines and enables you to draw freeform lines by pressing the Option (Windows: Alt) key.

8. **Click at the beginning of a straight section of the Fox sign. Release the mouse button (don't drag) and click again at the end of the straight section of the sign. Press and hold the Option (Windows: Alt) key and drag around the curved edge of the sign. Repeat this around the other side of the sign. When you're done, move your cursor over the beginning of the selection until you see a small circle. Then release the mouse button (and the Option key if you're holding it down) to close the selection.**

9. **Click with the Polygonal Lasso tool on one of the points in the star shape on the underside of the theater marquee. Click an inner corner to draw a straight line. Continue clicking around the star shape. Close the shape by clicking the beginning point of the selection when you see a small circle symbol.**
   When your entire selection is made up of straight lines, the Polygonal Lasso tool is easier to use than the regular Lasso tool. If you make a mistake while you create a selection with the Polygonal Lasso tool, press the Delete or Backspace key on your keyboard to remove the last segment of the polygon.

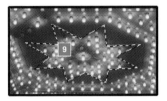

10. **Select the Zoom tool and click several times on the letter X in the Fox sign.**

11. **Select the Magnetic Lasso tool from the toolbox. If it isn't showing, click whichever Lasso tool is displayed and choose the Magnetic Lasso tool from the hidden menu.**

12. **Click any edge of the letter X in the sign. Move, but don't drag, your cursor around the edge of the X.**
    The Magnetic Lasso tool draws a selection border for you, placing points along the way. All you have to do is move your cursor around the edge of the X, without dragging. Once in a while (for example, at the inner edges and corners of the X), you may have to click to set a point manually if the Magnetic Lasso tool skips a spot. If you don't like the selection the Magnetic Lasso tool is making, press the Delete key to eliminate the last point set by the Magnetic Lasso. Repeat this to delete more than one point if necessary. Move your cursor backward along the selection boundary and then move the cursor forward, without dragging, to continue the selection.

13. **Choose File➔Save As. Save the file as** 07_tix_copy.psd **(whether you used your own file or the fresh file provided for you). Do not deselect.**
    Leave this file open for the next tutorial, in which you use the Quick Mask feature to clean up this selection.

<NOTE>
You can change the Width setting as you use the Magnetic Lasso tool to adjust how many pixels the Magnetic Lasso takes into account when it's looking for the edge of the image you select. Click the left bracket key to decrease this number if you work on an edge with tight turns and narrow crevices or if the selection you make jumps away from the edge of the image you select. Click the right bracket key if you work on a larger, uncluttered edge. If the Magnetic Lasso tool is still not doing a good job of selecting, try increasing the Edge Contrast setting in the Options bar, which helps the tool find the edge of a low contrast image. You can also try increasing the contrast in your image temporarily by adding a brightness and contrast, curves, or levels adjustment layer.

Tutorial
» Refining a Selection in Quick Mask Mode

The Quick Mask is an invaluable feature for augmenting selection tools. You can use it to correct and refine any selection. As you can tell by its name, the Quick Mask is really a mask that represents a selection. You can edit the mask by painting with the Brush tools, adding to or subtracting from any areas that you missed with your selection tools. Then with the click of a button, you can convert the mask back to a selection.

1. **Make sure that** 07_tix_copy.psd **is open from the previous tutorial and that there is a selection in the document. If for any reason there is not, repeat steps 10 through 13 of the preceding tutorial.**

2. **Zoom in to 300% magnification, if you have not already done so, so that you have a detailed view of the selection you made in the last tutorial.**

   Notice that the selection shown here doesn't reach all the way to the edges of the X in a few places. You fix that by painting in those areas in the Quick Mask in the following steps.

3. **Click the Quick Mask icon in the toolbox.**

   This puts the entire document into Quick Mask editing mode. The unselected portions of the document now appear covered with a semitransparent red.

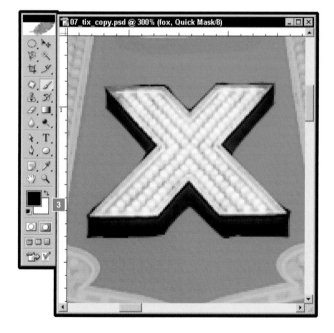

4. **Double-click the Quick Mask icon in the toolbox to open the Quick Mask Options dialog box. Change the Opacity to 70% to make the red mask less transparent so that there's more contrast between the mask and the selected image. Click OK.**

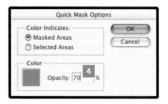

<NOTE>

If you ever work with selected content that doesn't contrast sufficiently with the color of the mask for you to see the difference between them, you can change the color of the mask by clicking in the Color field in this Quick Mask Options dialog box. If you prefer having the colored mask cover the selected area of the image, rather than the unselected area, you can click the Selected Areas button.

5. **Select the Brush tool in the toolbox and choose a hard, round small brush from the Brush pop-up palette on the left of the Options bar.**

If you don't see a small, hard round brush, click the arrow at the top right of the Brush pop-up palette and choose Reset Brushes.

6. **Click the Default Foreground and Background Colors icon at the bottom of the toolbox to set those colors to black and white, respectively. Then click the double-pointed Switch Foreground and Background Colors arrow to set the foreground color to white and the background color to black.**

It's important that you paint with black or white when working in Quick Mask mode in order to make pixels completely selected or deselected. Painting with a color results in partially selected pixels (such as the kind found in a gradual edge).

7. **Paint with white over all the areas in which the red mask infringes on the X, causing the mask to disappear from those areas.**
Use the Zoom tool to get in closer and the Hand tool to move the image around if necessary. If you make an error and paint too far into the red area, click the Switch Foreground and Background Colors arrow in the toolbox to change the foreground color to black and paint over your stray brush strokes, causing the red mask to reappear where you paint.

<TIP>
As you work in Quick Mask mode, you may have to reduce the brush size as low as 1 pixel to paint into corners and along edges. A shortcut for changing brush size on-the-fly is to click the left bracket key to reduce brush size and the right bracket key to increase brush size.

8. **Click the Standard Edit mode icon just to the left of the Quick Mask mode icon in the toolbox.**
This converts the mask (actually the inverse of the mask) back to a selection. The selection should now extend to all the corners and edges of the X.

9. **Press ⌘+D (Windows: Ctrl+D) to deselect.**

10. **Leave the file open for the next tutorial.**

Magic Wand Tool Options

When you click a pixel (or sample of pixels) with the Magic Wand tool, all pixels in the image that are similar in color to that pixel may be selected, depending on how you set the following:

>> Checking Contiguous in the Options bar limits the resulting selection to pixels that touch one another. If you uncheck this option, the Magic Wand selects all pixels within the appointed range anywhere in the image.

>> The Tolerance setting in the Options bar determines the range of colors that are selected (based on brightness values in each of the RGB color channels). Higher Tolerance values result in a broader selection.

>> Checking Anti-aliased ensures that the selection has a soft edge. (You learn more about anti-aliasing later in this session.)

>> Leaving Use All Layers unchecked tells the Magic Wand to consider the color of pixels only in the selected layer.

>> The number of pixels the Magic Wand samples depends on the Sample Size selected in the Options bar for the Eyedropper tool. Point Sample (which means 1 pixel) is the default.

Tutorial

» Selecting by Color with the Magic Wand Tool and Color Range Command

The selection tools that you've used so far have been selected based on shape and contrast. The Magic Wand tool and Color Range command are two selection methods based on the color of pixels. You learn how to use these features in this tutorial.

1. **Make sure that** `07_tix_copy.psd` **is still open from the previous tutorial and that the fox layer is selected in the Layers palette.**

2. **Select the Magic Wand tool in the toolbox. Leave the settings in the Options bar at their defaults for now (Tolerance: 32, Anti-aliased checked, Contiguous checked, and Use All Layers unchecked).**

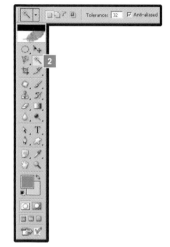

3. **Click the blue sky on the right side of the photograph to make your first selection.**
   It's unlikely that all neighboring pixels of sky will be selected, so in the next step you add to the selection.

4. **Hold the Shift key and continue to click in different areas of the sky outside the metal sign supports, until all the sky outside the sign is selected.**

   If you select too much, use the Quick Mask to paint that area out of the selection, as you learned to do in the last tutorial. The Shift key enables you to make multiple selections, adding to the selected area. The selections don't have to be contiguous. You can get the same result by clicking the Add to Selection button on the Options bar. Adding selections together makes more sense than trying to select the whole sky by increasing the Tolerance settings because any Tolerance setting is unpredictable.

5. **Select the Lasso tool in the toolbox. Holding the Shift key, draw a rough selection around the black area at the bottom right of the photograph to add it to the selection.**

   You can draw beyond the boundaries of the photograph because there is no content there on this layer. It often makes sense to use other selection tools in combination with the Magic Wand to add areas that weren't selected or to subtract areas you don't want to include in the selection.

< N O T E >

At first glance, the Magic Wand looks like the easiest of the selection tools to use. However, this tool suffers from unpredictability. It's impossible to know with certainty what selection will result from any click of the Magic Wand. The Magic Wand works best when the area that you want to select differs in brightness from the surrounding areas.

6. **Choose Edit→Cut from the menu bar at the top of the screen.**

   This cuts all the selected content out of the fox layer.

7. **Select the Polygonal Lasso tool and draw a rough selection around the remaining area of sky on the left of the Fox sign. Double-click to close the selection.**

8. **Click the Add to Selection button on the left side of the Options bar. Then draw a similar selection on the right.**

   These selections limit the area of the next Magic Wand selection. You may have tried to include these small inside areas of sky in your original selection and found that that caused other unwanted areas to be selected, too.

9. **Select the Magic Wand tool in the toolbox.**

10. **Uncheck Contiguous in the Options bar so that you can include the small isolated blue areas inside the sign supports in your next Magic Wand selection.**

11. **Click the Intersect with Selection button on the left side of the Options bar.**

   This button restricts combined selections to areas of selections that overlap. This stops a noncontiguous selection with the Magic Wand tool from spilling over the boundaries of your Polygonal Lasso selections.

12. **Click in the blue area of sky on either side of the sign.**

   This selects only the noncontiguous blue areas that are also surrounded by the Polygonal Lasso selections. Although the selection doesn't include every last bit of blue sky, it does a pretty good job.

13. **Choose Edit→Cut.**

The theater marquee is now free of sky and stands isolated against the gradient background on a lower layer.

<NOTE>

Another selection feature that selects by color values is the Color Range command, which you try out in the next steps.

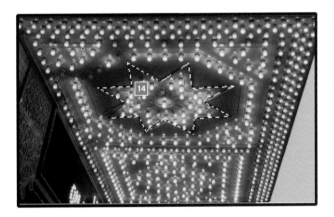

14. **Select the Polygonal Lasso tool in the toolbox and use it to draw a rough selection around the star shape under the marquee, as shown here.**

This isolates the effect of the Color Range command.

15. **Choose Select→Color Range from the menu bar at the top of the screen.**

16. **In the Color Range dialog box, set Selection Preview to Quick Mask.**
This lets you view the image through a mask, just like the Quick Mask feature you used earlier. The areas that you select with the Eyedropper tool are clear. The unselected areas are covered with a red mask.

17. **Click the Eyedropper tool in the Color Range dialog box and click one of the light bulbs inside the star selection in the masked image.**
The selected area appears light inside the black mask in the dialog box.

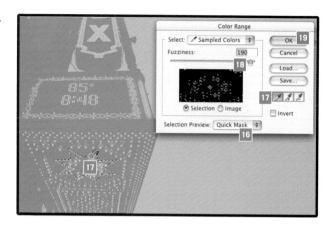

18. **Click the Fuzziness slider in the Color Range dialog box and move it to the right.**
As you do, the range of colors selected becomes broader. You see a preview of which areas are selected in two places—in the black mask in the dialog box and in the document window. The Fuzziness slider works similarly to the Magic Wand tool's Tolerance setting. Both determine a range of color values that will be selected. You have more control over the outcome with the Color Range feature than with the Magic Wand because you can adjust and readjust the Fuzziness slider as you select and because you can see a preview of the results.

19. **Click OK to close the Color Range dialog box and to make the selection.**

20. **Select the fox layer in the image. Choose a foreground color (such as rose) with which to fill the selected light bulbs and press Option+Delete (Windows: Alt+Backspace) to execute the fill.**

21. **Choose File→Save. Leave** 07_tix_copy.psd **open to use it in the next tutorial.**

< N O T E >

There are a number of useful options in the Color Range dialog box for you to try. The Select button gives you the choice of basing the selection on colors that you sample with the Eyedropper—predefined colors; shadows, midtones, or highlights; or even colors that are out of gamut for CMYK printing (so you can identify, select, and change those colors in advance of printing). The two other Eyedropper tools are for adding and removing colors from the sample on which the selection is based. The Selection Preview button gives you a choice of viewing the image as a quick mask, as a color image against a white background, as a color image against a black background, or in grayscale. You can also choose the kind of image that appears as a preview in the dialog box by toggling the radio buttons under that preview.

Tutorial

» Selecting and Changing Color with the Replace Color Adjustment

In the previous tutorial, you learned how to select parts of an image based on the color of the pixels using the Magic Wand tool and Color Range command. In this tutorial you learn how to use one more method—the Replace Color command. You create a temporary mask to select colors in an image and then replace those colors using the Color Picker. You can also replace color by setting the hue, saturation, and lightness of the selected areas.

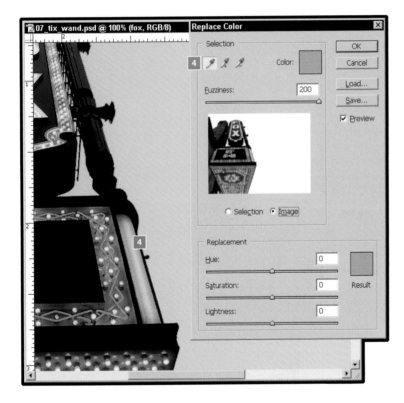

1. Use 07_tix_copy.psd, which you saved at the end of the preceding tutorial. Select the fox layer in the image.

2. Zoom into the image to see the vertical light to the right of the time and date sign.

3. Choose Image→Adjustments→Replace Color.
   The Replace Color dialog box opens. In the dialog box, the image displays in the preview area.

4. Click the Eyedropper tool in the dialog box, and click the lavender color in the light to sample it.
   You can sample either the image preview in the dialog box or the image itself. You can add more colors to the selection using the (+) eyedropper, or remove color using the (-) eyedropper.

5. **Click the Selection option below the preview area.**

   The selected areas are shown as white, and the rest of the image is masked out. The area that you want to recolor, along with the other portions of the theater marquee, are visible in the preview.

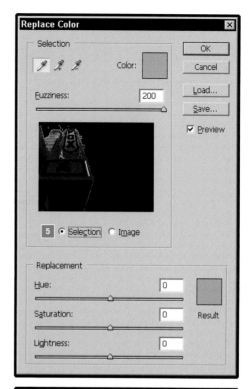

6. **Drag the Fuzziness slider left to approximately 90 to decrease the size of the selection until only the vertical light is visible in the preview.**

   You adjust the tolerance range of the mask using the slider or typing a value in the Fuzziness field. The higher the value, the greater the range of related color included in the selection.

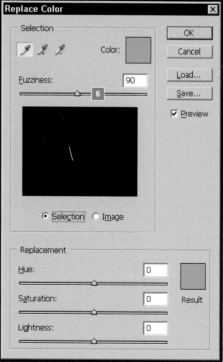

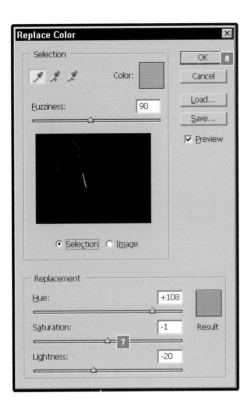

7. **Click the Result color swatch to open a Color Picker and choose a soft red color, or drag the Hue, Saturation, and/or Lightness sliders in the Replace Color dialog box to pick a red color.**
   The selected area, which was lavender, appears red in a live preview in the document window.

8. **Click OK to close the Replace Color dialog box.**
   The color is replaced in the image.

9. **Choose Edit →Undo and return the image to its original state.**
   Continue with the next tutorial. You don't have to save the image as you haven't made any permanent changes. You can start the next tutorial with the current file, or use a fresh file that is a replica of 07_tix_copy.psd.

Tutorial
» Modifying and Transforming Selections

After you create a selection, you don't have to live with it as it is. In this tutorial, you learn how to reshape and modify a selection using commands in the Select menu, including Transform Selection, Grow, Expand, Contract, and Smooth.

1. Use 07_tix_copy.psd, or open the fresh file 07_tix_wand.psd from the Session 7 Tutorial Files folder on your hard drive. Make sure that the fox layer is selected in the Layers palette.

2. Select the Magic Wand tool and set its options to Tolerance: 32, Anti-aliased, and Contiguous.

3. Click the purple light on the right side of the theater marquee, using the Magic Wand.
   This partially selects the purple light.

4. Choose Select→Grow several times, until the entire purple light is selected.
   The Grow command selects neighboring pixels incrementally, based on the tolerance set for the Magic Wand tool.

<NOTE>
The Similar command in the Select menu is like the Grow command except that Similar selects pixels that are non-adjacent too. This is useful for selecting large areas that have variations on a color. If you want to try this command, open 07_fox.psd again and make several small selections in the sky with the Rectangular Marquee tool. Then choose Select→Similar.

5. Select the Polygonal Lasso tool from the toolbox and click around the polygon shape in the lights under the marquee, as shown here.

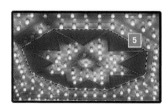

6. Choose Select→Modify→Expand, type 15 pixels, and watch the selection get larger.

7. Choose Select→Modify→Contract, type 15 pixels, and watch the selection get smaller.

8. Choose Select→Modify→Smooth, type 20 pixels, and watch the selection smooth out. Then choose Edit→Undo.

9. **Choose Select→Modify→Border and type** 10 **as the width of the Border. Press Option+Delete (Windows: Alt+Backspace) to fill the border with the foreground color.**

The Border command creates a soft-edged selection. You learn how to hide the marching ants of a selection in the next step.

10. **Press ⌘+H (Windows: Ctrl+H) to hide the marching ants of this selection. Now you can see the soft edge of the border more clearly. Repeat this key command to make the marching ants visible again.**

The marching ants that mark a selection often make it difficult to see the content of an image. It's very useful to be able to hide them without dropping a selection.

<CAUTION>

The trick when you hide a selection is remembering that there is a selection at all. If you don't remember that a hidden selection is active, you may be surprised that subsequent operations are limited to a particular area of your image. If something occurs in Photoshop that stumps you, press ⌘+H (Windows: Ctrl+H) to see if there is a hidden selection at work.

11. **Choose File→Step Backward several times if you don't want to keep the border in your collage.**

12. **Select the Rectangular Marquee tool and draw a selection to encompass as much of the black box on the theater marquee as possible.**

13. **Choose Select→Transform Selection to display a bounding box around your selection. Ctrl+click (Windows: right-click) inside the bounding box to display a drop-down menu of transform commands. Choose Distort from that menu.**

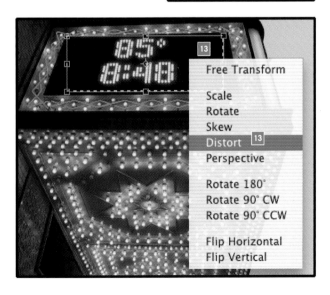

14. Click the points of the bounding box and pull them into position into the corners of the black box. Press Return or Enter to accept this transformation; press the Esc key on your keyboard to cancel a transformation.

<CAUTION>

Do not confuse transforming a selection outline, which is the subject here, with transforming the contents of a layer (by using the Edit➔Transform commands).

15. **Choose File➔Save As. Save the file as** `07_tix_wand.psd` **(whether you used your own file or the fresh file provided for you).** Leave the file open for the next tutorial.

Combining Selections

Another way to modify a selection is to combine multiple selections, which you did in preceding tutorials using a keyboard command (holding the Shift key to add to a selection) and using the combination buttons on the selection tools' Options bar. You've seen that one reason to combine selections is to limit the scope of a selection. Another is to resize or reshape a selection that isn't quite correct. For example, you may draw a selection that's too big. You can cut it down to size by choosing the Subtract from Selection combination button and drawing another selection that takes away part of the first selection. A more elaborate twist on that theme is the use of circular and rectangular selections in various combinations to build contoured shapes, such as Web navigation interfaces with rounded corners and cutouts.

Tutorial
» Creating Hard- and Soft-Edged Selections

Selections with hard, jagged edges are called aliased selections. Selections with soft edges are either anti-aliased or feathered selections. Anti-aliasing is the gradual softening of an edge between a foreground and background element, achieved by the partial selection of some pixels along that edge. When you color a selection that has an anti-aliased edge, some pixels are only partially filled with color, which gives the illusion of a smooth edge. Anti-aliasing is the default behavior of all the selection tools, except the Rectangular Marquee tools and the One Pixel Vertical and Horizontal tools, which don't need anti-aliasing because they don't draw curved selections. You'll find an Anti-aliased option, which is checked by default, on the Lasso selection tools, the Magic Wand, and the Elliptical Marquee tool. In this tutorial, you'll practice making these different kinds of selections and learn what the differences are between them.

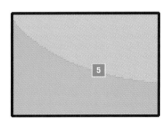

1. **Make sure that** `07_tix_wand.psd` **is still open from the previous tutorial.**

2. **Select the forms layer and click its eye icon to make that layer visible in the document.**

3. **Select the Elliptical Marquee tool. Uncheck Anti-aliased in the Options bar. Click and drag an ellipse.**

4. **Click the Quick Mask button in the toolbox.**
   It's easiest to see the hard-edged and soft-edged nature of selections in Quick Mask editing mode. You can't really see the difference in an unfilled selection in Standard Editing mode.

5. **Select the Zoom tool and zoom in until you can see the jagged edge of the aliased selection that you drew.**

6. **Click the Standard Editing mode button in the toolbox and zoom out.**
   In the next steps, you create an anti-aliased selection for comparison.

7. **Make sure that the Elliptical Marquee tool is still selected. Check Anti-aliased in the Elliptical Marquee tool's Options bar.**

8. **Click and drag an elliptical selection in the document.**

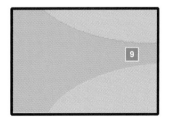

9. **Zoom in to see the relatively smooth edge of the anti-aliased selection (the selection on the bottom of the figure), as compared to the aliased selection (at the top of the figure).**
   Notice that there are partially selected pixels among the edge pixels of the anti-aliased selection. These pixels cause the edge to appear relatively smooth. An aliased selection is one with a jagged stair-stepped edge necessary to simulate a curved edge with rectangular pixels.

<CAUTION>

After you draw a selection with an aliased edge, there's no way to convert it into an anti-aliased selection.

10. **Click the Standard Editing mode button in the toolbox and zoom back out to 50% magnification.**

    In the next few steps, you make another sort of soft-edged selection—a feathered edge.

11. **Make sure that the Elliptical Marquee tool is still selected in the toolbox.**

12. **Type 7 in the Feather field in the Options bar.**

13. **Click and drag in the document to create a feathered selection.**

    Feathering creates a smooth-edged selection by blurring both the inside and outside of the edge of a selection. There are two ways to feather a selection. Enter a value between 1 and 250 (usually a low number is all you need) in the Feather field in the Options bar before drawing with a selection tool; or draw a selection, choose Select→Feather, and enter a value in the Feather Radius field of the dialog box and click OK.

14. **Click the Quick Mask button in the toolbox.**

    Notice the difference between the blurry edge of the feathered selection at the bottom of the figure and the edge of the anti-aliased selection at the top of the figure.

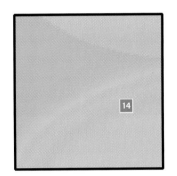

15. **Zoom in to the edge of this selection.**

    If you look closely, you can see that the blur goes both in and out from the edge of the selection.

16. **Zoom back out to 50%. Click the Standard Editing mode button to exit Quick Mask mode.**

17. **Leave this file open for the next tutorial.**

Using Feathering to Vignette an Image

A classic effect that you can achieve with feathering is a vignette (which was often done in the old days with portraits). You can feather a selection to paste into, as you did in an earlier tutorial in this session, or you can feather the selected content. To do the latter, select the Elliptical Marquee tool and type a value (try 10) into the Options bar. Select the fox layer. Click and drag an ellipse over a portion of the photograph in the document. Choose Edit→Copy and Edit→Paste. Select the Move tool and drag the copy to the right side of the document. That's all there is to creating a feathered vignette.

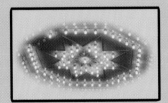

Tutorial

» Saving and Loading Selections as Alpha Channels

After you go to all the trouble of making a selection that you may use again, it makes sense to save it, rather than have to select it all over again. In Photoshop, you can save any selection as an alpha channel mask, which contributes little to file size and becomes a permanent component of the image. In this tutorial, you learn how to save a selection as an alpha mask and how to load it to use it again.

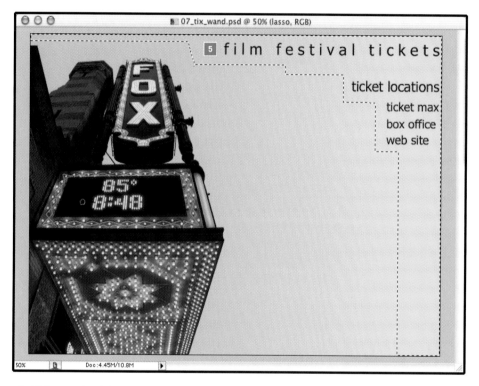

1. Make sure that 07_tix_wand.psd is still open from the previous tutorial.

2. Click the forms layer in the Layers palette and drag it to the Trash icon at the bottom of the Layers palette. Repeat this for Layer 1, which was created if you worked through the vignetting sidebar in the preceding tutorial.

3. Select the Polygonal Lasso tool in the toolbox. Make sure that Feathering is set to 0 and Anti-aliased is checked in the Options bar.

4. Drag the document window out so that it's larger than the image.

5. Click around the top and right side of the image to create a selection similar to the one shown here. (Yours doesn't have to match exactly.) Click the beginning point to close the selection.
It is easier to draw this selection to the edges of the document if you click outside of the document boundaries.

6. Select the Eyedropper tool in the toolbox and sample the yellow on the right side of the document.

7. Select the fox layer in the Layers palette, click the Create New Layer button, and make sure that the new layer is selected. Name the new layer menubar.

8. Press Option+Delete (Windows: Alt+Backspace) to fill with the foreground color.

9. Choose Select→Save Selection.

10. **In the Save Selection dialog box, make sure that Channel is set to New and type** menubar **in the Name field. Click OK.**

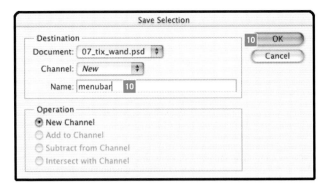

11. **Click the Channels tab in the same palette group as the Layers palette.**

    You'll see your selection saved there as a mask in a channel. The channel, known as an alpha channel, is a grayscale image. It is just another way, other than marching ants, of visually representing a selection.

12. **Click in the Visibility box to the left of the menubar channel to make the mask visible in the document.**

    Notice that this mask looks just like the Quick Mask that you used to modify a selection in an earlier tutorial. The difference between this alpha channel mask and a Quick Mask is just that this one isn't temporary.

13. **Turn off the Visibility icon on the menubar channel to return to the normal view of the image.**

14. **Choose File→Save and keep this file open for the next tutorial.**

Reusing an Alpha Channel Mask

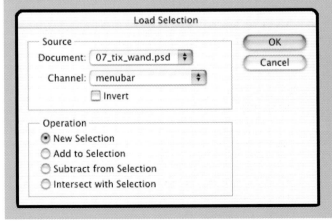

To reuse this alpha channel mask as a selection, choose Select→ Load Selection from the menu at the top of the screen. In the Load Selection dialog box, choose the menubar channel by name and click OK. Each separate layer in a document has a separate listing in the menu as a transparency, making it easy to load a selection in the shape of all the artwork in any layer. You can fill or otherwise use that selection on any layer in the document because an alpha channel isn't tied to a particular layer. You can also use the inverse of the selection as well. When you choose the channel in the Load Selection dialog box, click Invert to select everything but the alpha channel mask's area.

Tutorial

» Using the Extract Feature

The Extract feature is useful for separating a foreground object from a background. It does a pretty good job of detecting otherwise hard-to-select wispy edges, such as hair, tree branches, and fibers, as long as there's lots of contrast between the foreground object and the background. In this tutorial, you learn how to use the Extract tool to separate an object from its background for use in your collage.

1. **Open** 07_tickets.psd **from the Session 7 Tutorial Files folder on your hard drive.**

2. **Choose Filter→Extract from the menu bar at the top of the page.**

3. **Select the Highlighter tool from the left side of the Extract dialog box**.

4. **Set the Brush Size on the right side of the dialog box to around 24.**
   The brush should be just big enough to cover the edge between the tickets and their background. Use a slightly bigger brush when you come to the fibrous area at the top of the tickets by pressing the right bracket key on your keyboard to increase the size of the brush tip on-the-fly.

5. **Drag the highlighter around the tickets, making sure that the brush tip covers the edge of the tickets as you drag.**
   You can hold the Shift key and click from point to point on the straight edges if you prefer. Or try checking the Smart Highlighting box on the right side of the dialog box for help in finding the edges of the foreground item. Be sure to include the boundary of the document at the bottom of the image.

6. **Select the Paint Bucket tool from the left side of the dialog box and click inside the highlighted boundaries of the tickets.**
   If the paint runs out past the boundary of the highlighter, there's a hole in the boundary. Reselect the highlighter, fix the hole, and fill again.

7. **Click the Preview button at the top right of the dialog box.**

8. **Select the Cleanup tool from the top left of the dialog box. Hold the Option key (Windows: Alt key) and drag over areas in the tickets in which there are holes.**
   This restores any holes in the image caused by the extraction. If you restore part of the background by mistake, release the Option key and drag over that area with this same tool to delete the mistake.

9. **Select the Edge Touchup tool from the top left of the dialog box and drag along the edges of the tickets to sharpen those edges.**

<NOTE>

To save yourself Cleanup work, try some of the Extract options at the right of the Extract dialog box. You can choose options depending on the characteristics of your image. If the foreground image is a similar color, but a different texture than the background, select Textured Image to extract on the basis of texture (pattern) as well as contrast. Select Force Foreground if the object is especially intricate or lacks a clear interior.

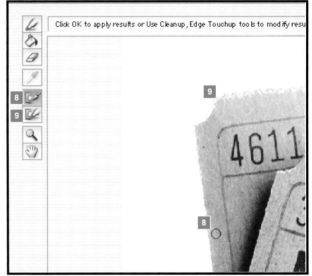

10. **Click OK in the Extract dialog box to perform the extraction of the tickets from the background.**
    The Extract tool affects the original image. If you didn't have a clean copy of the image on the CD-ROM, it would have been a good idea to make a copy of the image before you started extracting.

11. **Select the Move tool and drag the tickets into place in the open collage, 07_tix_wand.psd. Name the new layer tix and move it above the menubar layer.**

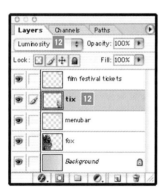

12. **Make sure that the tix layer is selected in the Layers palette. Click the button on the top left of the Layers palette to see a menu of blending modes. Choose Luminosity.**

    This colorizes the grayscale tickets, using the yellow from the Background layer below.

13. **Choose File→Save As and name the image 07_tix_end.psd. Save it in your collages folder for inclusion in your final project.**

    Now that you know all about selecting, you're ready for one of the most important sessions in the book, Session 8.

» Session Review

This session covers the many different selecting tools, options, and commands that you can use to select an area in an image.

1. Name any three things that you may want to do to an item in a document for which selecting is a prerequisite. (See "Tutorial: Selecting Geometric Forms with the Marquee Tools.")

2. How do you constrain a rectangular selection to a square? (See "Tutorial: Selecting Geometric Forms with the Marquee Tools.")

3. What do you press on your keyboard to reposition a selection while you're creating that selection? (See "Tutorial: Selecting Geometric Forms with the Marquee Tools.")

4. What kind of tool must be selected when you move a selection outline? (See "Tutorial: Moving and Copying Selections.")

5. How do you draw a selection with the Magnetic Lasso tool? (See "Tutorial: Using the Lasso Selection Tools.")

6. How do you enter Quick Mask Mode? (See "Tutorial: Refining a Selection in Quick Mask Mode.")

7. What colors should you paint with when you're working in Quick Mask Mode? (See "Tutorial: Refining a Selection in Quick Mask Mode.")

8. What does checking Contiguous do in the Magic Wand Options bar? (See "Tutorial: Selecting by Color with the Magic Wand Tool and Color Range Command.")

9. What does the Tolerance setting do in the Magic Wand Options bar? (See "Tutorial: Selecting by Color with the Magic Wand Tool and Color Range Command.")

10. What effect does moving the Fuzziness slider have in the Replace Color dialog box? (See "Tutorial: Selecting and Changing Color with the Replace Color Adjustment.")

11. Is transforming a selection the same thing as transforming layered artwork? (See "Tutorial: Modifying and Transforming Selections.")

12. What is an aliased selection? (See "Tutorial: Creating Hard- and Soft-Edged Selections.")

13. What is an anti-aliased selection? (See "Tutorial: Creating Hard- and Soft-Edged Selections.")

14. What is a feathered selection? (See "Tutorial: Creating Hard- and Soft-Edged Selections.")

15. What is an alpha channel used for? (See "Tutorial: Saving and Loading Selections as Alpha Channels.")

film festival tickets

ticket locations

ticket max
box office
web site

Session 8

Using Layers

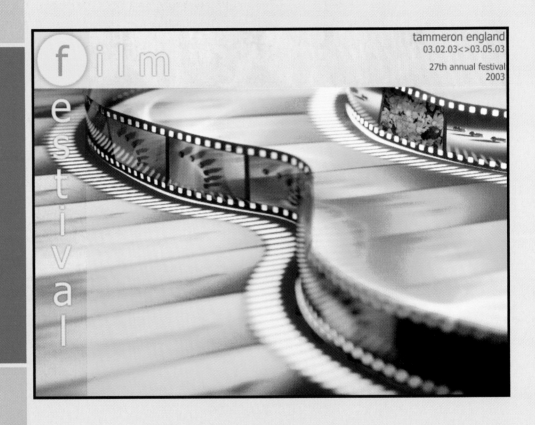

tammeron england
03.02.03<>03.05.03

27th annual festival
2003

Session Introduction

I remember using Photoshop back in version 2.5, when layers were just a gleam in Adobe's eye. Now, if I had to pick one feature in Photoshop that I couldn't live without, it would be layers. Layers have revolutionized the way that images are edited because they enable you to work on one piece of artwork without affecting the rest of the image. After you isolate artwork, it's easy to move, color, transform, filter, adjust, or apply effects to that item alone. In this session, you learn different ways to create layers. You practice working with the Layers palette—stacking, duplicating, deleting, locking, linking, and merging layers. You find out about layer visibility and how to move and transform the content of layers. You see how to group sets of layers and create layer comps that can be exported as separate images. You explore layer sets and nested layer sets and learn how to use adjustment layers and fill layers. If you're a Photoshop novice, this session is a must-read because it covers the all-important layers basics. If you're more advanced, this session contains tips that will help you use layers more productively than you may have been doing.

Your exploration of layers doesn't end here. In Session 9, you explore more advanced layers features, including layer blending, layer masks, and vector masks. And you find out about layer styles and other features that breathe life into the content of layers in Session 10.

TOOLS YOU'LL USE
Layers palette, Layer Comp palette, Layer sets, Auto Select Layer option, adjustment layers, and fill layers

CD-ROM FILES NEEDED
08_fest.psd, 08_fest_create.psd, 08_fest_eyes.psd, 08_fest_opacity.psd, 08_fest_links.psd, 08_fest_sets.psd, 08_logo.psd, 08_fest_end.psd, 08_fest_comps.psd, and 08_fest_comps_done.psd

TIME REQUIRED
60 minutes

Discussion
What Are Layers?

Layers are individual images on transparent backgrounds stacked on top of one another. The analogy I like to use is that a document with layers is like a stack of sheets of glass. Imagine that each sheet in the stack starts out perfectly clear and that you add solid or partially transparent artwork to each sheet as you work. If you looked down through the stack from above, you'd be able to see through to the sheets below wherever there was a clear or partially transparent area, but not where there was solid artwork. The same is true of a document with layers. Each layer starts out as transparent pixels. You add solid and partially transparent pixels of artwork to individual layers. When you view the image on a computer screen, artwork on the top layers obscures lower layers. Where there is no artwork, you can see through to lower layers.

The beauty of using layers is that the artwork on each layer is isolated so that it can be edited, moved, styled, and adjusted independently of the content of other layers.

Layer Transparency and Clipping Paths

You won't see anything in your document when you create a new blank layer because layers are transparent unless and until you fill them with content. If you look closely at a thumbnail in the Layers palette that corresponds to a new layer or a layer that is only partially filled with artwork, you can see the telltale gray-and-white checkerboard that indicates transparency. Option+click (Windows: Alt+click) the Eye icon on that layer to make all other layers in the document temporarily invisible. You can see the checkerboard in the document window. Unfortunately, Photoshop transparency isn't recognized by some object-oriented page layout programs and drawing programs, such as QuarkXPress and Macromedia Freehand. If you import a Photoshop image that has a transparent area into one of those programs, that area fills with a color. If you want to retain transparency so that the background you prepare in that program shows through, you must first add a vector clipping path around the artwork in Photoshop. This is most likely to come up if you want your artwork to appear nonrectangular. The alternative is to fill the background with pixels in Photoshop and bring the artwork into the object-oriented program as a rectangular, bitmapped image.

To practice adding a clipping path to an object, open `08_logo.psd` from the Session 8 Tutorial Files folder. Choose Select→Load Selection. Click the Make Work Path from Selection button at the bottom of the Paths palette. (Turn back to Session 6 if you need a refresher on paths.) Double-click your work path in the Paths palette and click OK to save it as a path. Click the arrow at the top right of the Paths palette and choose Clipping Path. Leave the Flatness value blank for now and click OK. (Flatness determines the shape of the polygon that is used to approximate the curved image when printing. Ask your printer what value he recommends.) To import the document to a page layout or illustration program with the clipping path intact, you would save it as a Photoshop EPS file.

Layers and File Size

Each layer that you add to a document increases the file size of the document. This is true even of new transparent layers that have no artwork on them. Although the ability to isolate pieces of artwork on separate layers is invaluable, it has its price in file size. Too many layers can make editing sluggish, slow down printing, and require lots of storage space. What can you do about this? Merge layers together when you finish working on them. (Click the arrow on the top right of the Layers palette and choose Merge Down to merge a selected layer into the layer directly beneath it, or Merge Visible to merge all the visible layers into the bottom-most layer. You can also merge layers that are linked or layers you put in a layer set.) Even better, juice up your computer with more RAM to increase performance while you're working and with a bigger hard drive for more storage space.

If you're curious about how much multiple layers add to file size, click the arrow at the bottom of the document window and choose Document Sizes from the pop-up menu. The number on the right (28.5 megabytes in the figure) is the size of the file with all its layers. The number on the left (4.45 megabytes) is an estimate of the size the file would be if all the layers were flattened into one.

Tutorial
» Creating Layers

There's more than one way to create a layer. In this session, you work through three ways to make a layer—from scratch, from a selection in another layer, and from another document. You've already seen some of the commands that you work with here in preceding tutorials, but this is where you pull it all together, along with details about each command and feature and a straightforward explanation of what layers are.

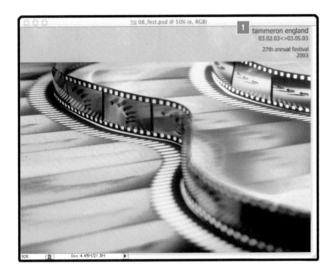

1. **Choose File→Open, navigate to** 08_fest.psd **in the Session 8 tutorial files on your hard drive, and click Open. If you are prompted to update text files, click Update.**

2. **Choose Window→Show Layers to open the Layers palette if it isn't already open on your desktop. Click and drag the scroll bar to see all the prebuilt layers in this document.**

3. **Click the top layer in the Layers palette (labeled tammeron england) to select that layer.**
   This ensures that the layer you're about to create will be located above the tammeron england layer. When a new layer is created, it's always placed directly above the selected layer. Layer stacking order is important because it determines which artwork will be visible and which will be hidden behind other artwork.

4. **Click the New Layer button at the bottom of the Layers palette.**
   This creates a new layer called Layer 1. That's how easy it is to make a new layer from scratch. The New Layer button creates an empty layer with default options (100% opacity and Normal blending mode). You can change these defaults to suit the content of the layer later.

<NOTE>
If you know which layer settings you want ahead of time, you may prefer setting those options when you create the layer. Choose Layer→New→Layer to open the New Layer dialog box. Set your layer options, type a layer name there, and click OK to create a layer.

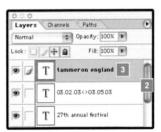

5. **Double-click directly on the Layer 1 name so that you can rename the layer. Type** corner square **as the new layer name and press Return (Windows: Enter) on your keyboard.**
   You have to click right on the layer name. Clicking anywhere else on the layer opens the Layer Style dialog box. It's important to give your layers meaningful names so that you can identify them as you work. Don't put off this step; you'll regret it later.

6. **Select the Rectangular Marquee tool in the toolbox. Click the Style button in the Options bar and choose Fixed Size from the menu. Type** 170 px **in both the Width and Height fields of the Options bar.**

7. **Click inside the document window to create a square selection and drag the selection into position at the top-left corner of the image.**

8. **Choose a yellow color (R:** 246**, G:** 224**, B:** 56**) in the Color palette. (If that palette isn't showing, choose Window→Color.)**

9. **Make sure that the corner square layer is selected in the Layers palette. If it's not, click that layer to select it. Press Option+Delete (Windows: Alt+Backspace) to fill the square selection with yellow.**
   The gray highlight in a layer in the Layers palette indicates that that layer is selected as the active layer. When a layer is selected, almost any editing operation that you do affects only that layer. Your yellow square is now isolated on the corner square layer. Any changes that you may make to it would not affect the artwork on other layers.

10. **Choose File→Open, navigate to** 08_logo.psd **in the Session 8 Tutorial Files folder, and click Open.**
    This source document contains artwork on a single transparent layer, the circle layer. If there were more than one layer in this document, you'd have to select the circle layer in the Layers palette before the next step.

11. **Select the Move tool in the toolbox. Click in the document window of the source document** 08_logo.psd**, drag to the document window of the destination document** 08_fest.psd**, and release the mouse button.**
    Alternatively, you can click the layer that you want to move in the Layers palette of the source document and drag to the document window of the destination document.

<NOTE>

If you're wondering why the logo looks bigger in the source document than in the destination document, it's because the destination document is set to 50% magnification and the source document opens at 100% magnification.

12. **Drag the logo into position on top of the yellow square.**

13. **Take a look at the Layers palette and notice that there's a new layer, named circle, just above the corner square layer.**

    The new layer was created automatically when you dragged content from the source document to the destination document. Where did the layer name circle come from? Photoshop was smart enough to take the new layer's name from the corresponding layer in the source document.

    <NOTE>

    Another source for a new layer can be an existing layer in the same document. In the next steps, you'll learn how to duplicate an entire layer and how to select and copy part of a layer.

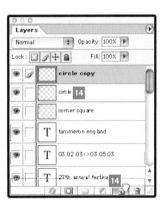

14. **Click the circle layer and drag it to the New Layer icon at the bottom of the Layers palette.**

    This creates a new layer, called circle copy, which is a duplicate of the circle layer. You can't see both layers in the document window because the duplicate is located right on top of the original. Click and drag with the Move tool to view the duplicate.

15. **Click the circle copy layer in the Layers palette and drag it to the Trash icon at the bottom of the Layers palette to delete that layer.**

    <CAUTION>

    The Layer palette Trash can can't be opened to retrieve deleted files like the regular Macintosh Trash or Windows Recycle Bin. After you drag a layer to the Trash in the Layers palette, the only way to get it back is with Edit→Undo or through the History palette.

16. **Select the Polygonal Lasso tool in the toolbox and click repeatedly around the edge of one of the film frames in the image to select that frame. Click the first point to close the selection.**

    <TIP>

    There's another way to make a duplicate layer that offers an additional useful option. Select the film layer in the Layers palette. Click the arrow at the top right of the Layers palette and choose Duplicate Layer. If you just clicked OK, you would get a duplicate layer in the same document, as you did in step 14. However, if you click Document and choose New, you get a separate document with a copy of the selected film layer. This would come in handy if you wanted to use this same layer to experiment with other collage ideas. For now, you can close this extra document.

17. **Ctrl+click (Windows: right-click) the film layer in the Layers palette to display a menu and choose Layer Via Copy.**
This creates a new layer above the film layer called Layer 1. Select the Move tool and click and drag in the document window to move the new Layer 1 away from the film layer so that you can see it.

18. **Click and drag Layer 1 from its current position in the Layers palette to just beneath the gradient layer. Wait until you see a black bar under the gradient layer to let go of the mouse button.**
That's all there is to reordering layers. If you ever lose the contents of a layer in the document window, it's probably because that layer is hidden under the artwork on another layer and needs repositioning in the stacking order of layers in the Layers palette.

19. **Drag Layer 1 to the Trash icon at the bottom of the Layers palette.**

20. **Choose File→Save. Leave** 08_fest.psd **open if you want to use it in the next tutorial.** You have the option of starting that tutorial with a fresh prebuilt file that's a replica of how 08_fest.psd should look now.

<NOTE>
There are a couple of other ways to create new layers, which you encounter elsewhere in this book. New layers are automatically created when you use the Type tool (see Session 11) and the Shape tools (see Session 6). Later in this session, you learn how to create two special kinds of layers—adjustment and fill layers.

Tutorial
» Converting a Background Layer

A Photoshop Background layer is a special kind of layer that has restrictions other layers do not. There are times, such as when you're trying to create a transparent GIF for the Web, that you want to eliminate the Background layer. This tutorial explains why and shows you how simple it is to convert a Background layer to a regular layer.

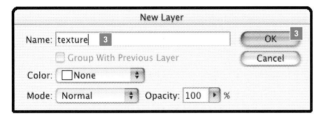

1. **Use the file that you saved at the end of the previous tutorial,** `08_fest.psd`, **or open the fresh file** `08_fest_create.psd` **from the Session 8 Tutorial Files folder on your hard drive.**
   You have the option of using the fresh file so that you can continue on even if you didn't complete the previous tutorial.

2. **Locate the bottom-most layer in the Layers palette, which is labeled Background in italics.**

3. **Double-click the Background layer. In the New Layer dialog box, you can accept the name that Photoshop suggests or type in a meaningful name, such as** texture. **Click OK.**
   That's all you have to do to convert a Background layer to a regular layer with none of the restrictions of a Background layer.

4. **Choose File→Save As. Save the file as** `08_fest_create.psd` **(whether you used your own file or the fresh file provided for you at the beginning of this tutorial). Leave the file open for the next short tutorial.**

What Is a Background Layer?

When you create a new document in the New dialog box, you must choose white, background color, or transparent as the content of that document. If you choose either white or background color, Photoshop creates a special kind of layer at the bottom of the layer stack labeled Background layer. A Background layer acts differently than a regular layer. You can't add another layer beneath it in the Layers palette, change its opacity, or move its contents around in the document window. If you try to erase in the Background layer, you may be surprised that you don't see the gray-and-white transparency checkerboard beneath it, but rather the color in the Background Color box in the toolbox. The most significant restriction of a Background layer is that it doesn't support transparency. Transparent pixels on a Background layer are treated as white. So if you want to create a transparent graphic (for example, a transparent GIF for the Web), you have to delete the Background layer, turn off its visibility before you save a flattened file, or convert the Background layer to a regular layer.

Tutorial
» Selecting Layers

You already learned that you have to select a layer in order to edit it. The trick is making sure that you select the right layer. More often than not, when you get stuck in Photoshop, it's because you're on the wrong layer. In this tutorial, you learn how to use the Auto Select layer features, which can help you avoid this problem.

1. **Check that the file you saved at the end of the previous tutorial, 08_fest_create.psd, is still open.**

2. **Select the Move tool in the toolbox. Click to put a check mark next to Auto Select Layer in the Options bar.**

3. **Click the circle logo at the top left of the image.**
   The circle layer is selected automatically in the Layers palette. Activating Auto Select Layer causes Photoshop to select the topmost layer in the Layers palette that's under your cursor in the document. This can boost your speed and accuracy in selecting a layer. What if, though, you're looking for a layer that's not at the top of the stack at that location? Try using the contextual menu covered in the next step.

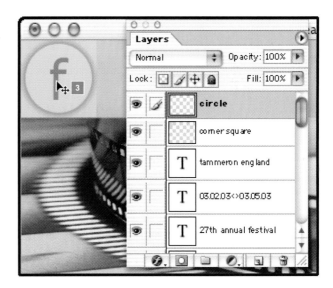

<CAUTION>
If you turn on Auto Select Layer, remember to turn it off when you're done using it. Otherwise, you may not know what's happening the next time that you click in a document with the Move tool and find yourself automatically switched to a layer you don't want.

4. **Ctrl+click (Windows: right-click) the circle logo in the document.**
   You see a contextual menu that lists all the layers on which there are nontransparent pixels at the location under your cursor.

5. **Choose corner square from the contextual menu.**
   The corner square layer is selected automatically in the Layers palette.

6. **Leave this document open for the next tutorial.**
   There's no need to save because you haven't changed any pixels in the image since the previous time that you saved.

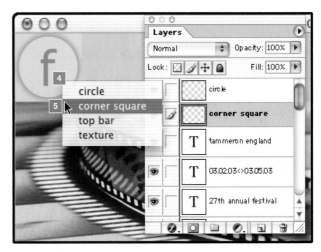

Tutorial
» Changing Layer Visibility

The ability to make layers disappear temporarily from the document window is one of the most useful layer features. After you see how easy it is, you'll use it frequently for a variety of tasks, ranging from deconstructing an inherited file to isolating a layer to work on to creating rollover buttons for a Web page. In this tutorial, you learn how and when to make a layer invisible.

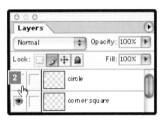

1. **Continue to use the file** `08_fest_create.psd`.

2. **Click the eye icon to the left of the circle layer to make the layer temporarily invisible.**

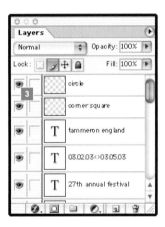

3. **Click in the empty Visibility field on the circle layer again to make the eye icon and the contents of the layer reappear.**

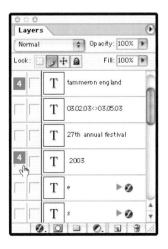

4. **Click the eye icon on the tammeron england type layer and keep the mouse button held down as you run it over the eye icons on the three layers beneath that layer (down through the 2003 layer).** This is a quick way to make multiple layers invisible.

5. **Click the empty Visibility field on the 2003 layer and slide back up the layer stack, turning on the eye icons up through the tammeron england layer.**

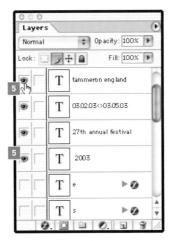

6. **Option+click (Windows: Alt+click) the eye icon on the negs layer.** This makes all the layers invisible except the negs layer. Leave the image like this for the next tutorial so that you can work on the negs layer unimpeded by the content of other layers.

7. **Choose File→Save. Leave** 08_fest_create.psd **open if you want to use it (instead of a fresh copy of this file) in the next tutorial.**

<N O T E>

Option+clicking (Windows: Alt+clicking) the eye icon on the negs layer a second time would make all the layers in the document visible that had been invisible before. This is a useful change from the previous version of the program, in which option+clicking (Windows: Alt+clicking) always made all layers visible.

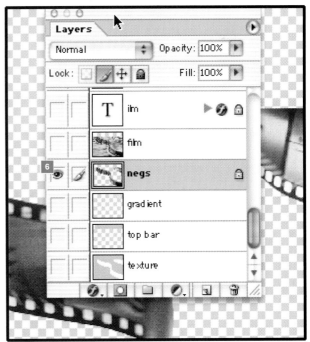

Tutorial
» Locking Layer Properties

The Layers palette contains four buttons (Lock Transparency, Lock Pixels, Lock Position, and Lock All) that you can use to protect various properties of a layer from change. You explore these layer locks in this tutorial.

1. **Use the file that was open at the end of the previous tutorial,** 08_fest_create.psd, **or open the fresh file** 08_fest_eyes.psd **from the Session 8 Tutorial Files folder. If you see an update prompt, click Update.** 08_fest_eyes.psd is a replica of 08_fest_create.psd as it should look at the end of the previous tutorial.

2. **Make sure that the negs layer is selected in the Layers palette and the visibility of all layers except the negs layer is off.**

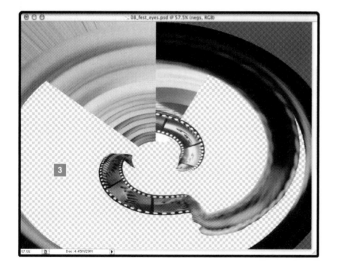

3. **Choose Filter→Distort→Polar Coordinates.** This filter normally distorts all the pixels on the layer, as you can see in the figure.

4. **Choose Edit→Undo.**

5. **Click the Lock Transparency button at the top of the Layers palette.** Notice the hollow lock icon that appears on the negs layer, indicating that this layer is partially locked.

6. **Choose Filter→Polar Coordinates.**

   As you can see, the effect of the filter is now limited to the nontransparent pixels on the layer.

7. **Choose Edit→Undo**.

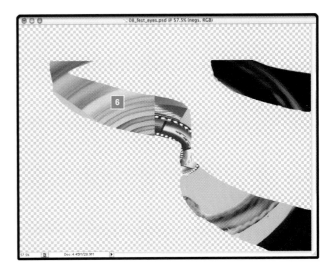

8. **Select the Brush tool in the toolbox and try to draw an X across one of the film frames and into the transparent area indicated by the gray checkerboard.**

   Notice that the paint only appears on the image, not in the transparent area.

9. **Choose Edit→Step Backwards until the X is gone.**

<T I P>
Another effect that you can achieve with the Lock Transparency button is custom-painted text. Use the Type tool and a thick font to type some words in a document. With the type layer selected, choose Layer→Rasterize→Type. (You find out more about rasterizing type in Session 12. For now, take my word for it that rendering is necessary because you can't paint on regular Photoshop type.) Activate the Lock Transparency button in the Layers palette. Then paint ribbons of color across the type. The color appears only on the letters and not on the transparent pixels between the letter forms.

10. **Click the Lock Pixels button at the top of the Layers palette.**

    This lock protects all pixels on a layer, nontransparent as well as transparent, from change. That's why the Lock Transparency button is also grayed out when you activate the Lock Pixels button.

11. **Try to paint anywhere in the document, and you get a warning that you cannot use the Brush tool because the layer is locked. Click OK in the warning box.**

    Although you can't modify any of the pixels on the layer, you can still move or transform the layer.

12. **Click the Lock Transparency and Lock Pixels buttons again to deactivate them.**

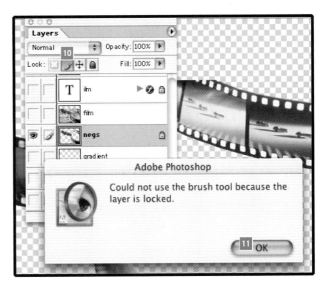

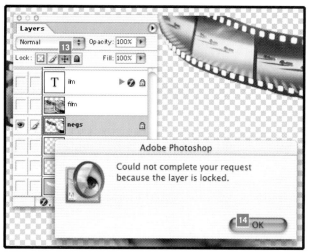

13. Click the Lock Position button in the Layers palette.

14. **Select the Move tool and try to move the content of the film layer. You get a warning that you can't because the layer is locked. Click OK in the warning box.**
    With the Layer Position lock on, you can make changes to pixels, but you can't move or transform the layer.

<TIP>

Instead of going to the toolbox to select the Move tool, you can press and hold the ⌘ key (Windows: Ctrl key) to switch to the Move tool temporarily. As long as you hold that modifier key down, you can use the Move tool.

15. Click the Lock All button at the top of the Layers palette.

16. **Try to move the negs layer with the Move tool. Click OK in the warning box. Then try to paint on the layer with the Brush tool. Again, click OK in the warning box. Neither operation is successful.**
    Lock All activates all three of the other locks at once, causing them all to be grayed out in the Layers palette. Lock All protects all the pixels on a layer from movement, as well as from pixel-changing operations such as filling, painting, and filtering. Notice that the lock icon on the negs layer is now solid, as compared to the hollow icon that appeared when you activated any of the other three locks.

17. **Choose Edit→Undo.**

18. **Choose File→Save and close the file.**

Tutorial
» Changing Layer Opacity

Layer opacity, in simple terms, is how much you can see through the artwork on a layer. Lowering layer opacity makes a layer more transparent so that you can see through to artwork on the layers below. This tutorial shows you how and when to change layer opacity and introduces you to Photoshop's Fill opacity slider.

1. Choose File→Open, navigate to 08_fest_opacity.psd in the Session 8 Tutorial Files folder, and click Open. If you see an update prompt, click Update.

2. Click the corner square layer and drag it to the New Layer icon at the bottom of the Layers palette to create a copy of that layer.

3. Make sure that the corner square copy layer is selected in the Layers palette, and click the Transparency Lock button. Choose Edit→Fill, and fill the layer with white.

4. Select the circle layer in the Layers palette. Click the arrow on the Opacity field at the top of the Layers palette and move the slider down to 40%.
   This causes the yellow circle and the magenta glow around the circle to become more transparent.

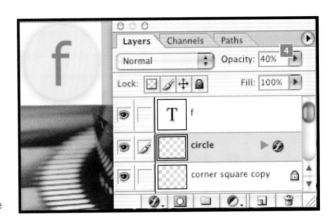

<NOTE>
There's a great shortcut for changing layer opacity. Select the Move tool and type a number between 1 and 100. The Opacity field in the Layers palette automatically reflects that number.

5. Return the Opacity slider to 100%.

6. Make sure that the circle layer is still selected. Click the arrow on the Fill opacity field at the top of the Layers palette and move that slider down to 25%. Leave the regular Opacity field set to 100%.
   Notice that the yellow circle in the document window becomes more transparent, but the magenta glow around the circle remains full-strength. Fill opacity affects only the opacity of art work on a layer; it doesn't affect the opacity of any layer style on that layer.

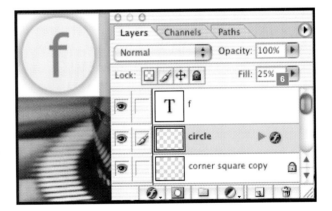

7. Return the Fill opacity slider to 100%.

Why Change Layer Opacity?

There are several reasons to change layer opacity, including the following:

» To composite layers: You do this in the next session.

» To position layers: If you try to align the artwork on separate layers, it's often useful to lower the opacity of the top layer temporarily so that you can see through the artwork below.

» To make rollovers and animations: You can change the opacity of a layer on individual rollover states so that an image appears more or less opaque as the viewer interacts with it. When you make an image in ImageReady, you can create two frames in which you vary the opacity of a layer. Then have the program automatically create in-between frames with varying levels of opacity to make an image appear to fade in or out.

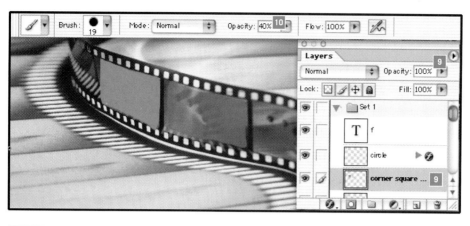

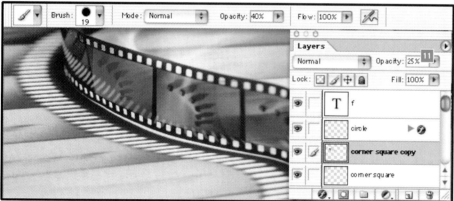

8. **Select the Brush tool in the toolbox and choose a blue color in the Color palette.**

9. **Select the corner square copy layer in the Layers palette and make sure that Opacity is set to 100%. Paint in one of the frames in the image.**

10. **Click the Opacity field in the Brush tool Options bar and reduce that Opacity slider to 40%. Leave Opacity set to 100% in the Layers palette.**
    The Brush tool has its own opacity control that is separate from the Opacity slider in the Layers palette.

11. **Click the Opacity field in the Layers palette and reduce it to 25%.**
    This reduces the opacity of the whole corner square copy layer, so both painted frames are more transparent. Notice that the frame on the right is even more transparent than when it was created at 40% opacity. Both of the opacity controls have had an effect on this frame.

<NOTE>
You may be wondering which opacity control to use when. Use the Opacity field on the Layers palette when you want to affect the opacity of an entire layer. You can't restrict the effect of that Opacity field to just a portion of a layer (even if you select part of the layer, as you may imagine). If you want to affect the opacity of part of a layer, you have to do so when you fill, paint, clone, or erase part of the layer. An Opacity control is on the Options bar for the Brush tools (the Brush and Pencil, the History and Art History brushes, the Gradient and Paint Bucket, the Clone, and the Eraser tools) and in the fill dialog boxes.

12. **Close the file without saving.**
    You use a different file in the next tutorial to learn how to use layer comps.

Tutorial
» Using Layer Comps

Photoshop CS has a terrific new feature called layer comps that shows you multiple versions of a layout in a single file. Using the Layers palette and the Layer Comps palette, you can record variations of a project with different combinations of layer properties—layer visibility, position, and appearance. The variations are all stored in one file for easy viewing. They also can be exported for viewing as a slide show, a Web Photo Gallery, or individual files. In this tutorial, you create a series of layer comps that display variations on a logo design and learn how to automatically export them as a slide show.

1. **Open** 08_fest_comps.psd **from the Session 8 Tutorial Files folder.**

2. **In the Layers palette, click in the empty Visibility field on the circle layer to make the contents of that layer visible.**
   This is the first of several design variations you record as a layer comp.

3. **Choose Window→Layer Comps to open the Layer Comps palette. If the palette opens in the Palette well, drag it onto your desktop. Click the Create New Layer Comp button at the bottom of the Layer Comps palette to open the New Layer Comp dialog box.**

4. **Type** visibility design **as the name of the layer comp. Type** circle layer made visible **in the Comment field. Make sure there are check marks next to all three layer properties—Visibility, Position, and Appearance. Click OK to close the dialog box.**
   The visibility design layer comp is now listed in the Layer Comps palette. Selecting all three layer properties in the New Layer Comp dialog box is the safest choice in most cases. This tells the program to record all these attributes of all layers at this point in time. Use the Comments field to describe what you do to each design or to make notes about a design, for example original design, preferred design, or source of design.

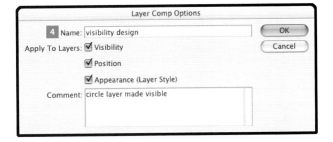

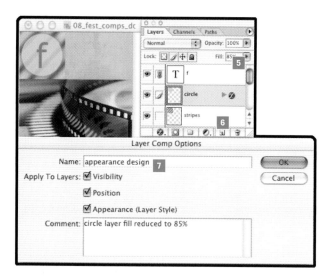

5. **Select the circle layer and type** 85% **in the Fill field in the Layers palette.**
   This reduces the opacity of the fill in the yellow circle.

6. **Click the Create New Layer Comp button at the bottom of the Layer Comps palette to open the New Layer Comps dialog box.**

7. **Type** appearance design **in the Name field, leave all three layer properties selected, and type** circle layer fill reduced to 85% **in the Comments field. Click OK to close the dialog box.**
   The new comp is listed in the Layer Comps palette.

<TIP>
You can reopen the New Layer Comp dialog box at any time to change a layer comp's options by clicking the arrow at the top right of the Layer Comp palette and choosing Layer Comp options.

8. **Select the Move tool. With the circle layer selected and linked to the** f **layer in the Layers palette, click in the document window and drag the logo down and to the right.**

9. **Repeat steps 6 and 7, typing the following in the New Layer Comp dialog box—Name:** position design, **Comment:** circle & layers moved.
   You have a total of three layer comps, each of which records the position, visibility, and appearance (which includes opacity, fill opacity, blending mode, and layer style) of all layers in the image at a particular point in time. Clicking an arrow next to a layer comp reveals your descriptive comment. In the next steps you learn how to apply and view your layer comps.

10. **In the Layer Comps palette click in the empty field to the left of the visibility design layer comp.**
    An Apply Layer Comp icon appears in the field and this layer comp is displayed in the image in the document window.

11. **Click on the Next or Previous buttons at the bottom of the Layer Comps Palette.**

12. **In the Layer Comps palette, click in the empty field to the left of the Last Document State.**
    An Apply Layer Comp icon appears in the field and the document window displays the last state of the image as it was before any layer comp was applied.

13. **Choose File→Save.**
    The 08_comp.psd file is saved with three layer comps. You can view the finished file by opening 08_comp_done.psd from the Session 8 Tutorial Files. In the next steps you learn how to export your layer comps for viewing as an animated slide show.

14. **Choose File→Scripts→Layer Comps to PDFs to open the Layer Comps To PDF window.**
    Photoshop CS ships with several scripts for exporting Layer Comps in special viewing formats. The script you've chosen exports layer comps as a slide show in PDF format. Alternatively, you can export layer comps as a Web Photo Gallery site that you can upload to the Internet, or as individual files.

15. **Click the Browse button and choose the Session 08 Tutorial Files folder as a destination for the PDF file. Leave Selected Layer Comps Only unchecked so that all your layer comps appear in the slide show.**

16. **Make sure Advance Every is checked, and type 3 in the Seconds field to cause your layer comp slides to change automatically every 3 seconds. Leave Loop after last page unchecked so your slide doesn't play over and over.**

17. **Click Run. If you see any Embedded Profile Mismatch prompts, click OK.**
    Photoshop begins the process of automatically creating a slide show in PDF format. The process pauses at each image that has an embedded color profile that differs from the RGB working space in your Color Settings so that you can tell the program how to handle the mismatch.

18. **Sit back and enjoy the slide show. When it's done, click the Esc (Escape) key on your keyboard to exit the full screen view.**
    When Photoshop has finished creating your slide show, Acrobat Reader or Acrobat launches automatically and displays the slide show, which runs against a full black screen. Each slide in the show is a design variation that you saved as a layer comp.

< N O T E >
Instead of saving a large number of Layer Comps each time you make changes to your document, you can update the ones you already have. If you have a Comp that you like, and make changes to a layer, select the Layer Comp in the palette, and then click the Update Layer Comp icon (the circling arrows) at the bottom of the Layer Comps palette.

< N O T E >
If you don't have Acrobat Reader or Acrobat installed on your computer, download the free PDF viewing program, Acrobat Reader, from the Adobe Web site, www.adobe.com.

< N O T E >
Exporting layer comps to a PDF slide show is an impressive way to show multiple design variations to clients. You can burn the PDF file onto a CD or DVD disk, post it on a Web site, or send it by e-mail. It's viewable by anyone who takes advantage of the free download of Acrobat Reader from the Adobe Web site.

Layer Comp Cautions

You can usually restore an image to its original state, so that it appears as it would with no layer comps applied, by clicking the empty field next to Last Document State in the Layer Comp palette. However, you may lose that ability and permanently alter existing layer comps if you make a nonreversible change to the image, such as merging layers, deleting layers, or changing image modes. When you make a nonreversible change, you see a yellow caution icon and a rollover message (Layer Comp Cannot Be Fully Restored) on each affected layer comp. At that point you can:

» Update layer comps by highlighting them and clicking the Update Layer Comps button. This changes layer comp parameters and removes the yellow icons.

» Ignore the cautions. This results in some changes to layer comps, although consequences are unpredictable. You can still remove the yellow icons by Ctrl+clicking (Windows: right-clicking) an icon and choosing one of the removal commands.

» Undo a nonreversible change by stepping backward in the History palette. This restores the existing layer comps but not the Last Document State.

Tutorial
» Linking Layers

You can link layers together for the purpose of moving them together, transforming them together, and aligning them to each other or to the document. You try all of this in this tutorial.

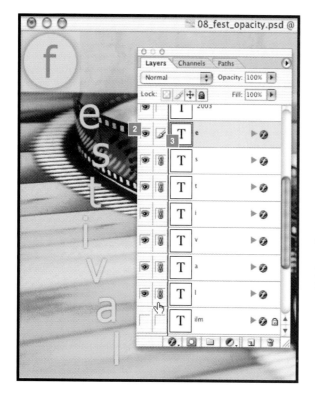

1. **Open** 08_fest_opacity.psd **from the Session 8 Tutorial Files folder on your hard drive or use the copy you worked with in an earlier tutorial. If you see an Embedded Profile Mismatch warning, click OK.**

2. **Click and drag the scroll bar in the Layers palette so that you can see the type layers labeled e, s, t, i, v, a, and l. Turn on the eye icons for each of these letter layers so that they are visible in the document.**

3. **Select the e layer in the Layers palette. Click in the Link field to the left of that layer and drag down through the Link fields to the l layer.**
   This adds a link to each of the letter layers, linking them all to the selected e layer.

<CAUTION>
Be careful not to click in the link field next to any other layer, or you will include it in this group of linked layers. You'll know if you've inadvertently included another layer because you'll see it moving as you proceed through this tutorial. If that happens, click in the link field of that layer again and move it back to its original location.

4. **Select the Move tool in the toolbox and click and drag in the document window to move the letter e into position under the f logo in the document, as shown in the figure.**
   Notice that all the other letters move with the e because they're linked to the selected e layer.

5. **Make sure that the e layer is still selected in the Layers palette and the Move tool is still selected in the toolbox. Click the Align Horizontal Centers button in the Options bar.**
   This vertically aligns all the linked letters to the letter e.

6. **Click the Distribute Vertical Centers button in the Options bar.**
   You see a slight movement in some of the letters in the middle of the group. This distributes the letters so that there is an equal amount of space between their centers.

7. **Choose Edit→Transform→Skew.**
   This creates a bounding box with editable points around all the artwork on the linked layers.

8. **Click one of the corner points and drag to slant the linked letters. Click the Cancel icon on the right side of the Options bar to cancel the transformation.**

Experiment with some of the other transformation choices if you like—scale, rotate, and flip. Distort and perspective aren't available unless you rasterize these type layers. You can choose from the commands in the Transform menu or use Free Transform from the Edit menu. To accept a transformation and dismiss the bounding box, press Return (Windows: Enter) on your keyboard.

<NOTE>

You can transform either linked layers as you did here, a single layer (select that layer in the Layers palette and use the Edit→ Transform commands), the contents of a selection (create a selection and then use the Edit→Transform commands), or even a selection outline (create a selection and choose Select→ Transform Selection).

Why Link Layers?

There are several reasons to link layers, including the following:

» To move multiple layers together.

» To align objects on individual layers to one another, as you do in this tutorial. This is also useful for making multiple buttons for a Web page, as you see in Bonus Session 1.

» To quickly create a layer set from linked layers, as you see in the next tutorial.

» To transform the artwork on multiple layers at once.

» To rasterize multiple layers at the same time (by choosing Layer→Rasterize→Linked Layers). You learn about rasterizing type layers in Session 12.

Aligning Linked Layers to the Document Window

The steps of this tutorial show you how to align and distribute objects on separate layers relative to one another, but what if you want to align layered artwork to the document? The secret is to select the whole document before aligning, which tells Photoshop to align to the selection. For example, to position these linked layers in the vertical center of the document window, choose Select→All from the menu bar at the top of the screen. Then click the Align Vertical Centers button on the Move tool Options bar. When you're done, deselect and choose Edit→Step Backward to send the letters back to the left side of the document.

9. **If you experimented with other transformations, as suggested in step 8, choose Edit→Step Backward to eliminate those transformations.**
   The letters should look as they do in this figure when you're done.

10. **Choose File→Save. Leave** 08_fest_opacity.psd **open.**

<CAUTION>
Each time that you accept a transformation, Photoshop resamples pixels, which can degrade the image. If you plan to do multiple transformations, do them all and then press Return or Enter.

Tutorial
» Organizing Layers in Layer Sets

Layer sets are great for organizing layers in the Layers palette, especially when you have lots of layers in a document. Layer sets are also useful for performing operations on multiple layers that you can't accomplish with linked layers, such as changing layer opacity, visibility, and blending modes. In this tutorial, you learn how to create and use layer sets.

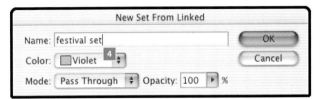

1. **Use the file that you saved in the previous tutorial, 08_fest_opacity.psd, or open the fresh file 08_fest_links.psd from the Session 8 Tutorial Files folder on your hard drive.**
   08_fest_links.psd is a copy of 08_fest_opacity.psd as the file should look at the end of the previous tutorial.

2. **Check that the letter layers e, s, t, i, v, a, and l are still linked in the Layers palette. If they're not, run your cursor down the column of link fields on these layers to relink the layers.**

3. **Select any of the linked letter layers in the Layers palette. Click the arrow at the top right of the Layers palette and choose New Set from Linked.**

4. **In the New Set From Linked dialog box, type festival set in the Name field. Choose a color code to apply to the layer set and each of its layers for quick identification. Leave Mode set to Pass Through and Opacity set to 100% (see the Layer Set Mode and Opacity sidebar for an explanation of these items). Click OK.**
   This is the fastest way to create a layer set that contains multiple existing layers.

5. **Click the arrow on the festival set in the Layers palette to open that set.**
   You see all the layers from which you made that set. Notice that each of the layers in the set is indented and bears the color code that you chose for the set.

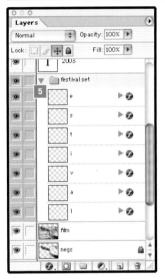

Layer Set Mode and Opacity

When you put layers into a layer set, you have the opportunity to apply a second round of layer blending and opacity; layer blending is covered in Session 9. Photoshop first blends together the layers in the set according to the blending modes and opacity of individual layers. Then it blends the entire layer set with other layers in the image using the blending mode and opacity assigned to the set. When you choose Pass Through as the layer set's blending mode, no additional blending is done. When you choose 100% as the layer set's opacity, there are no additional opacity changes.

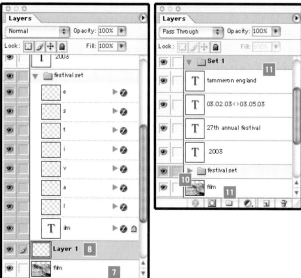

6. **Click the empty Visibility field on the type layer labeled ilm to make that layer visible in the document. Click that layer in the Layers palette and drag it on top of the festival set to add the layer to that set.**
This is how to add an existing layer to a layer set. Notice that the film layer is now indented under the festival set and bears the purple code of that set.

7. **Make sure that the festival set is open and any layer in the set, or the set itself, is selected. Click the New Layer icon at the bottom of the Layers palette.**
This creates a new layer inside the layer set, called Layer 1.

8. **Click Layer 1 and drag it on top of the festival set to remove it from the set and place it directly below the set.**
Another way to remove a layer from a set is to click and drag it elsewhere in the layer stack. I prefer the first way because I always know where to find the removed layer.

<CAUTION>
Notice that even though you removed Layer 1 from the layer set, it retained its purple color code. This defeats the purpose of color coding to indicate assignment to a layer set. To remove the color code, Ctrl+click (Windows: right-click) Layer 1 and choose Layer Properties from the contextual menu. This opens the Layer Properties dialog box in which you can click the Color button and choose a new color or none.

9. **Click Layer 1 and drag it onto the Trash icon at the bottom of the Layers palette.**

10. **Click the arrow on the festival set to close that set and shorten your Layers palette.**

11. **Click the tammeron england layer in the Layers palette. Click the New Layer Set icon at the bottom of the palette to create a new set, Set 1, above the selected layer.**

12. **Double-click Set 1 and rename it** headline set.

13. **Drag each of the four type layers located under the headline set in the Layers palette on top of that set to move them into the set. Then click the triangle on the headline set to close it.**
    If you want to give the headline set a color, Ctrl+click (Windows: right-click) the headline set and choose Layer Set Properties from the contextual menu. This opens the Layer Set Properties dialog box, in which you can click the Color button. When you're done, click the arrow on the headline set to close the set.

14. **Create one more layer set using the logo layers. Combine the f, circle, and corner square layers into a layer set named logo set.**
    This may not be the most exciting task in the world, but when you're done, you'll be happy to have a shorter, more manageable Layers palette. The layers at the bottom of the Layers palette are not part of a layer set. You use them to construct nested layer sets in the next tutorial.

<NOTE>
The introduction to this tutorial mentioned that the benefit of using layer sets, other than organization, is its ability to affect multiple layers with an operation. In the next steps, you'll try some examples of what I mean. In addition to these operations, you can apply a layer mask to a layer set, you can alter the blending mode of a layer set, and you can transform a layer set.

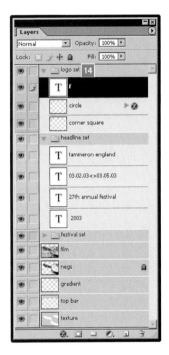

15. **Select the logo set in the Layers palette. Select the Move tool and click and drag in the document window to move all the layers in this set around in the document window together. When you're done observing this, choose Edit→Undo.**

<NOTE>
The rest of the steps in this tutorial are for more advanced users, so don't worry if you don't completely understand them. The main point to take from them is that you can change the opacity of all layers in a layer set together, after Photoshop accounts for opacity levels assigned to individual layers.

16. **Double-click (Windows: Alt+double-click) the f layer in the logo layer set.**
    This opens the Layer Style dialog box.

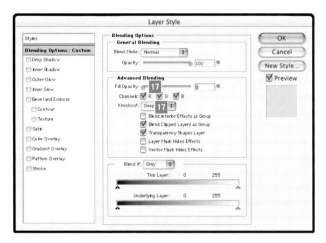

17. **In the Layer Style dialog box, move the Fill Opacity slider all the way to 0%. Then click the Knockout button and choose Deep.**
This makes the fill on the f layer completely transparent, enabling you to see all the way down to the transparent pixels behind the image. In the next step, you see a neat trick you can do only when you're working on a layer that's in a layer set.

< N O T E >
This Fill Opacity slider is a copy of the Fill Opacity slider on the Layers palette, which you worked with earlier in this session. The only difference is that this copy of the slider comes with options.

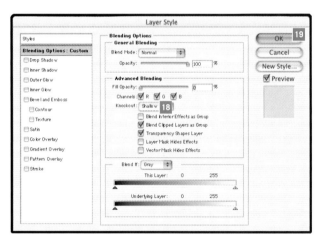

18. **Click the Knockout button again and choose Shallow.**
Now you can see through the fill on the f layer only down to the bottom-most layer in the logo layer set (the orange patterned layer called top bar).

19. **Click Cancel to exit the Layer Style dialog box without applying the new setting.**
You learn more about the Layer Style dialog box in Session 10.

20. **Choose File→Save As. Save the file as** 08_fest_links.psd, **regardless of whether you used your own file or the fresh file provided for you at the beginning of this tutorial. Leave the file open for the next exercise.**

Tutorial
» Adding a Nested Layer Set

In the previous tutorial you organized most of the layers in your project file into layer sets. Not only is it simpler to view the contents of your project in the Layer palette, but you also learned that you can apply an operation to the entire set at one time. In this tutorial, you learn how to nest a layer set within another layer set and how to work with the groups of layers.

1. **Use the file that you saved in the previous tutorial.**

2. **Select the film layer. Click the Link field on the negs layer to link the two layers.**
   You create a new layer set for the fields.

3. **Click the arrow at the top right of the Layers palette and choose New Set from Linked.**
   In the New Set From Linked dialog box, type **background set** in the Name field. Choose a color code. Click OK to close the dialog box.

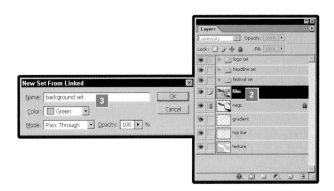

4. **Create one more layer set containing the gradient, sdfsfd, and texture layers. Name the layer set** background 2.

5. **Click the background 2 layer set label in the Layers palette. Drag it on top of the background layer set label and release the mouse.**
   The background 2 layer set is now nested within the background layer set. You can see in the Layers palette that the nested layer set is indented.

6. **Click the background 2 layer set label to select it. Click the Opacity field on the Layers palette and move the Opacity slider to 50%.**
   The opacity of the three layers in the background 2 layer set is lowered, but the images in the background layer set aren't affected.

7. **Click on the background layer set label. Type** 50% **in the Opacity field on the Layers palette.**

   The opacity of the film and negs layers in the background layer set decreases to 50%. The opacity of the gradient, top bar, and texture layers in the background 2 layer set also decreases (to around 25%), because these layers are in a layer set that is nested within the background 2 layer set. The opacity settings of the two layer sets are cumulative.

8. **Choose Edit→Step Backward until the two layer sets are 100% opaque again.**

9. **Drag the three layers from the background 2 layer set into the parent background set, keeping them in the same order.**

10. **Click the background 2 layer set label. Drag the empty background 2 layer set folder to the Trash icon.**

11. **Click the arrows on all the layer sets to close them.**

12. **Choose File→Save to save the file. Leave the file open for the next tutorial.**

Tutorial
» Editing with Adjustment Layers

There are two special kinds of layers—adjustment layers and fill layers—with which you can make changes to an image without affecting the pixels of the original layers. This nondestructive editing is a real advantage because it gives you the flexibility to change your design decisions without having to start over. In this tutorial, you are introduced to adjustment layers, which you can use to make editable adjustments to image color and tone. In the following tutorial, you work with fill layers, which you can use to add editable color, pattern, or gradient to your image.

1. **Make sure that** 08_fest_links.psd **is open from the previous tutorial or open** 08_fest_sets.psd **from the Session 8 Tutorial Files folder.**
   08_fest_sets.psd is a copy of 08_fest_links.psd, as the latter file should look at the end of the previous tutorial.

2. **Click the arrow on the background set to open that set.**

3. **Select the top bar layer in the Layers palette. Choose Select→ Load Selection. In the Load Selection dialog box, make sure that the Channel button is set to top bar Transparency. Click OK.**
   You may remember this technique for selecting all the artwork on a transparent layer from Session 7.

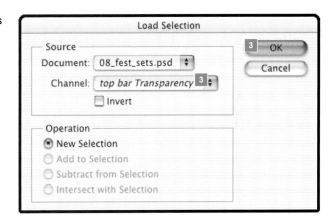

<NOTE>
You can apply an adjustment layer to a selected area or to the whole image. If you didn't want the adjustment to be limited to just a portion of the image, you would skip the step of making a selection before you create the adjustment layer.

4. **Click the New Fill or Adjustment Layer button at the bottom of the Layers palette and choose Hue/Saturation.**
   This opens the Hue/Saturation dialog box.

<NOTE>
There are many flavors of adjustments in this menu, including Levels, Curves, Variations, and some auto-adjustments. These are all different ways of adjusting the tonality and color of an image. You work with some of these other adjustments in Sessions 14 and 15.

<NOTE>
Don't confuse an adjustment layer with a regular adjustment (accessible from the Image→Adjustments menu). The difference is that a regular adjustment is applied directly to the selected layer, permanently altering the pixels of that layer. It's preferable to use the adjustment layer version of any of the adjustment commands because adjustment layers are nondestructive to the underlying image layers.

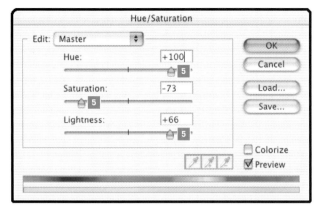

5. Drag the Hue slider to +100 to change the hue of the selected portion of the selected area to green. Drag the Saturation slider to −73 to desaturate the color and drag the Lightness slider to +66 to lighten the color. Click OK.

There is nothing magical about these particular numbers. I arrived at them by watching the live preview in the document window as I moved the sliders until I got the color I wanted.

< N O T E >

Notice the new Hue/Saturation adjustment layer in the Layers palette. It contains a thumbnail on the left that represents the adjustment and a thumbnail on the right that represents a layer mask defined by the selection that you made in step 3. This mask limits the effect of the adjustment layer to the top bar in the image.

< N O T E >

An adjustment layer affects pixels on all the layers beneath it in the Layers stack, unless you specfically restrict its effect to the layer directly beneath the adjustment layer. To do that, hold the Option (Windows: Alt) key and move your cursor over the line between the adjustment layer and the layer beneath it. Click when the cursor changes to an icon of two circles. This groups the two layers and limits the adjustment to the layer that's been grouped with the adjustment layer. Repeat this to ungroup these layers.

6. Turn the eye icon off on the adjustment layer, to see that none of the pixels of the underlying top bar layer have been changed. When you're done observing, turn the eye icon back on.

This illustrates the nondestructive nature of adjustment layers, which is one of the main advantages that they offer over other methods of correcting tone and color.

7. Double-click the thumbnail on the left side of the adjustment layer in the Layers palette to reopen the Hue/Saturation dialog box. Click the Hue slider and move it to −161 to change the color of the adjustment to blue. Click OK.

You can reopen and make changes in this dialog box as many times as you want without harming the original artwork. The ability to edit your adjustments is the other major benefit of using adjustment layers to control tone and color.

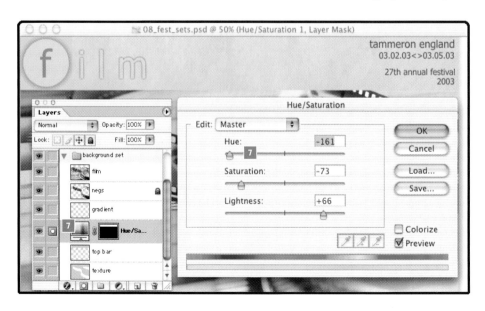

8. **Select the Rectangular Marquee tool in the toolbox. Click and drag to create a vertical selection on the left side of the document like that shown in the figure.**

9. **Click the New Fill or Adjustment Layer button at the bottom of the Layers palette and choose Hue/Saturation. Set Hue to +173, Saturation to –83, and Lightness to +44. Click OK.**
   This creates a vertical bar in the image made entirely of adjusted color in a second Hue/Saturation adjustment layer.

10. **Choose File→Save As. Save this file as** `08_fest_sets.psd`**, regardless of whether you used your own file or the fresh file provided for you at the beginning of this tutorial. Leave the file open for the next tutorial.**

Tutorial
» Using Fill Layers

Fill layers are similar to adjustment layers in that they don't permanently change the existing image and they are easily edited. Fill layers offer a means of adding editable solid colors, patterns, and gradients in selected areas of an image or across an entire image. Try them out in this tutorial.

1. **Make sure that** 08_fest_sets.psd **is open from the previous tutorial.**

2. **Select the film layer in the Layers palette.**

3. **Select the Polygonal Lasso tool in the Layers palette and click around the edges of one of the frames in the image to select that frame.**

4. **Choose Select→Feather and choose 1 pixel as the Feather Radius to soften the edges of the selection.**

5. **Click the New Adjustment or Fill Layer button at the bottom of the Layers palette and choose Pattern from the menu.**

6. **In the Pattern Fill dialog box, click the pattern sample down arrow to open the Pattern Picker.**

7. **Click the arrow on the Pattern Picker and choose Nature Patterns. Click OK at the prompt to replace the current patterns. Select the leaves pattern and click OK in the Pattern Fill dialog box.**
   This fills the frame with the pattern and creates a new fill layer in the Layers palette.

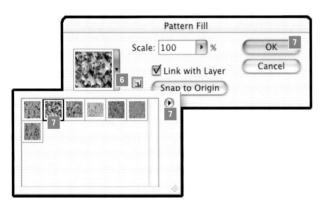

<N O T E>
Leaving the Link with Layer option checked in the Pattern Fill dialog box makes the pattern move when you move the layer. Clicking Snap to Origin returns the pattern to its original location. Scale transforms the pattern so that it appears bigger or smaller in the image. You can leave all of these Pattern Fill options at their defaults for now.

<N O T E>
A fill layer, like an adjustment layer, has two thumbnails. The thumbnail on the left represents the fill, and the thumbnail on the right represents the mask that determines where the fill is visible in the image.

8. **Double-click the pattern thumbnail on the left of the Pattern Fill layer to reopen the Pattern Fill dialog box. This time, choose the blue daisies pattern from the Pattern Picker. Click OK.**

   That's how easy it is to edit a Pattern Fill layer.

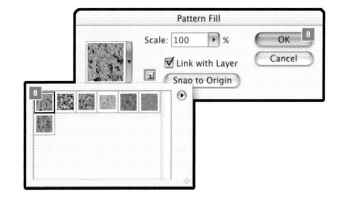

9. **Click the Layer Blending Mode button at the top left of the Layers palette and choose Multiply to blend the pattern with the underlying image.**

   You learn more about layer blending modes in Session 9.

10. **Repeat steps 2 through 7 on another frame in the image. Then choose Layer→Change Layer Content→Gradient.**

   This changes the nature of the fill from a pattern to a gradient and opens the Gradient Fill dialog box.

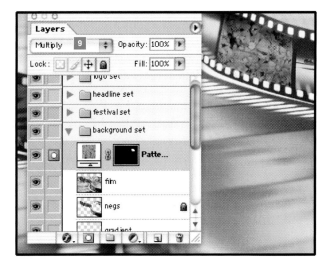

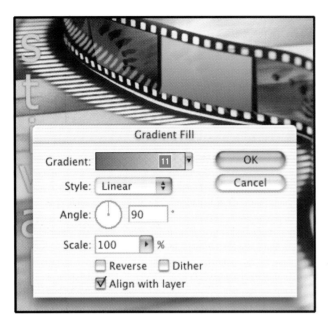

11. Click the gradient bar in the Gradient Fill dialog box to open the Gradient Editor. Create a magenta (R: 111, B: 41, G: 109) to yellow (R: 248, G: 229, B: 50) gradient. (If you've forgotten how to create your own gradient in the Gradient Editor, turn back to Session 5.) Click OK in the Gradient Editor and OK in the Gradient Fill dialog box.

12. Click the Layer Blending Mode button in the Layers palette and choose Overlay to blend the gradient fill with the image.

13. Repeat steps 2 through 5 on a new frame in the image, except this time choose Solid Color from the menu that appears when you click the New Adjustment or Fill Layer button on the Layers palette. This opens the Color Picker.

14. Choose a light orange (try R: 255, G: 210, B: 128) in the Color Picker and click OK.

15. Click the Layer Blending Mode button in the Layers palette and choose Color to blend the solid color fill with the image.

16. Click the arrow on the background set to close that layer set, so your Layers palette is neatly organized.

17. Choose File→Save As and rename the file 08_fest_end.psd. This is a final collage for your complete course project, so navigate to your collages folder and click Save to save it there.

» Session Review

This session covered layers. You learned to create layers from scratch, from another layer, and from another document. You practiced selecting layers with Auto-Select features. You learned how and when to change layer visibility, to lock layer properties, to work with layers, and to link layers. Then you created layer sets to manage your layers and work with multiple layers at once. Finally, you learned about two special kinds of layers—adjustment and fill layers. These questions will help you review this session.

1. Why is it important to give layers meaningful names? (See "Tutorial: Creating Layers.")

2. How do you rename a layer in Photoshop 7? (See "Tutorial: Creating Layers.")

3. When would you add a clipping path to an object on a layer? (See "Tutorial: Creating Layers.")

4. Do empty layers contribute to file size? (See "Tutorial: Creating Layers.")

5. Name one of the limitations a Background layer has. (See "Tutorial: Converting a Background Layer.")

6. How do you convert a Background layer to a regular layer? (See "Tutorial: Converting a Background Layer.")

7. What does the Auto Select Layer option do? (See "Tutorial: Selecting Layers.")

8. How do you turn off the visibility of a layer? (See "Tutorial: Changing Layer Visibility.")

9. How do you turn off the visibility of all layers except one? (See "Tutorial: Changing Layer Visibility.")

10. Name two reasons that you may want to change layer visibility. (See "Tutorial: Changing Layer Visibility.")

11. Name the four layer lock buttons on the Layers palette. (See "Tutorial: Locking Layer Properties.")

12. What does the Lock Transparency button on the Layers palette do? (See "Tutorial: Locking Layer Properties.")

13. Name one reason that you may want to change layer opacity. (See "Tutorial: Changing Layer Opacity.")

14. What's the difference between fill opacity and regular layer opacity? (See "Tutorial: Changing Layer Opacity.")

15. What's the advantage of using layer comps? What purposes can layer comps be used for? (See "Tutorial: Using Layer Comps.")

16. Are layer comps automatically created when you designate the layers for the comp? (See "Tutorial: Using Layer Comps.")

17. Name two reasons that you may want to link layers together. (See "Tutorial: Linking Layers.")

18. Name two benefits of using layer sets. (See "Tutorial: Organizing Layers in Layer Sets.")

19. What effect does making opacity changes to the parent layer set have on a nested layer set? (See "Tutorial: Adding a Nested Layer Set.")

20. Name one advantage of using an adjustment layer rather than a regular adjustment to edit tone or color. (See "Tutorial: Editing with Adjustment Layers.")

21. What is a fill layer? (See "Tutorial: Using Fill Layers.")

f ilm

festival

tammeron england
03.02.03<>03.05.03

27th annual festival
2003

Compositing Images

screenings
thursday 8 pm
friday 7 pm
saturday 8 pm
saturday 10pm
sunday 12 pm
sunday 4 pm

Session Introduction

Putting images together is what Photoshop is all about, but it isn't as easy as it looks. To do it right requires understanding some of the more advanced Photoshop features, such as layer masks, vector masks, Blending sliders, and layer blending modes. In this session, you are introduced to those features, and you learn how to use some tools—rulers, guides, and the Crop tool—that help you composite images. This session pulls together many of the skills that you learned in previous sessions.

TOOLS YOU'LL USE
Crop tool, layer mask, vector mask, Blending sliders, Measure tool, rulers, guides, and blending modes

CD-ROM FILES NEEDED
09_screening.psd, 09_curtain.psd,
09_screening_mask.psd, 09_screening_blend.psd,
09_screening_mode.psd, 09_screening_end.psd,
09_lens.psd, and 09_vintage.psd

TIME REQUIRED
60 minutes

Tutorial
» Making Images Compatible

You make your job easier and get better results if you take some time before you start compositing to make your images compatible in terms of size and style. In this tutorial, you change the magnification of two images to view their relative size, crop one of the images to match the other, and adjust color before beginning to collage the images.

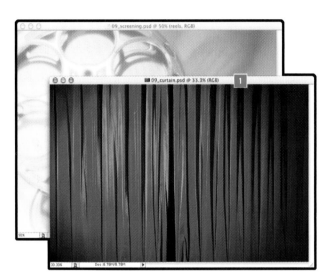

1. **Open two files from the Session 9 Tutorial Files folder on your hard drive**—09_curtain.psd **and** 09_screening.psd. Depending on the size of your monitor, the two images may open at different magnifications that make them look, at first glance, approximately the same size. However, this is deceptive. You can't get a true picture of the relative size of two documents on-screen unless they are set to the same magnification. You fix this in the next steps.

   <TIP>
   Of course, how the images look on your monitor and how much of them you see depends on their size as well.

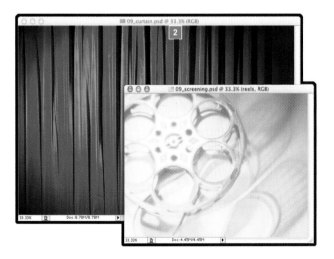

2. **Select the Zoom tool, set the tool to zoom in, and click one or both documents to set both to 33% magnification.** Now you can see that 09_curtain.psd is bigger than 09_screening.psd.

3. **Click the arrow at the bottom of either document window and choose Document Dimensions from the pop-up Information menu.**
You see the dimensions in pixels of both of the documents, confirming that 09_curtain.psd is the bigger document. The relevant unit of measurement when you're comparing images on-screen is pixels. If you see pixels here, go to Photoshop→Preferences→Units and Rulers (Windows: Edit→Preferences→Units and Rulers) and change the Rulers field to pixels.

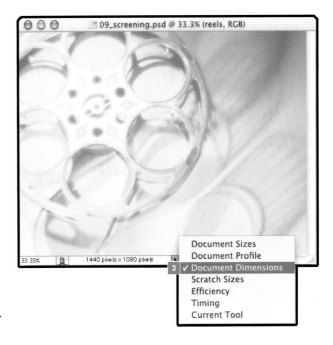

<NOTE>
09_screening.psd has been sized to fit on a page of your final project, so you have to match the size of 09_curtain.psd to 09_screening.psd (1440 pixels x 1080 pixels). This sounds like it might require some serious math, but it doesn't at all. Photoshop matches the two images for you with just a click of the Crop tool, as you see in the next steps.

4. **Select the Crop tool from the toolbox.**

5. **Click the Clear button on the Options bar to clear the option fields.**
This deletes any Crop tool settings that you may have made previously.

6. **Make sure that 09_screening.psd is the active image and click Front Image.**
This inserts the pixel dimensions and resolution of 09_screening.psd in the Crop tool Options bar. This information is applied when you use the Crop tool to crop another image.

<TIP>
The double arrows between the Width and Height fields on the Crop tool Options bar are a new feature that allows you to switch the values entered in those two fields.

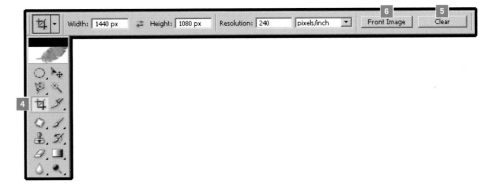

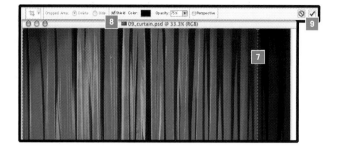

7. **Click and drag in the** `09_curtain.psd` **document window to drag the crop boundary.**

    A crop boundary looks just like a selection boundary. It's a little hard to see in the figure, but it is there.

8. **Uncheck Shield on the Options bar so that you can get a better view of the area to be cropped away.**

    You can click and drag to reposition or rotate the crop outline. Accept the default position for now.

9. **Click the Check Mark icon on the Options bar to accept your crop settings and initiate the crop.**

    Alternatively, you can press Return or Enter on your keyboard.

<N O T E >

Photoshop not only crops the curtain image, but also resamples the image so that it is the same size in pixels as `09_screening.psd`. This feature is a real time-saver!

<N O T E >

Another way to resize images to make them compatible for collaging is to use the Transform→Scale command. You try that in the tutorial "Using Blending Sliders to Composite" later in this session.

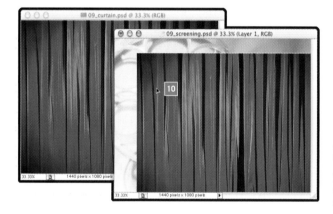

10. **Click inside** `09_curtain.psd` **and drag it into the** `09_screening.psd` **document window.**

    This copies the curtain image into the main image and creates a new layer in the Layers palette.

11. **Double-click the new Layer 1 in** `09_screening.psd` **and rename it** curtain.

12. **You can close** `09_curtain.psd` **without saving.**

<N O T E >

There are a lot of design considerations to take into account when you're choosing images to put together, ranging from the direction of shadows and light sources to texture, perspective, and point of view. An important design element that can make or break a composite image is color. In the next steps, you'll adjust the rich color of the curtain image to bring it into line with the softer gold theme of the main image.

13. **Select the curtain layer in the Layers palette. Choose Layer→New Adjustment Layer→Hue/Saturation.**

    This opens the New Layer dialog box.

14. **Click the Group With Previous Layer check box and click OK.**

    Normally an adjustment layer affects all the layers below it. Group With Previous Layer restricts the effect of an adjustment layer to the layer immediately below it. In the last session, you learned another way to do this—by Option+clicking (Windows: Alt+clicking) the border between layers after, rather than before, creating an adjustment layer.

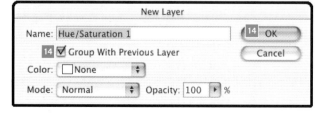

15. In the Hue/Saturation dialog box, change the Hue to +40 and the Lightness to +3 and click OK.

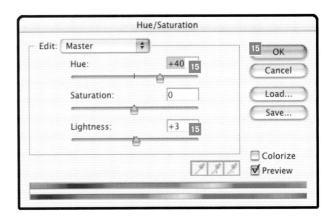

16. Select the curtain layer in the Layers palette and click and drag the curtain image in the document window to move it into position over the main layer.

17. Choose File→Save and leave 09_screening.psd open for the next tutorial.

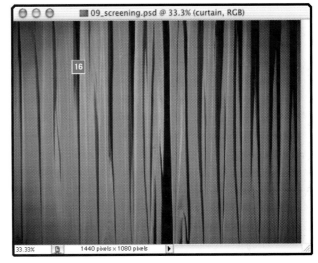

Match Color Adjustment

One way to adjust the color in the curtain layer is to match it to the color of the yellow reels layer using the powerful Match Color adjustment that is new to Photoshop CS. Start with a fresh copy of 09_screening.psd. Select the curtain layer in the Layers palette to tell the program that this is the target layer (the layer to be changed). Then choose Image→Adjustments→Match Color to open the Match Color dialog box. Make sure the Preview option is checked and the Source field is set to 09_screening.psd. Click in the Layer field and choose reels to set the reels layer as the source of color. The live preview in the document window displays the curtain layer with yellow hues sampled from the reels layer. Click on Fade and scrub to the right (using the new scrubby slider feature) to decrease the Match Color adjustment, moving the colors toward reddish-gold. Click on Luminance and scrub to the left to adjust brightness, and click on Color Intensity and scrub

to the left to adjust saturation. If the curtain layer still doesn't display the dark reddish-gold color you want, click the Cancel button, make a selection around a dark gold area in the reels layer, and redo the steps above. Click OK to apply the Match Color adjustment to the curtain layer.

The Match Color adjustment also comes in handy to match colors between two separate images, offering a quick way to correct a photograph that has a color cast or exposure problems. With both images open, click on the target image to make it active. Then choose Image→Adjustments→Match Color to open the Match Color dialog box and choose the filename of the other image in the Source field. To fine tune the results, use the sliders in the dialog box or go back and make selections around color areas in the source and/or target images.

Tutorial
» Joining Images with Layer Masks

A layer mask is a bitmapped grayscale image that you can attach to a layer of artwork. You can paint on a mask with black, white, or shades of gray to hide and reveal artwork on the attached layer. One popular use for layer masks is to gradually fade one layered image into another. You can accomplish this by painting on the mask with feathered fills, soft brushes, or gradients, as you do in this tutorial.

1. **Use** `09_screening.psd`, **which should be open from the previous tutorial.**

2. **Make sure that the curtain layer is selected in the Layers palette and click the Add Layer Mask icon on the bottom of the palette.**
   This adds a white thumbnail on the right side of the curtain layer. Another way to add this same kind of mask is to choose Layer→Add Layer Mask→Reveal All.

<NOTE>
The right thumbnail represents the layer mask, the left thumbnail represents the regular layer, and the link symbol is the tie between the two. When the link is showing, moving either the mask or the layer causes the other to move with it. If you deactivate the link (by clicking on it), the two components of this layer move separately. You can use this feature to reposition a layer mask or to animate a mask to create different frames for an animated GIF in ImageReady.

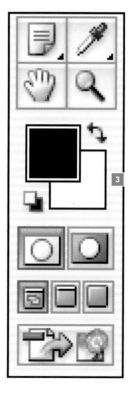

3. **Press the keyboard shortcut D to set white as the foreground color and black as the background color in the toolbox. Then press X to switch those colors so that black is the foreground color.**
   These shortcuts come in particularly handy when you work with masks because you generally use only black, white, and shades of gray on a layer mask. You use these shortcuts throughout this session.

4. **Select the Gradient tool in the toolbox. Click the Gradient bar in the Options bar to open the Gradient Editor.**

5. **Select the Foreground to Transparent gradient.**
   The icon for this gradient is black to transparent.

6. **Move the black stop on the gradient in the Gradient Editor to the far right so that there is just a small area of opaque pixels on the right side of the gradient. Click OK.**

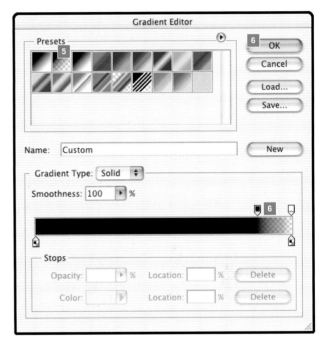

7. **Make sure that the layer mask thumbnail is selected on the curtain layer in the Layers palette.**
   A black border around that thumbnail indicates that it is selected.

<CAUTION>
If the layer thumbnail rather than the layer mask thumbnail is selected, you end up painting on the image, rather than on the mask. This is difficult to undo, short of using the History palette, so try to avoid this common mistake.

8. **Click at the far right of the document window and drag to just before the left edge.**

This draws a black to transparent gradient on the layer mask, hiding most of the image on the curtain layer. Where the mask is black, you can see through the curtain layer to the reels layer below. Where the mask is white (where the transparent part of the gradient lies), you see the curtains layer. Where the mask fades to gray, the two images gradually fade together.

< T I P >

The effect of drawing this gradient in the layer mask depends on the length and direction of your gradient line. If you don't like the gradient that you get, try drawing another gradient line over the first one until you're happy with the result. Each time you redraw the gradient line, it replaces the one before it.

< N O T E >

You could accomplish nearly the same thing by drawing a selection with the Rectangular Marquee tool to cover almost all the document except the area on the left edge. Choose Select➔Feather and type a relatively large number in the feather radius field (try 40). Press Option+Delete (Windows: Alt+Backspace) to fill the selection on the layer mask with black. The heavily feathered left edge provides a soft transition between images, much like the gradient.

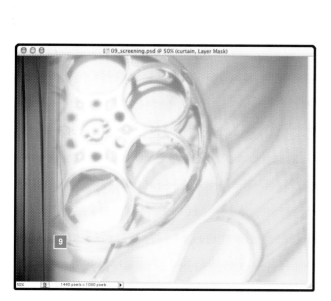

9. **Select the Brush tool in the toolbox and choose a big soft-edged brush from the Brush pop-up palette on the Options bar. Make sure that the layer mask thumbnail is still selected in the Layers palette. Paint with black wherever you want to paint away more of the curtain. Paint with white if you want to restore some of the curtain.**

10. **Option+click (Windows: Alt+click) the layer mask thumbnail in the Layers palette to see the actual layer mask.**

    This illustrates the point that a layer mask is a bitmapped image composed entirely of shades of gray. You can see the black area that normally hides the image on the attached curtain layer, the white area that reveals that image, and the gradual gray edge between the two through which that image is partially visible.

11. **Option+click (Windows: Alt+click) the layer mask thumbnail again to return the document window to the normal view.**

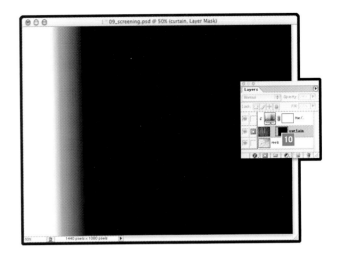

12. **Shift+click the layer mask thumbnail in the Layers palette to temporarily disable the layer mask, revealing the image on the attached curtain layer. Shift+click again to reactivate the layer mask.**

    This feature comes in handy when you try to reposition a layer mask and need to see what's beneath it. When the layer mask is disabled, you see a red X across the layer mask thumbnail in the Layers palette.

13. **Choose File➔Save. Leave** 09_screening.psd **open for the next tutorial, if you want to use it instead of the fresh file that has been provided for you to use there.**

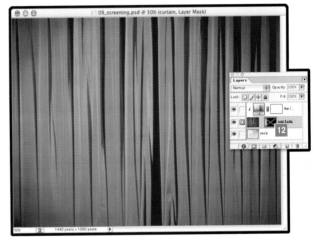

What's the Difference between a Layer Mask and a Vector Mask?

On a layer mask, the grayscale pixels that you add to the mask with Photoshop's regular painting and fill tools are what hide or reveal the image on the attached layer. You can paint soft-edged areas on a layer mask to create gradual transitions in the image, using the techniques that you learned in this tutorial.

On a vector mask, vector objects that you create with the Pen, Path, or Shape tools are what hide or reveal the image on the attached layer. Vector objects have smooth edges, as you may remember from Session 6. So vector masks create designs that have crisp edges in your image. Another unique feature of vector masks is that their shape is malleable. You can scale the shape of a vector mask with Transform commands or change the shape of

the mask with the Pen tools, just as you can with any vector object. You can use a vector mask to mask out smooth shapes in the artwork on a layer, so you can see through to the layer below. If you want to get really fancy, you can use a vector mask in combination with a layer mask, as you do in this tutorial.

The contents of a vector mask are vector objects, which can come from a few different sources. The objects that you add to a vector mask can be objects created with the Shape tools (as in this tutorial), paths that you draw with the Pen tools, or vector objects that you create in another program, such as Illustrator, and copy and paste into the vector mask.

Tutorial

» Combining a Vector Mask and a Layer Mask

Photoshop CS offers a powerful vector mask feature that you can use to add a crisp scalable vector object to a layer of soft-edged pixel-based artwork. You can even combine a vector mask with a layer mask, as you do in this tutorial. This is an advanced technique, so feel free to skip this tutorial if your brain is full.

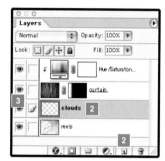

1. **Make sure that** 09_screening.psd **is still open from the previous tutorial or open** 09_screening_mask.psd **from the Session 9 Tutorial Files folder on your hard drive.**
   09_screening_mask.psd is a replica of how 09_screening.psd should look at the end of the previous tutorial. Use 09_screening_mask.psd if you didn't finish the previous tutorial or if you messed up the file that you were using in that tutorial.

2. **Select the reels layer in the Layers palette. Click the New Layer button at the bottom of the Layers palette. Double-click the new layer name and rename the layer** clouds.

3. **Click the eye icon on the curtain layer to hide that layer temporarily while you work on the layer beneath it.**

4. **Make sure that the clouds layer is still selected. Double-click the Foreground Color box in the toolbox to open the Color Picker. Choose a dark orange color (R:153, G:51, B:0). Press Option+Delete (Windows: Alt+Backspace) to fill the clouds layer with this color.**

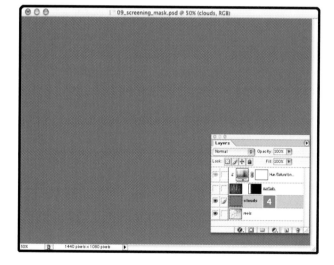

5. **Choose Filter→Render→Difference Clouds. Then choose Edit→Fade Difference Clouds and move the slider to 86%. Click OK to close the Fade dialog box.**

   This is a quick way to make a textured background. Although it looks "Photoshopped," most of this layer will be hidden from view by the vector mask that you add later, so it works fine here. You learn more about filters in Session 10.

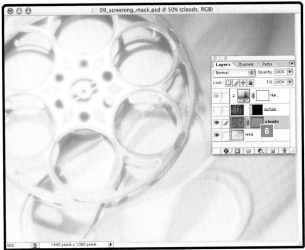

6. **Make sure that the clouds layer is selected and choose Layer→Add Vector Mask→Hide All.**

   This creates a mask that hides all the content of the clouds layer, so you see only the layer below. Notice that the layer mask thumbnail on the clouds layer is filled with gray indicating it is a "hide" mask, rather than a "reveal" mask.

7. **Click the Shape tool that is displayed in the toolbox and choose the Custom Shape tool from the hidden tools menu.**

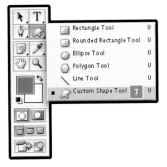

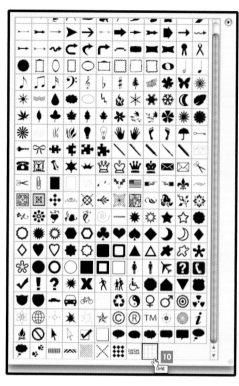

8. **Click the Paths button on the left side of the Options bar.**

   This causes the Custom Shape tool to draw a path, rather than create a shape layer, which is its default behavior.

9. **Click the Add to Path combination button on the right side of the Options bar.**

   If you don't choose the correct combination button, this tutorial won't work because the path inverts.

10. **Click the Custom Shape field's down arrow on the Options bar to open the Custom Shape Picker. Click the Grid shape at the bottom of the Custom Shape Picker. Click anywhere in the Options bar to close the Custom Shape Picker.**

    If you don't see the Grid shape in the Custom Shape Picker, click the arrow on the top right of that Picker, choose All from the menu of shapes, and click OK at the prompt. Click on the bottom right of the Picker and drag to expand it, or use the scroll bar to scroll to the bottom of the Picker.

11. **Press the keyboard shortcuts D and then X to set the foreground color in the toolbox to white.**

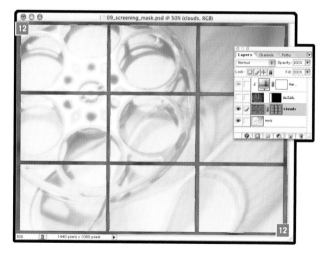

12. **Click in the very top-left corner of the document window and drag across the image to the bottom-right corner.**

    Drag carefully to make sure that the edges of the shape just fit against the boundaries of the document window. This particular shape is made up of multiple paths, so it would be hard to modify later with the Black and White Arrow tools (although it is possible, which is one of the benefits of a vector mask).

    That's all there is to adding a vector mask. Notice that the masked shapes have crisp, smooth edges. You can see the outlines of the vector shapes along the edges of the shapes. To hide those outlines, click another layer in the Layers palette. In the next steps, you add a layer mask to the same layer.

13. Take a minute to play. First go to the History palette and click the Camera icon to make a snapshot of the current state. Then draw some more custom shapes in the grid to make sure that you really understand how this works. Click a shape with the Black Arrow tool to select and move it. Click a point in a shape with the White Arrow tool to modify the shape (like the double note in the figure). When you're done, click the snapshot that you made in the History palette to return to the state with the grid shape.

14. **Make sure that the clouds layer is selected in the Layers palette. Click the Add Layer Mask icon at the bottom of the palette.**
This adds a third thumbnail to the clouds layer. This is a layer mask, like the kind you worked with in the last tutorial. It's not a vector mask.

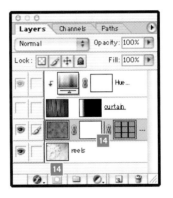

15. Select the Rectangular Marquee tool in the toolbox. Click and drag around the inside of the four-square on the top left of the document window, as shown in the figure. Try to make the selection butt sharply against, but not cut into, the edges of the bars that surround the selection.

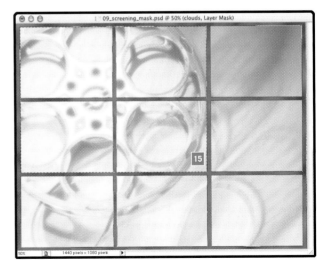

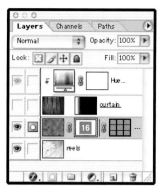

16. **Click the new layer mask thumbnail on the clouds layer in the Layers palette.**

It's very important that you click the right thumbnail. You see a black border around the layer mask thumbnail when it's selected.

17. **Press the keyboard shortcuts D and X to set the Foreground Color box in the toolbox to black.**

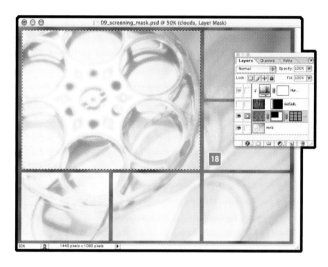

18. **Press Option+Delete (Windows: Alt+Backspace) to fill the selection on the layer mask with black. Press the shortcut ⌘+D (Windows: Ctrl+D) to deselect the filled selection.**

This hides the clouds image on the clouds layer that was previously visible through the vector mask, enabling you to see through this area of the grid to the reels layer below.

19. **Repeat steps 15 through 18 on the two-square on the bottom left of the document window, to match this figure.**

<NOTE>
Comprehending the way multiple masks interact can be mind-bending. So if you don't understand all the twists and turns yet, just remember that a vector mask and a layer mask can interact on the same layer, determining which part of an image is visible or invisible.

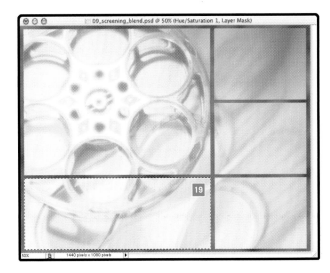

20. **Click the eye icon on the curtain layer in the Layers palette to redisplay that image and its layer mask.**
As you can see, you can have multiple layers with masks, all of which interact.

21. **Choose File→Save and close the file.**

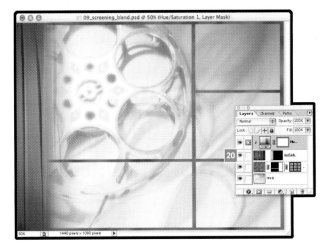

Tutorial
» Using Blending Sliders to Composite

The Blending sliders in the Layer Style dialog box offer a quick and easy way to blend images on separate layers based on the brightness of pixels in both images. This feature can be used to completely knock out bright or dark pixels in a layer. This makes it easy to eliminate the white backgrounds that you often see in studio photographs like the one you use in this tutorial. You also use the Transform feature to scale images to match as you composite.

1. **Open** 09_screening_blend.psd **from the Session 9 Tutorial Files folder.**

2. **Open a second file,** 09_vintage.psd, **from the Session 9 Tutorial Files folder.**
   If you get a message about missing file information, ignore it and click OK. It's irrelevant to what you're working on here.

3. **Select the topmost layer, the Hue/Saturation layer, in** 09_screening_blend.psd.

4. **With the Move tool selected, click and drag** 09_vintage.psd **from its document window into the** 09_screening_blend.psd **document window.**
   If you get a warning about missing file information, ignore it and click OK. This creates a new layer in the destination document (09_screening_blend.psd) called Layer 1.

5. **Close** 09_vintage.psd.

6. **Double-click Layer 1 and rename it** camera.

7. **Double-click the thumbnail on the camera layer to open the Layer Style dialog box.**

<NOTE>
The Layer Style dialog box can be intimidating at first. It has several different controls and takes up almost the whole screen on a laptop! Fortunately, you only have to focus on one small part of this monster for now—the Blend If section at the bottom of the Blending Options panel. You find out more about other features of this dialog box in Session 10.

8. Click the white slider on the right side of the bar labeled This Layer and drag it to around 230.

The white area around the vintage camera disappears.

< N O T E >

You're probably wondering what made the white background of the camera disappear. That requires some further understanding of the Layer Style dialog box. Blending Options determine how the pixels in the selected layer (here the camera layer) blend with pixels in the layers below. The This Layer slider controls which pixels are included in and excluded from that layer blend. The bar represents 255 brightness values with dark on the left and bright on the right. Photoshop blends only those tones between the dark and light sliders. Any tones that fall outside of those sliders are excluded, so they won't be visible in the blended image. When you moved the white slider to the left, you excluded all the bright tones to the right of the slider. That's why the bright whites disappeared from the image. They are actually still there; you just can't see them.

9. Option+click (Windows: Alt+click) the left side of the white slider and drag to the left to around 210.

This eliminates some of the stray white pixels that were still hanging around the edges of the image.

< N O T E >

Splitting the sliders like this when you move them is a good idea. It helps with the stray pixel problem and gives you a softer, blended edge around an object. That's because Photoshop partially blends any pixels that contain tones that fall between the two parts of the white slider or between the two parts of the black slider.

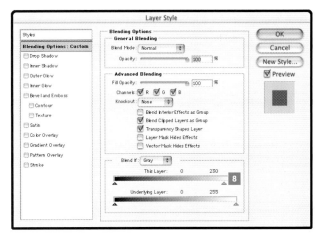

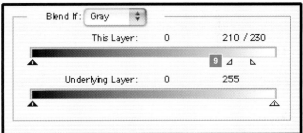

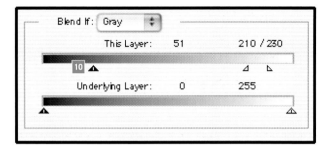

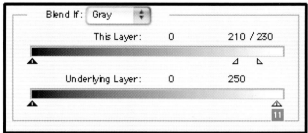

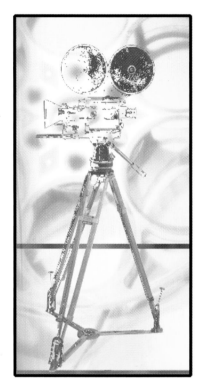

10. **Drag the black sliders on the This Layer bar to the right to see what they do. Then pull them back to their original position.**

    These sliders work like the white sliders on the This Layer bar, but in the opposite direction. Pulling them to the right causes all darker pixels in the camera layer (those to the left of 51 in the example illustration) to disappear from the image.

11. **Drag the white sliders on the Underlying Layer bar to the left. When you're done, pull them back to their original position.**

    The sliders on the Underlying Layer bar are somewhat different than the sliders on the This Layer bar. Moving the white Underlying Layer sliders to the left causes all brighter tones in the reel layer (those to the right of 250 in the example illustration) to break through the selected camera layer.

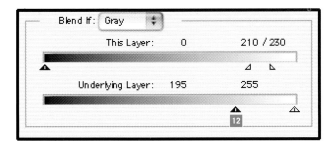

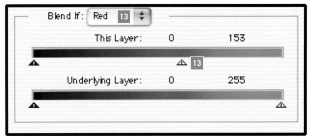

12. Drag the black sliders on the Underlying Layer bar to the right. Then pull them back to their original position.

Moving the black Underlying Layer sliders to the right causes all darker tones in the reels layer (those that are darker than 195 in the example illustration) to show through the selected camera layer.

13. Click the Blend If button and change it from Gray to Red. Move the white This Layer slider to the left. When you're done, return the slider to its original position.

The bright reds in the camera legs start to disappear. That's because you're now working in one of the color channels in the image and taking the color of pixels, rather than just their brightness, into account. The ability to exclude pixels on the basis of color gives you even more compositing options.

14. Click OK in the Layer Style dialog box to close it.

You can reopen it at any time to make further modifications to a layer by double-clicking on the layer thumbnail.

15. Make sure that the camera layer is selected and choose Edit➔ Transform➔Scale from the menu bar at the top of the screen.

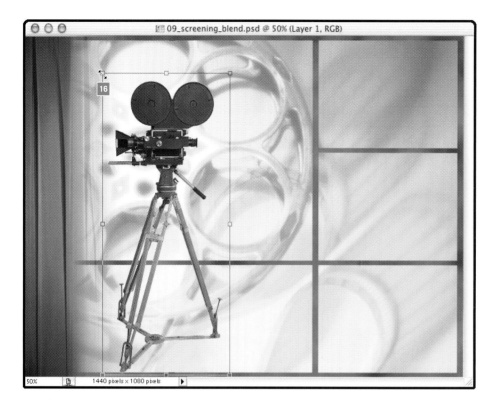

16. **Hold the Shift key, click one of the corner points of the bounding box, and drag toward the center of the bounding box to make the camera image slightly smaller to match the figure. Press Return (Windows: Enter) on your keyboard to accept the transformation and eliminate the bounding box.**

    If the camera is in a different position than the camera shown in the figure, select the Move tool and reposition it.

17. **Choose File→Save and leave** 09_screening_blend.psd **open for the next tutorial.**

Tutorial
» Using the Measure Tool, Rulers, and Guides

Photoshop has some tools that I think of as handy utilities. They don't do anything fancy, but they're integral to getting the job done efficiently, and they're useful in lots of situations. Rulers, guides, and the Measure tool are that kind of flexible, reliable utility. In this tutorial, you practice using them to position artwork in a composite.

1. **Make sure that** 09_screening_blend.psd **is still open from the previous tutorial.**

2. **Click the Eyedropper tool in the toolbox to display a hidden menu of tools and choose the Measure tool.**
   This is a relatively unknown tool that's useful for measuring distances and angles.

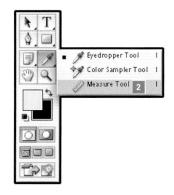

3. **Click the top line made by the vector shape in the right corner of the document window and drag down to the next line of the vector shape to measure the number of pixels of height in that space.**
   Take a look at the H field in the Options bar, which reads approximately 352 pixels.

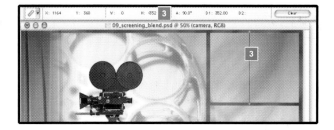

<NOTE>
The Measure tool has another feature that comes in really handy if you have an image that needs to be straightened, like a scan that came out a little crooked (as often happens). Locate a portion of the image that should be straight and click and drag across that area with the Measure tool. Click the end points of the line drawn by the Measure tool to adjust the line. Then choose Image→ Rotate→Arbitrary. Photoshop compares the angle of the Measure tool's line to the angle of the image and rotates the image to make it straight.

<TIP>
When you're finished with a measure line, remove it from the visible portion of the document by clicking and dragging it off the side of the document. If you expand your canvas, you see that it's still sitting out there, but it won't print with the document. Another way to measure is with the rulers and guides.

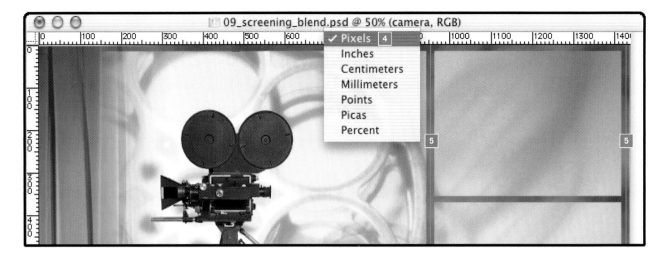

4. **Choose View→Rulers to make the vertical and horizontal rulers around the document visible.**
   If your rulers display inches, change them by Ctrl+clicking (Windows: right-clicking) directly on a ruler and choosing Pixels from the menu that pops up.

5. **Select the Move tool in the toolbox. Click inside the vertical ruler on the left of the screen and drag to the right to bring out a vertical guide. Position the guide in the middle of the bar made by the vector shape at the far right of the document ruler. Drag out a second vertical ruler and position it in the next vector shape bar to the left.**
   The guides are hard to see on the blue bars in the figure, but they are there.

<NOTE>
To reposition a guide, select the Move tool and move the cursor over the guide until the cursor becomes a double-pointed arrow. Then click and drag.

<NOTE>
There's an invisible grid underlying the document window, which helps position objects symmetrically on the screen. You can see the grid if you choose View→Show Grid. (Dismiss the grid by repeating that command.) Objects snap to the intersections of the grid lines if the Snap To feature is activated. To deactivate Snap To, choose View→Snap To→Grid to uncheck that option.

6. **Click in the top-left corner of the document window, where the two rulers meet, and drag to the first guide in order to reposition the 0, 0 point of the rulers. Take a look at the horizontal ruler on the top of the screen and note that the width of the space between the two guides is about 475 pixels.**

<TIP>
Keep track of the measurements that you've made (width = 475 pixels and height = 352 pixels) for the next tutorial.

7. **Choose View→Clear Guides to dismiss all the guides.**
Alternatively, you can drag each guide off the edge of the document window using the Move tool. Or you can leave the guides where they are because guides don't print with a document.

8. **Double-click in the small box where the rulers meet at the top left of the document window to return the 0, 0 point of the rulers to its default.**

9. **Choose File→Save and close** 09_screening_blend.psd.

Tutorial
» Applying Layer Blending Modes

Blending modes are a collection of prebuilt formulas that control how pixels in a layer interact with pixels in the layers below. You can do some nice work with minimal effort using blending modes. You try some of my favorites in this tutorial.

1. **Open** 09_screening_mode.psd **from the Session 9 Tutorial Files folder.**

2. **Open a second document,** 09_lens.psd, **from the Session 9 Tutorial Files folder.**
   Your task is to put the lens image into the box formed by the grid at the top right of 09_screening_mode.psd. When both images are magnified to the same percentage, it's obvious that the lens image is way too big. In the next steps, you use the Crop tool to bring it down to size.

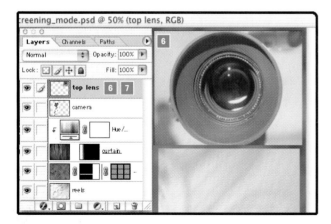

3. **Select the Crop tool from the toolbox. Type the dimensions that you measured in the last tutorial — Width:** 475 px, **Height:** 352 px—**into the respective fields on the Options bar. Leave the resolution at 240, which is the resolution of the destination document.** Photoshop needs the resolution to resample the image; otherwise, it just crops out part of the image with the specified dimensions.

4. **Click and drag in the document window of** 09_lens.psd, **reposition the cropping selection as you feel necessary, and press Return or Enter.**

5. **Make sure that the topmost layer—the camera layer—is selected in the Layers palette of** 09_screening_mode.psd.

6. **Select the Move tool in the toolbox and click and drag the single layer from the** 09_lens.psd **Layers palette (or document window) into the** 09_screening_mode.psd **document window. Position the lens image in the rectangle at the top right of the image.**
   This creates a new layer in the destination document.

7. **Double-click the new layer and name it** top lens. **Then hold the Option key (Windows: Alt key), click the lens image in the document window, and drag down to the next grid box.**
   This creates a copy of the image and a new layer in the Layers palette called top lens copy.

8. **Double-click the top lens copy layer and rename it** middle lens. **Hold the Option key (Windows: Alt key), click the middle lens image in the document window, and drag down to the bottom grid box.**
   This creates yet another layer in the Layers palette called middle lens copy.

9. **Double-click the middle lens copy layer in the Layers palette and rename it** bottom lens.

10. **Select the top lens layer in the Layers palette. Click the Blending Mode button on the top left of the palette and choose Overlay.**
    The Overlay mode is one of my favorites. It darkens some pixels in the selected layer and lightens others depending on the pixels in the underlying layer. This often results in a painterly image that doesn't look too distorted.

11. **Click the Opacity field in the Layers palette and lower the opacity of the layer to around 82%.**
    Lowering the opacity makes the effect of the blending mode more subtle.

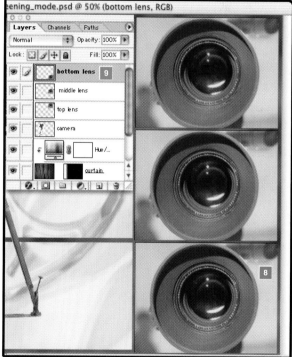

Blending Mode Details

Blending modes are grouped into logical categories, which proves useful when you're trying out different blending modes but have only a general idea of the result that you're looking for. There is a group of modes that always darkens (Darken through Linear Burn), a group that always lightens (Lighten through Linear Dodge), and a group that darkens or lightens depending on the colors involved (Overlay through Hard Mix). Photoshop 7 introduced several new blending modes—Linear Burn, Linear Dodge, Vivid Light, Linear Light, and Pin Light. Photoshop CS adds one more blending mode, Hard Mix, which applies a hard light and decreases the number of tones in the image creating blocks of color. In the following steps, you apply various layer blending modes to the three lens layers for a posterized effect. If you'd like to read a technical explanation of each blending mode, take a look at the Photoshop Help Files. My view is that this is a feature you have to use to understand. Each blending mode offers different results in different situations. So I suggest that you try out a few on the same image and compare the results, as shown in this tutorial.

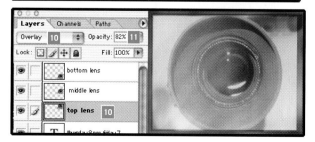

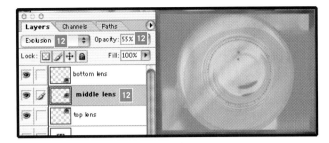

12. **Repeat steps 10 and 11 on the middle lens layer, but choose the Exclusion blending mode. Lower the opacity to around 55%.**

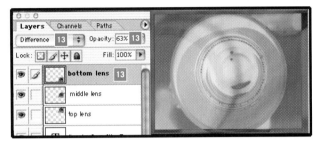

13. **Repeat steps 10 and 11 on the bottom lens layer, but choose the Difference blending mode. Lower the opacity of the layer to around 63%.**

< T I P >

You may be wondering why I chose these particular blending modes and opacities. Unfortunately, there is no secret formula that I can share. I suggest that you experiment like crazy and see what works, keeping basic principles of good design and your own artistic style in mind. For example, in this case I looked for blending modes that honored the color palette of the image, and I tried to put the heavier, more dramatic effect on the bottom image to avoid creating imbalance.

14. **Select the Type tool. In the Options bar, set Font to Tahoma, Size to 18 pt, Anti-aliasing to Smooth, and Color to a burnt orange (R:172, G:77, B:46). Type screenings. Select the Move tool and drag the type into place.**

Selecting the Move tool also serves to accept the type, so you don't have to click the Check Mark icon on the Options bar.

15. **Change Size to 12 pt in the Options bar. Click in the document again and type a few more lines of text to match those shown in the figure.**

< N O T E >

You learn how to work with text in Sessions 11 and 12.

16. **Choose File→Save As, navigate to your collages folder, and rename the document 09_screening_end.psd. Save it as a final collage for your program guide project.**

» Session Review

In this session, you learned some techniques for compositing images. You used the Crop tool to make images compatible. You applied layer masks and a vector mask to hide and reveal artwork on layers. You learned how to use the blending sliders in the Layer Style dialog box and blending modes in the Layers palette. You also got a taste of Photoshop's utility tools — rulers, guides, and the Measure tool. These questions will help you review this session.

1. What tool can you use to resample and match the size of one image to another? (See "Tutorial: Making Images Compatible.")

2. What do you have to do to two documents to get a true picture of their relative size on-screen? (See "Tutorial: Making Images Compatible.")

3. What kind of image is a layer mask? (See "Tutorial: Joining Images with Layer Masks.")

4. What would you use a layer mask for when compositing? (See "Tutorial: Joining Images with Layer Masks.")

5. What does pressing the keyboard shortcuts D and then X accomplish? (See "Tutorial: Joining Images with Layer Masks.")

6. What colors should you usually use to paint on a layer mask? (See "Tutorial: Joining Images with Layer Masks.")

7. Name two ways to create a soft edge on a layer mask. (See "Tutorial: Joining Images with Layer Masks.")

8. Can you have more than one mask on a layer? (See "Tutorial: Combining a Vector Mask and a Layer Mask.")

9. Name one difference between a layer mask and a vector mask. (See "Tutorial: Combining a Vector Mask and a Layer Mask.")

10. Name two different tools that you can use to put a vector object on a vector mask. (See "Tutorial: Combining a Vector Mask and a Layer Mask.")

11. How can you change the scale or shape of an object on a vector mask? (See "Tutorial: Combining a Vector Mask and a Layer Mask.")

12. How do you make a Shape tool draw a path, rather than create a shape layer? (See "Tutorial: Combining a Vector Mask and a Layer Mask.")

13. What does sliding the white slider on the This Layer bar in the Layer Style dialog box accomplish? (See "Tutorial: Using Blending Sliders to Composite.")

14. How do you turn on rulers? (See "Tutorial: Using the Measure Tool, Rulers, and Guides.")

15. How do you change the units of measurement used by the rulers? (See "Tutorial: Using the Measure Tool, Rulers, and Guides.")

16. How do you create a guide? (See "Tutorial: Using the Measure Tool, Rulers, and Guides.")

17. What's the Measure tool used for? (See "Tutorial: Using the Measure Tool, Rulers, and Guides.")

18. What does the blending mode of a layer do? (See "Tutorial: Applying Layer Blending Modes.")

screenings

thursday 8 pm
friday 7 pm
saturday 8 pm
saturday 10pm
sunday 12 pm
sunday 4 pm

Filters, Layer Styles, and Special Effects

tammeron
film festival

2004

Session Introduction

Photoshop is famous for its special effects. It comes with dozens of decorative and functional filters you can apply to photographs, graphics, shapes, and text. It also offers a wide range of layer styles for embellishing images with effects ranging from a simple drop shadow to a customized combination of styles. In this session, you work with individual filters and you use the new Filter Gallery to preview and apply multiple filters at once. You learn to make realistic-looking wood with the new Fibers filter and the Liquify filter interface. You take a look at the new Photo Filter adjustment, which simulates real photographic filters. You use the History brush to create a unique look by painting with filter effects. And you add light to your work with the Lighting Effects filter. You also learn to use layer styles, with which you can add effects that are customizable and editable and do not impact the underlying art work. You learn that you can create a customized layer style, save it in the Styles palette, and easily reapply it to other art work.

TOOLS YOU'LL USE
Gaussian Blur filter, Fibers filter, Liquify filter, Filter Gallery, Photo Filter Adjustment, Lighting Effects filter, History Brush tool, and Layer Styles

CD-ROM FILES NEEDED
10_effects.psd and 10_effects_end.psd

TIME REQUIRED
45 minutes

Tutorial
» Filtering a Layer

In this tutorial, you apply a Gaussian Blur filter to a layer of art work, getting a glimpse into the importance of functional filters like this one for creating realistic imagery. Along the way, you learn some filter basics, including how to preview filter effects and how to reapply an individual filter to intensify its effect.

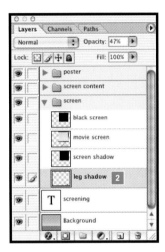

1. **Choose File→Open, navigate to** 10_effects.psd **in the folder of Session 10 tutorial files on your hard drive, and click Open. Click Update if you see a warning that some text layers need to be updated.**

<NOTE>

This is an RGB color image. Many filters (such as the Lighting Effects filter, which you use later in this session) are only available for use on RGB color images and don't work on CMYK images. If you want to use these filters on an image destined for a commercial printer, you can edit in RGB mode and then convert to CMYK mode (Image→Mode→CMYK). Keep in mind that there may be a color shift when you convert from RGB to CMYK mode.

2. **Click the screen folder in the Layers palette to open the screen layer set, and select the leg shadow layer.**
   You must select a layer before you apply a filter because a filter affects the active layer only, not the entire image.

3. **Choose Filter→Blur→Gaussian Blur.**
   The Gaussian Blur dialog box opens. This filter, like many individual filters, has a dialog box with filter settings and a small preview pane in which you can view the effect of the filter at selected settings. Now you see only a checkerboard pattern because the preview pane centered on a transparent area of the leg shadow layer.

4. **Move your cursor into the document window so that it changes to a square and click on the shadow of the movie screen legs.**
   This centers the shadow in the filter's preview pane.

<TIP>
Another way to change the view in a filter's preview pane is to click inside the preview pane, automatically changing the cursor to a hand icon. Then drag to preview other parts of the active layer.

5. **Click the minus icon in the Gaussian Blur dialog box to zoom out so that you can see more of the shadow in the preview pane.**

6. **Make sure that there's a check mark in the Preview box in the Gaussian Blur dialog box so that you can see a live preview of your filter settings in the document window.**
   The live preview gives you a better view of the final result than the preview in the Gaussian Blur dialog box. However, the live preview takes a lot of processing power. If previewing filter effects on your computer is slowing you down, uncheck the Preview box.

<NOTE>
Not all filters offer a live image preview in the document window.

7. **Type** 2.0 **in the Radius field in the Gaussian Blur dialog box. Click OK.**
   The Radius setting determines the amount of blur. Although the current setting does soften the shadow, more softening is required to make the shadow look real. In the next step you learn a quick way to reapply the Gaussian Blur filter to intensify the blur effect.

8. **Click Filter in the menu bar at the top of the screen and choose Gaussian Blur from its new position at the top of the Filter menu.**
   This reapplies the Gaussian Blur filter with the same Radius setting that you chose in the last step. Reapplying a filter is a way to intensify its effect. Photoshop saves the most recent filter settings as the top entry in the Filter menu, so you don't have to reopen the filter dialog box and choose filter settings again.

<TIP>
The keyboard shortcut to repeat a filter is ⌘+F (Windows: Ctrl+F).

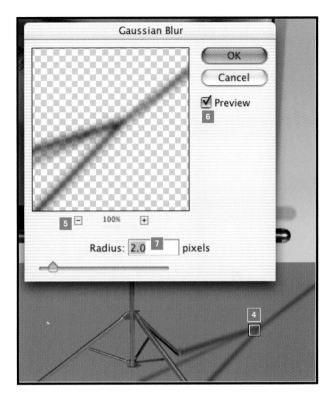

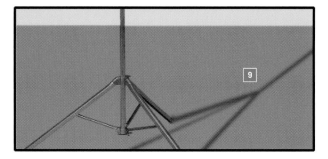

9. **Repeat step 8.**

   The Gaussian Blur filter has now been applied three times in total. The shadow should look similar to the one shown here.

   < N O T E >

   The results of your successive applications of the Gaussian Blur filter could have been accomplished in one step by specifying a higher radius number when the filter was first applied. However, there are times when it is better to work in small steps. When you lightly apply a filter and then repeat to intensify the effect, you can experiment until you get to just the right amount of filtering.

10. **Click the arrow to the left of the screen layer set to close that layer set for now, keeping the multiple layers in this file more manageable.**

    < N O T E >

    Filters are not just for embellishing art work, as you've just seen. Some, like the Gaussian Blur filter, are useful for producing realistic-looking art work. Others—like the new Lens Blur filter for simulating shallow depth-of-field and the Unsharp Mask filter for sharpening a photograph—are essential for photographic processing. These specialized, photographic filters are covered in the later session on Using Darkroom Tools.

11. **Choose File→Save and leave the document open for the next tutorial.**

    In this tutorial you applied the Gaussian blur filter to an entire layer to make the shadow on that layer look more realistic.

Using Filters Wisely

Photoshop's filters can create some striking and useful effects, but you should be aware of their downsides. For one thing, filters produce standardized effects that can make your images look like everyone else's if you're not careful. Don't let this stop you from using filters, but do think about whether applying a filter will serve a real purpose. One legitimate purpose for which you use certain filters is to correct flaws in an image. For example, you've seen in this tutorial that the Gaussian Blur filter is useful for softening the look of hard-edged art work. Along the same lines, the Dust & Scratches filter (in the Noise filter submenu) is useful for eliminating small spots and imperfections, and the Unsharp Mask filter (in the Sharpen filter submenu) is great for sharpening scanned and retouched images. Another problem with filters is that they permanently change the pixels of art work that they affect. That leaves you little room for changing your mind after you apply a filter to a layer, other than one chance at the Fade command or backing up

to a previous state in the History palette. There are several ways around this limitation:

» Make a copy of a layer before you apply a filter. You can use a layer blending mode to blend the filtered copy layer with the unfiltered original, and you always have the original to return to if you change your mind.

» A similar solution is to create a layer filled with a shade of black that is neutral in a particular blending mode and apply the filter to that layer, as you do in the tutorial on the Lighting with a Filter later in this session.

» Another alternative is to create effects with layer styles, which are always editable, rather than filters. You learn about layer styles later in this session.

Tutorial
» Filtering a Selection

Sometimes you want to apply a filter to just part of the art work on a layer, rather than to the entire layer. You can use any of Photoshop's selection tools to restrict the area to which a filter is applied. In this tutorial, you select part of the background layer and create a realistic wood floor from scratch inside that selection, without affecting the rest of the art work on the active layer. You use the new Fibers filter, which comes in handy for making surfaces and textiles, along with the Liquify Filter for making knots in the wood.

1. **With** `10_effects.psd` **still open from the last tutorial, open the Color palette (Window→Color). With the Foreground Color box in that palette selected, set the R slider to 228, the G slider to 191, and the B slider to 102.**
   The Foreground Color box fills with light gold.

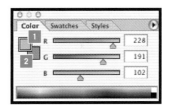

2. **Click on the Background Color box in the Color palette and set the R slider to 197, the G slider to 142, and the B slider to 46.**
   The Background Color box fills with darker gold.

3. **With the Background layer selected, click on the New Layer icon at the bottom of the Layers palette to create a new layer. Double-click the layer name and rename the layer** floor.

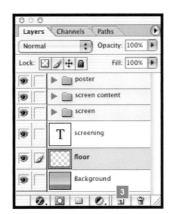

4. **Choose the Magic Wand tool in the toolbox. Leave the Options settings at their defaults.**

5. **Select the Background layer. Click in the olive rectangular area in the image to select that area.**

6. **Select the floor layer. Press Option+Delete (Windows: Alt+ Backspace) to fill the rectangular selection with the light gold Foreground Color.**

7. **Choose Filter→Render→Fibers in the menu bar.**
   The Fibers filter dialog box opens.

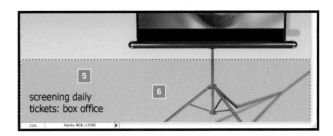

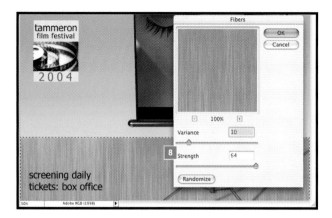

8. **Set Variance to 10 and Strength to 64 in the Fibers filter dialog box and click OK.**

   The selection in the floor layer fills with a pattern of the Foreground and Background colors that resembles woodgrain. The Variance setting affects the color variance in the pattern (the higher the setting the more the color variance); the Strength setting affects the appearance of the pattern (the higher the setting the thinner the fibers in the pattern).

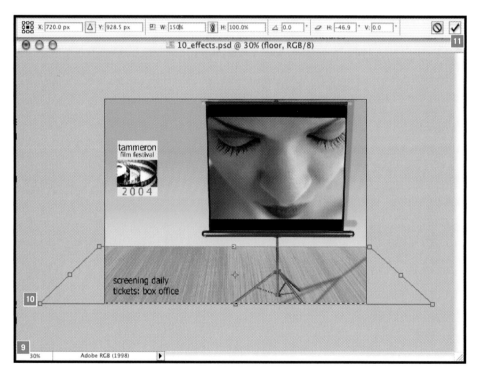

9. **Click in the zoom box at the bottom-left corner of the document window, type 30, and press Return (Windows: Enter).**

   The document window zooms out to 30% so you see gray space around the image.

10. **Choose Edit→Transform→Perspective. Click on the anchor point at the bottom-left corner and drag to the left until the Width field in the Options bar reads 150%.**

11. **Click the Commit Transform button (the check mark on the Options bar) to apply the transformation.**

    This changes the shape of the patterned selection, adding perspective to the wood floor you created.

12. **Zoom out to 50% and press ⌘+D (Windows: Ctrl+D) to deselect.**
    The floor should look like the illustration.

13. **With the floor layer still selected, choose Filter→Liquify in the menu bar.**
    The Liquify interface opens. It offers a suite of tools on the left, a preview pane in the middle, and options on the right. You use this filter to add knots to your wood floor to make it look more realistic.

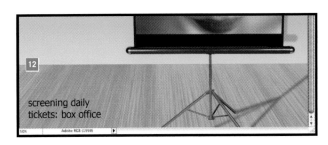

<NOTE>

The Liquify filter distorts an image by attaching an invisible mesh framework that you can twirl, pinch, bulge, push, pull, and otherwise modify with an impressive array of tools. The details of your art work follow the mesh. This is more than just a fun feature. You can use it to create artistic effects like smoke, steam, fire, clouds, reflections, patterns, and the wood knots you make in this tutorial.

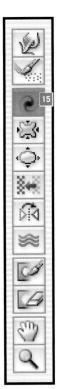

14. **Click the zoom box at the bottom left of the Liquify dialog box and choose Fit on Screen.**
    You can see a preview of all the art work on the floor layer.

15. **Select the Twirl Clockwise tool from the toolbox on the left side of the Liquify dialog box.**

Filter News

The Fibers filter isn't the only new filter in Photoshop CS. The new Lens Blur filter simulates the differential blur effect you would get by manipulating the aperture on a traditional camera lens (see the session on Using Darkroom Tools for more on the Lens Blur filter). The new Average filter (Filter→Blur Average) calculates the average color of an image or selection and fills that area with that color. This is useful for replacing a dithered or patterned area with a related solid color, or for making flat art from a photograph. The Extract Filter has a new Textured Image option that selects on the basis of texture, making it easier to isolate an object with a unique texture or pattern against a background of a similar color. And the Liquify filter has new mask and view options.

16. **Set Brush Size to 130, Brush Density to 25, Brush Pressure to 40, Brush Rate to 100 in the Tool Options section of the dialog box.** Brush Size is the size of the distortion tool. Brush Density is the amount of feather on the brush. Brush Pressure controls the speed of distortion when the cursor is dragged. Brush Rate controls the speed of distortion when the cursor stays in one place. And Turbulent Jitter controls the tightness of the distortion.

< N O T E >

It isn't necessary to view the mesh as you distort the image, but it's easier to understand what's happening when you see the mesh moving. Choose Show→Mesh in the Liquify dialog box if you want to see the mesh.

17. **Click and drag to draw several vertical lines on the woodgrain floor in the Liquify dialog box, pausing here and there to let the Twirl tool form a knot. Draw some of the lines in the reverse direction by holding the Option key (Windows: Alt key) as you drag.** For a realistic result, don't draw too many lines or knots. If you make a mistake, use the undo commands or the Reconstruct tool from the Liquify toolbox.

18. **Still in the Liquify dialog box, select Show Backdrop, Use All Layers, and Behind, and leave Opacity set to 50 so you can see how the distortion looks with the other art work in the image.**
If Opacity is not low enough, you won't see the distortion you drew in the woodgrain.

<NOTE>
You can save a distortion and reapply it to other art work using the Save and Load Mesh buttons in the Liquify dialog box.

19. **Click OK to apply the distortion.**
Your floor should resemble the one in the illustration. You created a realistic wood floor by applying the new Fibers filter and the Liquify filter to a selection in your image.

20. **Choose File→Save and leave the file open for the next tutorial.**

Tutorial
» Applying Multiple Filters in the Filter Gallery

The Filter Gallery is a welcome new feature in Photoshop CS. It includes filter thumbnails that illustrate what each filter does, so you don't have to remember Photoshop's many filters by name. It contains a large, expandable preview pane. And best of all, in the Filter Gallery dialog box you can preview how your image would look with multiple filters applied. You can also change the stacking order of filters, modify filter options, and apply multiple filters all at once, as you do in this tutorial.

1. **In the Layers palette of** 10_effects.psd, **which should be open from the previous tutorial, click on the arrow to the left of the screen content folder to open that layer set. Select the portrait layer.**

2. **Choose Filter→Filter Gallery from the menu bar.**
   The Filter Gallery dialog box opens.

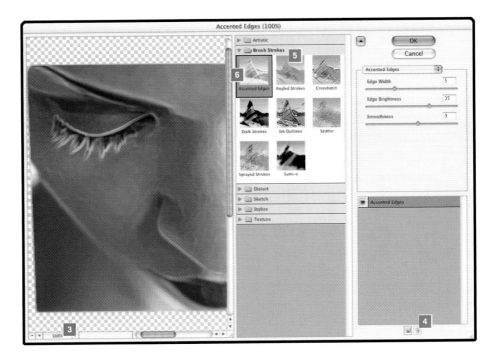

3. **Set the preview magnification to 100% in the box at the bottom left of the dialog box. Click and drag the preview of the woman's face so that you can see as much of it as possible in the preview pane.**

4. **If there is more than one effects layer at the bottom right of the dialog box, remove the additional effects layers by selecting them one by one and clicking the Trash icon at the bottom right of the Filter Gallery dialog box.**
   Effects layers represent filters that have been selected in the Filter Gallery dialog box. The list of effects layers retains the last values to which it was set, so you might see some leftover effects layers in your copy of the program.

5. **Click the Brush Strokes category in the middle section of the dialog box.**
   A menu of filter thumbnails in the Brush Strokes category appears. Each thumbnail represents the effect that that filter generates.

6. **Click on the filter thumbnail labeled Accented Edges.**
   The preview of the woman's face in the dialog box appears as it would with the Accented Edges filter applied with default option settings. The selected filter appears in the list of effects layers at the bottom right of the dialog box.

7. **In the top right of the Filter Gallery dialog box, set options for the Accented Edges filter as follows: Edge Width: 5, Edge Brightness: 35, and Smoothness: 9.**
   These options change the appearance of the live preview in the dialog box. Options are specific to the filter that is selected.

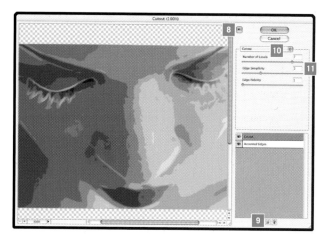

8. **Click the Show/Hide Thumbnails icon in the dialog box.**

   This closes the thumbnail portion of the dialog box, freeing up more space for the image preview. This view gives you a better idea of how filters will look when applied, so it's often preferable to the default thumbnails view.

<NOTE>

The Show/Hide Thumbnails icon looks like a double arrow on Windows.

9. **Click the New Effect Layer button at the bottom right of the dialog box.**

   This adds an additional effect layer to the list of filters you selected, defaulting to the last filter selected—Accented Edges. The image preview now displays a double Accented Edges effect.

10. **With the top Accented Edges effect layer highlighted, click the Filters pop-up menu above the filter options and choose Cutout from that menu.**

    The Cutout filter replaces the second Accented Edges filter in the image preview and in the effect layer list. This menu is an alternative to choosing a filter from the filter thumbnails.

<CAUTION>

The Filters pop-up menu displays the names of all the filters in the Filter Gallery. Some familiar Photoshop filter names are missing from this list. That's because the Filter Gallery doesn't include all of the filters that ship with Photoshop; it contains only the art filters that were called Gallery Effects filters in previous releases.

11. **Set the options for the Cutout filter to: Number of Levels: 7, Edge Simplicity: 3, and Edge Fidelity: 1.**

    The image now has a posterized look, as if it were made of pieces of cutout paper.

12. **Repeat steps 9 through 11, but this time choose the Accented Edges filter again and set its options to: Edge Width: 1, Edge Brightness: 20, and Smoothness 9.**

<NOTE>

You can change the order in which filters are to be applied by clicking and dragging effects layers to reorder them in the effects layers list. This would change the look of the image in the preview.

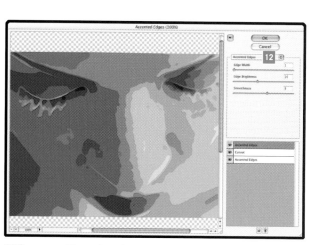

13. **Repeat steps 9 through 11 one more time, choosing the Poster Edges filter and setting its options to Edge Thickness: 1, Edge Intensity: 0, Posterization: 1.**

    There are now four filter effect layers, all of which are visible in the image preview.

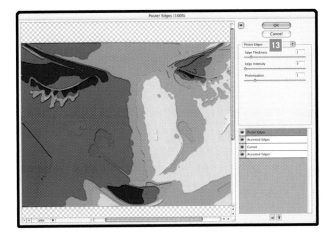

<TIP>

You can hide a filter effect temporarily so that it doesn't appear in the image preview, by clicking in the Visibility field to the left of the effect layer to remove that Eye icon. If you decide you don't want to apply a filter that you previewed, leave it hidden or remove it permanently by selecting it and clicking on the trash can at the bottom right of the Filter Gallery dialog box.

14. **Choose OK to close the Filter Gallery dialog box.**

    The combination of four filters is applied to the woman's face on the portrait layer.

15. **Choose File→Save and leave the file open for the next tutorial.**

    The image on the movie screen has been modified with a combination of filters from the Filter Gallery. Move on immediately to the next tutorial. If you close the file, the next tutorial won't work.

Tutorial
» Painting with Filters and the History Brush

You can achieve a unique painterly look by painting filter effects into your image, rather than applying them wholesale to a layer or selection. The History Brush tool and the History palette are the features you use for this unusual technique. In this tutorial, you selectively paint into the image the filter effects you generated in the last tutorial.

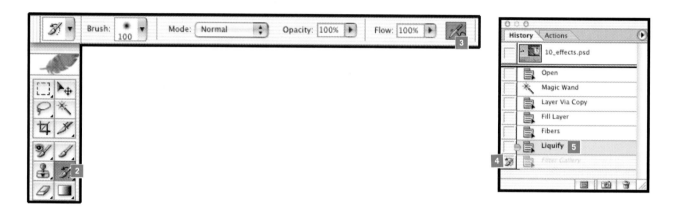

1. **Working in `10_effects.psd` from the last tutorial, make sure the portrait layer is still selected in the Layers palette.**
   If you closed the file at the end of the previous tutorial, this tutorial won't work; so move on to the next tutorial.

2. **Select the History Brush tool in the toolbox.**
   Don't confuse the History Brush tool with the Brush tool or the Color Replacement Brush tool, which are located near it in the toolbox. The History Brush tool is grouped with the Art History Brush tool.

<NOTE>
The Art History Brush works similarly to the History Brush, except that when you paint with the Art History Brush the underlying content is revealed in a spiral or curl pattern, allegedly representing a style of painting.

3. **In the Options bar, choose a 100-pixel soft round brush from the Brush picker, set brush Opacity to 100%, and click the Airbrush icon. Leave the other settings at their defaults.**

4. **Open the History palette (Window→History) and click with the History Brush tool in the box to the left of the Filter Gallery state (the last state in the History palette).**
   This identifies the Filter Gallery state (the way the image looked just after you applied the combined filters in the Filter Gallery) as the "paint" you're about to selectively apply with the History Brush tool.

<NOTE>
The History palette lists each of the last 20 operations you performed on this image, with each entry acting as a snapshot of the state of the image at that juncture. Don't worry if the states in your palette are slightly different than those in the illustration. It just means you did something slightly out of the order of the instructions.

5. **Select the state just above the Filter Gallery state in the History palette; this should be the Liquify state if you followed the tutorial instructions.**
   This moves the image back in history to just before you applied the Filter Gallery, causing the Filter Gallery effects to disappear from the image, because in theory they haven't yet been applied. It's okay if you see a different name on the state above your Filter Gallery state. As long as this state is something you did just before entering the Filter Gallery and you still have the portrait layer selected, this tutorial should work for you. If it doesn't, double-check that the portrait layer is selected in the Layer palette and try again.

6. **Click and drag in the image, painting the Filter Gallery effects back in where you want them to appear.**

   In the illustration, the Filter Gallery effects were painted in everywhere except the model's eyelashes, lips, neck, and shoulders. If you look closely at the illustration, you can see that these areas don't have the posterized look of the rest of the image. This results in an interesting painterly effect that you can't get if you apply filters wholesale.

<NOTE>

Use the Undo commands if you want to correct a paint stroke as you go. If you have to make a big change, you may find it easier to select a History state prior to the Filter Gallery state and reopen the Filter Gallery, where the last filters are still selected.

7. **When you're satisfied with the result, choose File→Save and leave the image open for the next tutorial.**

Tutorial

» Applying a Photo Filter Adjustment

Photographers often attach colored glass filters to the front of the camera lens to compensate for an unwanted color cast or to introduce a color tint as a special effect. Photoshop CS has a new feature that simulates the work of photographic filters. It's called, appropriately enough, the Photo Filter adjustment. In this tutorial, you use a Photo Filter adjustment layer to add a blue decorative tint to the portrait in the image you're building.

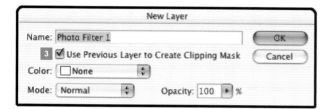

1. **Make sure the portrait layer is still selected in** 10_effects.psd.

2. **Choose Layer→New Adjustment Layer→Photo Filter from the menu bar.**
   This opens the New Layer dialog box.

3. **In the New Layer dialog box, put a check mark next to Use Previous Layer to Create Clipping Mask.**
   This identifies the underlying portrait layer as a clipping mask for the Photo Filter adjustment layer, so that the adjustment will appear only where there is content on the portrait layer (in the rounded rectangle of the portrait). The rest of the image will maintain its unadjusted color.

4. **Click OK in the New Layer dialog box.**
   This opens the Photo Filter dialog box and adds a Photo Filter adjustment layer above the portrait layer. The down-pointing arrow on the indented Photo Filter layer indicates that this adjustment layer is masked by the underlying portrait layer.

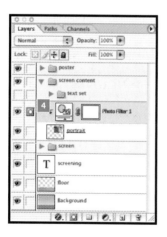

<NOTE>
Another way to create a Photo Filter adjustment layer is to click the New Fill or Adjustment Layer icon at the bottom of the Layers palette and choose Photo Filter. You would then create a clipping mask by Option+clicking (Windows: Alt+clicking) the border between the Photo Filter adjustment layer and the portrait layer, as you learned to do earlier in the tutorial on creating a clipping mask in the session on Special Text Effects.

Advantages of a Photo Filter Adjustment Layer

You can apply a Photo Filter adjustment as a direct image adjustment rather than as an adjustment layer by selecting Image→Adjustments→Photo Filter in the menu bar. However, it's preferable to apply a Photo Filter as an adjustment layer for all the reasons that make adjustment layers so useful:

» A Photo Filter adjustment layer can be edited at any time by clicking its leftmost thumbnail in the Layers palette to reopen the Photo Filter dialog box.

» As an adjustment layer, the Photo Filter is nondestructive of the underlying image pixels.

» And a Photo Filter adjustment layer can be modified using the layer opacity and layer blending mode controls on the Layers palette.

5. **In the Photo Filter dialog box, make sure Preview is checked so that you can see a live preview of the Photo Filter adjustment in your image.**

6. **Choose Cooling Filter (80) from the Filter menu in the Photo Filter dialog box.**
   The Filter menu is a list of preset Photo Filters. Choosing Cooling Filter 80 changes the Color field in the dialog box to a medium blue and adds a blue tint to the affected area of the image below.

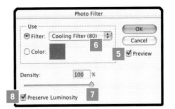

7. **Move the Density slider in the dialog box to 100%.**
   Density controls the strength of a Photo Filter adjustment. For more realistic effects you would set Density to a lower value.

8. **Leave Preserve Luminosity selected to compensate for the tendency of a photo filter to make an image darker.**
   Advanced users may want to turn this option off and adjust exposure more precisely using Curves or other tonal adjustment features.

What the Preset Photo Filters Do

The two Cooling Filters in the list of preset filters simulate blue photographic filters that are commonly used to compensate for warm light sources. Cooling filters are used to reduce the red rays of sunset or to correct the orange cast that can ruin indoor shots taken with a camera loaded with daylight film. The two yellow/orange Warming Filters do the opposite. They are typically used to compensate for the bluish cast of fog, distance, or predawn light. Warming Filters are also useful for fixing the blue cast you see in outdoor photographs taken with tungsten film that is balanced for indoor lighting.

Photoshop also comes with a variety of colored filters that neutralize their complementary colors in a photograph. These are useful for correcting color casts. For example, you can apply the Magenta filter to absorb the greenish cast of a photograph taken under flourescent lighting, or use the Yellow filter to neutralize the blue color cast you often get in photographs of snow from the reflection of a blue sky.

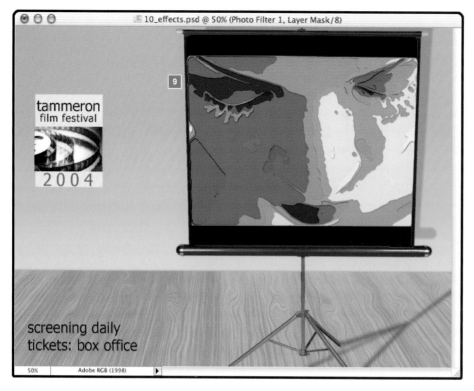

9. **Click OK in the Photo Filter dialog box to apply the Photo Filter adjustment.**

   The Photo Filter dialog box closes. It can be reopened at any time for editing by clicking the leftmost thumbnail on the Photo Filter 1 layer. Your image should resemble the illustration.

10. **Close the screen content layer set for now.**

11. **Choose File→Save and leave the file open for the next tutorial.**

Create Custom Photo Filters

You aren't limited to using only the preset Photo Filters that ship with Photoshop. You can create your own photo filter by clicking the color field in the Photo Filter dialog box to open the Color Picker, selecting a color, and clicking OK. Then click OK again in the Photo Filter dialog box.

If you want to reuse a custom Photo Filter, you can create and save it as part of a swatch in the Swatches palette. To do that, click the Foreground color box in the toolbox and choose a color for your custom Photo Filter. Open the Swatches palette (Window→Swatches) and click the arrow at the top right of that palette to open the palette menu. Choose Photo Filter Colors from the list of Swatches in that palette menu and click OK at the

prompt. This loads the Photo Filter Colors swatch, with one square for each of the Photo Filter Colors, into the Swatches palette. Click in a blank area of the Swatches palette to add the Foreground color you just selected. Give the new color whatever name you want your new Photo Filter to have. Then choose Save Swatches from the Swatches palette menu, name the swatch Photo Filter Colors.aco, and save it over the existing swatch of that name in the following location: Photoshop CS application folder\Presets\Color Swatches\Adobe Photoshop Only. Finally, close and relaunch Photoshop so that the new filter name appears in the Filters menu in the Photo Filter dialog box.

Tutorial
» Lighting with a Filter

Light is one of the most difficult effects to create. Luckily, Photoshop provides a full lighting toolbox with many adjustable attributes in its Lighting Effects filter. In this tutorial, you create a custom spotlight effect to add drama and interest to the scene you're building. You also learn how to apply a filter to a neutral-colored layer so that the filter doesn't alter the pixels of the layer that it affects. This gives you the option of deleting the filter effect at any time.

1. **With** 10_effects.psd **still open from the last tutorial, select the Poster layer set in the Layers palette.**

2. **Choose Layer→New→Layer.**
   The New Layer dialog box opens.

3. **Type** lighting **as the name of the new layer in the New Layer dialog box. Choose Multiply from the Mode menu and put a check mark in the Fill with Multiply-neutral color (white) check box. Click OK to close the New Layer dialog box.**
   The new lighting layer appears above the Poster layer. The lighting layer is filled with white and is set to blend with the underlying layers using the Multiply layer blending mode. White is a neutral color in Multiply mode, which means that it becomes invisible in that blending mode, leaving only the filter effect that you're about to add to the lighting layer.

4. **With the lighting layer selected in the Layers palette, choose Filter→Render→Lighting Effects.**
   The Lighting Effects dialog box opens, offering many options for controlling lighting.

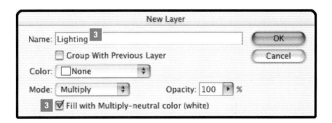

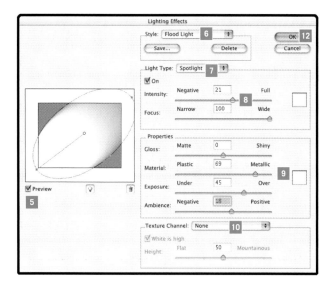

5. **Make sure that the Preview option is checked in the Lighting Effects dialog box.**

   This displays a preview of the lighting effect in the Lighting Effects dialog box. Unfortunately, you can't see the underlying image in this preview, and there is no live image preview in the document window for this filter. This means that you have to use trial and error to get just the right lighting effect when you are working on a neutral color layer. (If you were working directly on an image layer, the image would be visible in the preview pane of this dialog box.)

6. **Choose Flood Light from the Style menu.**

   Each preset style in this menu sets the other controls in the Lighting Effects dialog box. You can customize these settings to get the effect that you want, as you do in the next steps.

7. **Choose Spotlight from the Light Type menu.**

   Spotlight creates a beam of light that is bright at its source and tapers off.

8. **Drag the slider bars to set each of the following attributes for Light Type: Focus: 100, Intensity: 21.**

   Focus controls the reach of the spotlight's beam. Intensity controls the brightness of the spotlight. The color field in the Light Type section enables you to change the color of the spotlight. Leave it white for now.

9. **Drag the slider bars in the Properties section of the dialog box to match the following settings: Gloss: 0, Material: 69, Exposure: 45, Ambience: 18.**

   Gloss and Material control how the light appears to reflect off the underlying image. Exposure affects the brightness of all the lights in the image, including the general ambient light. Ambience controls the level of that general light. The color field in the Properties section enables you to change the color of the ambient light. Leave it white for now.

10. **Leave Texture Channel set to None.**

    Texture Channel can be used to make one of the color channels in the image into a texture map that controls the brightness and darkness of different areas of the image.

< T I P >
You can add multiple lights to an image by clicking the light bulb icon under the preview pane in the Lighting Effects dialog box.

11. **Drag the small white circle in the preview pane to reposition the light.**

12. **Drag the gray points on four sides of the ellipse to resize and rotate the light. Don't worry if your preview pane doesn't look exactly like the one in the figure.**

    Notice that the ellipse extends outside of the preview pane in this example.

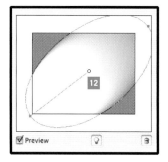

13. **Click OK to apply the Lighting Effects filter to the lighting layer.**
    The lighting effect adds dimension and life to the image.

<CAUTION>

Applying this filter is the only way to test the effect in your document because the Lighting Effects filter has no live image preview. If you aren't happy with the result, you can delete the Lighting layer and start over. The settings that you used will still be in place in the Lighting Effects dialog box. The Lighting Effects filter is tricky to work with. You may have to start over several times to make your document look like the final illustration in this tutorial.

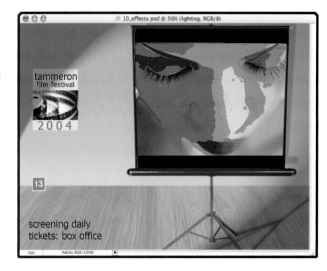

14. **Click the New Snapshot button at the bottom of the History palette (Window→History).**

15. **Experiment with reducing the opacity of the Lighting layer, turning its visibility on and off, and even deleting the layer, just as you could with any layer.**
    Isolating the filter on a neutral layer gives you this editing flexibility that's otherwise lacking when you use a filter and preserves the original art work.

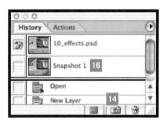

16. **Click the Snapshot 1 state at the top of the History palette to return the image to the way that it looked before your experiments.**

17. **Choose File→Save and leave the document open for the next tutorial.**

Tutorial
» Creating a Layer Style

Layer styles are a more flexible method of applying special effects than filters. A layer style doesn't alter the actual pixels of the layer that it affects. You can edit, hide, or delete a layer style at any time. Also, layer styles come with many options, making them fully customizable. In this tutorial, you learn how to create and customize layer styles.

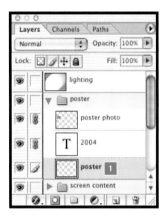

1. In `10_effects.psd`, **which is still open from the previous tutorial, click the arrow to the left of the poster folder to open the poster layer set. Select the poster layer.**

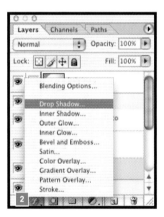

2. **Click the Add Layer Style button (the button with the *f* symbol) at the bottom of the Layers palette and choose Drop Shadow from the menu of layer styles.**
   This adds a Drop Shadow layer style to the poster layer and opens the Layer Style dialog box, in which you can customize that drop shadow.

3. **Check that the Drop Shadow option in the Styles section displays a check mark and is highlighted.**
   The check mark indicates that the Drop Shadow layer style is active on the selected layer. The highlight is what makes the Drop Shadow settings appear on the right side of the Layer Style dialog box.

<CAUTION>
It's easy to forget that a layer style must be highlighted, rather than merely checked, to be subject to editing. Put this on your list of common mistakes to watch out for.

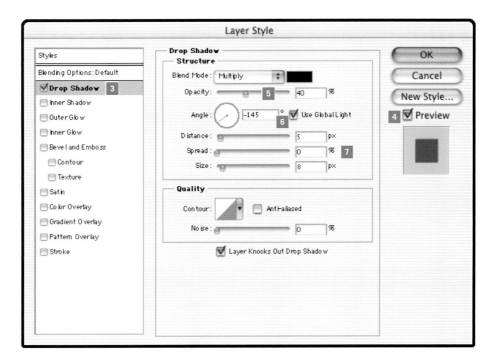

4. **Make sure that there is a check mark in the Preview checkbox.**
   This enables you to see a live preview of the layer style that you're creating in the document window. This preview updates as you change the settings in the Layer Style dialog box.

5. **Drag the Opacity slider to 40% in the Drop Shadow options section of the dialog box.**
   Reducing the opacity of a shadow helps create a natural look.

6. **Set the angle to –145. Make sure that Use Global Light is checked.**
   Angle controls the direction of the shadow. The check mark next to Use Global Light ensures that this layer style shares the same lighting direction as other layer styles that you may add to this image. If you already had a shadow, bevel, or other directional layer style on another layer, changing the Angle to –145 here would change that layer style too. Keeping shadows and other effects at a consistent angle makes images look more realistic.

7. **Drag the Size slider to 8 and the Distance slider to 5.**
   Size and Distance determine how far the shadow extends beyond the edge of the art work. Increasing the size of a shadow provides a softer effect.

8. **Click OK to accept the changes and return to the document.**
Notice the drop shadow effect on the Poster layer in the document window and in the Layers palette.

< T I P >

You can edit the settings that you applied to this drop shadow layer style at any time by double-clicking its name in the Layers palette to reopen the Layer Styles dialog box.

< T I P >

Layer styles are very flexible. You can hide, delete, copy, or collapse an existing layer style straight from the Layers palette, as follows:

- To hide an individual layer style, click its eye icon in the Layers palette. To hide all the layer styles on a layer, click the eye icon next to the word Effects on that layer.

- To delete a layer style, click it and drag it to the Trash button at the bottom of the Layers palette. To delete all the layer styles on a layer, click the word Effects and drag it to the same Trash button.

- To copy a layer style from one layer to another, click the layer style in the Layers palette and drag it just beneath the other layer until you see a black bar.

- To collapse your view of layer styles in order to tidy up the Layers palette, click the triangle next to the word Effects.

9. **Select the poster photo layer in the Layers palette, click the *f* icon at the bottom of the palette, and choose Color Overlay.**
The Layer Style dialog box opens with the Color Overlay style highlighted in the Styles section. This style defaults to red.

10. **Click Color Overlay in the Styles section of the Layer Style dialog box, highlighting that style.**

11. **Click the Color field in the Layer Style dialog box to open the Color Picker. Make sure Web Colors Only is unchecked. Type the following values in the RGB fields in the Color Picker: R: 26, G: 81, B: 128. Click OK. Make sure the Blend Mode field is set to Color. Click OK.**
The picture on the poster in the image changes to a tinted blue.

12. **Double-click the Screening layer in the Layers palette.**
The Layer Style dialog box opens for editing.

< C A U T I O N >

Be careful not to click directly on the layer name, or you highlight the layer name for renaming rather than open the Layer Style dialog box.

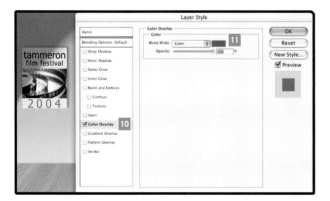

13. **Click the Drop Shadow item in the Styles section of the Layer Style dialog box, highlighting that item.**

    This applies a drop shadow to the selected screening layer (yet another way of creating a layer style) and opens the Drop Shadow settings on the right side of the dialog box.

14. **Set the opacity to 25%, the distance to 28 px, the spread to 2, and size to 7. View the preview of this shadow in the image, and if you're satisfied, click OK.**

    As the distance setting increases, a shadowed object appears to be farther away from the background. It is a good idea to create a light, soft shadow when using higher distance values, as you've done here. Don't click OK yet.

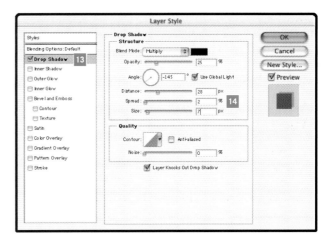

15. **Click Color Overlay in the Styles section of the Layer Style dialog box.**

    This adds another layer style to the selected layer, and the Color Overlay options appear in the right pane. Note that the color of the screening text in your document changes to red, the default color for the color overlay.

16. **Click the Color field in the Layer Style dialog box to open the Color Picker. Type the following values in the RGB fields in the Color Picker: R:** 67, **G:** 109, **B:** 7. **Click OK.**

    The screening text in the image changes to dark purple.

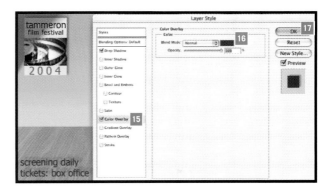

17. **Click OK to accept the layer style settings and return to the document.**

18. **Close the poster layer set in the Layers palette.**

19. **Choose File→Save and keep the document open for the next tutorial.**

Tutorial
» Saving and Reusing a Layer Style

Photoshop takes much of the work out of creating special effects, but often you create a unique combination of layer styles that could be useful in the future. Photoshop provides the Styles palette to collect and save styles, an efficient way to reduce the time spent creating special effects and to guarantee consistency. It's easy to reapply these styles to a different layer or even to a different document. In this tutorial, you create a custom layer style, save it to the Styles palette, and then apply it to a different layer.

1. Make sure that 10_effects.psd is still open from the last tutorial.

2. Expand both the Screen Content layer set and its nested text set in the Layers palette. Turn on the Visibility of the text set and select the film layer.

3. Click the New Layer Style button at the bottom of the palette and choose Outer Glow from the menu of layer styles.
   The Layer Style dialog box opens with the Outer Glow settings displayed. An outer glow applies a gentle color around the outside of an object—in this case, text.

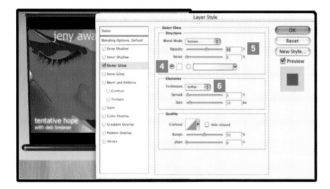

4. Click the Color field in the Structure section of the Outer Glow settings to open the Color Picker. Select R: 255, G: 255, B: 255 from the Color Picker and click OK.
   This sets the color of the outer glow to white.

5. Set the opacity to 55%.
   It's typical to have to increase the opacity of the default Outer Glow layer style to be able to see it against certain backgrounds.

6. In the Elements section, set Technique to Softer, Spread to 3%, and Size to 10 px.
   These settings control the look and size of the glow.

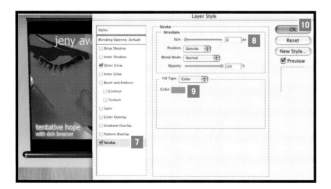

7. Click Stroke in the Styles section of the Layer Style dialog box.

8. In the Structure section of the dialog box, set the Size of the stroke to 3.

9. Click the Color field in the Fill Type section to open the Color Picker. In the Color Picker choose a medium blue (R: 136, G: 149, and B: 241). Click OK.

10. Click OK to close the Layer Style dialog box.
    Now that you have this combination of custom glow and stroke layer styles defined and applied, you can save them as a single style in the Styles palette for later use.

11. **Choose Window→Styles.**

    The Styles palette opens.

    <CAUTION>

    Don't be confused by the similarity of the terms *layer style* and *style*. A layer style can stand alone or be a component of a style. A style is made up of a combination of layer styles and is stored in the Styles palette.

12. **Click the arrow on the right side of the Styles panel and select New Style.**

    The New Style dialog box opens.

13. **Type** white glow blue stroke **as the style name. Make sure that there's a check mark next to Include Layer Effects to ensure that the outer glow and stroke layer styles are included in the style. Click OK.**

    The new style appears in the Styles palette.

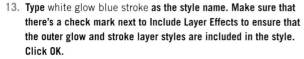

14. **Move your mouse over the last thumbnail in the Styles palette. Its name, white glow blue stroke, appears in a ToolTip.**

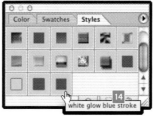

15. **Select the Jeny layer in the Layers palette.**

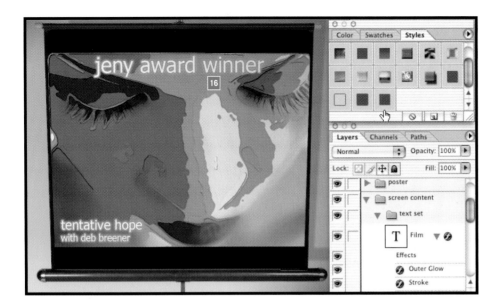

16. **Click your new white glow blue stroke style in the Styles palette.**
The layer style is automatically applied to the Jeny layer, and
the words "jeny award winner" in the image display the same
style as the words on the film layer. That's all there is to applying a custom style to the art work on a layer.

17. **Choose File→Save As, rename the file** `10_effects_end.psd`,
navigate to your collages folder, and click Save.

» Session Review

You covered a lot of territory in the Photoshop special effects world. You now have the basics to do much more exploring. Special effects are best learned by wandering through the menus and experimenting with different combinations. Before you head off to discover your own style for special effects, check to see how much you remember from this session.

1. What is the effect of applying the same filter to a layer multiple times? (See "Tutorial: Filtering a Layer.")

2. What is the Fibers filter useful for creating? (See "Tutorial: Filtering a Selection.")

3. How can you reduce the effect of a filter after it is applied? (See "Tutorial: Filtering a Selection.")

4. What is the purpose of the mesh when creating a Liquify effect? (See "Tutorial: Filtering a Selection.")

5. Can you preview the effect of more than one filter at a time in the Filter Gallery? (See "Tutorial: Applying Multiple Filters in the Filter Gallery.")

6. Does the Filter Gallery include all Photoshop filters? (See "Tutorial: Applying Multiple Filters in the Filter Gallery.")

7. What does painting with the History Brush do? (See "Tutorial: Painting with Filters and the History Brush.")

8. Is the Photo Filter feature really a filter? If not, what is it? (See "Tutorial: Applying a Photo Filter Adjustment.")

9. What is the name of the filter that creates sophisticated lighting effects? (See "Tutorial: Lighting with a Filter.")

10. How do you reposition or resize a lighting effect? (See "Tutorial: Lighting with a Filter.")

11. What is a layer style? (See "Tutorial: Creating a Layer Style.")

12. How does a layer style differ from a filter? (See "Tutorial: Creating a Layer Style.")

13. What effect does a color overlay layer style apply? (See "Tutorial: Creating a Layer Style.")

14. How do you apply a saved style to a new layer? (See "Tutorial: Saving and Reusing a Layer Style.")

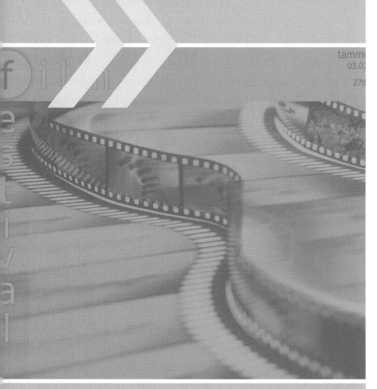

Part V
Text

Creating and Formatting Text

Session Introduction

Photoshop offers powerful tools for working with text. In this session, you'll learn to use the Type tools as you add text and manipulate it with character and paragraph controls. You will also learn to work with Photoshop's spell check and find and replace features to ensure accuracy in your text.

TOOLS YOU'LL USE
Horizontal Type tool, Vertical Type tool, Options bar, Character palette, Check Spelling command, and Find and Replace Text command

CD-ROM FILES NEEDED
11_type.psd and 11_type_end.psd

TIME REQUIRED
45 minutes

Tutorial
» Using the Type Tools

When you select a type tool and click in your document, Photoshop automatically creates a type layer. This special kind of layer contains only text, which is vector-based and editable. In this tutorial, you learn the basics of creating text in Photoshop, including how to use the Horizontal Type and Vertical Type tools, how to set type options on the Options bar, and how to recolor existing text.

1. Open `11_type.psd` from the Session 11 Tutorial Files folder on your hard drive.

2. Open the Character palette. Click the arrow on the top right of that palette to open the palette menu and choose Reset Character.

3. Select the topmost layer (the Ticket Background layer) in the Layers palette. Click the New set button at the bottom of the Layers palette to create a new layer set.

4. Double-click the Set 1 name and rename the layer set Ticket text.

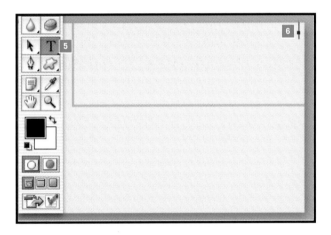

5. Select the Horizontal Type tool in the toolbox.
   The Horizontal Type tool is the default type tool. If it's not showing, click whichever type tool is displayed and choose the Horizontal Type tool from the fly-out menu.

6. Click inside the green rectangular outline on the top right of the ticket in the image.
   When you click with the Horizontal Type tool in the image, a new type layer, Layer 1, is created in the Layers palette. Layer 1 is automatically included in the Ticket text layer set, because that layer set is selected.

Photoshop's Vector-Based Type

Photoshop type is vector-based, which means that it consists of resolution-independent mathematical font definitions rather than pixels. As a result, the text that you create in Photoshop has smooth outlines and can be scaled up or down without harming its appearance, as long as it is printed on a post-script printer or saved in Photoshop EPS format or Photoshop PDF format with the Include Vector Data option turned on in the Save settings.

However, if you print on an inkjet printer, text becomes pixel-based and no longer has these qualities, and if you zoom into Photoshop type on-screen, you see pixels, because your monitor is pixel-based. Text on a type layer is always editable with the Photoshop type tools, unless you rasterize the layer (convert its contents from vector to pixel-based format) in order to add special effects, as you do in Session 12.

7. **Choose the following font settings in the Options bar—font family: Tahoma; font style: Regular; font size: 18 pt.**
Font family sets the typeface. Font style sets the style of that typeface (such as regular, bold, italic, or bold italic). Font size is reported in points, the unit of measurement commonly used in print projects.

<TIP>
You can change the unit of measurement for font size by selecting Preferences➜Units and Rulers➜Type from the Photoshop menu (Windows: the Edit menu) and choosing pixels or millimeters instead of points.

<NOTE>
The font family and font style menus list fonts installed in your system, as well as fonts installed in the Library/Application Support/ Adobe/Fonts folder (Windows: the Program Files/Common Fonts/ Adobe/Fonts directory). The latter appear only in Adobe applications.

<TIP>
The font style menu displays only those styles that are native to the selected typeface. If a typeface doesn't have a native bold or italic style, you can simulate that style using the Faux Bold or Faux Italic buttons that are located at the bottom of the Character palette (Window➜Character).

8. **Click the anti-aliasing button in the Options bar and choose Sharp as the anti-aliasing style.**
Anti-aliasing gradually blends text into the background by creating partially filled pixels along the edges of text characters. You can choose from four anti-aliasing styles: Sharp produces the sharpest anti-aliased text, Crisp the next sharpest, Strong the boldest, and Smooth the smoothest. Choosing None in the anti-aliasing field produces aliased text with jaggedy edges.

<TIP>
Text in print projects usually is anti-aliased. Aliased text typically is used on small text for the Web, which could be hard to read if it were anti-aliased because the edges of individual characters might blur into one another on-screen.

9. **Click in the Color field on the Options bar to open the Color Picker. Enter R: 204, G: 204, B: 0 to set the color for all the text that you enter on this type layer.**
Another way to set the color of text before it's entered is to set the Foreground color by double-clicking the Foreground Color box in the toolbox and choosing a color from the Color Picker.

10. **Leave the default left text alignment button depressed in the Options bar.**

<NOTE>
You can create multiple lines of text on a single type layer by pressing the Return or Enter key between lines. The text alignment setting determines how multiple lines of text will align with one another. The position of the small dot that appears on the text baseline in text edit mode indicates left, center, or right text alignment

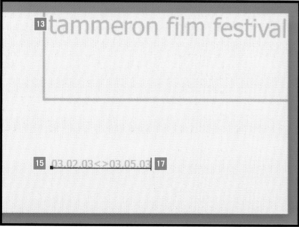

11. **Type** tammeron film festival **in the image.**
    The text appears in the image on a baseline.

12. **Click the Commit button (the large check mark icon on the right side of the Options bar).**
    This confirms your text edits and exits text edit mode, so that you again can perform all operations in Photoshop. The text baseline disappears, and the name of the type layer automatically changes to the first few words of text that you typed.

<NOTE>
There are several other ways to exit text edit mode, including selecting another tool, or clicking in any palette other than the Character and Paragraph palettes. Clicking the Cancel button in the Options bar undoes your text edits and exits text edit mode.

<CAUTION>
If you can't perform an operation after you've made a text edit, it's probably because you haven't exited text edit mode. You know that you're still in text edit mode if you see the Commit and Cancel buttons in the Options bar.

13. **Select the Move tool and drag the tammeron film festival text to the correct location in the image, as shown in the figure.**

14. **Select the Horizontal Type tool again.**

15. **Click anywhere in the image away from the tammeron film festival text to generate a new type layer.**

<CAUTION>
You have to click far away from the existing text in order to create a separate type layer. If you click too close to existing text, Photoshop thinks that you want to edit that text and doesn't create a new layer for the text you're about to type.

16. **Change the font size in the Options bar to** 8pt **for the new type layer.**

17. **Type the dates** 03.02.03<>03.05.03.

Changing Partial Text Color

To change the color of just part of the text on a type layer, select the Type tool and click and drag across that part of the text. Click ⌘+H (Windows: Ctrl+H) to hide the text highlighting so you can see a live preview of color changes as they occur. Open the Color palette (Window→Color) and move the sliders to try different colors, which you can see changing in the image. Or open the Swatches palette (Window→Swatches) and click some swatches to try those colors. When you decide on a color, click the Commit button on the Options bar. You see a question mark in the Color field in the Options bar whenever you reselect this type layer because the layer now contains more than one color of text.

18. **Select the Move tool and move the date text into position just above the horizontal green line on the ticket. The right edge of the text should be close to the right edge of the ticket.**
Selecting the Move tool automatically exits text edit mode.

19. **Select the Horizontal type tool again. With the 03.02.03<>03.05.03 type layer selected in the Layers palette, click the Color field on the Options bar to open the Color Picker. Choose black (R: 0, G: 0, B: 0) from the Color Picker and click OK.**
This recolors all the text on the selected type layer to black. This is the quickest way to change the color of an existing type layer because you don't have to highlight any text.

20. **Click and hold the Horizontal Type tool in the toolbox to display the fly-out menu of type tools. Select the Vertical Type tool.**

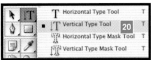

21. **Click in the top-left corner of the ticket to create another type layer.**

22. **In the Options bar, make sure the font family is set to Tahoma, the font style is set to Regular, and the font color is set to black. Type 16 pt in the Font Size field and press Return or Enter on your keyboard.**

23. **Type admit one.**
The text is positioned vertically in the image. The vertical line through the text is the type baseline.

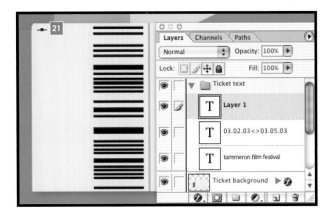

24. **Select the Move tool to adjust the position of the text if necessary.**
This commits this line of type and exits text edit mode.

< T I P >
Vertical text is created with each letter in an upright position. You can change all the letters on a vertical type layer so that they are still in a vertical column but are lying on their sides by opening the Character palette (Window→Character), clicking the arrow at the top right of that palette, and choosing Rotate Character.

< T I P >
You can convert vertical text to horizontal text at any time (and vice versa) by selecting the type layer, selecting a type tool, and clicking the Text Orientation button on the top left of the Options bar.

25. **Choose File→Save and leave this file open for the next tutorial.**
Photoshop offers two kinds of type—point and paragraph type. The type you created in this tutorial was point type—independent lines of type, as distinguished from type that wraps from line to line in paragraph style. Point type is useful for short pieces of text, like headlines and tag lines. In the next tutorial you learn about paragraph type, which is used for longer passages of text.

Tutorial
» Creating Paragraph Type

This tutorial covers paragraph type—text that is created inside of a bounding box. Paragraph type wraps automatically from line to line to fit the size and shape of its bounding box. Paragraph type is used for substantial passages of text or when you require flexibility in the shape or alignment of a block of text.

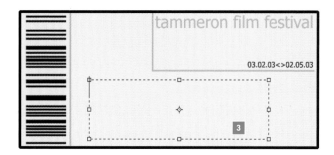

1. **Make sure that** `11_type.psd` **is still open from the preceding tutorial.**

2. **Select the Horizontal Type tool.**

3. **Click in the lower portion of the ticket and drag to create a rectangular bounding box.**
   A new text layer is created, and dotted lines define a bounding box for text. Don't worry if your bounding box is a different size or shape than the one in the figure. You adjust the box shortly.

4. **Set font size to** `12 pt` **in the Options bar.**
   The other type options should be as they were at the end of the last tutorial—font family: Tahoma; font style: Regular; anti-aliasing: Sharp; alignment: left; and color: black.

5. **Type the following, without correcting the spelling errors:** thank you for supporting the 27th annual tammeron festival. we appericiate your patronage. the selected films are explorations into the human concious and subconcious. enjoy
   Note that two spaces follow the first and second periods, and the words *appericiate*, *concious*, and *subconcious* are misspelled on purpose so that you have some text to correct in a later tutorial on spell checking.

< N O T E >

If you drew your bounding box to approximately the same size as the one in the figure, only part of the text appears in the bounding box, and you see a small cross in the handle at the bottom right corner of the bounding box. The cross indicates that the bounding box isn't big enough to accommodate the text.

6. **Move your cursor over any handle of the bounding box. When the cursor changes to a double-pointed arrow, click and drag until you see all the text you entered.**

   The text reflows to fit in the expanded bounding box. The lines of text now end at different points than they did before.

7. **Click the Commit button on the top right of the Options bar to accept the text edits.**

   The bounding box disappears as you exit text edit mode.

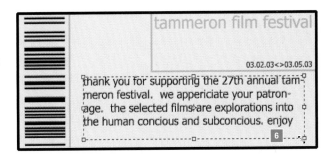

<TIP>

If you ever want to resize, rotate, or distort this text again, select a type tool and click the text in the document to make the paragraph bounding box reappear. Then use the appropriate transform commands to affect the type in the bounding box.

8. **With the thank you . . . type layer selected and the Horizontal Type tool selected, change the font size in the Options bar to** 8.

   All the text in the layer changes size, and Photoshop automatically rewraps the resized text to fit the bounding box. This is the same technique you use to change font family, color, or other formatting attributes of all the text on a paragraph type layer at any time after text has been committed. If you make a similar change before committing text, you have to click and drag to select the text first.

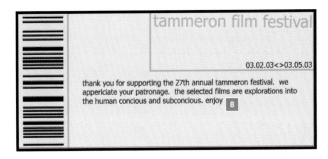

9. **Select the Move tool to move the text into position just above the bottom of the ticket area, as shown here.**

10. **Choose File→Save and leave this file open for the next tutorial.**

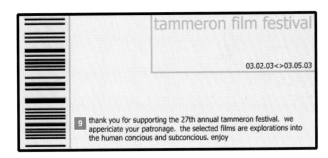

<TIP>

You can change your mind about whether to use point or paragraph format after you enter your text by converting from one format to the other. Select your type layer in the Layers palette and choose Layer→Type→Convert to Point Text or Layer→Type→Convert to Paragraph Text, as appropriate. Make sure that all the paragraph text is visible before converting to point text because any text that falls outside the bounding box is deleted on conversion.

Tutorial
» Formatting Type

Creating words in a document is just the start if you want to produce attractive, legible text. In this tutorial, you get to know the Character and Paragraph palettes and some of the powerful typographic features that they offer for formatting text.

1. Use `11_type.psd` from the last tutorial.

2. **Select the Horizontal Type tool from the toolbox. Click the Palette button on the right side of the Options bar to open the Character palette.**
   Alternatively, you can open the Character palette by choosing Window→Character.

   \<NOTE\>
   The Character palette offers controls for formatting individual characters. Some of its settings are the same as those on the Options bar; others are unique.

3. **Locate "27th" in the paragraph type that you created in the previous tutorial. Click and drag to select the** *th*.

4. **Click the Superscript button (T^1) in the Character palette.**
   Photoshop automatically reduces the size of the selected text and raises its baseline above the other letters.

5. **Click the Commit button on the Options bar to confirm the change.**

6. **Create a new layer of point text by clicking just below the green line and near the right edge of the ticket in the image.**

7. **Set the font size to** 10 pt **in the Character palette. Check that font color is still set to black, font family to Tahoma, and Font Style to Regular from the last tutorial.**
   Alternatively, you can set all of these character formatting options in the Options bar.

8. **Click the Paragraph tab to switch to the Paragraph palette. Then click the right alignment button.**
   The Paragraph palette offers settings—including alignment, justification, and hyphenation—that pertain to entire paragraphs of type, rather than to individual characters.

9. **Type the following two lines of text on the same layer, pressing the Return or Enter key after england to create a line break:**
   tammeron, england
   27th annual

10. **Click and drag to highlight the first line of the text you just typed.**

11. **Click the Character tab and type** 500 **in the Tracking field of the Character palette.**

12. **Highlight the second line of text you typed. In the Character palette, type** 745 **for the Tracking value.**

13. **Click the Color field to open the Color Picker. Set the font color to R: 204, G: 204, B: 0 and click OK.**

14. **Set the font size to** 8 pt **in the Character palette.**

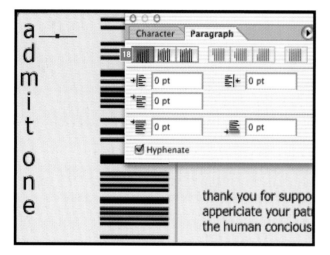

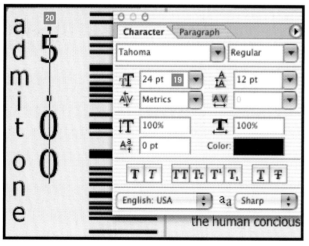

15. **Highlight both lines of text in this layer in the document window. Click the leading field down arrow in the Character palette and choose 12 pt as the leading value.**

    The distance between the lines increases with this value.

<NOTE>

Some of the fields in the Character palette now display no values. This is because those values are different in each line of text that is selected. The Color field in the Character palette, like the one in the Options bar, displays a question mark because there are now two colors on the same layer.

16. **Click the Commit button on the Options bar to confirm the text changes.**

<TIP>

If you want to see the results of these changes without the highlighting, press ⌘+H (Windows: Ctrl+H).

17. **Select the Vertical Type tool. Click beside the words *admit one* in the document to create a new point type layer.**

18. **Click the Paragraph tab to display the Paragraph palette and click the Top Align button.**

19. **Click the Character tab to switch to the Character palette. In the Character palette, set font size to 24, Color to black, and tracking to 0.**

20. **Type 5.00 in the image.**

21. **Insert the cursor between the 5 and the . (period). Click the kerning field down arrow and choose 100.**

    The space between the 5 and the period increases.

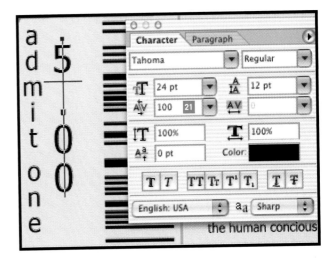

22. **Insert the cursor between the . (period) and the first 0. Type** 500 **in the kerning field for the kerning value to increase that space. Repeat this for the space between the 0 and 0.**

23. **Select the Move tool and move the 5.00 type layer if necessary to match the illustration.**

24. **Choose File→Save and keep this document open for the next tutorial.**

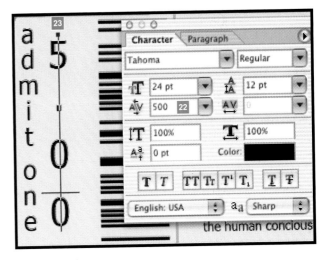

Tracking, Kerning, and Leading

Tracking, kerning, and leading are classic typography spacing techniques that are controlled from the Character palette in Photoshop. *Tracking* spaces all characters in a selection equally. *Kerning* is used to adjust the spacing between characters, often to correct awkward gaps or lack of space caused by character combinations. *Leading* adjusts the spacing between lines.

Tutorial
» Using Photoshop's Word-Processing Features

You may not add large areas of text to your Photoshop documents often. But when you do, you'll appreciate Photoshop's spell checker and find and replace features, which give you the kind of control over type content that you expect in a word-processing program.

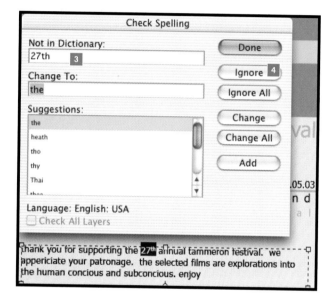

1. Check that 11_type.psd is still open from the last tutorial.

2. Select the Horizontal type tool. Click in the image after the word enjoy to select the layer of paragraph text.
   The paragraph type bounding box appears.

3. Choose Edit→Check Spelling.
   The Check Spelling dialog box appears with the word 27th highlighted in the text. The spell checker stops on the first word that is not in its dictionary, assuming it might be misspelled, and suggests a correct spelling.

4. Click Ignore to leave the word 27th unchanged.
   The spell checker continues on to the next word it does not recognize—*tammeron*.

5. Click Ignore again to leave the word tammeron unchanged.
   The spell checker stops next at the misspelled word *appericiate*.

\<NOTE\>
If you often use a word that is identified as an error, you can add that word to Photoshop's dictionary by choosing Add. Photoshop won't see that word as an error in future checks.

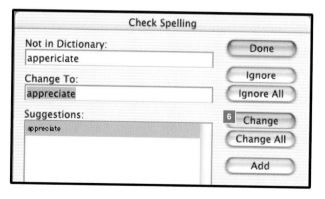

6. Click Change to accept appreciate as the correct spelling.
   The corrected word now appears in the document, and the next misspelled word is highlighted.

7. Click Change twice more when the spell checker stops on the misspelled words concious and subconcious to correct the spelling of those words (to conscious and subconscious).

8. Click OK at the spell check complete prompt to exit the spell checker.

9. Add an ! (exclamation point) at the end of the paragraph text and click the Commit button on the Options bar to accept the text edits.

10. With the Horizontal Type tool selected, reactivate your layer of paragraph type by clicking before the words *thank you*.

11. Choose Edit→Find and Replace Text from the menu bar.
    The Find And Replace Text dialog box opens.

12. **With your cursor in the Find What field, press your space bar twice.**

13. **With your cursor in the Change To field, press the space bar once.**

14. **Click Find Next.**
    Photoshop finds the double-space between *festival* and *we* and highlights that area in the document.

15. **Click Change/Find.**
    Photoshop makes the correction and proceeds to search for another instance of double spacing.

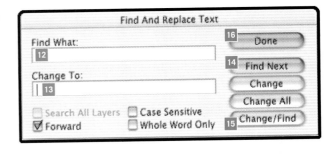

< T I P >
You can also use the Change All setting in the Find And Replace Text dialog box. This setting replaces all search terms with the replacement with one click. However, it is a good idea to test a few replacements before you use the Change All setting.

16. **Click Done to exit the Find And Replace Text dialog box.**

17. **Open the Layers palette (Window→Layers) if it isn't open already.**
    Your Layers palette should have all text layers residing in the Ticket text set. If this is not the case, drag any stray text layers into the Ticket text set as you learned to do in the layers session.

18. **Select the Ticket text layer set in the Layers palette. Click the arrow beside the layer set name to collapse the set.**

19. **Click the Link field beside the Ticket background layer.**
    The Ticket background layer and the Ticket text layer set are now linked and will move as a unit.

20. **Choose Edit→Transform→Rotate.**
    A bounding box appears around the ticket area of the document.

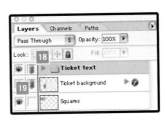

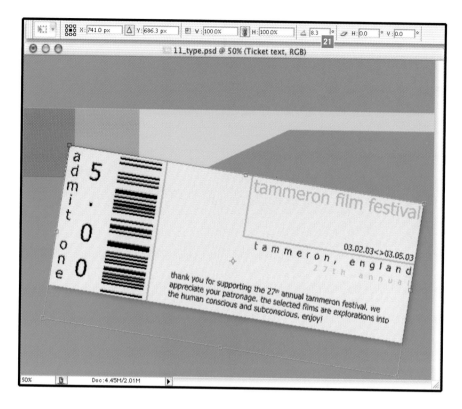

21. **Type** 8.3 **in the Rotation angle field on the Options bar.**

22. **Click the Commit button on the Options bar to commit the transformation.**

    The Options bar for the Transform commands has a Commit button for confirming changes just like the Options bar for the Type tool.

23. **Choose File→Save As, rename the document** 11_type_end.psd, **navigate to your collages folder, and click Save.**

    Congratulations! You finished another collage for your final project.

» Session Review

This session covers how to create point type and paragraph type, how to edit and format text, and how to check your text for accuracy with Photoshop's spell check and find and replace features. The following questions will help you review the materials in this session. You can find the answer to each question in the section noted.

1. How do you know when you're in text edit mode? (See "Tutorial: Using the Type Tools.")

2. Name three ways of exiting text edit mode. (See "Tutorial: Using the Type Tools.")

3. How do you create vertical text? (See "Tutorial: Using the Type Tools.")

4. What is the difference between point type and paragraph type? (See "Tutorial: Creating Paragraph Type.")

5. Name a situation to which point type is best suited and a situation to which paragraph type is best suited. (See "Tutorial: Creating Paragraph Type.")

6. How do you make paragraph type reflow? (See "Tutorial: Creating Paragraph Type.")

7. Can you convert point type to paragraph type, and vice versa? (See "Tutorial: Creating Paragraph Type.")

8. Name three places in Photoshop where you'll find controls for formatting text. (See "Tutorial: Formatting Type.")

9. What is the general purpose of the formatting controls in the Character palette? In the Paragraph palette? (See "Tutorial: Formatting Type.")

10. Define tracking, kerning, and leading. (See "Tutorial: Formatting Type.")

11. Name two features in Photoshop that you can use to make the content of text more accurate. (See "Tutorial: Using Photoshop's Word-Processing Features.")

admit one

5.00

0

tammeron film festival

03.02.03<>03.05.03

tammeron, england

27th annual

thank you for supporting the 27th annual tammeron festival. we appreciate your patronage. the selected films are explorations into the human conscious and subconscious. enjoy!

Special Text Effects

Session Introduction

In this session, you move beyond the basics of working with Photoshop type tools to apply special effects to text. You learn to distort text using the Warp Text feature. You are introduced to curves and learn how to use a curves adjustment layer to create a backdrop that makes text legible against a photograph. You learn how to rasterize a type layer so that you can apply filters and other pixel-based features to text. You discover how to display an image inside text and convert text to a shape. With these methods in hand, you have the power to create dynamic, artistic text effects.

TOOLS YOU'LL USE
Type tool, Warp Text feature, Curves dialog box, Rasterize command, filters, Grouping command, Convert to Shape command, type on a path feature

CD-ROM FILES NEEDED
`12_texteffects.psd`, `12_textimage.psd`, and
`12_texteffects_end.psd`

TIME REQUIRED
60 minutes

Tutorial
» Warping Text

Prior to the introduction in Photoshop CS of the type on a path feature—which you explore later in this session—the Warp Text feature was the only way to distort the shape of text and keep it editable. Warping text still comes in handy as a quick and easy way to distort Photoshop's vector-based type, with both the type and the warp effect remaining editable, as you see in this session.

1. Open `12_texteffects.psd` **from the folder of Session 12 tutorial files on your hard drive.**

2. **Select the Horizontal Type tool in the toolbox. If it's not showing, click whichever Type tool is displayed and choose the Horizontal Type tool from the fly-out menu.**

3. **Click the Palette button on the Options bar to open the Character palette it if is not already showing. Click the arrow on the top right of the Character palette to display the palette menu. Choose Reset Character.**
   This resets the fields in the Character palette to their default settings.

4. **In the Character palette, set the font family to Tahoma, the font size to 24, and the Color to black in the Character palette. Type** `175` **in the Tracking field.**

Tweaking Warped Text

Warped text remains editable in the same way as text on any type layer, which means that you can change its color, font, size, kerning, and other attributes in the Character palette, Paragraph palette, and Options bar, as you learned to do in the previous session. The warp effect that you applied also remains editable. To change or remove the distortion of warped text, select its layer in the Layers palette and click the Warp Text button on the Options bar to reopen the Warp Text dialog box. Change the settings as desired. Choosing None from the Style menu in the dialog box removes the warp effect and changes the Warp Text icon on the type layer back to a type icon.

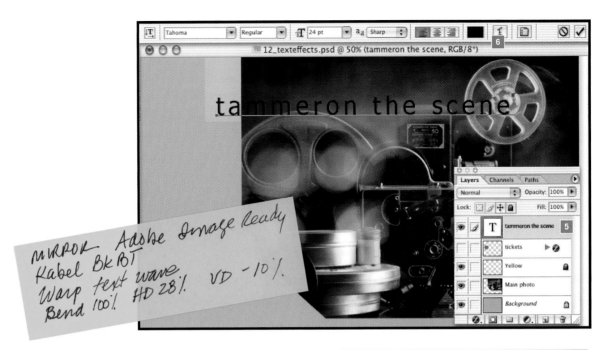

MIRROR — Adobe Image Ready
Kabel Bk BT
Warp text wave
Bend 100% HD 28% VD -10%

5. **Select the topmost layer in the Layers palette. Click near the bottom-left corner of the yellow square in the image. Type** tammeron the scene.
A new type layer appears in the Layers palette.

6. **Click the Warp Text button on the Options bar.**
The Warp Text dialog box opens.

7. **Select Arc from the Style menu in the Warp Text dialog box. Move the Bend slider to +20.**
The text in the document is now curved, as determined by the settings in the Warp Text dialog box. Experiment with some other settings if you like, but return to these settings before moving on to the next step.

8. **Click in the document and drag to move the warped text into place to match the figure.**
Warping the text moves it from its original starting point. This is all you have to do to reposition it while the Warp Text dialog box is open.

9. **Click OK to close the Warp Text dialog box.**
A new warp text icon appears in place of the type icon in the Layers palette.

10. **Click the Commit button on the Options bar to confirm your warp text edit.**

11. **Choose File→Save and keep this document open for the next tutorial.**

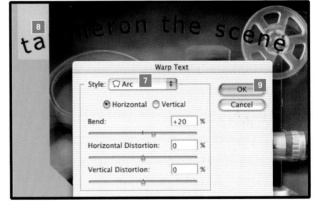

<NOTE>
The text may not show up clearly over dark areas of the image, but you fix that in the next tutorial.

An Introduction to Curves

The Curves adjustment is a powerful tool that gives you precise control over the brightness and contrast of individual tones in an image. This makes Curves superior to the general Brightness and Contrast adjustment that adjusts all tones in an image the same way. The Curves dialog box may look intimidating at first, but it makes sense when you break it down. Here's a brief explanation of how it works.

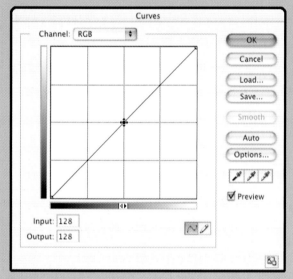

The horizontal bar at the bottom of the diagram is a scale that represents 256 grayscale tones (the maximum number of tones in an RGB image) from black on the left to white on the right. The horizontal scale is used to identify the original tones in an image. The vertical bar on the left side of the diagram is an identical tonal scale turned on its side, which is used to identify the tones to which you remap the original tones. The diagonal curve line represents the tones in the open image. It always starts as a straight diagonal line. To adjust a particular tone in an image, you click that tone's representative spot on the curve line and drag up to lighten and down to darken. Nearby tones on the curve move with the selected tone.

For example, click near the middle of the diagonal curve line and look at the horizontal bar directly below that point for a visual representation of the middle gray tone that you selected.

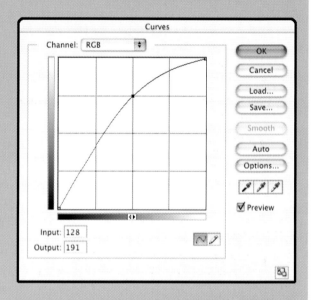

Drag the selected point up to the first intersection above it, as shown in the second figure. Look at the tonal bar directly to the left of the new location of that point, where you see a lighter shade than middle gray. You've mapped the original middle gray tone to this lighter tone wherever the original tone appeared in the image. You've also lightened neighboring tones because dragging the selected point upward changed other points on the curve, too. You could have limited the effect on neighboring tones by clicking other places on the curve to add control points before dragging.

To cancel the adjustment and return the curve to its original state, press the Option (Windows: Alt) key to temporarily change the Cancel button to a Reset button and click the Reset button. In this tutorial, you apply what you learned here to lighten a selected area in the open image so that the text on top of that area is more legible.

Tutorial
» Making Type Visible on Top of a Photograph

The text that you added in the preceding tutorial is not easily legible because there is too little contrast between the dark values in the photograph and the text. In this tutorial, you learn how to solve this common problem by adding a curves adjustment layer above the layer that contains the photograph. This lets the tones of the underlying image come through, while providing a lightened background against which the text is legible.

1. **Use** `12_texteffects.psd` **for this tutorial. That file should still be open from the preceding tutorial.**

2. **Click whichever Lasso tool is showing in the toolbox and select the Polygonal Lasso from the fly-out tool menu.**

3. **Click from point to point to draw a polygonal selection similar to the one shown here.**
   The selection defines the area you're about to lighten. Don't worry if your selection doesn't match this one exactly. Just make sure that it covers all the warped text.

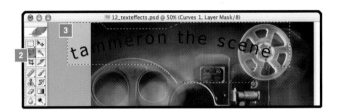

4. **Press ⌘+H (Windows: Ctrl+H) to hide the selection so you get a better view of the adjustment you're about to make.**

5. **Select the Main photo layer in the Layers palette. Choose Layer→New Adjustment Layer→Curves. Click OK in the New Layer dialog box.**
   This creates an adjustment layer called Curves 1 above the Main photo layer and opens the Curves dialog box.

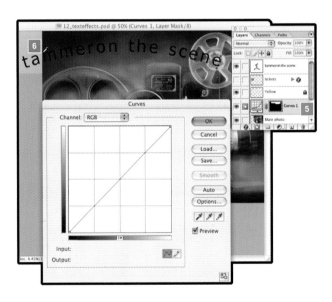

<TIP>
Another way to create a curves adjustment layer is to click the New Fill or Adjustment Layer button (the black and white button) at the bottom of the Layers palette and choose Curves from that menu.

<NOTE>
Notice that the Curves 1 adjustment layer contains two thumbnails. The thumbnail on the left represents the adjustment. You can double-click that thumbnail at any time to reopen the Curves dialog box and edit the curve. The thumbnail on the right represents a layer mask that limits the effect of the adjustment to the area that you selected in step 3 (the white area of the mask).

6. **Move your cursor over the document window (where it changes to an eyedropper) and ⌘+click (Windows: Ctrl+click) the darkest part of the image that is under the text, as shown here.**
   This sets a point on the bottom left of the curve line representing the tone on which you clicked. You lighten this and neighboring tones shortly.

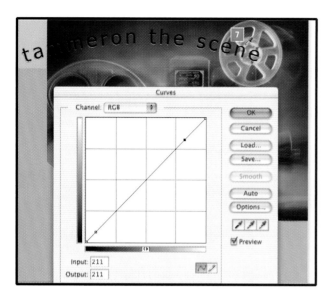

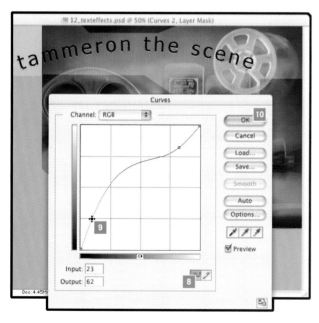

7. **⌘+click (Windows: Ctrl+click) a highlighted area in the middle of the reel on the right side of the image, as shown here.**
This sets a point on the top right of the curve that acts as a control point, protecting highlighted areas that are brighter than this tone from becoming lighter when you lighten the dark areas. Making highlighted areas too bright would cause them to lose all detail.

8. **Make sure there is a check mark next to Preview and the Point tool (the wavy line icon) is selected, both on the bottom right of the Curves dialog box.**

9. **Click the solid point that you created on the bottom left of the curve line and drag straight up to the first horizontal guide, as shown here.**
This lightens the darkest part of the selected area and neighboring tones. You can preview the change in the document as you drag to ensure that you lighten the selected area enough to make the text legible.

10. **Click OK to close the Curves dialog box.**

<NOTE>
The active selection that you made in step 3 limits the effect of this adjustment to the selected area. If you didn't have an active selection, the adjustment would affect the entire image on the layers below the curves adjustment layer.

<TIP>
If you ever want to limit an adjustment layer to just the layer immediately below it, Option+click on the line between those two layers in the Layers palette. This groups the adjustment layer and the single affected layer.

11. **Press ⌘+D (Windows: Ctrl+D) to eliminate the selection you made earlier.**

12. **Choose File→Save. Leave** 12_texteffects.psd **open for the next tutorial.**

<NOTE>
A common, but less successful solution to the text-on-photograph problem is to add a layer between the photograph and the text, draw a white rectangle on that layer, and lower the opacity of that layer to create a light area on which the text can be read. That isn't the best method because it treats the entire area the same way, flattening tone and losing detail in the image. Applying a curves adjustment layer instead lets the tonal variation in the underlying image show through. It also gives you more control over which tones to lighten.

Tutorial
» Rasterizing Type

All the type that you worked with so far has been editable vector-based type. You can customize this kind of type with many of Photoshop's features, ranging from layer styles to adjustment layers. However, there are a few pixel-based features, like some filters, that you can't apply to a type layer. You have to first rasterize the type layer, which changes the text on that layer from vector-based type to a bitmapped image of type. You learn how to rasterize a type layer in this tutorial.

1. **Make sure that** `12_texteffects.psd` **is open from the preceding tutorial.**

2. **Select the Yellow layer in the Layers palette.**

3. **Select the Horizontal Type tool and click the Palette icon on the Options bar to open the Character palette.**

4. **In the Character palette, set font family to Tahoma, font style to Regular, and font size to 30. Choose 100 for the tracking value.**

5. **Click the color well in the Character palette to open the Color Picker. Position the cursor over the yellow rectangle at the top of the image and click to sample the color under the eyedropper (R:**246, **G:**210, **B:**10**). Click OK.**
   The cursor changes to the Eyedropper tool when you move it over the document, enabling you to sample any color in the document.

6. **Click in the image and type** festival**.**

7. **Select the Move tool and drag to position the text at the bottom-right edge of the photograph, as shown here.**

8. **Click the commit button on the Options bar to confirm these text edits.**

9. **Click the festival type layer and drag it to the New Layer button at the bottom of the Layers palette to duplicate that type layer. Turn off the visibility of the festival copy layer by clicking its eye icon. Make sure that the festival layer is selected before the next step.**
   This step is just a precaution before you rasterize the festival layer in the next steps. Rasterizing converts editable type to a static bitmapped image. It's wise to keep a duplicate copy of the layer as editable type until you're satisfied with the rasterized layer.

10. **Choose Filter→Texture→Texturizer from the menu bar at the top of the screen.**
    This opens a warning dialog box, telling you that the type layer must be rasterized before proceeding, and cautioning that once rasterized, the text is no longer editable.

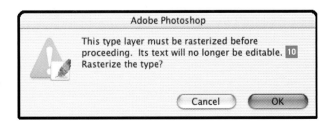

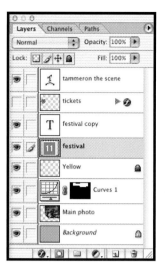

11. **Click OK in the warning dialog box to rasterize the type.**
The appearance of the text hasn't changed in the document, but the T icon marking the type layer has disappeared from the Layers palette. The festival layer is now a regular layer rather than an editable type layer. Clicking OK also opens the Filter Gallery dialog box.

12. **In the Filter Gallery dialog box, open the Texture category, choose the Craquelure thumbnail, and set the filter options to Crack Spacing:** 10, **Crack Depth:** 6, **Crack Brightness:** 7. **Click OK to close the Filter Gallery dialog box and apply the filter. The new Filter Gallery is covered in more detail in Session 10.**
This filter adds texture to make the text stand out from the background image.

13. **Click the festival copy layer and drag it to the Trash icon at the bottom of the Layers palette when you're satisfied with the look of the rasterized festival layer.**

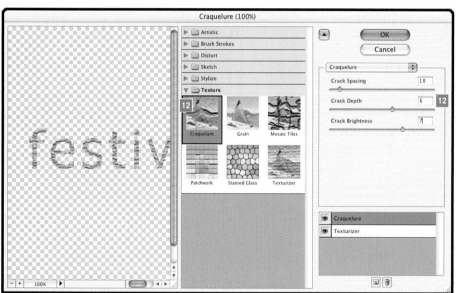

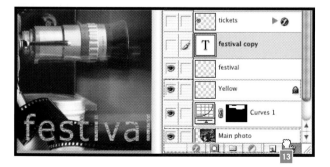

When to Rasterize Type

Here's a brief list of situations in which you'll want to rasterize a type layer:

>> You must rasterize in order to apply a filter, as you've seen in this tutorial. Photoshop warns you of this and does the rasterizing for you when you try to invoke a filter.

>> You must rasterize before you use any painting tool or fill feature on text. This means that you have to rasterize a type layer if you want to paint on text with the Brush tool, clone text with the Rubber Stamp tool, retouch text with the Healing Brush tool or Patch tool, erase text, use a History Brush on text, or use a darkroom tool on text. You must also rasterize before using the Gradient tool, Pattern tool, or gradient and pattern Fill options on text (although you can apply a Gradient Overlay or Pattern Overlay layer style to a type layer). You also have to rasterize before using the Stroke command, as you do in this tutorial. In most of these cases, you won't see a warning other than a small symbol. You have to figure out what the problem is and rasterize manually by choosing Layer→Rasterize→Type or

Ctrl+clicking (Windows: right-clicking) the type layer in the Layers palette and choosing Rasterize Layer from the contextual menu.

>> You must rasterize type layers in order to combine them using the layer Merge commands.

>> It's a good idea to rasterize type layers if your PSD file will be viewed on a computer on which the font you used isn't installed. Otherwise, the font will be converted to a different font on that computer, and the type won't look as you intended.

Keep in mind that when you rasterize a text layer, you lose all the editing power that Photoshop's vector text provides. A small change such as adjusting the tracking for a word becomes difficult—sometimes impossible—on a rasterized layer. Try to retain vector format at all times, unless you have a solid reason to rasterize text. Even if rasterizing is essential, delay the action as long as you can in case edits in other parts of your document demand edits in size, content, or color for your text.

---

14. **Choose the Vertical Type tool from the fly-out menu behind the Horizontal Type tool.**

15. **In the Character palette, leave Tahoma as the font family and change the font style to Bold. Type** 40 **as the font size. Set tracking to –50.**

    It doesn't matter what text color you use because you change it shortly.

16. **Select the Yellow layer in the layers palette. Type** admit one. **Use the Move tool to position the vertical text at the top left of the document, as shown here.**

17. **Click the color well in the Character palette to open the Color Picker. Move the cursor into the document window, where it turns to an eyedropper. Click the green background to change the admit one text to that color. Click OK to close the Color Picker.**

    The admit one text in the document is invisible (although it's still there), because it is now the same color as the background.

18. **Choose Layer→Rasterize→Type from the menu bar at the top of the screen.**

    The T icon disappears from the admit one layer in the Layers palette. You have to rasterize this type layer in order to use the Stroke command in the next step.

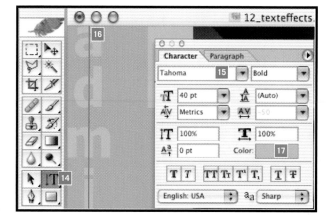

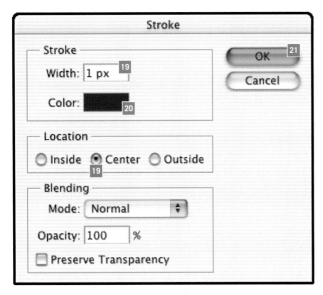

19. **Choose Edit→Stroke. In the Stroke dialog box, specify** 1 px **for the stroke width and Center for the location.**

20. **Click the Color field in the Stroke dialog box to open the Color Picker. Type the following values in the Color Picker to set the stroke color: R:** 76, **G:** 49, **B:** 30. **Click OK to close the Color Picker.**

21. **Click OK to close the Stroke dialog box.**
    The stroked text is now visible in the image.

22. **Choose Filter→Blur→Gaussian Blur.**

23. **In the Gaussian Blur dialog box, set the Radius value to 1.0, and click OK.**
    The Gaussian Blur softens the stroke. I suggest you use the Stroke command, rather than a Stroke layer style to outline the text because a similar Gaussian Blur applied on top of a Stroke layer style would have produced a hard edge instead of this soft-edged blur.

24. **Set the Opacity of the admit one layer to 50% in the Layers palette to soften the effect further.**

25. **Choose File→Save. Keep this document open for the next tutorial.**

Tutorial
» Using Text as a Clipping Mask

In this tutorial, you add another special skill to your text toolbox. You learn how to use text as a clipping mask for a photographic image so that the text appears to be filled with the photograph. This great-looking effect is simple to create.

1. Make sure that 12_texteffects.psd is open from the last tutorial.

2. Select the Horizontal Type tool in the toolbox. If it's not showing, click the Vertical Type tool and choose the Horizontal Type tool from the fly-out menu.

3. If the Character palette is not showing, click the Palette button on the Options bar. In the Character palette, leave the font set to Tahoma Bold. Type 150 in the font size field. Set the tracking to 0 for now.
   The text color that you use doesn't matter because you replace the color with an image later in this tutorial.

4. Select the festival layer in the Layers palette.
   This locates the type layer you're about to create directly above the festival layer.

5. Click in the lower-left portion of the document and type film.
   Don't worry about precisely where your text is located. You reposition the text to the correct spot at the end of this tutorial.

6. With the Horizontal Type tool still selected, click between the *f* and *i* in the word *film* and set the kerning to 25 in the Character palette.
   Kerning is usually required to achieve balanced spacing between characters when you're working with very large fonts. That's because the automatic spacing included with most fonts is often set for smaller text.

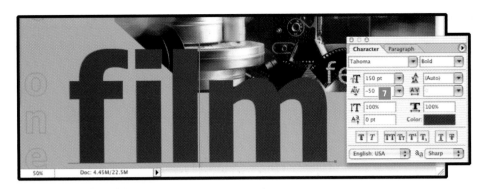

7. Click between the *i* and *l* in the word *film* and set the kerning to –50. Click between the *l* and *m* and set the kerning to –50.

8. Click the Commit button on the Options bar to confirm the text edits.

9. Open the photograph `12_textimage.psd` from the Session 12 Tutorial Files folder on your hard drive.

10. Position `12_texteffects.psd` and `12_textimage.psd` on your screen so that you can see them both, by clicking and dragging each by its title bar.

11. With the Move tool, click in the `12_textimage.psd` **document window and drag that photograph to the** `12_texteffects.psd` **document window. Release the mouse button.**
This copies the photograph into `12_texteffects.psd` and creates a new layer, labeled image, in `12_texteffects.psd`.

12. Click the title bar of `12_textimage.psd` **to make sure it's the active document window and choose File→Close.**
This leaves only one document open on your screen— `12_texteffects.psd`.

13. **In the** `12_texteffects.psd` **Layers palette, drag the film layer immediately above the image layer, if it does not already occupy that position.**

14. **With the image layer selected, click and drag in the document window to position the photograph over the word** *film.*

15. **Press the Option (Windows: Alt) key and move the cursor over the line between the image layer and the film layer until you see an icon with two circles. Click to create a clipping mask.**
    In the document window, the word *film* now appears to be filled with the photograph. Behind the scenes, the text on the film layer is acting as a clipping mask for the photograph on the layer above, allowing the photograph to appear only where there is content on the film layer.

<NOTE>
The Layers palette offers several clues that there is a clipping mask at work. The film layer is underlined, indicating that it is the base layer—the layer that is acting as the mask. The image layer is indented and displays a curved arrow (officially a clipping mask icon) indicating that this layer is subject to the mask.

<TIP>
One base layer can act as a clipping mask for multiple layers. To make a multilayered clipping mask, stack the layers to be masked directly above the base layer and Option+click (Windows: Alt+click) on each of the borders between the layers.

<NOTE>
Clipping masks are not a new feature in Photoshop CS, but they do have a new name. In previous releases, they were called Clipping Groups.

16. **With the Move tool and the image layer still selected, click and drag in the document window to move the photograph around inside the text until you're satisfied with portion of the photograph that is showing.**
    The layers in a clipping mask arrangement move independently of one another by default. You can move either one without the other, giving you control over which part of the masked image layer appears in the text.

17. **With the image layer selected, click in the Link field to the left of the film layer to link the two layers together. Click and drag to move the two layers together to the position shown here.**
Leave a small area of space between the bottom of the characters in the word *film* and the bottom of the document, in preparation for the next tutorial.

18. **Select the film layer in the Layers palette. Click the Add Layer Style button at the bottom of the Layers palette and choose Drop Shadow. Click OK in the Layer Style palette to apply a drop shadow with default options to the word *film*.**
This makes the text and its masked photograph stand out more against the background.

19. **Choose File→Save and leave the document open for the next tutorial.**

Tutorial
» Converting Type to Shapes

There may be times when you want to change the shape of individual characters in text. In order to do that, you have to first convert a type layer to a path, as you do in this tutorial. This tutorial comes in handy for creating unusual letters to introduce a text block or for creating typographic artwork.

1. **Make sure that** `12_texteffects.psd` **is open from the last tutorial.**

2. **Select the film layer in the Layers palette and choose Layer→Type→Convert to Shape from the menu bar.**
   The layer changes from a type layer to a shape layer in the Layers palette, and the text in the document now shows a thin vector outline. (Turn back to Session 6 "Drawing with Vectors" if you need some review on shape layers.)

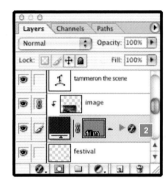

< N O T E >
You can also convert type to editable paths so that you can reshape individual characters. Follow the instructions for changing text to a shape, but choose Layer→Type→Convert to Work Path in step 2. You can edit paths created from type in the same way as any other paths (see Session 6 "Drawing with Vectors").

3. **Select the Direct Selection tool (the white arrow) in the toolbox.**
   If it's not showing, click the Path Selection tool (the black arrow) to reveal the fly-out menu of arrow tools and select the Direct Selection tool from there.

4. **With the film layer selected, click the letter *f* in the word *film* in the document to reveal the hollow anchor points on the vector outline.**

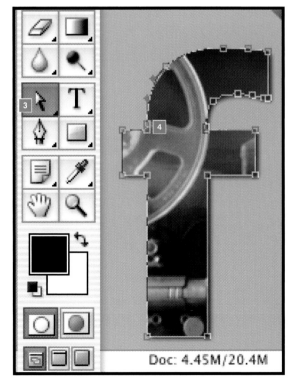

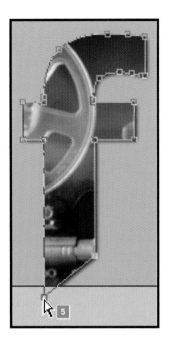

5. Click the point at the lower-left edge of the letter *f,* hold the Shift key to constrain movement to a straight line, and drag that point down to touch or go slightly below the bottom of the document. Repeat on the point at the lower-right edge of the letter. To reveal the gray area outside the image, click on the bottom-right corner of the document window (Windows: the application window) and drag.

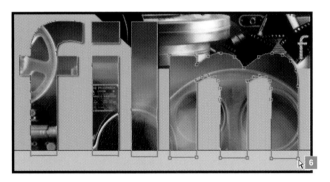

6. Repeat steps 3 through 5 on each letter in the word *film.* The end points of each letter should touch or go slightly past the lower edge of the document.

   Check that the image showing through the characters goes all the way to the bottom of the characters after this adjustment. If not, click in the Link field next to the image layer to unlink the layers and move the image within the text as you did in the last tutorial.

7. Choose File→Save and leave the file open for the last tutorial in this session.

Tutorial
» Creating Text on a Path

Photoshop CS offers a new feature that designers will appreciate—the ability to create text on a path. You can generate vector-based type on any closed or open path or shape without any special tools, as you see in this tutorial.

1. **With** 12_texteffects.psd **open from the last tutorial, click in the Visibility field to the left of the ticket layer in the Layers palette.**
   A roll of movie tickets appears in the image.

2. **Select the Ellipse tool from the fly-out menu of shape tools in the toolbox.**

3. **Click the arrow to the right of the shape icons in the Options bar.**
   The Ellipse Options palette opens.

4. **In the Ellipse Options palette, select Unconstrained and From Center.**
   With these options selected, you can draw a noncircular shape from the center outward.

5. **Select the Path icon in the Options bar.**
   This option causes any shape tool to draw a vector-based path, rather than a filled shape. The resulting path is just like a path you might draw by hand with the pen tools, but a lot quicker and easier to create.

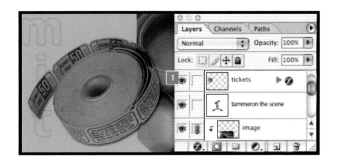

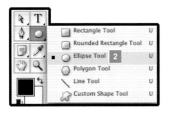

<CAUTION>
It's a common mistake to forget to select the Path icon in the Options bar before attempting to create a path. If you forget to do this, you end up with a filled shape, rather than an empty path. If that happens to you, undo, select the Path icon, and try again.

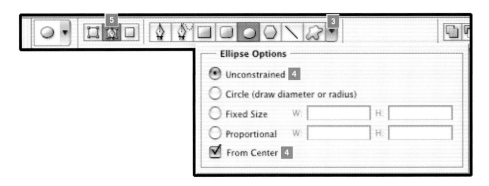

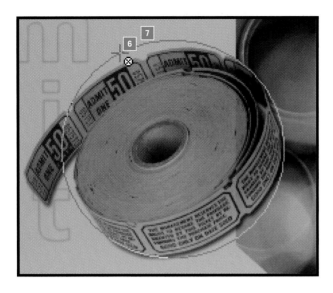

6. **Click in the center of the ticket roll and drag toward its outside edge to create a path as close as possible to the outside edge of the ticket roll. Do not release the mouse yet!**

7. **With the mouse still held down from the last step, press the space bar and drag to move your path slightly toward an edge of the ticket roll. Then release the space bar, but do not release the mouse yet. To further change the shape of the ellipse, continue to drag with the mouse held down. If necessary, repeat this entire step, keeping the mouse held down all the while.**

   Don't be discouraged if your path is not as close to the edge of the ticket roll as you would like. You can fix that later in this tutorial.

<CAUTION>

Do not release the mouse until you are done drawing your elliptical path. As long as the mouse is depressed, you can alternate between changing the shape of the path and holding the spacebar to move the path. The combination of these methods gets you as close as possible to creating a path that follows the edge of the ticket roll.

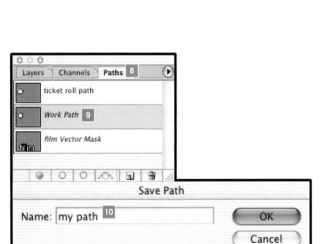

8. **Click on the Paths tab to open the Paths palette. If you do not see that tab, choose Window→Paths.**

9. **Double-click the path labeled Work Path.**

   This opens the Save Path dialog box.

10. **In the Save Path dialog box, type** my path **as the name of the path. Click OK to close the Paths dialog box.**

    This saves the path as a permanent path.

<CAUTION>

A work path is a temporary path that is easily lost, as you learned in Session 6 "Drawing with Vectors." Make it a practice to save a work path as a permanent path as soon as possible to safeguard your work.

11. **With my path selected in the Paths palette, choose Edit→Transform Path→Distort from the menu bar.**

    This generates a bounding box with open points around the path.

12. **Click in any of the points on the transform bounding box and drag to fine tune the path. Click the Commit button in the Options bar to apply this transformation.**

13. **In the Paths palette click on the my path name to make that path visible in the document.**

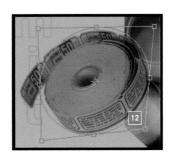

<NOTE>
If you prefer, you can use the ticket roll path, which I prepared and saved for you in case you were having trouble creating your own path. To use that path for the rest of this tutorial, click on the ticket roll path name in the Paths palette.

14. **Select the Horizontal Type tool in the toolbox. In the Options bar, set font family to Tahoma, font style to Regular, font size to 15 pt, and anti-aliasing to Sharp. Click the Left Align Text button. Click in the Color field to open the Color Picker. Choose a bright yellow (R: 246, B: 210, G: 10) and click OK.**

15. **Select the topmost layer in the Layers palette.**
This ensures that the type layer you're about to create by generating type on a path is located at the top of the layer stack.

16. **Move your I-beam cursor over the top-left part of the path until the horizontal line in the I-beam is over the path. Then click to change the cursor to a blinking bar.**
The horizontal line represents the type baseline.

Text on a Hand-Drawn Path

Text can be created on any path, including any open or closed path you might draw by hand. If you want to try creating a hand-drawn path around the ticket roll, select the Pen tool in the toolbox, and the Path icon in the Options bar. Click once at the edge of the ticket roll to begin the path. Click again further along the edge, but this time drag in the direction of the path you are drawing, causing the path to curve. Do this several times as you continue around the ticket roll. When you get back to the beginning of the path, move your cursor over the initial anchor point until you see a hollow circle. Then click to close the path. Once you complete your path, follow the steps in this tutorial for generating text on that path. For more information on drawing paths, review Session 6 "Drawing with Vectors."

17. **Type** actors - directors - producers, **with spaces between the words and hyphens.**
The text wraps around the path, and a new type layer is created in the Layers palette.

18. **Click the Commit button on the Options bar to accept this text and exit text edit mode.**

19. **Click Enter or Return on your keyboard to hide the path.**

< N O T E >
You can move type along a path with the Path Selection tool (the black arrow). Move the cursor over the path until you see an I-beam with a black arrow. Click and drag along the path to move the type. If you drag across the path, the type flips to the other side of the path.

< T I P >
When you move or change the shape of a path, the type attached to that path follows. To move a path and its type, click and drag with the Move tool. To change the shape of a path and its type, click and drag the points and handles on the path with the Direct Selection tool (the white arrow).

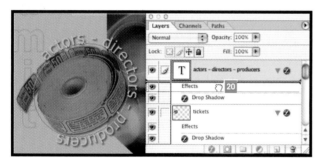

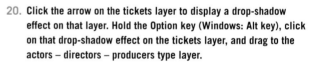

20. **Click the arrow on the tickets layer to display a drop-shadow effect on that layer. Hold the Option key (Windows: Alt key), click on that drop-shadow effect on the tickets layer, and drag to the actors – directors – producers type layer.**
This copies the drop shadow effect from the tickets layer to the type layer. Adding a drop shadow makes the type on the path more visible against the background.

21. **Choose File→Save As. In the Save As dialog box, rename the file** 12_texteffects_end.psd, **and save it in your collages folder for use in the final film festival program guide that you put together at the end of the book.**
You can find a copy of this finished file in the Session 12 Tutorial Files folder under the name 12_texteffects_end.psd.

» Session Review

This session covers Photoshop's more advanced capabilities for working with text. You distorted text with the Warp Text feature and manipulated a photograph with a curves layer so that your text would be easy to read. You rasterized text layers in order to apply filters and other effects to your type; you used text as a clipping mask for a photograph; you converted text to shapes, which enabled you to manipulate individual text characters; and you created type on a path. Take a look at the following questions to remind you of how much you have learned.

1. How can you tell that a Warp Text effect is applied to text? (See "Tutorial: Warping Text.")

2. Does text with a Warp Text effect applied remain editable? (See "Tutorial: Warping Text.")

3. Why is it preferable to use curves, rather than layer opacity, to prepare an area on which to place type over a photograph? (See "Tutorial: Making Type Visible on Top of a Photograph.")

4. When you are preparing an area on which to place type over a photograph, how can you limit the area that will be affected by your curves adjustment layer? (See "Tutorial: Making Type Visible on Top of a Photograph.")

5. What does it mean to rasterize a text layer? (See "Tutorial: Rasterizing Type.")

6. How does the appearance of a type layer change in the Layers palette when that layer has been rasterized? (See "Tutorial: Rasterizing Type.")

7. What do you have to do before applying a filter to text in Photoshop? (See "Tutorial: Rasterizing Type.")

8. What are the reasons to delay or avoid rasterizing text layers? (See "Tutorial: Rasterizing Type.")

9. Name three situations in which you would have to rasterize a type layer to apply a feature. (See "Tutorial: Rasterizing Type.")

10. What text adjustment is usually necessary when working with large fonts? (See "Tutorial: Converting Type to Shapes.")

11. What command do you use to make text appear as if it is filled with a photograph? (See "Tutorial: Converting Type to Shapes.")

12. How do you manipulate the shape of text after converting from a type layer to a shape layer? (See "Tutorial: Converting Type to Shapes.")

13. Name two ways to create a path for type. (See "Tutorial: Creating Type on a Path.")

14. If you move or change the shape of a path, does type attached to the path change too? (See "Tutorial: Creating Type on a Path.")

Part VI
Working with Photographs in the Digital Darkroom

Session 13

Using Darkroom Tools

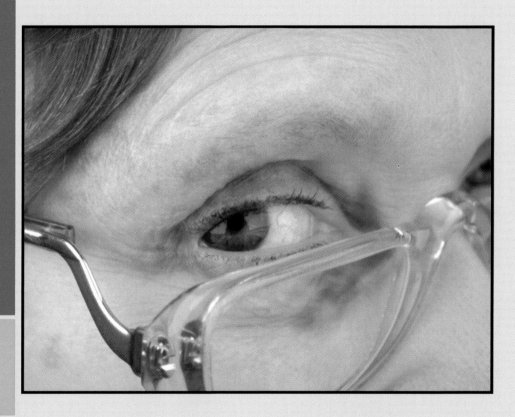

Session Introduction

It's hard to think of Photoshop without thinking of photographs. Photoshop has always been an undisputed leader as a photo manipulation and correction tool. Nearly every image that is captured with a digital camera or scanned needs some adjustment, retouching, or repair.

In this session, you learn basic image-correction skills using Photoshop's digital darkroom features. These features do the job of traditional darkroom tools and more. You crop and straighten multiple images with the new Crop and Straighten command. You correct imperfections in a photograph using the Clone Stamp tool, the Healing Brush, and the Patch tool. You use the Dodge and Burn tools to adjust exposure and the Sponge tool to modify saturation. You use the Sharpen and Blur tools to adjust focus. You change a model's eye color with the new Color Replacement tool. You create a shallow depth of field effect with the new Lens Blur filter, and you sharpen the image with the Unsharp Mask filter.

TOOLS YOU'LL USE
Crop and Straighten feature, Clone Stamp tool, Healing Brush tool, Patch tool, Dodge tool, Burn tool, Sponge tool, Blur tool, Sharpen tool, Color Replacement tool, Lens Blur filter, and Unsharp Mask filter.

CD-ROM FILES NEEDED
13_textframe.psd, 13_scan.psd, 13_darkroom.psd, and 13_darkroom.end.psd

TIME REQUIRED
90 minutes

Tutorial
» Cropping and Straightening a Scan

No one likes to spend time scanning photographs one by one and then cropping and straightening each scan by hand. You never have to do that again thanks to Photoshop's new Crop and Straighten Photos command. Now you can place multiple photographs on a scanner bed without worrying about whether they're crooked, scan them all at once, and save them as one image. Then sit back while the Crop and Straighten Photos feature automatically crops them into individual images, straightening each one for you, as you see in this tutorial.

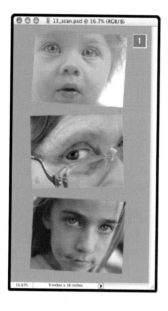
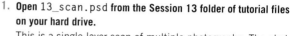

1. **Open** 13_scan.psd **from the Session 13 folder of tutorial files on your hard drive.**

   This is a single layer scan of multiple photographs. The photographs in the scan are slightly crooked and misaligned, which is common when you lay photos on a scanner bed.

2. **Choose File→Automate→Crop and Straighten Photos.**

   The program quickly crops and straightens each of the three photographs in the scan and opens each as a separate document in Photoshop.

3. **Click on the original scan,** 13_scan.psd, **and choose File→Close.**

4. **Click on the title bars of the three automatically created smaller images and drag them apart so you can see that they are separate documents that have been cropped and straightened.**

5. **Click on the title bar of the photograph of the baby, choose File→Close, and click Don't Save at the prompt. Repeat this step on the photo of the young girl.**

   You won't be using these two photos again.

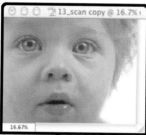

6. **Click on the remaining photograph—the closeup of a woman's eye— and choose File→Save As. Name the file** 13_darkroom.psd, **navigate to the Session 13 Tutorial Files folder on your desktop, and click Save. Leave this photograph open for the following tutorial.**

   A copy of 13_darkroom.psd is located in the Session 13 Tutorial Files folder on the CD-ROM. You can use this file if you ever return to this session to review any of its individual darkroom techniques.

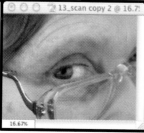

<CAUTION>

Files generated by the Crop and Straighten Photos command are not automatically saved. If you close them without saving, they are deleted from your hard drive.

Tutorial

» Removing Content with the Clone Stamp Tool

The Clone Stamp tool, sometimes called the Rubber Stamp tool, copies pixels from one area of an image and paints them onto another area. It is useful for covering unwanted content from a photograph—scratches, dust spots, and even people or objects—as well as for repeating content. It can be used on a single layer, between layers, or even between documents.The Clone Stamp tool works best when the source and destination areas share similar color, lighting, and texture. Otherwise, try using the Healing Brush tool or the Patch tool, which are covered later in this session. In this tutorial, you use the Clone Stamp tool to remove unsightly redness from a model's eye.

1. **With** 13_darkroom.psd **open from the preceding tutorial, select the Zoom tool in the toolbox. Select the Zoom In button and the Resize Windows to Fit check box in the Options bar. Click and drag around the woman's eye to zoom in on that area.**
   It's useful to zoom in on a subject for accuracy when you're working with the Clone Stamp and other darkroom tools. However, you should return to 100% view from time to time to check on how the changes you make appear in the final view.

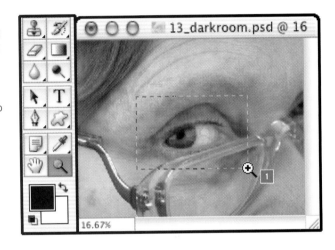

2. **Select the Clone Stamp tool in the toolbox. If it is not showing, click the Pattern Stamp tool and choose the Clone Stamp tool from the fly-out menu of tools in that group.**

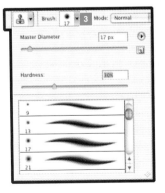

3. **Click the Brush Sample in the Options bar to open the Brush pop-up palette. Choose the soft round 17 px brush. Increase the hardness of that brush by dragging the Hardness slider to around 30%.**
   A soft-edged brush often works best to blend the edges of cloned pixels with the original. However, Photoshop's default soft brushes, which are set to 0% Hardness, sometimes make the cloned area look too blurry. Increasing brush hardness slightly avoids this problem.

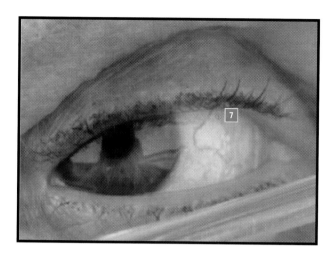

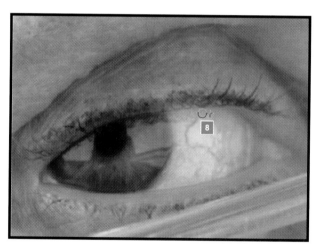

4. **Drag the Opacity slider in the Options bar to around 90%.**
Lowering the Opacity setting slightly from its default of 100% helps blend cloned pixels with the original pixels they cover. The best Opacity setting varies from image to image, but is usually somewhere between 80% and 100%.

5. **Leave the check mark in the Aligned box on the Options bar.**
When the Aligned option is checked, as it is by default, Photoshop starts sampling from a new location each time you click as you're painting with cloned pixels. Aligned usually is the preferred option, because it avoids repeating the same source pixels in different destinations, making your cloning less obvious. When Aligned isn't checked, the original sample spot is always used as the initial source of cloned pixels.

6. **Select Use All Layers in the Options bar. In the Layers palette, click the New Layer icon to create an empty layer on which to paint cloned pixels. Click the new layer's default name and rename it cloned pixels. Leave the other settings in the Options bar at their defaults.**
When Use All Layers is checked, Photoshop samples pixels from all layers in a document and paints the merged sample on the active layer. Cloning to the new cloned pixels layer, rather than to the original *Background* layer, preserves the original image and allows you to erase any mistakes. It also lets you compare a before and after view by turning the visibility of the cloned pixels layer off and on.

7. **With the cloned pixels layer active, Option+click (Windows: Alt+click) just to the right of the red vein to set the first sampling point.**
The cursor changes to a target symbol. The pixels under the target are copied.

8. **Click on the red vein in the eye immediately to the left of where you took the sample.**
The Clone Stamp tool paints with the pixels that you sampled in step 7, covering the red vein where you click.

9. Click repeatedly along the red vein, covering it with pixels that you copy from sampling points that move along with your cursor. From time to time, Option+click (Windows: Alt+click) again next to the vein to set a new sampling point, in order to avoid creating a visible pattern of cloned pixels.

Each sampling point is marked by a cross and each target point by the round brush symbol.

10. If a click creates a spot that doesn't blend well, choose Edit→Undo Clone Stamp. Then Option+click (Windows: Alt+click) in a different location to sample from a new point and continue to clone along the red vein.

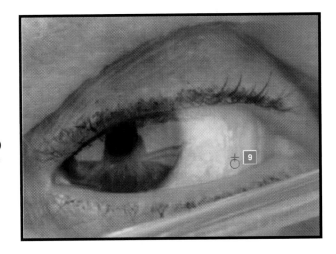

11. To see a before and after cloning view of the image, turn the eye icon on the cloned pixels layer off and then on.

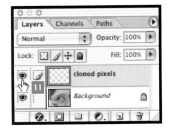

< T I P >

You can clone between images as well as within an image. Option+click (Windows: Alt+click) in the first image to set a sampling point and click to paint in the other image. You can also clone from one layer to another in the same document by unchecking Use All Layers and switching active layers as you sample and paint.

12. Choose File→Save. Leave this image open for the next tutorial.

Tips for Successful Cloning

Here are a few things that you can do to make your cloning more blended and less obvious:

» Avoid dragging the cursor when you paint with cloned pixels, which can result in a repetitive or striped look. Instead click from point to point to dab the cloned pixels onto the image.

» Use a variety of sample points by Option+clicking (Windows: Alt+clicking) from time to time on different sides of the area that you're trying to cover.

» If you're cloning from a dark to a lighter area (for example, if you're trying to cover light dust spots), set the blending Mode to Darken on the Options bar. And if you're cloning from a light to a darker area (for example, if you're trying to cover a dark blemish), try setting Mode to Lighten.

Tutorial
» Retouching with the Healing Brush Tool

The Healing Brush tool is a lifesaver for anyone who uses Photoshop to retouch photographs. It is similar to the Clone Stamp tool, but produces a more subtle, blended effect. Instead of just painting pixels over an area, the Healing Brush automatically preserves the lighting, texture, and tones of the corrected area. In this tutorial, you use the Healing Brush tool to remove a dark blemish from the model's face.

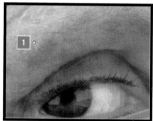

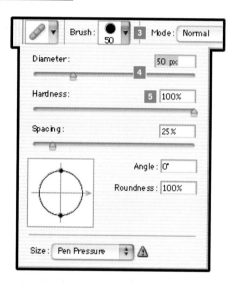

1. **You should still be zoomed in to the eye area of** `13_darkroom.psd` **from the previous tutorial. Click and drag with the Hand tool to reposition the image, if necessary, so that the model's eyebrow is showing.**

2. **Select the Healing Brush tool in the toolbox. If it is not showing, click the Patch tool or Color Replacement tool and choose the Healing Brush tool from the fly-out menu of tools in that group.**

3. **Click the Brush sample on the Options bar to open the Brush pop-up palette.**
   You have to use the Brush pop-up palette, rather than the Brushes palette, with the Healing Brush tool. The Brushes palette is grayed out.

4. **Set the Diameter of the brush to 50 px.**

5. **Leave the other settings in the Brush pop-up palette at their defaults, including the default Hardness setting of 100%.**
   A hard-edged brush usually works better than a soft-edged brush with the Healing Brush tool.

<TIP>

There is one situation in which a soft-edged brush is the best choice with the Healing Brush tool. If you're correcting an image that has a lot of noise, such as film grain, use a soft-edged brush with the Mode setting on the Options bar set to Replace. The Replace blending mode helps eliminate the fuzzy edges that you might otherwise see on the correction.

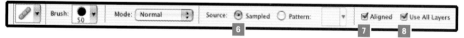

6. **Leave Source set to Sampled on the Options bar.**
   This tells the program to use pixels that you sample as the healing pixels. If you chose pattern, the program would use one of Photoshop's prebuilt patterns as the source of healing pixels.

7. **Put a check mark in the Aligned box on the Options bar.**
   The Aligned option works the same way with the Healing Brush tool as it does with the Clone Stamp tool, as explained in the previous tutorial.

8. **Select Use All Layers in the Options bar. In the Layers palette, click the New Layer icon to create an empty layer on which to place the healing pixels. Click the new layer's default name and rename it healing pixels. Leave the other settings in the Options bar at their defaults.**
   The Use All Layers option, which is new in Photoshop CS, works the same way as it does with the Clone Stamp tool.

<NOTE>

The Healing Brush tool doesn't have an Opacity setting on the Options bar like the Clone Stamp tool. Although you can't alter the opacity of the Healing Brush tool, you can get a similar effect by choosing Edit➔Fade Healing Brush from the menu bar immediately after you use the Healing Brush tool. Lower the Opacity slider in the Fade dialog box and click OK. However, if you take any other action after applying the Healing Brush you won't be able to access the Fade option.

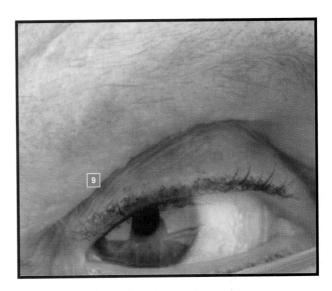

9. **With the healing pixels layer selected, Option+click (Windows: Alt+click) just below the age spot.**
   The cursor changes to a target icon and takes an initial sampling of the pixels that the Healing Brush tool will use to correct the area.

10. **Click and drag across the area to be corrected (the brown age spot).**
    The sampling points, represented by the plus symbol, move along with your cursor, represented by the round brush icon. Don't worry that the tool creates a dark area in the image as you drag. You won't see the true effect of the Healing Brush tool until you release the mouse button. At that point, the tool does its work, blending the texture, lighting, and tonality of the pixels surrounding the target area with the sampled pixels.

11. **Turn the eye icon on the healing pixels layer off and then on to see a before and after view of the correction you made with the Healing Brush tool.**

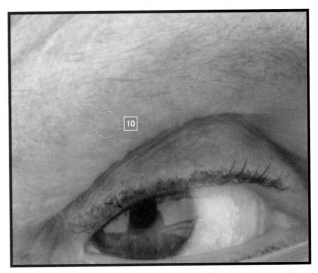

<NOTE>

The Healing Brush tool works well on blemishes and similar imperfections. It may be less successful on areas of substantial damage, such as a tear or deep scratch in a photograph, because this tool attempts to repair, rather than cover up a damaged area. In that case, try the Clone Stamp tool, which covers the target area, or the Patch tool, which is the subject of the next tutorial.

<TIP>

You can use the Healing Brush tool to copy pixels from image to image and from layer to layer, just as you can with the Clone Stamp tool.

12. **Choose File➔Save and leave this document open for the next exercise.**

Tutorial
» Working with the Patch Tool

The Patch tool is another very useful retouching tool. It works in a similar way to the Healing Brush tool, blending the sampled pixels with pixels to be corrected. However, instead of sampling and painting with a brush, the Patch tool uses selections. In this tutorial, you use the Patch tool to hide blemishes and wrinkles.

1. **With** 13_darkroom.psd **open from the previous tutorial, select the Zoom tool in the toolbox and Option+click (Windows: Alt+ click) to zoom out to 50%.**
   When using the Patch tool, you are working with selections rather than brushes, so you don't need to work at a high magnification.

2. **Click the Healing Brush tool in the toolbox and select the Patch tool from the fly-out tool menu.**

3. **Make sure Source is selected on the Options bar. Leave the other options at their defaults.**
   Source tells the program that you intend to select the damaged area and drag the selection to the healthy pixels that will be the source of the repair. The other choice, destination, would tell the program you intend to select healthy pixels and drag them to the destination that needs repair. You can use the Patch tool either way. I prefer to leave it set to Source, because then I can draw the selection to fit the damaged area as closely as possible. A smaller selection usually produces a less noticeable patch.

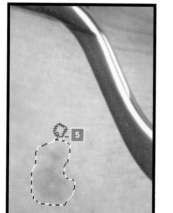

4. **Click and drag the Background layer in the Layers palette to the New Layer icon, creating a Background Copy layer. Make sure the Background Copy layer is selected.**
   The Patch tool makes repairs directly on the selected layer. It has no option for using all layers like the Clone Stamp tool and the Healing Brush tool. Working on a copy layer preserves the original pixels.

5. **Click and drag a selection with the Patch tool around the blemished skin on the subject's left cheek.**
   Make sure to include all the damaged area in the selection, but don't make the selection any bigger than necessary. You want the selection to just fit the damaged area because the Patch tool uses the edges of the selected area to make its blending calculations.

6. **Position your cursor inside the selection. Click and drag the selection over a nearby unblemished area of the cheek.**
   As you drag, the original selection around the blemish displays a preview of the pixels you're sampling. This new addition to the Patch tool helps you avoid including extraneous pixels (like the edge of the model's glasses) in the sampled area.

7. **Release the mouse button.**
   When you release the mouse button, the selection outline snaps back to the damaged area, and the Patch tool goes to work, blending the unblemished sample with the damaged area, taking into account the brightness, texture, and tonality of the pixels at the edges of the damaged area.

8. **Press ⌘+D (Windows: Ctrl+D) to cancel the selection.**
   The damaged area appears completely healed.

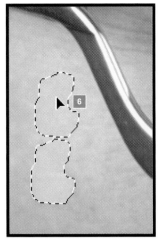
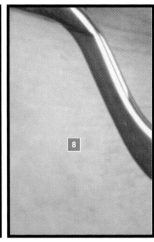

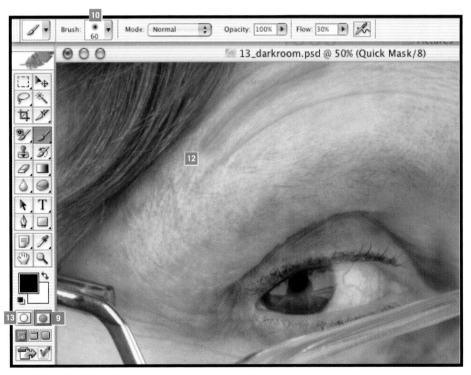

9. **Double-click the Quick Mask icon in the toolbox to open the Quick Mask Options dialog box. Choose Selected Areas and click OK.**

10. **Select the Brush tool in the toolbox and set the brush Diameter to around 60 in the Options bar.**

11. **Click D to set the Foreground color to black.**

12. **Click and drag over one of the wrinkles in the model's forehead.**

13. **Click the Standard Mode icon in the toolbox.**
    The wrinkle is selected.

<NOTE>
You can use any of the regular selection tools or methods, rather than the Patch tool itself, to make a selection that is used with the Patch tool. Painting in Quick Mask mode is an easy way to select a long, narrow area.

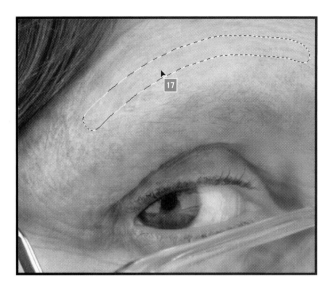

14. **Select the Patch tool in the toolbox.**

15. **With the Background Copy layer selected in the Layers palette, drag the selection to some unblemished pixels just below the wrinkle, being careful not to include unwanted pixels in the preview. Release the mouse.**
    The wrinkle disappears.

<TIP>
The Patch tool is a good choice for fixing wrinkles, as well as bags under eyes in portraits.

16. **Press ⌘+D (Windows: Ctrl+D).**

17. **Repeat steps 10 through 16 on the other large wrinkle on the model's forehead to cover that wrinkle.**

18. **Use the Healing Brush tool, if necessary, to clean up the patched area.**

19. **Turn the eye icon next to the Background copy layer off and then on to see how much better the model looks after application of the patch tool.**

<TIP>
The Patch tool, like the Healing Brush tool, has no Opacity option. To reduce the opacity of the patch, you can choose Edit➜Fade Patch Selection immediately after applying the Patch tool. Lower the Opacity slider in the Fade dialog box and click OK.

20. **Choose File➜Save and leave this document open for the next tutorial.**

Tutorial
» Dodging and Burning

Photoshop offers tools for selectively adjusting the exposure in an image, duplicating the effects known as *dodging* and *burning* in the traditional darkroom. The Dodge tool lightens areas of an image, simulating decreased exposure, and the Burn tool darkens, simulating increased exposure. In this tutorial, you lighten the subject's eye socket and darken the frame of her glasses.

1. With `13_darkroom.psd` **open from the previous tutorial, select the Zoom tool in the toolbox. Click on the eye to magnify the view to 66.67%.**

2. **Select the Dodge tool in the toolbox.**

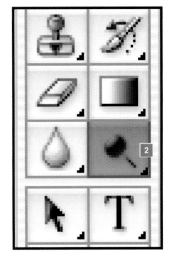

3. **Click the Brush sample on the Options bar and select the 65 px soft round brush from the Brush pop-up palette. Set the range to Shadows and the exposure to 20%.**
   Setting Range to Shadows makes the Dodge tool affect dark areas of the image more intensely than lighter areas. Exposure controls the strength of the tool's lightening effect.

4. **With the Background copy layer still selected in the Layers palette, click your cursor in a random pattern over the inside eye socket area that you want to lighten.**
   Don't try to accomplish the entire job of lightening the area at this point. Using a variety of shadows, midtones, and highlight settings to adjust the exposure of an area gives a more natural result.

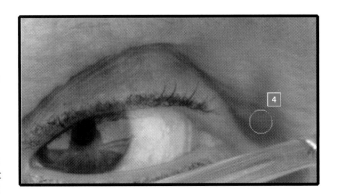

5. **Select Midtones from the Range field on the Options bar. Repeat step 4.**
   The Midtones range affects all pixels except very dark and very light pixels.

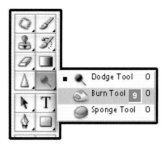

6. **Select Highlights from the Range field on the Options bar and lower the Exposure setting to 10%.**

   Setting the range to Highlights makes the Dodge tool have its greatest effect on light areas of the image.

7. **Continue alternating between Shadow, Midtones, and Highlight settings on the Options bar as you click in the correction area until you are satisfied with the result.**

   Use the Edit→Undo command at any time if necessary.

8. **Select the Hand tool in the toolbox. Click and drag in the image until you see the silver arm of the glasses frame.**

9. **Click the Dodge tool in the toolbox and select the Burn tool from the fly-out tool menu.**

   The Burn tool works in the same way as the Dodge tool, except that it darkens pixels instead of making them lighter.

10. **Choose the 45 px Soft Round brush from the Brush pop-up palette. Leave the other settings on the Options bar at their defaults— Range: Midtones and Exposure: 50%.**

    Because you are simply darkening an object rather than working with the subtleties of correcting flaws in human skin, you can apply the effect more aggressively.

11. **With the Background Copy layer still selected, click and drag along the arm of the glasses frame to darken the color.**

    Respect the original lighting pattern of the image. Leave small areas untouched, especially at the top of the frame where there are bright highlights.

12. **Choose File→Save. Leave the document open for the next tutorial.**

Tutorial
» Adjusting Saturation

The Sponge tool adjusts color saturation to intensify or mute colors. In this tutorial, you increase the saturation, or *intensity*, of the color in the subject's eye to increase the reflection and add interest.

1. With 13_darkroom.psd still open from the previous tutorial, select the Hand tool in the toolbox and move the image in the document window, if necessary, so that the eye is displayed.

2. Click the Burn tool in the toolbox and select the Sponge tool from the hidden menu.

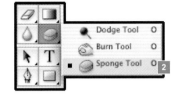

3. Choose the soft round 65 px brush from the Brush pop-up palette. Set Mode to Saturate and leave Flow at its default of 50% in the Options bar.

   A soft brush prevents brush lines from forming as you apply the tool. The Flow setting controls how fast saturation changes.

4. With the Background copy layer selected in the Layers palette, click around the iris area.

5. Choose File→Save. Leave the document open for the next tutorial.

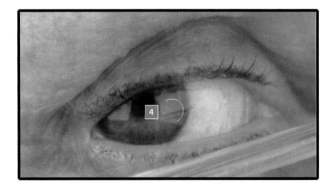

Tutorial

» Applying the Color Replacement Tool

Photoshop CS has a new tool—the Color Replacement tool. You can use this tool to fix the red-eye effect you often see in flash portraits or to quickly recolor an item. In this tutorial, you use the Color Replacement tool to change the color of the model's eye.

1. **With 13_darkroom.psd open from the previous tutorial, click on the Patch tool in the toolbox and choose the Color Replacement tool from the fly-out tools menu.**

2. **Click the Brush sample in the Brush pop-up palette on the Options bar and set brush diameter to 50. Leave the other brush options at their defaults.**

3. **In the Options bar leave blend Mode set to Color.**
   This mode blends the hue and saturation of the replacement color with the luminosity of the color below so that catchlights and other subtleties in the model's eye are retained.

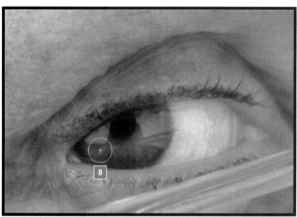

4. **Leave Sampling set to its default—Continuous.**
   This determines which colors are replaced. It tells the tool to target colors to replace by sampling continuously as you paint with the replacement color. Choosing Once would target all instances of the first color on which you click. Choosing Background Swatch would target all instances of the Background color in the toolbox.

5. **Leave Limits set to Contiguous.**
   This ensures that only areas of color contiguous to your cursor are replaced. Find Edges is similar to Contiguous with special attention paid to preserving shape edges.

6. **Leave tolerance set to its default of 30% and anti-aliased selected.**
   The higher the tolerance, the more colors are replaced. Anti-aliasing smooths the edges of areas in which color is replaced.

7. **Click the Foreground Color box and choose an olive-khaki color (R: 176, G: 155, B: 80) in the Color Picker. Click OK.**

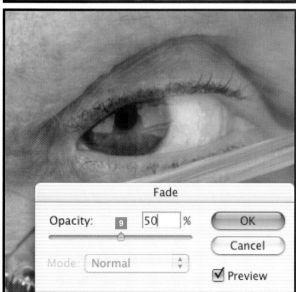

8. **Make sure the Background copy layer is still selected, and click and drag around the iris.**
   Do not take any other action before the next step or you won't be able to access the Fade dialog box.

9. **Choose Edit→Fade Color Replacement Tool from the menu bar. In the Fade dialog box, lower Opacity to 50%.**
   This makes the color replacement more subtle.

10. **Choose File→Save, and leave the image open for the next tutorial.**

Tutorial
» Using the Blur Tool

There are a number of blur filters that are used to blur selections or entire layers. But when you want to blur just a local area, the Blur tool sometimes comes in handy, as you see in this tutorial.

1. **With** 13_darkroom.psd **open from the preceding tutorial, double-click the Zoom tool to zoom in to 100%. Use the Hand tool to move the eye to the middle of the document window.**

2. **Select the Blur tool in the toolbox.**
   You use the Blur tool to soften the hard line of the crease in the eyelid.

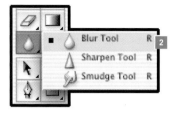

3. **Choose the 45 px soft round brush from the Brush pop-up palette. Leave mode set to Normal and strength to 50% on the Options bar.**
   Choosing a large, soft brush helps the correction to blend into the surrounding pixels. Strength controls the intensity of the blur effect.

4. **With the Background copy layer selected, drag along the crease of the eyelid.**
   The pixels that are touched by the brush blend into each other, softening the line. Repeat this step until you are satisfied with the look.

5. **Choose File→Save and keep the document open for the next tutorial.**

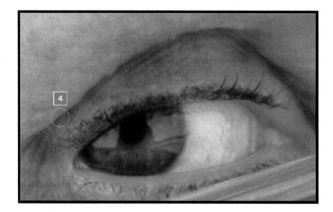

Tutorial

» Sharpening an Image with the Unsharp Mask Filter

The Unsharp Mask filter is one of Photoshop's most frequently used filters. It is rare to work with an image that doesn't need some level of sharpening with this filter. Images digitized by scanning or created with a digital camera always need sharpening, as do images that have been resized or transformed. The Unsharp Mask filter is usually the last operation in photo correction. In this tutorial, you apply it to the entire photograph that you corrected in this session.

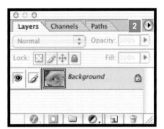

1. `13_darkroom.psd` **should still be open from the previous tutorial, zoomed in to 100%.**
   It is important to view your image at 100% as you apply the Unsharp Mask filter. Viewing at actual size provides an accurate view of how the filter is affecting the image.

   <CAUTION>
   The Unsharp effect looks more pronounced on-screen than it does in high-quality print output, due to the difference in resolution between screen display and print output. If you are sending files to a high-quality printer (above 133 lpi), you may want to provide a test file to the service bureau so that sharpening can be adjusted if necessary.

2. **Click the arrow at the top right of the Layers palette and choose Flatten Image from the palette menu.**
   Flattening allows you to sharpen all of the content at once.

3. **Choose Filter→Sharpen→Unsharp Mask from the menu bar.**
   The Unsharp Mask dialog box opens, providing a preview of your image as well as the filter controls.

4. **Confirm that the Preview check box in the Unsharp Mask dialog box is checked.**
   The Preview option temporarily applies the Unsharp Mask controls to the image in the document window, where you can make a better overall assessment of how each setting affects the image than with the small preview pane in the dialog box.

5. **Move the Amount slider in the Unsharp Mask dialog box to 150. Leave the other settings at their defaults.**

   Check the results in both the preview pane of the Unsharp Mask dialog box and the document. The amount of sharpening required normally goes up as file resolution increases.

6. **Click the Preview check box in the Unsharp Mask dialog box to uncheck it.**

   Toggling the preview in the document on and off is an excellent way to see the full extent of the effect.

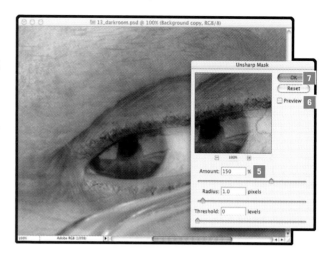

< C A U T I O N >

Pay attention to all areas of the image. Applying a strong amount of the Unsharp Mask effect may provide excellent results for most of the image but produce unacceptable hard lines or artifacts in another.

7. **Click OK to return to the document and accept the Unsharp Mask settings.**

< T I P >

If sharpening appears too strong, you can decrease it by choosing Fade➜Unsharp Mask from the menu bar and reducing opacity.

8. **Choose File➜Save and leave the document open for the next, and final, tutorial in this session.**

Unsharp Mask Controls

The Unsharp Mask filter in Photoshop comes with three separate controls. The Amount setting controls the overall strength of the Unsharp Mask filter. Lower numbers have less effect. Values of 50 to 100% are common for low-resolution images, such as those for the Web. Images prepared for high-quality printing usually demand settings from 150 to 200% or more.

The Radius setting controls the number of pixels along an edge (a place where contrast changes) that are used for sharpening the image. Between 0.5 and 1 px is usually correct for low-resolution images. Higher-resolution images commonly require a setting between 1 and 2 px.

Threshold controls the amount of contrast that is required for Photoshop to determine what is an "edge." The default value of 0 levels sharpens every pixel and is often an acceptable setting. Increasing the value excludes some pixels and may help to prevent unwanted artifacts from appearing.

Tutorial
» Creating a Depth-of-Field Effect with the Lens Blur Filter

Photoshop CS has a new feature that simulates the way a camera lens whose aperture is open wide would blur a scene. This creates a shallow depth-of-field effect, in which part of an image is in focus, but much of the image is out of focus. This has the effect of drawing attention to the part that's in focus. In this tutorial, you add a lens blur around the model's eye to make the eye take center stage.

1. **With** 13_darkroom.psd **still open from the previous tutorial, select the Zoom tool in the toolbox and zoom out until the entire image fits on your screen.**

2. **Click D to switch the Foreground and Background color boxes in the toolbox to their defaults—black and white respectively.**

3. **Select the Gradient tool in the toolbox.**

4. **Click the Radial Gradient icon in the Options bar to set the gradient style.**

5. **Click the Gradient sample in the Options bar to open the Gradient Editor.**

6. **In the Gradient Editor, click on the Foreground to Transparent gradient thumbnail and click OK.**

7. **Drag the single Background layer to the New Layer icon at the bottom of the Layers palette.**
   This creates a Background copy layer.

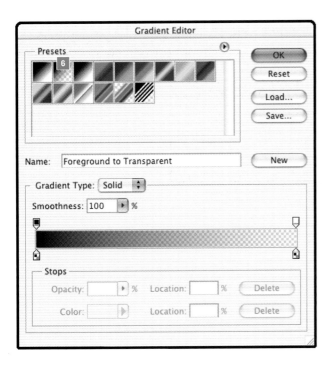

8. **With the Background copy layer selected in the Layers palette, click the New Layer Mask icon at the bottom of the Layers palette.**
   This adds a white (reveal all) layer mask to the Background copy layer. Make sure the layer mask thumbnail, rather than the image thumbnail, is selected on this layer. A double border around the layer mask thumbnail indicates that it is selected.

9. **With the Layer Mask icon highlighted in the Layers palette, click in the model's eye in the image and drag diagonally to the top-left corner of the document window.**
   This creates a radial gradient in the layer mask. Your layer mask generates an alpha channel, which you can see in the Channels palette, that becomes the depth map for your lens blur effect.

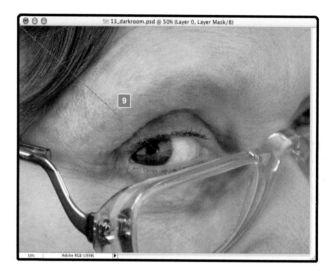

10. **Click on the image thumbnail, rather than the layer mask thumbnail, on the Background copy layer in the Layers palette.**
    A double border around the image thumbnail indicates that it is selected.

11. **Choose Filter→Blur→Lens Blur.**
    The Lens Blur dialog box opens. You can make the dialog box fill your screen by clicking the arrow on the bottom right and choosing Fit on Screen. You can also control its magnification from this menu.

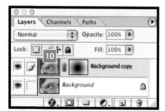

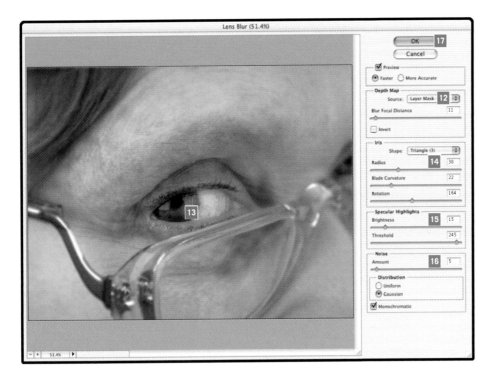

12. **In the Lens Blur dialog box, set the source of the Depth Map to Layer Mask.**

    The black to white pixels on the layer mask are a depth map that determines the appearance of the lens blur in the photograph. The most blur occurs where the layer mask is white (around the edges of this photograph), the least where it is black (around the model's eye). There is a gradually increasing amount of blur where the gradient on the layer mask progressively fades from black to white through gray tones.

13. **Click in the iris (the colored area) of the model's eye in the image to automatically set the Blur Focal Distance in the Lens Blur dialog box.**

    This determines the areas that are most in focus in the image.

14. **Set the Iris Shape to Triangle, Radius to 30, Blade Curvature to 22, and Rotation to 164 in the Lens Blur dialog box.**

    These settings control the size and shape of the simulated iris. Radius is particularly important because it determines the amount of blur (the higher the Radius value, the more the blur). Iris Shape affects the shape of the in-focus area of the image; Blade Curvature controls how rounded that shape is; and Rotation controls how much that shape is rotated.

15. **In the Specular Highlights section of the Lens Blur dialog box, set Brightness to 15 and Threshold to 245.**

    This compensates for that fact that blurring the image made the bright white highlights a little more gray. The brightness setting adds a little more brightness to those specular highlights. The threshold setting determines which pixels get that boost (only those above the threshold tonal value).

16. **Set Noise Amount to 5 and Distribution to Gaussian, and put a check mark next to Monochrome in the Lens Blur dialog box.**

    This adds a little noise to simulate film grain, which is usually decreased by blurring.

17. **Click OK to apply the Lens Blur filter.**

18. **Choose File→Open, navigate to the file** 13_textframe.psd **in the Session 13 Tutorial Files folder on your hard drive, and click Open.**

Depth Map and Blur Focal Distance

The depth map (in this case a layer mask with a black-to-white gradient) determines which areas are in focus and which are blurred in the image. The Blur Focal Distance determines the location of the plane of focus (the area that is most in focus). Blur Focal Distance can be set either by clicking on a particular location in an image (which has a corresponding grayscale tone in the depth map), or by dragging the slider in the Lens Blur dialog box to a number between 1 and 255. Areas on the depth map that have tonal values higher than the Blur Focal Distance value (lighter tones) are considered to be in back of the focal plane; numbers with lower values (darker tones) are considered to be in front of the focal plane.

In this example, clicking the model's eye set the focal plane to 11 (a dark value in the gradient on the layer mask depth map). Higher-numbered tones (which are lighter) are considered to be in back of this focal plane and, therefore, cause progressively more blur.

You do not have to use a layer mask as a depth map. You could use a layer with transparency, in which case the image would get blurrier as the depth map became more transparent. Or you could forego a depth map, in which case the image would be uniformly blurry.

19. **Select the Move tool in the toolbox. Then click in the** 13_textframe.psd **document window and drag that image and text into** 13_darkroom.psd **on your desktop.**

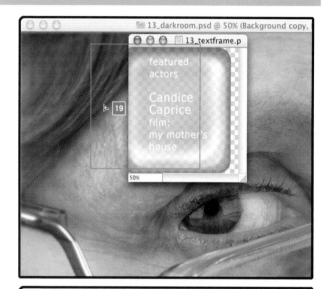

20. **Drag the glass text frame and text into place at the top left of** 13_darkroom.psd **to match the illustration.**

21. **Choose File→Save As, rename the image** 13_darkroom_end.psd, **and save it to your collages folder for use in the final project.**

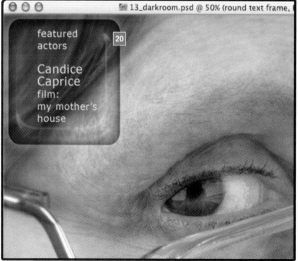

» Session Review

This session covers the many aspects of editing and adding effects to photos in Photoshop. It includes lessons on cloning, retouching images with the Healing Brush and Patch tools, adjusting exposure, adjusting saturation, sharpening, blurring and saturating an image, and creating depth of field. Here are some questions to help you review the information in this session. You find the answer to each question in the tutorial noted in parentheses.

1. What is the Crop and Straighten Photos feature used for? *Hint:* Not just straightening a single photo. (See "Tutorial: Cropping and Straightening a Scan.")

2. When using the Clone Stamp tool, what happens when you sample pixels? (See "Tutorial: Removing Content with the Clone Stamp Tool.")

3. How does the Healing Brush tool differ from the Clone Stamp tool? (See "Tutorial: Retouching with the Healing Brush Tool.")

4. When you select an area using the Patch tool, what is the difference between specifying Source or Destination in the Options bar? (See "Tutorial: Working with the Patch Tool.")

5. What does the Patch tool preview show you? (See "Tutorial: Working with the Patch Tool.")

6. What do the Dodge and Burn tools do? (See "Tutorial: Dodging and Burning.")

7. Why change the range from Shadows to Midtones to Highlights when using the Dodge or Burn tools? (See "Tutorial: Dodging and Burning.")

8. Which tool can be used to soften a hard line of pixels? (See "Tutorial: Using the Blur Tool.")

9. Name two uses for the Color Replacement tool. (See "Tutorial: Applying the Color Replacement Tool.")

10. At what point in the image correction workflow is it most common to apply the Unsharp Mask filter? (See "Tutorial: Sharpening an Image with the Unsharp Mask Filter.")

11. How can you preview the effect of an Unsharp Mask filter in the document window? (See "Tutorial: Sharpening an Image with the Unsharp Mask Filter.")

12. What do the Threshold and Radius settings for the Unsharp Mask filter control? (See "Tutorial: Sharpening an Image with the Unsharp Mask Filter.")

13. What photographic effect does the Lens Blur filter simulate? (See "Tutorial: Creating a Depth-of-Field Effect with the Lens Blur Filter.")

14. Why might you use a layer mask with the Lens Blur filter? (See "Tutorial: Creating a Depth-of-Field Effect with the Lens Blur Filter.")

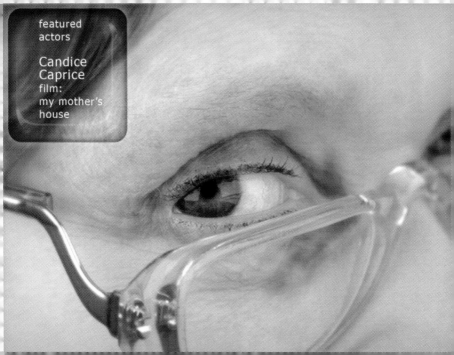

Session 14

Controlling Tone

featured
actors

Allison
Reverent
film: finish line

Session Introduction

Almost every photograph that you acquire, perhaps with the exception of an image that's professionally scanned at a service center, requires some tonal adjustment. Desktop flatbed scanners and digital cameras often produce images lacking optimal brightness and contrast. There is no one method or formula for tonal correction that's best for all images. Photoshop offers a number of tools for adjusting brightness and contrast. The trick is knowing how and when to use each, which is what you learn in this session. You apply and customize Photoshop's automatic tonal correction commands—Auto Levels and Auto Contrast. You become acquainted with the new Shadow/Highlight adjustment, which is great for quickly correcting under-exposed and over-exposed photographs. And you learn more sophisticated and effective correction methods using Levels and Curves adjustments.

TOOLS YOU'LL USE
Auto Levels command, Auto Contrast command, auto-correction options, Shadow/Highlights adjustment, Levels adjustment, Curves adjustment, Save Levels command, and Save Curves command

CD-ROM FILES NEEDED
14_tone.psd, tone_levels.alv, tone_curves.acv, and 14_tone_end.psd

TIME REQUIRED
90 minutes

Tutorial
» Applying a Shadow/Highlight Adjustment

Don't be so quick to throw away dark, underexposed photographs or shots that have bright, overexposed areas. The Shadow/Highlight adjustment, which is new to Photoshop CS, can save incorrectly exposed photos that you might otherwise have abandoned. In this tutorial, you apply the Shadow/Highlight adjustment to a photograph for your film festival brochure, exploring the inner workings of this useful new feature.

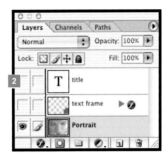

1. **Open** `14_tone.psd` **from the Session 14 Tutorial Files folder on your hard drive.**

2. **Click in the Visibility fields on the text frame layer and the title layer to remove the eye icon from those layers.**
   Hiding these two decorative layers gives you a better view of the photograph you correct.

3. **Squint your eyes and take a look at this photograph to get a sense of its tonal qualities. Notice that it is too light overall and lacks contrast between light and dark tones.**
   Analyzing the tones in a photograph is the first step in correcting any image. Squinting as you view an image can minimize the impact of color and help you get a sense of tonal qualities—the distribution of white, black, and gray tones in an image.

\<N O T E\>
A photograph with good contrast typically has some areas of true white, some areas of rich black, and a complete range of tones between white and black. This photo lacks rich blacks, resulting in an image that appears muddy and dull. To correct this, you need to make adjustments that expand the tonal range, with emphasis on darkening the darkest areas of the photograph (often referred to as the shadow areas).

4. **Select the Portrait layer in the Layers palette.**

5. **Choose Image→Adjustments→Shadow/Highlight.**
   The Shadow/Highlight dialog box opens. By default, the Shadows→Amount slider is set to 50, which automatically applies an adjustment to the shadow areas in your image causing immediate improvement.

6. **Leave the Show More Options checkbox unchecked for now.**
   If you're a novice, you'll appreciate how simple the dialog box appears without the extra options.

7. **Uncheck and then recheck the Preview checkbox to compare the before and after effect of this automatic adjustment.**

< N O T E >
Notice that the Highlights→Amount slider is set to 0 by default. This means that there has been no automatic adjustment to the highlight areas of the photograph. The beauty of the Shadow/Highlight adjustment is that it can impact the shadow and highlight areas of an image separately.

8. **Click Cancel to close the Shadow/Highlight dialog box without applying the adjustment. Leave this image open for the next tutorial.**
   This keeps the image in its original, unadjusted state in preparation for the tutorials that follow, in which you try out other tonal correction methods.

<NOTE>

The Shadow/Highlight adjustment is ideal for correcting photographs that have both shadow areas that are too dark and highlight areas that are too bright. This problem often exists in a backlit photograph, in which the light source is coming from behind the subject. The Shadow/Highlight adjustment is also useful for fixing photos that have been over-flashed, causing the foreground to be too bright and the background too dark. Adjusting the Amount sliders in the collapsed Shadow/Highlight dialog box can significantly improve an image. However even more can be done to improve a photo by clicking the Show More Options check box at the bottom of the dialog box to reveal additional Shadow/Highlight adjustment controls. The table that follows describes each of the controls in the expanded Shadow/Highlight dialog box, along with tips about when and how to use the controls.

Table 14-1: Shadow/Highlight Adjustment Controls

Setting	Function	Tips
Shadow➜Amount	Controls how much shadows (ie. dark tones) in the image are lightened .	Dragging this Amount slider to the right lightens shadows.
		Values range from 0 (no change) to 100 (maximum change)—similar to the increasing steepness of a curve adjustment. The default value of 50 causes a moderate lightening of shadows.
		A shadow adjustment to brighten a backlit subject may cause a decrease in contrast between the subject and neighboring pixels. Try fixing this by increasing the Midtone Contrast slider at the bottom of the dialog box.
Shadow➜Tonal Width	Controls the range of tones that are affected by the Shadow➜Amount slider).	Setting this Tonal Width to a low value causes the darkest tones to be most affected by a shadow adjustment.
		When Tonal Width is set to 0 only dark shadows are notably affected by the Amount slider. When Tonal Width is set to 1, dark shadows are lightened the most, midtones are lightened half as much, and highlights are not affected.
		Dragging this slider to the right expands the range of affected tones, which is useful when you want to lighten midtones and highlights along with shadows.
		Default value is 50.
Shadow➜Radius	A shadow adjustment is applied to individual pixels depending on the darkness or lightness (luminance) of neighboring pixels. Radius determines the size of the neighborhood of pixels taken into account in this determination.	Too small a Radius can reduce the contrast between the subject that is lightened and the rest of the image.
		Too high a Radius can result in an overall lightening of the image, rather than the disparate lightening of the dark subject.
		Apply a trial and error approach in every image to find a value between these two extremes.

Setting	Function	Tips
Highlight→Amount	Controls how much highlights (ie. bright tones) are darkened .	Dragging this Amount slider to the right darkens highlights .

Values range from the default value of 0 (no change) to 100 (maximum change).

A highlight adjustment may give the image a cyan cast, which you can fix with the Color Correction slider or with the Edit→Fade Shadow/Highlight command (see below). |
| Highlight→Tonal Width | Controls the range of tones that are affected by the Highlight→Amount slider. | Setting this Tonal Width to a low value causes the brightest tones to be most affected by a highlight adjustment.

When Tonal Width is set to 0, only bright highlights are notably affected by the Amount slider. When Tonal Width is set to 1, bright highlights are darkened the most, midtones are darkened half as much, and highlights are not affected.

Dragging this slider to the right expands the range of affected tones, which is useful when you want to darken midtones and shadows along with highlights.

Default value is 50. |
| Highlight→Radius | See the explanation of Shadow→Radius above. | Too small a Radius can reduce the contrast between the subject that is darkened and the rest of the image.

Too high a Radius can result in an overall darkening of the image, rather than the disparate darkening of the bright subject.

Apply a trial and error approach in every image to find a value between these two extremes. |
| Adjustments→Color Correction | Corrects color only of pixels that are changed by a shadow or highlight adjustment | Use to remove color cast that may be generated by shadow or highlight adjustment.

Alternatively, immediately after applying a Shadow/Highlight adjustment, choose Edit →Fade Shadow/Highlight and lower the Opacity setting in the Fade dialog box. |
| Adjustments→Midtone Contrast | Adjusts contrast in the midtones. | Use to increase contrast of nearby midtone pixels after you lighten a backlit subject with a shadow adjustment . |

Tutorial
» Applying Auto-adjustments

When you need a quick tonal fix, you may be tempted to use either Auto Levels or Auto Contrast, which are commands that auto-matically adjust image brightness and contrast. These commands are sometimes all you need to quickly adjust a snapshot or a photograph you use for compositing. However, they aren't recommended for professional tonal correction because they aren't as precise as the manual correction methods that you study in later tutorials. Professional correcting requires more direct and spe-cific control over correction settings than these automatic methods allow. In this tutorial, you apply the default Auto Levels and Auto Contrast adjustments to an image, analyzing how these features work and what they produce.

1. **With `14_tone.psd` open from the previous tutorial, select the Portrait layer and choose Image→Adjustments→Auto Levels from the menu bar at the top of the screen.**

   Auto Levels adjusts brightness values and contrast to give the image a bolder, less washed-out appearance. However, con-trast is now a little strong, and there is loss of detail in the shadows on the left side of the photo, as you can see in this figure. The adjustment has also given the image a greenish cast that might be avoided by using a different automatic adjustment method—Auto Contrast.

   <NOTE>

   Auto Levels adjusts brightness and contrast by remapping the lightest highlights in an image to white and the darkest shadows in the image to black. It also redistributes the gray values across the brightness scale between the black and white points. Although you want a true black and true white point in an image, you don't want important shadow areas to become so dark or important highlight areas to become so light that you lose detail in those areas.

   <NOTE>

   Auto Levels works independently on each of the red, green, and blue channels in the image. This can sometimes shift color bal-ance, giving an image an unwanted color cast, particularly if brightness and contrast vary among channels.

2. **Choose Edit→Undo Auto Levels.**

   This undoes the last adjustment to return to the original image.

3. **Choose Image→Adjustments→Auto Contrast from the menu bar.**
   Auto Contrast, like Auto Levels, improves the contrast of the
   image, but also results in a slight loss of detail in the shadow
   areas, as you can see in this figure. You can also see that
   there is less of a greenish cast than there was when you
   applied Auto Levels.

<N O T E>
Auto Contrast is similar to Auto Levels in that it shifts the darkest
image values to black and the lightest to white. The difference
between the two commands is that Auto Contrast doesn't treat
each color channel independently. Instead, it works on a composite
of all channels. As a result, you don't see a dramatic color shift
when you apply Auto Contrast.

4. **Choose Edit→Undo Auto Contrast. Keep the file open for the next
   tutorial.**
   You again undo the last adjustment to return to the original
   image. Because both Auto Levels and Auto Contrast produced
   less than satisfactory results (loss of detail in shadow areas),
   you try other correction methods on this image as this session
   moves on.

<N O T E>
It's common that the default auto-correction methods are not sufficient for serious attempts at tonal adjustment. However, they are
so easy to apply and to remove if necessary that it sometimes
makes sense to include them in your workflow, particularly when
you work on non-professional projects.

Tutorial
» Changing Auto-adjustment Defaults

When you use the auto-correction tools, the amount of correction is controlled by default settings established upon installation of the program. When adjustments made with auto-correction tools are too strong, you can override Photoshop's defaults with user-defined settings. In the preceding tutorial, the brightness and contrast adjustments made by Auto Levels and Auto Contrast were too extreme. To apply a more subtle correction, you can adjust the default auto-correction settings, as you do in this tutorial.

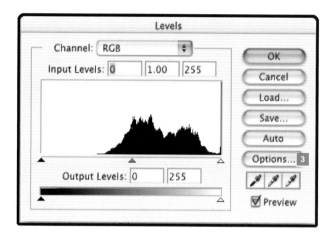

1. **14_tone.psd should still be open from the last tutorial. If it's not, open it from the Session 14 Tutorial Files folder on your hard drive.**
   You must have an image open in the document window before attempting to change the auto-correction defaults. Otherwise, you won't be able to launch the Levels dialog box from which the auto-correction options are accessed.

2. **With the Portrait layer still selected in the Layers palette, choose Image→Adjustments→Levels from the menu bar.**
   This opens the Levels dialog box.

3. **Click the Options button in the Levels dialog box.**
   This opens the Auto Color Corrections Options dialog box, in which you can make changes that affect the behavior of the auto-correction features.

<TIP>
If you attempt to open the Levels dialog box and the command is grayed out, you may have a layer selected to which levels can't be applied. Invisible layers, layers with vector objects, type layers, and other adjustment layers can't accept a levels adjustment.

The Levels Histogram

When you first open the Levels dialog box, take a moment to observe the bar chart, known as a histogram. This Levels histogram is one of two histograms in Photoshop CS. You learn about the other freestanding histogram in the next session. The Levels histogram shows you the entire range of possible grayscale values in an 8 bit image—from 0 (representing pure black) on the left to 255 (representing pure white) on the right. The black bell curve is actually a group of thin vertical bars symbolizing the data in this image. Each bar represents the frequency with which a particular tone is used in the image. Notice that no data appears on the far left side of the histogram. This means that there is an absence of black in this image, and the skew is in the direction of white, resulting in a light image. The sliders below the histogram can be adjusted to control brightness and contrast in the image, as you learn to do in the tutorial "Adjusting Brightness and Contrast with Levels" later in this session.

4. **Type** 0.01 **in the Shadows Clip box, replacing the default value of 0.10.**

   This reduces the amount of shadow clipping that is applied when you use any of the auto-correction features. Shadow clipping is the conversion of dark tonal values to pure black, as explained in the nearby Shadow and Highlight Clipping sidebar.

5. **Type** 0.01 **in the Highlights Clip box, replacing the original default value of 0.10.**

   This reduces the amount of highlight clipping that is applied when you use the auto-correction tools. Highlight clipping is also explained in the sidebar.

6. **Check the Save as Defaults checkbox in the Auto Color Correction Options dialog box.**

   This changes the Clip values that are used by all auto-correction tools, including Auto Levels, Auto Contrast, and Auto Color, and by the Auto buttons in the Levels and Curves dialog boxes.

7. **Click OK to close the Auto Color Correction Options dialog box, and OK again to close the Levels dialog box.**

   This applies an automatic Levels correction with your corrected Clip values to the image, giving you the result that you see in the figure. The shadows on the left side of the image are not as dark and have slightly more detail than they did when you applied Auto Levels with the default Clip values in the previous tutorial.

Shadow and Highlight Clipping

To get a grasp on what the term *clipping* means, try the following in the Levels dialog box (after the Auto Color Correction Options dialog box is closed): Move the black Input slider below the histogram to the right past the beginning of the data displayed in the bell-shaped curve. The data to the left of the black slider is cut off, or *clipped*, meaning that all values in the image that are darker than the value at which you placed the black slider become pure black. (Return the black slider to the far left after you observe this.) Moving the white slider to the left would have a parallel effect on the highlights. As a general rule, the more clipping that you apply to an image, the stronger the contrast appears. In the previous tutorial, you applied auto-corrections using Photoshop's default Clip values. The result was too much clipping, which produced an image with too much contrast. By adjusting the defaults and reducing the amount of clipping, you see less extreme brightness and contrast changes when you apply an auto-correction.

8. **Review this figure, which compares the application of Auto Levels and Auto Contrast adjustments with and without the modification you made to the Auto Color Correction Options in steps 4 and 5.**
The images in the top row were adjusted with Auto Levels and Auto Contrast adjustments, respectively, using Photoshop's default auto-correction settings. The two images in the bottom row were adusted with Auto Levels and Auto Contrast, respectively, with the Clip values in Auto Color Correction Options reduced to 0.01, as you did in steps 4 and 5.

9. **Choose File→Revert.**
This returns you to the original image.

10. **Leave this file open for the next tutorial. Don't bother saving.**
Table 14-2 summarizes each of the features Photoshop offers for correcting brightness and contrast. Study this chart and use it as a reference.

Table 14-2: Understanding Photoshop's Tonal Controls

Menu Command	Function
Auto Levels	When using Auto Levels, Photoshop analyzes the image and finds the lightest pixel and shifts it to white. That lightest pixel could be a 10% gray, 20% gray, or any other gray value. The point is that it's the lightest pixel in the document, and Photoshop makes it pure white. Then it finds the darkest pixel and makes it black. The remaining pixels are stretched out across a range of grays between the new white and new black. Depending on the amount of brightness in the original lightest and darkest pixels, Photoshop may make the overall image appear too dark or too light. In order to effectively use Auto Levels, start with a good scan with the lightest point close to white, the darkest point close to black, and an even range of tones in between. In most cases, your scans won't be evenly distributed between a white and black, and you'll need to use other methods for correcting the image brightness and contrast.
Auto Contrast	This command sets monochromatic contrast. In other words, it applies an adjustment to a composite RGB channel as opposed to individual channels like the Auto Levels adjustment. The command works best on images with wide tonal ranges that are already in color balance.
Brightness/Contrast	Novice users are tempted to use the Brightness/Contrast command, which adjusts the entire image the same way, causing new problems even as it tries to fix an existing problem. You won't see any mention of this command beyond this point in the book. It will ruin the data in your file and should never be used. Forget it exists.
Curves	The Curves dialog box offers you even more control than the Levels dialog box for tonal corrections. You can adjust brightness values and reshape histograms for any of the 256 gray values. For correcting color, the Curves dialog box is the best tool in Photoshop.
Levels	The Levels command should always be your first stop when adjusting brightness and contrast or even just examining an image to determine where the gray values fall. By adjusting the input sliders, you can add snap and crispness to your images. Following the Levels adjustment, you can color correct or tweak grays in the Curves settings.

Tutorial

» Adjusting Brightness and Contrast with Levels

Whereas the auto-correction tools enable you to make only two adjustments at fixed values, the Levels dialog box offers you more control over midtones as well as highlights and shadows in an image. Although the auto-correction tools are quick and easy, you almost always get better results with the Levels command, which will frequently be your first stop when you correct an image. In this tutorial, you learn how to use the Levels dialog box to adjust brightness values and contrast in an image.

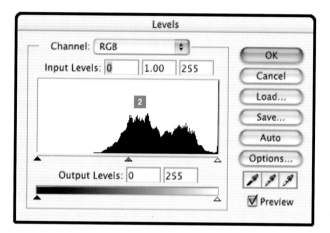

1. **Use the file** 14_tone.psd **that you left open from the last tutorial.**

2. **Choose Image→Adjustments→Levels.**
   The Levels dialog box opens. The tall lines in the middle of the histogram indicate that there are a lot of the corresponding medium gray colors in this image, and the short vertical lines on the right side of the histogram indicate that there are very few of those particular shades of light gray in this image. In the following steps, you learn how to adjust the range of tones in this image by moving the input sliders located directly below the histogram.

<NOTE>

The Input Levels fields tell you the numerical value of the tone just above each slider. Notice that the value at the far left of the histogram (above the black slider) is 0 (zero) and the value at the far right (above the white slider) is 255. Zero is counted as one value; hence the total number of grays in this 8-bit image equals 256.

3. **Click the left slider below the histogram and move it to where the data first appears on the left side of the histogram. Make sure that the left Input Levels box reads 83 after you move the slider.**
   Before you moved the slider, the histogram revealed no data above the left input slider. The histogram was skewed to the right, indicating that there was no true black in the original image and that the image contained more light than dark tones. By moving the left input slider to the right, you turned lighter pixels into darker pixels resulting in an overall improved contrast.

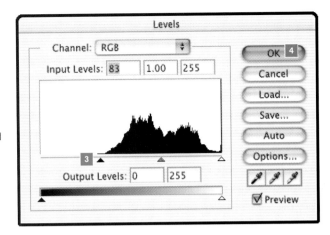

<NOTE>
The right side of the histogram contains sufficient data; therefore, there is no need to move the white slider to the left.

4. **Click OK in the Levels dialog box.**
   This applies your levels adjustments to the image.

<NOTE>
Moving sliders in the Levels dialog box is a bit of guesswork. Although Photoshop provides you with dynamic feedback, you may be confused as to where exactly the slider belongs and how much clipping will occur in the image. Macintosh users have more help from Photoshop than Windows users.

5. **Choose Edit→Undo Levels.**

6. **Choose Image→Adjustments→Levels to reopen the Levels dialog box.**

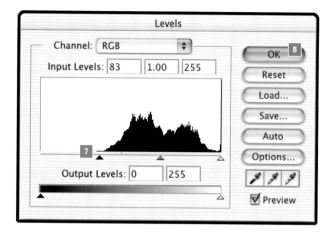

7. **Press the Option key (Windows: Alt key) on your keyboard and drag the left Input slider to the right. Stop the slider when you first begin to see pixels appear in the document window (which should correspond with an input level of about 83).**
   Photoshop dynamically shows you which pixels will be clipped (turned to pure black) as the Input slider is moved. You don't want to shift too many pixels to black because you lose detail in the shadow areas. As long as the pixels that you see are separated by some white space (rather than appearing as a solid clump), the area that includes these black pixels will retain detail.

8. **Click OK to apply the Levels adjustment to the image with your manually adjusted settings.**

9. **Keep the file open and move immediately on to the next tutorial.**
   Don't take a break yet, if you can help it, because the next two tutorials depend on leaving this file open and working on it further without closing.

<NOTE>
RGB files contain three separate channels of color information, which contain gray levels for the red, green, and blue colors in an image. You can apply levels corrections for each individual channel in order to adjust color balance. At the top of the Levels dialog box, the Channel button shows the composite RGB channel selection. Click that button to open a drop-down list from which you can select the red, green, or blue channel. Then move the sliders to adjust levels for the selected color channel. For more information regarding channels, see the next session.

<NOTE>
After you set the black and white points in the Levels dialog box, you may still find that an image is too dark or too light overall. In that case, click and drag the gray Input slider in the Levels dialog box to adjust the gray midtone without further affecting the very white highlights or the very black shadows. If a simple adjustment of the gray slider doesn't get you the look that you want, move on to adjust gray tones with the Curves dialog box, as you learn to do in the next tutorial.

Tutorial
» Adjusting Tonality with Curves

In this tutorial, you learn how to use Curves to adjust tonal range in an image with the highest level of control.

1. **With** `14_tone.psd` **still open from the last tutorial, choose Image→Adjustments→Curves.**
   The Curves dialog box opens. The diagonal line that begins at the lower left of the Curves dialog box and extends to the upper-right corner represents the linear progression of grays from 1 (black) to 255 (white). You can make tonal adjustments to any one of the 256 gray tones using curves.

2. **Click in the middle of the curve line to add a point to the line.**
   Adding one or more points to the curve line is the first step in making a tonal adjustment. The Input and Output fields at the lower left of the Curves dialog box give you a numerical read-out of the location of the selected point.

<TIP>
If you didn't click exactly at the middle point of the curve line, you can center the point numerically. Make sure the point is selected on the line (it should be solid instead of hollow) and type **128** in the Input field and **128** in the Output field.

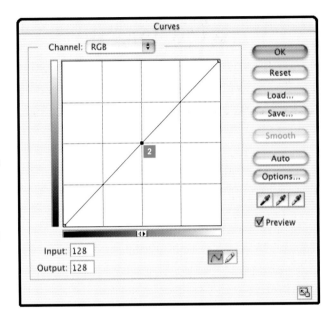

3. **Click on the point you added and drag slightly upwards until the Output box at the lower left of the dialog box reads 130. The Input box should still read 128.**
   This lightens the whole image slightly. This adjustment is so slight that you may find it easier to type **130** directly into the Output box with the point selected. Curves adjustments should be slight if you begin with an image with a good tonal range. (Following the Levels adjustment in the last tutorial this image has a fairly good tonal range.)

<NOTE>
To make tonal corrections to an image, you first click the line to add one or more points to the line. You drag a point up and to the left on the diagram to bend the line in that direction and lighten the image; you drag a point down and to the right to bend the line the other way and darken the image. The resulting shape of the curved line determines how tones are remapped in the image.

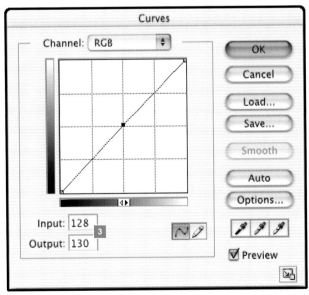

Using Levels and Curves Together

As a common practice, using Levels to adjust brightness and contrast is a good first step because the Levels histogram shows you where all the image pixels fall and gives you a clue as to where to move the sliders for making brightness and contrast adjustments. However, with Levels you can adjust only a single midtone point by moving the center Input Level slider. Using Curves, you can change any of 256 gray tones and make any one of those grays darker or lighter, resulting in a change to the midtones between the black and white points. In a typical workflow, you first adjust the black and white points in the Levels dialog box and then move to the Curves dialog box to adjust midtones.

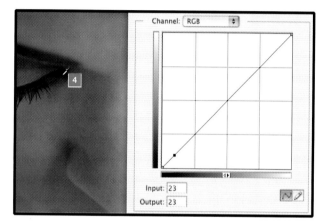

4. ⌘+click (Windows: Ctrl+click) in the part of the image that you think should be pure black, such as the model's right tear duct.
   A solid circle appears on the bottom left of the curve line, the part of the line that corresponds to the dark areas of the image. Don't worry if your point isn't at the exact location or your Input and Output numbers aren't exactly the same as those shown here.

<NOTE>
Alternatively you could plot the potential black point by hand. Option+click (Windows: Alt+click) in several of the darkest areas of the image. Each time you click, a hollow circle appears temporarily on the curve line, telling you that this is the part of the line that controls the dark parts of the image. Then just click on the line in that vicinity to plot a point.

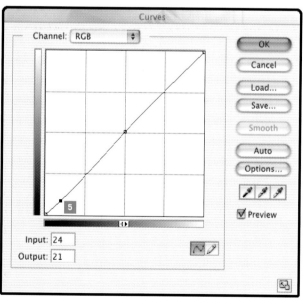

5. Click on the point that you created in step 4 and drag down slightly toward the bottom of the curve diagram.
   The whole image was lightened slightly back in step 3. This restores the darker shadow areas, keeping a true black in the image, without affecting the highlight areas. They are protected from moving by the point that you set in the middle of the curve line.

Understanding Curves

Here's a technique that helps you visualize what any point on the curves line represents and what you accomplish when you adjust that point. Create a point anywhere on the line and move your eye down to the black-to-white horizontal bar directly beneath that point to see a visual representation of the tone of gray that that point represents. Move the point slightly up or down. Now move your eye to the vertical bar on the left of the diagram to see the tone of gray to which you remapped the original tone. The numbers in the Input and Output boxes are numerical representations of the same thing. Numerical values in the Input box correspond to shades on the horizontal bar, and values in the Output box correspond to shades on the vertical bar.

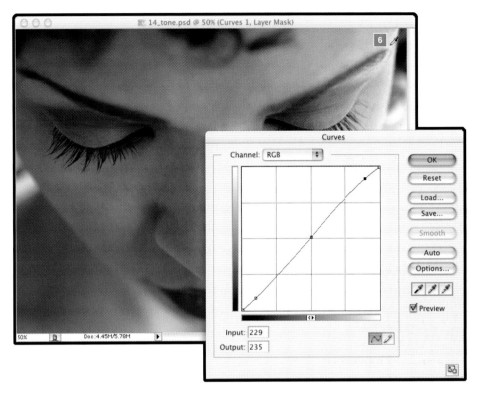

6. ⌘+click (Windows: Ctrl+click) in an area of the image that has the brightest highlight in which you'd like to retain detail (such as the area to the right of the model's left eyebrow).

You see a solid circle appear on the top right of the line in the Curves dialog box, in approximately the location that you see in the figure. Again, don't worry if your point isn't at the exact same location or your Input and Output numbers aren't exactly the same as those shown here.

7. Click the point that you created in step 6 and drag down to move it toward the bottom of the diagram very slightly.

This adjustment restores a little highlight detail.

8. Click OK in the Curves dialog box.

9. Keep the file open and move immediately on to the next tutorial.

Notice that the Curves adjustments were slight. The Levels adjustment that you made in the preceding tutorial was almost adequate to correct the brightness and contrast in the document. The slight Curves adjustments for midtones, shadows, and highlights preserve the highlight and shadow details.

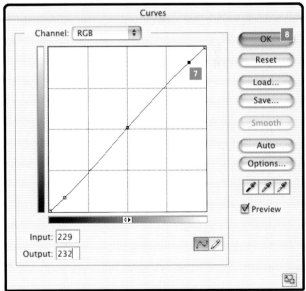

<TIP>

When you adjust in the Curves dialog box, don't make severe adjustments, or the image can become posterized or appear to have dull flat tones instead of crisp contrast.

Tutorial

» Saving and Loading Brightness Adjustment Settings

In the previous two tutorials, you made Levels and Curves adjustments. In some workflows, you may have a number of images that need the same brightness adjustments. Rather than individually apply new settings to each image, you can save the adjustments made to an image and load the same adjustments into other images. In this tutorial, you learn how to save and load Levels and Curves settings.

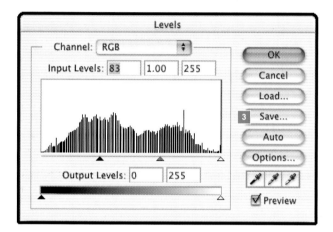

1. **Use the file** 14_tone.psd **with the Levels and Curves adjustments from the last tutorial.**

2. **Press ⌘+Option+L (Windows: Ctrl+Alt+L).**
   When you use these modifier keys to reopen the Levels dialog box, you see the last settings applied in the dialog box. If your file has remained open since the tutorial in which levels were discussed, you should see the Input slider for the black point resting at 83 in the Input Levels box. If you didn't keep your file open, open the original 14_tone.psd file and make the Levels adjustment again.

3. **Click the Save button in the Levels dialog box.**
   The Save dialog box opens.

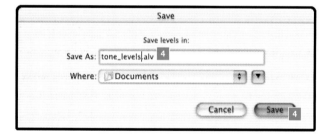

4. **Name the file** tone_levels.alv **and click the Save button in the Save dialog box.**
   The .alv extension is Photoshop's default file extension for Levels settings. Be sure to save the file in a folder that you can easily find on your hard drive.

5. **Click Cancel in the Levels dialog box.**

6. **Press ⌘+Option+M (Windows: Ctrl+Alt+M).**
   The Curves dialog box opens displaying the last adjustments made.

7. **Click the Save button.**

   The Save dialog box opens.

8. **Type** tone_curves.acv **and click the Save button in the Save dialog box.**

   The .acv extension is Photoshop's default file extension for Curves settings. Be certain to save the file in the same folder as the Levels settings.

9. **Click Cancel in the Curves dialog box.**

10. **Choose File→Save As and save** 14_tone_curves.psd **to your desktop. Do not save over the tutorial file of the same name that is on your hard drive. Close the file after saving.**

    The Levels and Curves adjustments have been made to this image. Saving the file preserves the brightness, contrast, and tonal corrections that you made. The settings have all been saved in two separate files.

11. **Open the original uncorrected file** 14_tone.psd **from the Session 14 Tutorial Files folder on your hard drive.**

    The file needs the same tonal corrections made in the previous tutorials. Rather than revisit the dialog boxes, you load the settings saved from steps in this tutorial.

12. **Choose Image→Adjustments→Levels.**

    The Levels dialog box opens.

13. **Click Load.**

    The Load dialog box opens.

14. **Navigate to** tone_levels.alv **and click the Load button.**

    Photoshop returns you to the Levels dialog box, and the adjusted Input Levels setting appears and is applied to the image. Note that a copy of this levels file is in the Session 14 Tutorial Files folder if you need it.

15. **Click OK in the Levels dialog box to accept the settings.**

16. **Choose Image→Adjustments→Curves.**

    The Curves dialog box opens.

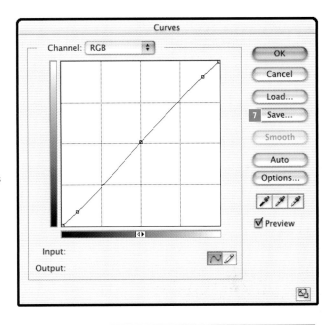

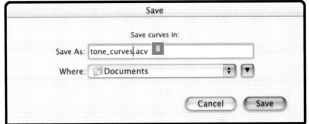

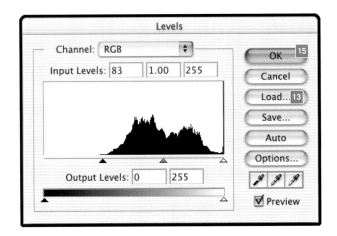

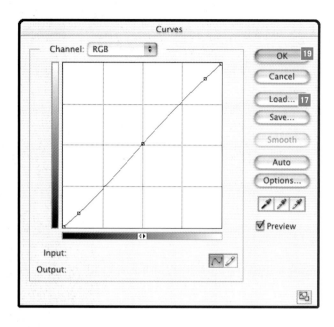

17. **Click Load.**

    The Load dialog box opens and displays all files with an `.acv` extension.

18. **Navigate to `tone_curves.acv` and click the Load button.**

    Photoshop returns you to the Curves dialog box, and the settings are applied to the Curves adjustment. Note that a copy of this curves file is in the Session 14 Tutorial Files folder if you need it.

19. **Click OK to accept the settings.**

20. **Choose File→Save As, name the image `14_tone_end.psd`, and save it to your desktop.**

    You use this file again in the next session.

» Session Review

This session covers how to adjust tonal values (brightness and contrast) in images. You first learned how to adjust brightness and contrast automatically using the Auto Levels and Auto Contrast commands, and then you worked in the Levels dialog box where you applied adjustments manually for brightness and contrast changes. Later, you made adjustments for tonal corrections in the Curves dialog box and learned how to save and load settings.

1. How do you use auto-correction tools? (See "Tutorial: Applying Auto-adjustments.")

2. When would you use Auto Levels and Auto Contrast? (See "Tutorial: Applying Auto-adjustments.")

3. How do you control the amount of adjustment with auto-correction tools? (See "Tutorial: Changing Auto-adjustment Defaults.")

4. What is a histogram? (See "Tutorial: Adjusting Brightness and Contrast with Levels.")

5. If there are 256 levels of gray in an 8-bit image, why does the largest number in the Levels dialog box appear as 255? (See "Tutorial: Adjusting Brightness and Contrast with Levels.")

6. What's bit depth? (See "Tutorial: Adjusting Brightness and Contrast with Levels.")

7. What's the difference between 8-bit and 16-bit images? (See "Tutorial: Adjusting Brightness and Contrast with Levels.")

8. When are curves used? (See "Tutorial: Adjusting Tonality with Curves.")

9. What are curves input and output levels? (See "Tutorial: Adjusting Tonality with Curves.")

10. How can you apply the same brightness, contrast, and tonal adjustments to several images? (See "Tutorial: Saving and Loading Brightness Adjustment Settings.")

featured
actors

Allison
Reverent
film: finish line

Session 15

Adjusting Color

Tutorial: **Adjusting Color Balance**

Tutorial: **Adjusting Hue/Saturation**

Tutorial: **Adjusting Color with Curves**

Tutorial: **Adjusting Color with Variations**

Tutorial: **Using the Match Color Command**

Session Introduction

After you address brightness and contrast corrections in images, the next step involves correcting color. Even with some of the best desktop scanners and digital cameras, you'll typically find a need for making some kind of color correction. In this session, you look at methods used in Photoshop for correcting color, including adjustments using the Color Balance, Hue/Saturation, Curves, and Variations features. You're also introduced to the new Histogram palette that gives you information about your image as you color correct, and the Color Match feature that applies the colors from one image to another image.

TOOLS YOU'LL USE
Color Balance command, Hue/Saturation command, Curves command, Channels command, and Variations command, Info palette, Histogram palette, Color Match command

CD-ROM FILES NEEDED
15_lipstick.psd, 15_tone.psd, 15_tone_clean.psd, and 15_tone_end.psd

TIME REQUIRED
90 minutes

Tutorial
» Adjusting Color Balance

Photoshop offers a number of color-correction tools. The Color Balance adjustment is one of the easiest to use, but it also offers you less control than more sophisticated color correction methods such as curves. Other methods are preferable if you do professional color correction, but Color Balance may be sufficient when you need a quick color correction fix for a snapshot or personal project. You practice applying a Color Balance adjustment in this tutorial.

1. **Open the file** 15_tone.psd **from the Session 15 Tutorial Files folder. This is a copy of the file** 14_tone_end.psd **that you completed and saved to your desktop in Session 14, so you can use that file if you prefer. Choose Window→Histogram to open the Histogram palette.**

   The file was corrected for brightness and contrast in Session 14.

2. **Make sure that the Portrait layer is selected in the Layers palette. Choose Layer→New Adjustment Layer→Color Balance and click OK in the New Layer dialog box.**

   This creates a new Color Balance adjustment layer above the Portrait layer and opens the Color Balance dialog box. Take a good look at the image to try to determine whether it has an unacceptable color cast and to determine how to correct that color cast or other problem.

<NOTE>
You could color correct directly on the Portrait layer by choosing Layer→Adjustments→Color Balance, but it makes sense to perform color corrections on separate adjustment layers because adjustment layers don't affect the original pixels of artwork; they can be reopened and edited at any time, and they can be deleted at will.

<NOTE>
When you're considering whether and how to correct the color of an image, keep in mind that each of the primary colors in an RGB image has a complementary color. The color complements are red/cyan, green/magenta, and blue/yellow. Adjusting the problem color or its complement is often all the color correction that you need to do. In this case, the image needs a slight bit of red to bring the flesh tones to a more neutral appearance. In the Color Balance settings, you add a little red and make some slight adjustments to the Green and Blue channels.

Detecting Color Cast with the Info Palette and the Histogram Palette

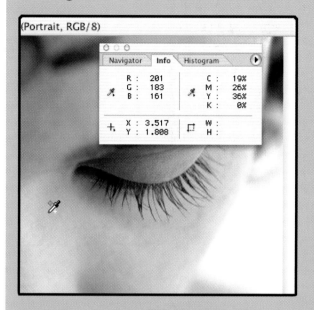

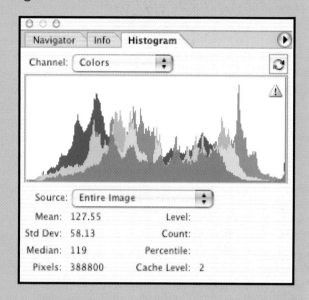

The Info palette has always been useful when you evaluate color in an image. One way to detect a color cast is to select the Eyedropper tool in the toolbox and move it over an area of your image that you think should be neutral gray, keeping your eye on the RGB readout in the Info palette. The R, G, and B values in an area of neutral gray should be equal. If any one of those colors is significantly greater than the other two, there is a color cast of that hue.

You can also use the floating Histogram palette, which is new in Photoshop CS, to spot a color cast. The Histogram is a visual representation of the distribution of tones in an image, similar to the static histogram in the Levels dialog box with which you're already familiar.

Open the Histogram palette (Window→Histogram). Click the arrow at the top right of the palette to display the palette menu and choose Expanded view. Then click the Channel menu at the top of the palette and choose Colors. This gives you a color, composite view of each of the R, G, and B channels in the image along with the luminosity channel.

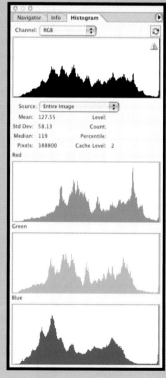

If you choose View All Channels and Show Channels in Color from the palette menu, you get separate color histograms of each of the channels. You can make a rough judgment from these diagrams as to whether any color predominates. If you notice that there is a lot more of one color than others in the middle of the histogram (the midtones), chances are there is a color cast.

You should be pleased to know that you can have the Histogram palette open while you work with any of the adjustment features, including Color Balance, Curves, and Levels. And if Preview is turned on in the adjustment feature's dialog box, you can see a before and after view of how the histogram is affected by the adjustment. You can view a histogram for an entire image, for a layer, or for an adjustment layer and all layers below it by choosing one of those options from the Source menu. A selection limits the histogram to the selected area, and you can see statistics for a particular area of the histogram by clicking and dragging in the histogram.

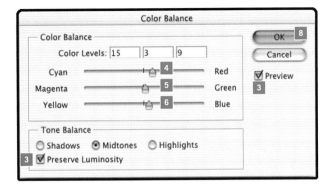

3. **Make sure that Preview is enabled in the Color Balance dialog box so that you can see a live preview of your adjustments in the document window. Select Midtones to work on the color of the midtones first. And make sure that Preserve Luminosity is checked in order to protect the tonal balance that you worked so hard to correct in the previous session.**

   Preserve Luminosity keeps the overall image brightness fixed while you make adjustments to color balance. You can adjust colors in the shadows, midtones, and highlights separately using the radio buttons in this dialog box.

4. **Move the Cyan/Red slider away from Cyan and toward Red, until 15 appears in the first Color Levels box.**

   You may be wondering how to know exactly where to set any of the color sliders. One way to work is to move the slider to an exaggerated position to see the results of the adjustment and back it off by moving slowly back toward the middle. With Preview enabled, Photoshop offers you dynamic viewing as the sliders are moved.

5. **Click the Magenta/Green slider and move it away from Magenta toward Green, until the second Color Levels box at the top of the dialog box reads 3.**

   Moving the slider away from magenta reduces the magenta in the image.

6. **Click the Yellow/Blue slider and move it toward Blue to 9.**

   This adjustment adds a little blue and reduces the yellow slightly.

7. **Uncheck and then recheck the Preview box to compare the way that the image looked before and after this adjustment.**

   Notice that the color adjustment is slight.

8. **Click OK to accept the changes.**

9. **Choose File→Save and keep** 15_tone.psd **open for the next tutorial.**

   Adjusting the color balance changes the mix of colors in the image. However, changes in color or the intensity of the color aren't handled in the Color Balance dialog box. For these changes, you need to use Hue/Saturation corrections. Therefore, this tutorial is one-half of the equation that may be needed for some images. To continue your color correction, move on to the Hue/Saturation dialog box, as explained in the next tutorial.

Tutorial
» Adjusting Hue/Saturation

In the previous tutorial, you adjusted color balance and made corrections for any color cast that may appear in an image. The color value and intensity of a color are handled in the Hue/Saturation dialog box. In this tutorial, you learn how to apply a Hue/Saturation adjustment.

1. **Make sure that** 15_tone.psd **is still open from the previous tutorial.**

2. **Choose Layer→New Adjustment Layer→Hue/Saturation and click OK in the New Layer dialog box.**
   This adds a Hue/Saturation adjustment layer above the Color Balance adjustment layer in the Layers palette and opens the Hue/Saturation dialog box.

3. **Make sure that Colorize is disabled in the Hue/Saturation dialog box, Master is selected in the Edit drop-down list, and there's a check mark next to Preview.**
   If Colorize is selected, the entire image is shifted to the same Hue and Saturation, with only brightness varying from pixel to pixel. When you adjust color, you want Colorize to be disabled. Master applies the adjustments that you're about to make to all the colors in the image equally, rather than to just a particular range of colors (such as reds, yellows, and so on).

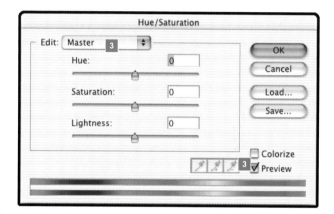

<NOTE>
The Hue/Saturation dialog box enables you to adjust three different parameters of color: Hue, Saturation, and Lightness. *Hue* means the color value. Moving the Hue slider applies colors as if you were moving 360° around a color wheel. *Saturation* means the intensity of color. *Lightness* means the brightness of color. The Lightness slider affects all tones in an image equally, so it's best to avoid using this slider and adjust brightness in the Levels or Curves dialog box instead.

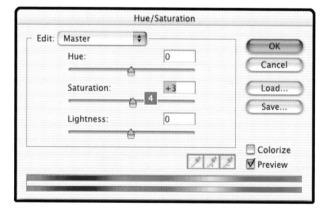

4. **Drag the Saturation slider to +3. Click OK in the Hue/Saturation dialog box.**
   This adjustment makes all the colors in the image slightly more vibrant. There's no reason to change the Hue or Lightness setting of this image in the Hue/Saturation dialog box because the brightness of this image was already adjusted in the previous session, and the Hue was addressed in the previous tutorial when you adjusted color balance.

5. **Choose File→Save and keep this image open for the next steps.**
   To gain a little more understanding about how Hue/Saturation adjustments affect an image, you learn how to use this feature to apply a special effect in the following steps.

<NOTE>
The combination of the Color Balance and the Hue/Saturation adjustments brings the sample image into a better color balance, resulting in more neutral skin tones. These adjustments were minor because this image didn't have much of a color cast or saturation problem at this point.

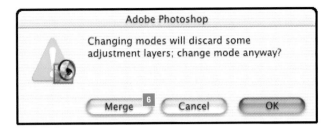

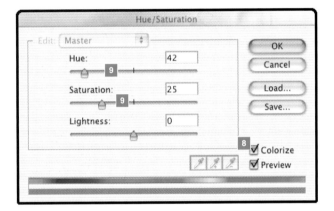

6. **Choose Image→Mode→Grayscale. You see a warning that changing modes will discard adjustment layers (because grayscale mode doesn't support adjustment layers). Click Merge.**
   This eliminates all color from the image in preparation for adding a sepia tone to the image using Hue/Saturation adjustments. Sepia toning is often applied to old photos for photo restoration. Before you begin to colorize an image with a sepia effect, you must first strip all color from the image, as you did in this step.

7. **Choose Image→Mode→RGB Color.**
   In order to colorize an image, you must convert it back to RGB mode because the file needs to be in a mode that can accept the application of color.

8. **Choose Layer→New Adjustment Layer→Hue/Saturation and click OK in the New Layer dialog box. In the Hue/Saturation dialog box, click the Colorize check box.**
   Colorize is the secret to this effect. It enables you to add a monochrome hue to the entire image.

9. **Move the Hue slider to the left to 42 to change the color. Move the Saturation slider to the left to 25 to tone down the effect. Click OK in the Hue/Saturation dialog box.**
   The image appears with a sepia effect.

10. **Close the file without saving.**

< N O T E >
Photoshop provides you with another, automatic method for sepia toning in the Actions palette. Actions are a series of Photoshop commands that can be applied to multiple images in batch mode or individually to separate images. To use the Sepia toning action, eliminate all color from your photos by choosing Image→Mode→Grayscale and then convert them back to RGB by choosing Image→Mode→RGB Color. Open the Actions palette and select Sepia toning (layer) in the palette and click the right pointing arrow at the bottom of the dialog box. Photoshop runs through a series of steps and converts the image to a sepia tone.

Tutorial
» Adjusting Color with Curves

The best tonal and color control feature in Photoshop is the Curves adjustment. In Session 14, you used Curves to correct the tonal range of an image, making adjustments to brightness in the midtones, highlights, and shadows. The Curves command can also be used for color balance. In this tutorial, you learn how to use the Curves dialog box to correct color.

1. **Open** 15_tone_clean.psd **from the Session 15 Tutorial Files folder. Make sure the Histogram palette is still open.**
   This file is another copy of the file that you completed at the end of the previous session, 14_tone_end.psd. The image has been corrected for brightness and contrast only. Make sure that you don't use a file in which you have already made color adjustments.

2. **Choose Layer→New Adjustment Layer→Curves and click OK in the New Layer dialog box.**
   The Curves dialog box opens.

3. **Make sure Preview is selected, and select Red from the Channel drop-down list.**
   A little red needs to be added to the image to warm it up. You can make adjustments to individual channels in the Curves dialog box.

4. **Click in the center of the Curves line to create a point there. Type** 128 **in the Input box and** 138 **in the Output box.**
   Notice that the point moves up slightly. This moves the red channel towards white, allowing more red light to show through the Red channel and increasing the red tint of the image.

5. **Click OK and observe the results.**
   The image could use a little more warmth and a little bit of saturation. To saturate the entire image, you use the Hue/Saturation tool.

6. **Choose Layer→New Adjustment Layer→Hue/Saturation and click OK in the New Layer dialog box. Move the Saturation slider to the right to +5.**

7. **Click the Preview check mark off and on for a comparative view of the effect of increasing the saturation. When you're done, click OK to accept the adjustment.**
   Notice that the flesh tones appear more neutral after making this adjustment in the Hue/Saturation dialog box.

8. **Close this file without saving. It's important that you don't save over** 15_tone_clean.psd **in the Session 15 Tutorial Files folder because you use that file again in the next tutorial.**

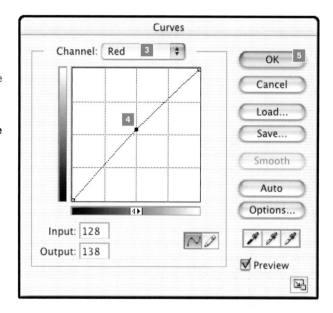

<NOTE>

As you become more experienced in Photoshop, you'll find the Curves adjustment a more sophisticated approach for adjusting color. The ability to access each individual channel and adjust any one of the 256 gray levels in the channels provides you with many more options than those found in the Color Balance and Hue/Saturation dialog boxes.

Using Curves for Color Correction

When you shoot your own images for Web hosting or printing, it is often advantageous to use a gray card. You can obtain a 10% gray card at a photo finishing laboratory or a photo supplier. When you shoot your own images, place the gray card in a visible area of the image.

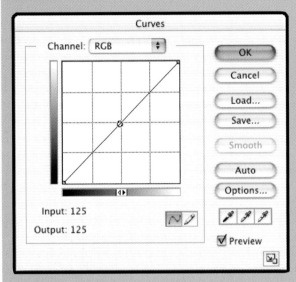

After scanning a photo or acquiring a digital camera image, open the Info palette in Photoshop and then open the Curves dialog box. Move the cursor to the image of the gray card in the photo. Click the mouse button and move the cursor around the photo until the bubble appearing on the Curve line is positioned close to the midpoint.

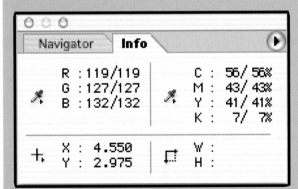

Observe the readout in the Info palette for the RGB values. A true neutral gray results in all three RGB values at 128. Write the values from the Info palette on a piece of paper. If, for example, your

readout is R: 119, G: 127, B: 132, these values should all be brought to the same value if the sampled pixel is a neutral gray. To bring each channel to the same value as the other two respective channels, identify the value between the extremes. In this example, the mid value is the Green channel at 127. Thus, the Red channel at 119 and the Blue channel at 132 need to be moved to the Green value of 127.

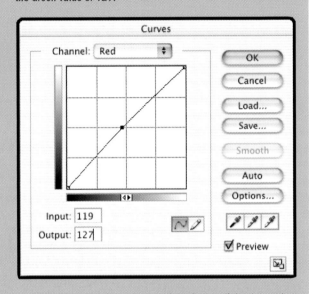

From the drop-down list at the top of the Curves dialog box, select the Red channel. Click along the curve line at any point. Enter the Red point value from the readout made in the Info palette into the Input box (in this example, 119). For the Output value, enter the midpoint value (in this example, the Green value of 127).

Perform the same steps for the Blue adjustment: Select Blue from the Channel drop-down list. Click a point on the Curve line and enter an Input value of 132 and an Output value of 127. The result of these adjustments is remapping the two channels to the third channel at the midtone range. This method provides a way to do quick color adjustments without having to do a lot of guesswork.

Tutorial

» Adjusting Color with Variations

If you've been struggling with color correction up to this point, fear not. The Variations tool can help the most novice user correct color in Photoshop documents. You still need to work with an image where the brightness and contrast corrections have been made. At that point, you can apply color correction in a more intuitive manner with Variations. This tutorial teaches you how to use the Variations tool.

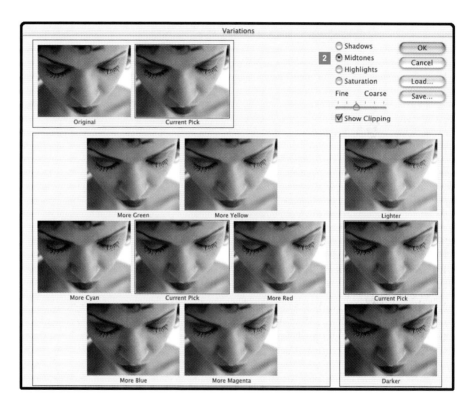

1. **Open** 15_tone_clean.psd **again from the Session 15 Tutorial Files folder. Make sure Portrait layer is selected.**
   Once again, you use the image that's been corrected for brightness and contrast.

2. **Choose Image→Adjustments→Variations. Click the radio button for Midtones at the top of the dialog box, if it isn't currently selected.**
   In the Variations dialog box, you see thumbnail views of the current image and the image as it would look after various adjustments to color and brightness.

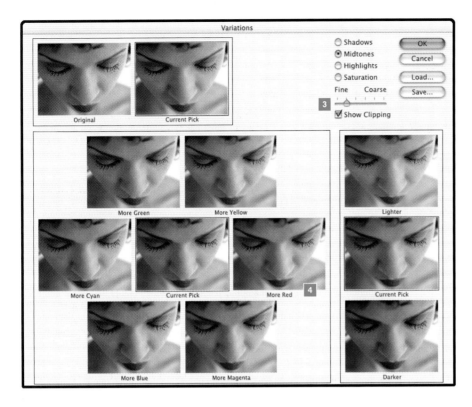

3. **Select the slider in the top-right corner of the Variations dialog box and move it to the left toward Fine. Rest the slider at the second hash mark from the left.**

   When you apply Variations, you can control the amount of adjustment applied to your image by moving the slider toward Coarse for a stronger change in color or toward Fine for less application. This image needs only a slight adjustment. Therefore, you move the slider to a finer setting.

4. **Click the More Red thumbnail.**

   Notice that when you click, the center thumbnail shows you the result of your adjustment, and all the other thumbnail views are updated to show you what the image will look like if you click another thumbnail.

   < N O T E >

   Notice that the Variations dialog box enables you to combine adjustments for color balance, brightness, and saturation. Unlike the tools used in previous tutorials, you can make all your color corrections in a single dialog box.

5. **Click OK in the Variations dialog box. Press ⌘+Z (Windows: Ctrl+Z) twice to toggle back and forth between the changes made and the original image as it was opened in Photoshop.**

   Note that Variations is an intuitive, visual approach for making color corrections. The use of the thumbnail views and the ability to address all the color correction parameters in a single dialog box afford you a much easier approach for adjusting color.

6. **Make sure that you redo the last correction that was applied to the document.**

7. **Leave the file open for the next tutorial without saving.**

   < N O T E >

   There's another automatic color correction tool called Auto Color. It is designed to eliminate color casts from photos. However, like the other automatic correction tools (Auto Levels and Auto Contrast), it doesn't work on all images (including the image that you've been using in this session). Auto Color works by finding the average lightest and darkest pixels in an image and using them as the black and white points. It also attempts to adjust midtones to neutral. If you're interested in trying this feature, choose Image➔ Adjustments➔Auto Color.

Tutorial
» Using the Match Color Command

Photoshop CS introduced another quick way to correct color images—by matching them to the color of other images. Match Color is useful when you need to achieve consistent color in a product, fashion, or catalog shoot; when you want to match photographs taken in different lighting conditions; or when you have images that you would like to have share a color palette. You can also use match color to tone a photograph with color tints borrowed from other images. In this tutorial, you use the Match Color command to put some virtual makeup on your model.

1. **Select the Portrait layer in** 15_tone_clean.psd, **which should still be open from the previous tutorial, and drag that layer to the New Layer icon at the bottom of the Layers palette to make a copy.**
The Match Color feature works directly on the image pixels, so making a copy of the layer to be affected is a way to play it safe. This also allows you to blend the result of the color match with the layer below using layer opacity and layer blend modes, as you do at the end of this tutorial.

2. **Choose Select→Load Selection and choose lips from the Channel menu. Click OK.**
This loads a feathered selection of the model's lips that was saved for you with the image. If you prefer, make your own selection around the model's lips using the Lasso tool and/or Quick Mask mode.

<NOTE>
The Match color feature works best if you make a selection in both the source and target images before invoking the command. The selection in the source image is used to create the color palette to which the target image is matched, so try to include a range of tones—from shadows to midtones to highlights in the selected area in the source image.

3. **With the selection active, click the add layer mask icon at the bottom of the Layers palette.**
This adds a layer mask to the Portrait copy layer that protects everything but the lips from the planned color change.

4. **Open the file** 15_lipstick.psd **located in the Session 15 Tutorial Files folder on your hard drive.**

5. **Use the Lasso tool and/or QuickMask mode to make a selection around the red lipstick in the foreground. Don't include any of the silver or white background.**

6. **Click on** 15_tone_clean.psd **to make that file active. Select the image thumbnail on the left side of the Portrait copy layer. Choose Image→Adjustments→Match Color.**
The Match Color dialog box opens. The file you want to correct (your target file) should be active before you invoke the Match Color dialog box.

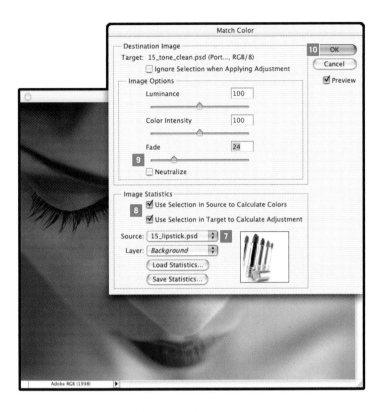

7. **In the Match Color dialog box, make sure Preview is checked. Choose** `15_lipstick.psd` **in the Source field.**

8. **Select Use Selection in Source to Calculate Colors and Use Selection in Target to Calculate Adjustment.**
   This narrows the range of colors involved, making a successful result more likely.

<NOTE>

If you select Ignore Selection when Applying Adjustment, the program includes the selected areas in its calculations, but applies the results to the entire image.

9. **Drag the Fade slider to around 24 to reduce the intensity of the color shift in the target image.**

<TIP>

If your target image has a color cast, try clicking the Neutralize check box. The purpose of that feature is specifically to reduce color cast.

10. **Click OK to apply the match. Choose ⌘+D (Windows: Ctrl+D) to deselect the lips.**
    Photoshop chooses the color palette from the selected area of the source image, `15_lipstick.com`, and attempts to match the palette of the target image, `15_tone_clean.psd`, to that of the source image.

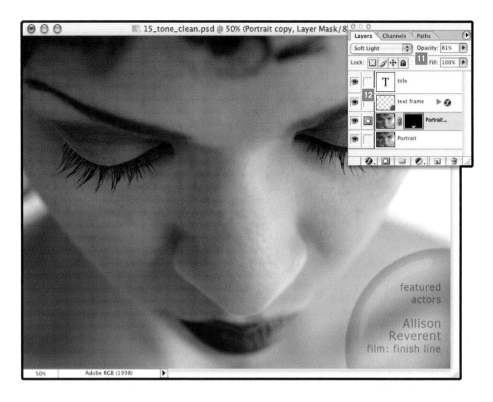

11. **With the Portrait copy layer selected, reduce layer opacity to around 80% and change the layer blending mode to Overlay or Soft Light.**
    This gives you further control over the appearance of the matched (and masked) copy layer.

12. **Click in the Visibility field on the text frame and title layers in the Layers palette to make the logo visible in the document.**
    If you're interested in how the glass effect was made, click on the layer styles to open the Layer Style dialog box, where you can try your hand at deconstructing the effect.

13. **Choose File→Save As, name the file** 15_tone_end.psd, **navigate to your collages folder, and click Save. Close** 15_lipstick.psd **without saving.**
    Congratulations! You completed another page of your film festival brochure.

» Session Review

This session covers how to correct color in images scanned from desktop scanners or acquired from digital cameras. You experimented with different color adjustment tools, including Color Balance, Hue Saturation, Curves, and Variations.

1. How is a color cast removed from an image with the Color Balance feature? (See "Tutorial: Adjusting Color Balance.")

2. What does the Histogram palette display about an image? (See "Tutorial: Adjusting Color Balance.")

3. What are hue and saturation? (See "Tutorial: Adjusting Hue/Saturation.")

4. How do you colorize an image? (See "Tutorial: Adjusting Hue/Saturation.")

5. How do you adjust color with the Curves dialog box? (See "Tutorial: Adjusting Color with Curves.")

6. How do you adjust color in only one channel? (See "Tutorial: Adjusting Color with Curves.")

7. How do you increase or decrease the amount of color in an image using Photoshop's Variations feature? (See "Tutorial: Adjusting Color with Variations.")

8. How can you adjust for color cast and saturation in a single dialog box? (See "Tutorial: Adjusting Color with Curves.")

9. Should you add a selection to your source and target images when using the Match Color command? (See "Tutorial: Using the Match Color Command.")

featured
actors

Allison
Reverent
film: finish line

Editing High-Bit Images

Session Introduction

In Session 2, you looked at the File Browser and learned what kinds of information can be stored with a file. That information included settings used for the actual capture of the image if certain cameras are used. In this session, you work with an image's raw data in Photoshop's Camera Raw plug-in. You learn how to view a camera's data and how to work with it directly, bypassing the camera's settings and filters.

You work with a 16-bit image in this session. Starting from a captured image, you modify it in the Camera Raw plug-in and then work with it in Photoshop. As you will see, most of the same options are available when you're working with a 16-bit image as with a regular 8-bit image. In this session, you create a multilayered image file using a 16-bit image and then composite it into a larger movie-poster image.

TOOLS YOU'LL USE
Camera Raw plug-in, File Browser, Elliptical and Rectangular Marquee tools, Gaussian Blur filter, guides, layer masks, layer styles, Levels command, Merge Visible Layers command, Noise filter, Photo Filter adjustment, Rasterize Type command, Text tool, Transform command

CD-ROM FILES NEEDED
16_church.psd, 16_church_end.psd,
16_church_layers.psd, 16_church_text.psd,
16_movie_poster.psd, 16_poster_end.psd, and
Wrig_002_original.nef

TIME REQUIRED
90 minutes

Discussion
Working with 16-Bit Images

In older versions of Photoshop, you were restricted to a maximum bit-depth of 8-bit-per-channel color. That still leaves plenty of colors to choose from—about 16 million. In Photoshop CS, you can work with 16-bit color per channel, which offers billions of potential colors! The advantage of 16-bit color is that it vastly increases the amount of color data in an image, which gives you more leeway to adjust the image without causing abrupt jumps in color or tone called posterization.

Plan carefully before creating or modifying images to use 16-bit color. Although the images' colors are more distinct, the file size is twice that of a regular 8-bit-per-channel image.

Here are some things to keep in mind when considering working with 16-bit color:

» You can use any layer functions, including adjustment layers, with 16-bit images.

» You can use any of the tools in the toolbox except for the Art History Brush tool with 16-bit images.

» You can use all color and tonal adjustment commands except Variations with 16-bit images.

» You can only use a limited number of filters, and you can't use the Extract, Liquify, or Pattern Maker commands.

» You can't use 16-bit images in Premiere Pro.

If you need to use some of the commands or filters that aren't available, you can quickly change a 16-bit image to an 8-bit image. Choose Image→Mode→8 Bits/Channel (choose Image→Mode→16 Bits/Channel to convert an 8-bit image to a 16-bit image).

How can you acquire a 16-bit image? Create one from scratch by choosing 16 bit from the bit-depth menu in Photoshop CS' File→New dialog box. Scan an image using a scanner capable of capturing 48 bits of data (3 channels of 16-bit color = 48 bits). Or shoot a photograph with a digital camera that saves images in raw format. In the following tutorials you learn how to use the Camera Raw plug-in that's integrated into Photoshop CS to process and import raw photographs as 16-bit files.

Tutorial
» Previewing and Opening a Camera Raw File

When you shoot an image with a digital camera, the raw image data is written to the camera's sensors. If you work with certain cameras, you can use the Camera Raw plug-in that comes with Photoshop CS to open the raw image and to adjust it yourself rather than have the camera do the processing and conversion. In this tutorial, you learn how to find information about a Camera Raw file, and learn about the different types of data stored with a Camera Raw file.

1. **Click the File Browser icon to open the browser, or Choose File→Browse. Choose the Session 16 folder in the Tutorial Files in the Folders area of the browser.**
    The folder contents display in the thumbnails area.

2. **Click the** `Wrig_002_original.nef` **thumbnail in the preview area to select it.**
    The file extension `.nef` represents the proprietary raw image file format produced by Nikon cameras. Different camera manufacturers have different raw file formats.

3. **In the Metadata palette, click the arrow to the left of File Properties, if that category is not already open, to display basic information about the image.**
    Scroll to the Bit Depth property and notice that bit depth is listed as 16, 16, 16—indicating that there are 16 bits of information in each of three channels of this high-bit image. Click the arrow again to close the display.

4. **Click the IPTC (International Press Telecommunications Council) heading to open the display.**
    You add author and copyright information.

5. **Click the Author field to make it active, and type** Carol Steele Photography, Torquay, UK; **click the Copyright field and type** 2003.
    You attribute the image's source to its author.

6. **Click anywhere on the File Browser outside the fields you used in step 5. A message displays stating you have to apply the changes to the metadata. Click Apply to close the message. Another message opens, describing where the metadata will be located. Click OK.**
    The final message closes, and a new file, `Wrig_002_original.xmp`, is added to the Session 16 folder.

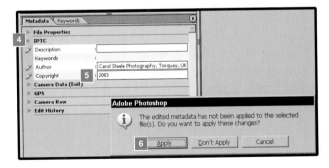

<NOTE>
The new file is referred to as a *sidecar* file. The metadata is saved in this kind of file because this image is in raw format and therefore cannot be rewritten. The sidecar file is located in the same folder as the image file with which it's associated. If you transfer this image to another location, be sure to keep the sidecar file with it or the metadata will be lost.

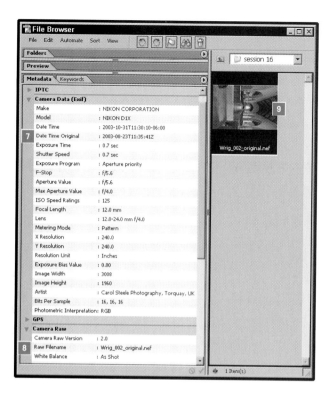

7. **Click the arrow next to Camera Data (Exif) to display the contents of the metadata category.**

   Scroll through the information; you see details about the camera, the exposure, f-stop and other camera data.

8. **Scroll down the Metadata palette, and click the Camera Raw heading to display its contents.**

   The settings for the Camera Raw process are listed. You can see that some basic options have values, such as brightness, contrast, and noise reduction. You modify some of these settings in the Camera Raw plug-in.

9. **Double-click the** Wrig_002_original.nef **thumbnail to open the image.**

   The Camera Raw dialog box opens. Opening a raw file launches the Camera Raw interface. The raw image data must be processed before it can be brought into Photoshop proper.

10. **Leave the Camera Raw dialog box open and continue with the next tutorial.**

    You learned how to preview a raw format image, how to preview its data in the File Browser, and how to open a raw image in the Camera Raw interface.

Advantages of Using Camera Raw

A camera raw file is like a digital negative. It contains image data in its purest, unprocessed form. The data must be converted before it can be opened in Photoshop. Until recently, raw image conversion was done inside of digital cameras using each camera manufacturer's proprietary algorithm. If a camera saved an image in JPEG format, image information was lost, because JPEG is a lossy file format. By contrast, the Camera Raw plug-in that is included with Photoshop CS converts raw data inside your computer. It gives you access to high-quality raw data and allows you, rather than the camera, to control this stage of processing. In addition, it avoids potential loss of data from in-camera JPEG compression.

Processing in the Camera Raw interface takes place before an image is brought into Photoshop proper. You can adjust white balance, exposure, contrast, saturation and more in the Camera Raw dialog box, as you do in the next tutorial. Clicking OK opens the adjusted image inPhotoshop, where you can perform further corrections and save the file in a non-raw format like PSD, TIFF, or JPEG.

Tutorial

» Processing a Camera Raw Image

In the previous tutorial, you learned how to find and understand the information that is included with a Camera Raw image file, and added more metadata, saved in a sidecar file. You opened the image in the Camera Raw plug-in. In this tutorial, you process the raw data file in the Camera Raw interface by specifying bit-depth, size, exposure, and other parameters with which the image will be brought into Photoshop.

1. **The image** Wrig_002_original.nef **should be open in the Camera Raw window.**
   If not, follow the instructions in the previous tutorial for opening a Camera Raw file.

2. **Click the Depth arrow and choose 16 Bits/Channel.**
   This sets the bit depth at which the raw image is brought into Photoshop's main interface at the end of the tutorial. Your project in this session uses a 16-bit file.

3. **Click the Size menu to open a list of file sizes. Click the 1572 by 1024 (-) pixel option.**
   You can choose from two file sizes smaller and three file sizes larger than the original, which was shot at 3008 x 1960 pixels. If you want to make a file larger than its original size, do so here in the Camera Raw dialog box, rather than in Photoshop, because there is a better up-sampling algorithm in Camera Raw.

4. **Click the Resolution field and type** 300. **Leave the pixels/inch default.**
   You use the image in a poster having a 300 pixels/inch resolution, and want the image's resolution to match that of the poster.

5. **Click the Rotate image 90 degrees counterclockwise icon below the preview area.**
   Rotate the image to display correctly; the image preview also resizes itself to fit the preview area.

<TIP>
You can see the RGB values for any sampled area display below the preview by moving any of the tools over the surface of the image, including the Zoom tool, Hand tool, or White Balance tool (eyedropper).

<NOTE>
Toggle the Preview check box off to see the original image; click the check box to view the modified image. You can toggle the Preview as necessary while you're making adjustments to your image.

6. **With the Basic radio button selected, click the Adjust tab in the Settings area to display exposure settings. Make changes by dragging the sliders or selecting the fields and typing the values:** Exposure: –0.35, Shadows: 52, Brightness: 10, Contrast: 27, and Saturation: –100.

   Lowering exposure darkens the image slightly. Increasing the Shadow slider clips the shadows, pushing them to black with no detail and increasing image contrast. Moving those two sliders is similar to adjusting the white and black points in an image in Photoshop, did in Session 13. Decreasing the Brightness slider darkens all tones in the image. Decreasing the Contrast slider reduces contrast in the midtones. And, moving the Saturation slider down to -100 removes all color, changing the image to monochrome.

   < N O T E >

   Holding the Option key (Windows: Alt key) as you drag the Exposure slider shows which highlights are pure white with no detail. Holding the Option key (Windows: Alt key) as you drag the Shadow slider shows which shadow areas are clipped to pure black with no detail.

7. **Click the Advanced radio button in the Camera Raw window.**
   Two additional tabs display in the Settings area.

8. **Click the Lens tab to display Lens settings.**

9. **In the Lens settings, change the Vignetting Amount to +100.**
   Vignetting is a lens defect where the edges of an image are darker than the center. Moving this setting to the right brightens the edges. The Vignetting Midpoint setting becomes active as soon as you adjust the vignetting setting.

10. **Set the Vignetting Midpoint to 45.**
    The default value is 50; decreasing the amount applies the adjustment to a larger area away from the corners than the default.

11. **Click OK to close the Camera Raw interface.**
    The raw file is processed according to the settings you made in the Camera Raw dialog box. Click OK if you see an Embedded Profile Mismatch message. A copy of the image opens in the document window in Photoshop proper.

12. **Choose File→Save. Save the file as** 16_church.psd**.**
    Note that the file identification information at the top of the image includes RGB/16, which means the RGB image is a 16-bit image. Leave the file open for the next tutorial.

    < N O T E >

    The Camera Raw settings you applied to the image are saved in the accompanying sidecar .xmp file. If you select the raw file thumbnail in the File Browser, you see those settings in the Camera Raw section of the Metadata palette. If you open the raw file again, you see those values in the Camera Raw dialog box.

Tutorial
» Filtering a High-Bit Image

Now you have an image that was corrected and modified in the Camera Raw window using the raw image file. In this tutorial, you make some size adjustments to the image, and then add some more layers. You should have the 16_church.psd file you saved in the previous tutorial open in the program. If not, locate the file in your storage folder and open it in Photoshop.

1. **Press ⌘+A (Windows: Ctrl +A) to select the entire image, and then press ⌘+Shift+J (Windows: Ctrl+Shift+J).**
   The image is cut and pasted to a new layer named Layer 1 above the Background layer.

2. **Double-click the default name or choose the Layer Properties option from the Layers palette menu to activate the Layer 1 name. Rename the layer** Church.

3. **In the Layers palette, select the Church layer and drag it to the Create a New Layer icon at the bottom of the palette to add a new layer named Church copy. Rename the new layer** Church Blur.

4. **With the Church Blur layer active, choose Filter→Blur→ Gaussian Blur.**
   The Gaussian Blur dialog box opens.

< N O T E >
When you open the Filter menu, you notice that not all the filter categories are available. This is because you are working with a 16-bit image. The Lens Blur filter is one of the filters you can't use with a 16-bit image, so you use a workaround to create a similar shallow depth-of-field effect in the following steps.

5. **Drag the Radius slider to 10 in the Gaussian Blur filter dialog box. Click OK to close the dialog box and apply the blur to the Church Blur layer.**

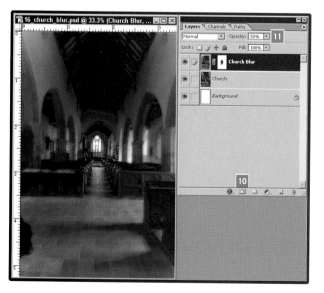

6. **Select the Elliptical Marquee tool.**

7. **Set the feathering for the tool to 40 px in the Options bar.**

8. **Draw an oval around the window at the center of the image.**
   You want the selection to include the window and part of the central aisle of the church as shown in the figure.

9. **Press ⌘+Shift+I (Windows: Ctrl+Shift+I) to inverse the feathered oval selection.**

10. **With the Church Blur layer still selected, click the Add Layer Mask icon at the bottom of the Layers palette.**
    A mask is added to the Church Blur layer, creating a depth-of-field effect.

11. **Click the arrow to open the Opacity slider. Decrease the blur layer's opacity to 50%.**

12. **Choose File→Save.**
    You added new layers to the church image and created a depth-of-field effect using a blur. Leave the image open for the next tutorial.

Tutorial
» Working with Layers in a High-Bit Image

In Photoshop CS all of the program's layer features are available when you are working with a 16-bit image. In this tutorial you work with layers in the 16-bit image you converted from the Camera Raw plug-in. You add and fill a layer, change the blending mode of a layer, and add multiple adjustment layers, including a new Photo Filter adjustment layer.

1. **Continue with the** 16_church.psd **file open from the previous tutorial.**

2. **Click the New Layer icon at the bottom of the Layers palette to add another layer to the file. Press Option+Delete (Windows: Ctrl+Backspace) to fill the layer with white.**

3. **Name the layer** Soft Noise.

4. **Choose Filter→Noise→Add Noise.**
   The Add Noise dialog box opens.

5. **Drag the Amount slider to 25% in the Add Noise filter dialog box.**

6. **Choose Uniform Distribution, and add a checkmark in the Monochromatic Field.**
   The noise converts from color to black and white.

7. **Click OK to close the dialog box and apply the filter.**

8. **Choose Filter→Blur→Gaussian Blur. Set the Radius slider to 1.0 and click OK to close the dialog box and apply the blur.**

9. **Leave the Soft Noise layer selected. Click and drag the mask from the Church Blur layer to the Add Layer Mask icon at the bottom of the Layers palette.**
   A copy of the Church Blur layer's mask is added to the Soft Blur layer. The church window shows through the center of the mask.

10. **Click the Layer Blend Mode list and choose Soft Light.**
    You can now see the rest of the scene.

11. **With the Soft Noise Layer still selected, choose Image→ Adjustments→Levels to open the Levels dialog box.**
    The image is quite dark; you make adjustments to the medium and light pixels to lighten it.

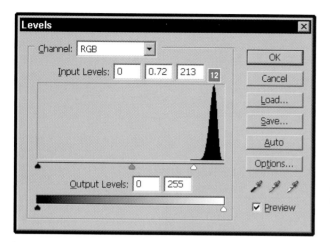

12. **Change the Input Levels to** 0, .72, **and** 213. **Click OK to close the dialog box.**

    You reset the midrange and light pixel distribution in the image making it brighter overall. Although you made adjustments for tone and exposure earlier in the Camera Raw plugin, you can further adjust those properties after the image is brought into Photoshop proper, as you've done here.

13. **Click the New Fill or Adjustment Layer icon at the bottom of the Layers palette to open a menu, and choose Photo Filter.**

    The Photo Filter dialog box opens.

    <NOTE>

    You can use Adjustments and Adjustment Layers with 16-bit images.

14. **In the Photo Filter dialog box, click the Filter menu and choose Warming Filter (85) if it isn't already showing.**

    Leave the default orange color that displays with the filter.

15. **Leave the Preserve Luminosity option checked; increase the Density slider to 97%.**

    This darkens the photo filter adjustment.

16. **Click OK to close the dialog box and apply the adjustment.**

    The image takes on a warm gold tint.

17. **Choose File→Save.**

    You copied a layer mask between layers, applied a layer blending mode, adjusted a layer's levels, and added an adjustment layer to this 16-bit image. Leave the image open for the next tutorial.

    <NOTE>

    It may take a while to save this file. That's because a 16-bit file is larger in file size than the 8-bit files you're used to, and adding layers has increased the file size substantially to around 33 megabytes. Reducing the dimensions of the image in the next step will bring this number down.

Tutorial
» Resizing the Image

In this tutorial you finish the assembly of the poster image. You add the final touches to the 16-bit image, crop it, and resize it in preparation for adding text, the final stage before you construct the poster. You used the smallest image size available from the options when you modified the original image in the Camera Raw window, but you need a smaller size to use in the poster.

1. **Make sure that** `16_church.psd` **is still open from the previous tutorial. Click the Church layer in the Layers palette to make it active.**
   You resize the layer.

2. **Press ⌘+T (Windows: Ctrl+T) to activate the Free Transform handles.**

3. **In the Options bar, type** 115% **for both horizontal and vertical scaling. Press Return (Windows: Enter) to rescale the layer, or click the check mark on the Options bar.**
   The rescaled layer creates a ghosting effect on the image.

4. **Choose Image→Image Size to open the Image Size dialog box.**
   You adjust the size of the image. In the Camera Raw dialog box, you used the smallest dimensions available; you need a smaller size for use in the poster.

5. **Type** 785 **in the Width field in the Pixel Dimensions area at the top of the Image Size dialog box. The Height field changes to 1205 pixels.**
   Click OK to close the dialog box and set the dimensions.

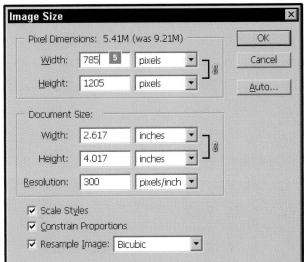

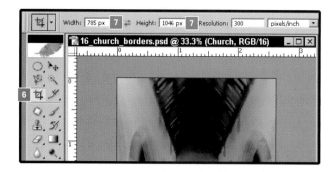

6. **Click the Crop tool in the Toolbox.**
   The Crop settings display in the Options bar.

7. **Type** 785 **in the Width field and** 1046 **in the Height field to set a size for the Crop tool. Type** 300 **in the Resolution field to match the current resolution of the image.**
   Make sure the resolution is displaying at 300, the resolution of the image.

8. **Click the bottom-right corner of the document window and drag out to add some gray area around the image. Click and drag with the Crop tool to draw a fixed size marquee on the image. Click and drag inside the crop boundary to position the crop boundary to match the figure.**
   The constrained size you set in step 7 means the full width of the image remains, but some of the height is cropped.

9. **Press Return (Windows: Enter) to commit the crop.**
   The image is resized.

10. **Choose File→Save As to save the layered image. In the Save As dialog box, name the file** 16_church_layers.psd**.**
    You resized the image to the final size used in the poster. In the next tutorial, you flatten the image, so make sure to save a layered copy as instructed here. A copy of the layered image complete to this point is on the CD in the Tutorial Files, named `16_church_layers.psd`.

Tutorial
» Framing the Image with a Border

In this tutorial you flatten the layers in the image and add a border. You can start this tutorial with the layered file 16_church_layers.psd that you saved from the last tutorial. If you prefer working with a fresh file, open 16_church_layers.psd from the Session 16 Tutorial Files folder on your hard drive.

1. **Choose Layer→Merge Visible to flatten the layers of the 16_church_layers.psd image.**
   The image is flattened to a locked background layer and maintains its 16-bit settings.

2. **Double-click the layer to open the New Layer dialog box. Name the layer church and click OK to close the dialog box and create an active layer.**

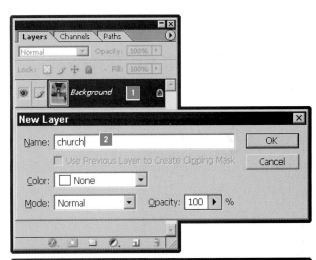

3. **Choose View→Rulers if your rulers aren't displayed in the document window. Ctrl+click (Windows: right-click) in a ruler and choose inches if your rulers aren't showing inches. Drag guides from the top and left rulers to identify a location ⅛ inch from all four edges of the image.**
   You resize the image based on the guides.

4. **Press ⌘+T (Windows: Ctrl+T) to activate the Free Transform handles. Resize the image to snap to the guides, leaving a blank border around the image. Choose View→Clear Guides to dismiss all the guides.**

5. Click the Paint Bucket tool in the Toolbox to select it. Click the blank border on the image to fill it with the black foreground color.

6. Press ⌘+D (Windows: Ctrl+D) to deselect the border.

7. Choose File→Save As. In the Save As dialog box, name the file 16_church_flat.psd. The poster image is complete. In the next tutorial, you add text layers. Leave the 16_church_flat.psd file open for the next tutorial.

Tutorial
» Creating Text for the Poster Image

In this tutorial, you add several layers of text to the image, completing the poster image. You use guidelines to help position the text. When you finish assembling the text for the poster, you add a copy of the image as a final overlay to add dimension and depth. There are no limits to the number of layers you can use with a 16-bit image aside from file size. Remember that a 16-bit image is roughly twice the size of an 8-bit image.

1. **In** `16_church_flat.psd`, **which you left open from the previous tutorial, drag a horizontal guide slightly less than ½ inch from the top of the image.**
   You use the guide for placing the first two pieces of text.

2. **Select the Horizontal Text tool in the toolbox, and type** SMITH **along the guide and approximately ¼ inch from the left border.**
   If necessary, move the text to the correct position.

3. **From the Properties toolbar or the Character palette, choose these settings for the text:**
   Font: Swis721 BlkCn BT (or another similar condensed black font)
   Font Size: 13 pt (you may have to experiment with the font size depending on what font you use)
   Color: white

4. **Click the Text tool in the toolbox, and type** JONES **along the guide and approximately ¼ inch from the right border. Use the same settings from step 3.**
   If necessary, move the text to the correct position. You completed the first text elements.

5. **Drag a horizontal guide at approximately the 3¼ inch mark.**
   You add another line of text at this level.

6. **Type** SCARY ENTERPRISES PRESENTS A COMPLETE COURSE PRODUCTION A FATEFUL GRAPHICS FILM. **Center the text horizontally. In the Character palette, choose these settings for the font:**
   Color: white
   Font: Swis721 BlkCn BT (or another similar condensed light font)
   Font Size: 6 pt (may vary depending on the font you use)
   Horizontal Scale: 85%

7. **Select the words PRESENTS A and reset the font size to 4 pt (although this may vary slightly depending on the font you use). Repeat this for PRODUCTION A and FILM.**
   You create two sizes of text in the same row.

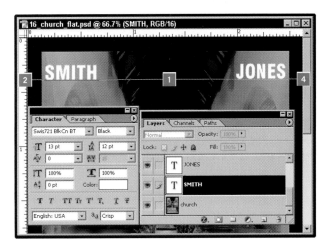

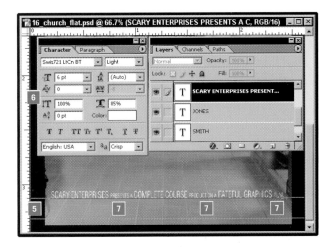

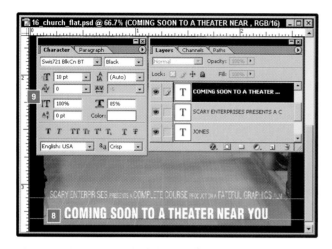

8. Drag a horizontal guide just past the 3½-inch level to place another line of text.

9. **Type** COMING SOON TO A THEATER NEAR YOU. **In the Character palette, choose these settings:**
   Font: Swis721 BlkCn BT (or another similar condensed black font)
   Font Size: 10 pt (may vary depending on the font you use)
   Horizontal Scale: 85%

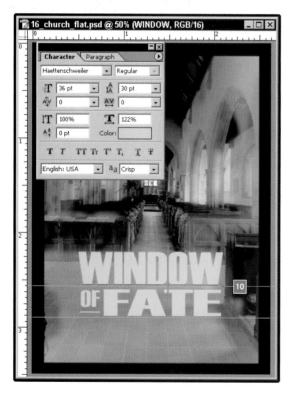

10. **Add three more pieces of text to make the title for the movie. Type** Window, OF, **and** FATE. **Use Haettenschweiler font (or a font that looks similar to the illustration), and a dark yellow (the sample uses R=255 G=204 B=0) and adjust the text in the Character palette using these settings for each text element:**
    Window: Use 36 pt font and horizontally scale to 122%.
    OF: Use 18 pt font and horizontally scale to 125%, use the underline option.
    FATE: Use 36 pt font, horizontally scale to 200%, vertically scale to 80% and adjust font sizes as necessary if you use a different font.

<TIP>
If you like, select pairs of letters in the word FATE and adjust the horizontal tracking between the letters to maintain separation.

11. **Toggle the visibility of all layers except the three text layers you added in step 10 to off. Make sure one of the three text layers added in step 10 is selected in the Layers palette.**

12. **Choose Layer→Merge Visible.**
    The three layers merge to one layer.

13. **Choose Layer→Rasterize Type.**
    You convert the text to a bitmap layer to add effects.

14. **Choose Filter➞Noise➞Add Noise to open the Noise dialog box. Set the noise level to 10%, choose Uniform distribution, and click Monochromatic.**

15. **Click OK to close the dialog box.**
    The noise is added to the text.

16. **Click the Add a Layer Style icon at the bottom of the Layers palette.**
    The Layer Style dialog box opens.

17. **Click the Drop Shadow style in the list at the left side of the dialog box.**
    The Drop Shadow settings display.

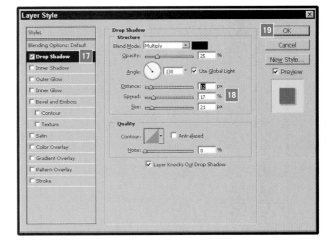

18. **Modify the settings to: Angle** 130 **degrees, Distance** 12 **px, Spread** 17**, Size** 21.
    You create a soft blurry shadow.

19. **Click OK to close the dialog box and apply the shadow.**

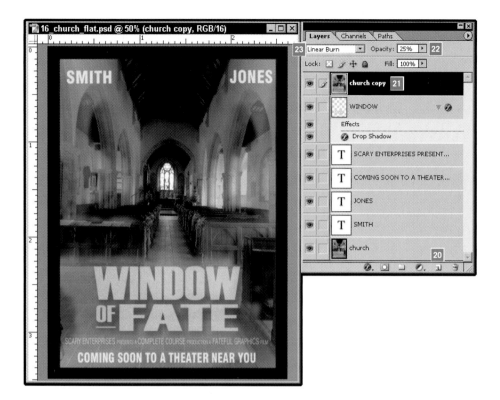

20. **In the Layers palette, click the church layer and drag it to the Add New Layer icon.**
    You add a copy of the layer.

21. **Drag the layer to the top position in the Layers palette.**
    You use the layer as a final overlay for the image and the text.

22. **Click the Opacity arrow and decrease the layer's opacity to 25%.**
    You want to see only a slight hint of the image overlay the text.

23. **Click the Blending Mode arrow and choose Linear Burn.**
    The final image takes on a faint color cast.

24. **Choose File→Save.**
    You save a final copy of the image with its layers.

<NOTE>

A copy of the file complete to this point is on the CD, named 16_church_text.psd. It contains all the text layers you have worked with in this tutorial. If you open this file and see yellow triangles on the text layers, it just means that you don't have the original font on your computer. You can ignore the triangles.

25. **Choose Layer→Flatten Image.**
    You create a flattened copy to add to the poster.

26. **Choose File→Save As.**
    Name the file 16_church_end.psd. Leave the flattened image open for the next and final tutorial.

Tutorial
» Finishing the Poster Layout

Your poster image is complete. In this tutorial, you place the finished image in the movie poster's file, which is also a 16-bit image. In order to maintain quality, you should use 16-bit images with other 16-bit images. If you try to add a 16-bit image to an 8-bit image, a message displays explaining the image quality could be degraded. You should have the 16_church_end.psd file open from the previous tutorial.

1. **From the Session 16 Tutorial Files folder, open 16_movie_poster.psd. Click Update if you see a message about updating text layers.**
   The poster contains a number of layers for the final poster.

2. **Drag guides from the rulers ½ inch from the top, the right, and the bottom of the poster. Place a guide at 3¼ inches.**
   You place the poster image within these guides.

3. **Click the line layer in the Layers palette.**
   You add the poster image in a new layer at this position.

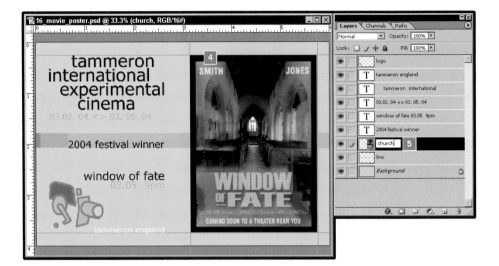

4. If you don't have the `16_church_end.psd` file open from the previous tutorial, open `16_church_text.psd` from your Session 16 tutorial files folder and flatten the image. Align the movie poster and the image file on the screen. Drag the `16_church_end.psd` image from its file to the movie poster file, and place it within the guides you added in step 2.

5. Click the Layer 1 default name in the Layers palette. Rename the layer church.

6. Choose File→Save As and save the image as `16_poster_end.psd`. Your movie poster is complete.

» Session Review

This session covered working with 16-bit images. You learned how to read and understand the information stored in an image's file. You learned how to edit an image in the Camera Raw window using the image data. You learned how to work with a 16-bit image. The initial image converted from the Camera Raw file is shown in this session's opening image. You created a multi-layered 16-bit image used as a movie poster shown in the final image in this session. The following questions will help you review the information you learned in this session.

1. Are there differences in file size between an 8-bit and a 16-bit image? What is the difference? (See "Discussion: Working with 16-Bit Images.")

2. Are there restrictions when working with 16-bit images? Can you use all the Photoshop tools you use with an 8-bit image? (See "Discussion: Working with 16-Bit Images.")

3. When you shoot an image with a camera, where is the image's data written? What is the benefit of being able to access the data? (See "Tutorial: Previewing and Opening a Camera Raw File.")

4. In an image's metadata, what does a Bit depth listed as "16,16,16" refer to? (See "Tutorial: Previewing and Opening a Camera Raw File.")

5. When additional information is added to a file's IPTC content, how is the information stored? (See "Tutorial: Previewing and Opening a Camera Raw File.")

6. In the Camera Raw window, how does the histogram work? When does it update? (See "Tutorial: Processing a Camera Raw Image.")

7. Can you change the image's resolution in the Camera Raw dialog box? Can you change its size? Are there any restrictions? (See "Tutorial: Processing a Camera Raw Image.")

8. What is lens vignetting? Where does it occur? (See "Tutorial: Processing a Camera Raw Image.")

9. Are all the filters available to work with a 16-bit image that you can use for an 8-bit image? (See "Tutorial: Filtering a High-Bit Image.")

10. Can you use Adjustments and Adjustment Layers with 16-bit images? (See: "Tutorial: Working with Layers in a High-Bit Image.")

11. Can you resize and crop a 16-bit image? Can you specify a precise size for an image when modifying the image originally in the Camera Raw window? (See "Tutorial: Resizing the Image.")

12. If you flatten a layered image, can it be saved as a 16-bit image? (See "Tutorial: Framing the Image with a Border.")

13. Are there any restrictions on the number of layers you can use with a 16-bit image? (See: "Tutorial: Creating Text for the Poster Image.")

14. Should you combine 16-bit and 8-bit images? Are there any restrictions? (See: "Tutorial: Finishing the Poster Layout.")

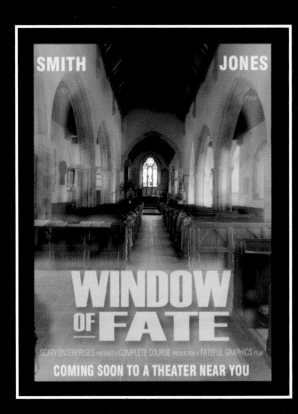

Part VII
CD-ROM Bonus Material:
Preparing Art for Print and Web

Bonus Session 1 **Using Photoshop and ImageReady for the Web** on CD-ROM

Bonus Session 2 **Printing** on CD-ROM

Bonus Session 1

Using Photoshop and ImageReady for the Web (CD-ROM)

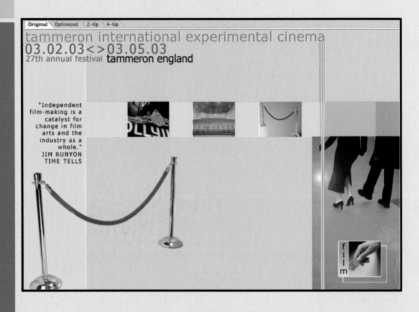

Session Introduction

Designing a Web site to complement print collateral has become a common task. In this bonus session located on the CD-ROM at the back of the book, you work on the opening page of a Web site that goes along with the film festival program guide you made in the sessions of the book. You start with a page layout created in Photoshop. Then you move to ImageReady to build a navigation bar, slice the page, create rollovers, and make an animation. You optimize the slices for fast Internet download and save images and HTML code from ImageReady, which generates functional, interactive Web pages ready to be incorporated into a Web site. Along the way, you learn tips and tricks for designing for the Web. Finally, you use Photoshop's Web Photo Gallery feature to automatically create an entire Web site from a folder of images.

Printing (CD-ROM)

tammeron england
03.02.03<>03.05.03

27th annual festival
2003

Session Introduction

In this bonus session located on the CD-ROM at the back of the book, you learn how to prepare image files for print in Photoshop, print to a desktop printer, and set up files for professional printing at a service bureau. You use the project files that you created as you worked through the book, printing composites of the final pages of the film festival program guide on your desktop printer and preparing the final files for professional printing.

All the steps in the printing tutorials in this bonus session assume that you have a desktop color printer. If you have a grayscale laser printer, you can follow the same steps to produce a composite grayscale proof. If you don't have a printer attached to your computer, you can prepare the file for printing and take it to a service center where a composite color proof can be obtained. You also learn how to create more kinds of specialized output. In Session 2, you saw how to use the Photomerge command; in this bonus session, you learn how to use Picture Package and PDF presentation options for displaying your work.

What's on the CD-ROM

This appendix provides you with information on the contents of the CD-ROM that accompanies this book. For the latest and greatest information, please refer to the ReadMe file located at the root of the CD-ROM. Here is what you will find:

» System Requirements

» Using the CD-ROM with Windows and Macintosh

» What's on the CD-ROM

» Troubleshooting

System Requirements

Make sure that your computer meets the minimum system requirements listed in this section. If your computer doesn't match up to most of these requirements, you will be unable to run Photoshop CS and may have a problem using other contents of the CD-ROM.

For Windows:

» PC with an Intel Pentium class III or 4 processor running Microsoft Windows 2000 with Service Pak 3, or Windows XP

» At least 192MB (256 MB recommended) of total RAM installed on your computer

» At least 280MB of free hard drive space

» A color monitor with at least 1024 x 768 resolution and a 16-bit video card

» A CD-ROM drive

For Macintosh:

» Macintosh OS computer with a G3, G4, or G5 PowerPC processor running Mac OS X v.10.2.4 through v.10.3

» At least 192MB (256 MB recommended) of total RAM installed on your computer

» At least 320MB of free hard drive space

» A color monitor with at least 1024 x 768 resolution and a 16-bit video card

» A CD-ROM drive

Using the CD-ROM with Windows

To install the items from the CD-ROM to your hard drive, follow these steps:

1. Insert the CD-ROM into your computer's CD-ROM drive.

2. The interface will launch. If you have autorun disabled, choose Start→Run. In the dialog box that appears, type **D:\setup.exe**. Replace D with the proper letter if your CD-ROM drive uses a different letter. (If you don't know the letter, see how your CD-ROM drive is listed under My Computer.) Click OK.

3. A license agreement appears. Read through the license agreement and then click the Accept button if you want to use the CD-ROM. (After you click Accept, you'll never be bothered by the License Agreement window again.) The first screen of the CD-ROM interface appears. The interface coordinates installing the Tutorial Files, the two Bonus Sessions, and a free copy of Adobe Reader.

4. For more information about an item, click the item's name. Be sure to read and follow the information that appears before you try to view any item.

5. To view an item, click the appropriate button.

6. To view other items, repeat these steps.

7. When you've finished viewing, click the Quit button to close the interface. You can eject the CD-ROM now. Carefully place it back in the plastic jacket of the book for safekeeping.

<NOTE>
To use the tutorial files, you need to copy them from the CD-ROM to your computer. To do this, simply drag the files directly from the window opened by the interface into a folder on your local hard drive. You can repeat this process with individual files at any time if you need fresh copies of those files. If you're using a Windows operating system other than Windows XP, you have to change the read-only status of the copied tutorial files. Otherwise, you won't be able to write over the files as you work through the tutorials. To do so, select all the files in a folder that you've copied to your computer. Right-click one of the files and choose Properties. In the Properties dialog box, uncheck Read-only.

Also, I suggest that you instruct Windows to display the filename extensions of the copied tutorial files (if your operating system isn't already set up to show them) so that you can see the file formats (.psd, .tif, .jpg, and so on). Find your Folder Options dialog box. (It's located in a slightly different place in different versions of Windows; in Windows XP, it's in the Appearance and Themes Control Panel; in Windows 2000, it's in the My Computer→Tools folder.) Click the View tab. Uncheck Hide File Extensions for Known File Types, which is checked by default.

Using the CD-ROM with the Macintosh OS

To install the items from the CD-ROM to your hard drive, follow these steps:

1. Insert the CD-ROM into your CD-ROM drive.
2. Double-click the icon for the CD-ROM after it appears on the desktop.
3. Double-click the License Agreement icon. This is the license that you are agreeing to by using the CD-ROM. You can close this window after you've looked over the agreement.
4. Some programs come with installers; for those, simply open the program's folder on the CD-ROM and double-click the Install or Installer icon. Note:
   To install some programs, just drag the program's folder from the CD-ROM window and drop it on your hard drive icon.

<NOTE>
You can browse and view the tutorial files directly from the CD-ROM, but in order to use them you will need to copy them from the CD-ROM to your computer. To do this, simply drag the files directly from the CD-ROM onto your local hard drive.

What's on the CD-ROM

The following sections provide a summary of the software and other materials that you'll find on the CD-ROM.

Tutorial Files

All the tutorial files that you use when working through the tutorials in this book are on the CD-ROM in the folder named "Tutorial Files." Within the Tutorial Files folder are subfolders containing the tutorial files for each session. In each session subfolder, you find all the files referenced in that session, in most cases including a file with the word _end in the filename. The _end file is an example of how the collage that you work on in that session should look at the end of the session.

Use the process described in the preceding sections to copy the files to your hard drive.

Bonus Sessions

The Bonus Sessions folder on the CD-ROM contains two extra sessions on special topics. Bonus Session 01, Using Photoshop and ImageReady for the Web, covers using these programs to create page layouts, graphics, rollovers, animations, and Web Photo Galleries for display on the World Wide Web. Bonus Session 02, Printing, covers printing your project on a desktop printer; preparing items for commercial printing; and outputting contact sheets, picture packages, and PDF presentations from Photoshop.

Applications

The following application is on the CD-ROM:

Adobe Reader

Freeware version for Windows and Macintosh. This program enables you to view and print PDF files. Go to www.adobe.com for more information and product updates.

Troubleshooting

If you have difficulty installing or using any of the materials on the companion CD-ROM, try the following solutions:

>> Turn off any antivirus software that you may have running. Installers sometimes mimic virus activity and can make your computer incorrectly believe that it is being infected by a virus. (Be sure to turn the antivirus software back on later.)

>> Close all running programs. The more programs you're running, the less memory is available to other programs. Installers also typically update files and programs; if you keep other programs running, the installation may not work properly.

>> Reference the ReadMe file: Please refer to the ReadMe file located at the root of the CD-ROM for the latest product information at the time of publication.

If you still have trouble with the CD-ROM, please call the Wiley Publishing Customer Care phone number: (800)762-2974. Outside the United States, call 1(317)572-3994. You can also contact Wiley Publishing Customer Service by e-mail at techsupdum@wiley.com. Wiley Publishing will provide technical support only for installation and other general quality control items; for technical support on the applications themselves, consult the program's vendor or author. To report any errata you find in the book, e-mail the author Jan Kabili at kabili@saga2.com.

Index

About Seybold Seminars and Publications

Seybold Seminars and Publications is your complete guide
to the publishing industry. For more than 30 years it
has been the most trusted source for technology events,
news, and insider intelligence.

SEYBOLD
CONSULTING PUBLICATIONS sm

SEYBOLD
SEMINARS

Produced by

K3M Key3 Media Group

PUBLICATIONS

Today, Seybold Publications and Consulting continues to guide publishing professionals around the world in their purchasing decisions and business strategies through newsletters, online resources, consulting, and custom corporate services.

○ **The Seybold Report: *Analyzing Publishing Technologies***
The Seybold Report analyzes the cross-media tools, technologies, and trends shaping professional publishing today. Each in-depth newsletter delves into the topics changing the marketplace. *The Seybold Report* covers critical analyses of the business issues and market conditions that determine the success of new products, technologies, and companies. Read about the latest developments in mission-critical topic areas, including content and asset management, color management and proofing, industry standards, and cross-media workflows. A subscription to *The Seybold Report* (24 issues per year) includes our weekly email news service, *The Bulletin,* and full access to the seyboldreports.com archives.

○ **The Bulletin: *Seybold News & Views on Electronic Publishing***
The Bulletin: Seybold News & Views on Electronic Publishing is Seybold Publications' weekly email news service covering all aspects of electronic publishing. Every week *The Bulletin* brings you all the important news in a concise, easy-to-read format.

For more information on **NEWSLETTER SUBSCRIPTIONS,** please visit **seyboldreports.com**.